The Conduct of Inquiry in International Relations

The Conduct of Inquiry in International Relations provides an introduction to philosophy of science issues and their implications for the study of global politics. The author draws attention to the problems caused by the misleading notion of a single unified scientific method, and proposes a framework that clarifies the variety of ways that IR scholars establish the authority and validity of their empirical claims. Jackson connects philosophical considerations with concrete issues of research design within neopositivist, critical realist, analyticist, and reflexive approaches to the study of world politics. Envisioning a pluralist science for a global IR field, this volume organizes the significant differences between methodological stances so as to promote internal consistency, public discussion, and worldly insight as the hallmarks of any scientific study of world politics.

In this second edition, Jackson has centralized the philosophical history of the "science question" into a single chapter, providing a clearer picture of the connections between contemporary concerns about the status of knowledge and classic philosophical debates about the relationship between human beings and the world they inhabit. The central chapters feature more detailed and pedagogically useful illustrations of the methodological positions discussed, making the book even better suited to clarify the philosophical distinctions with respect to which a scientific researcher must locate herself.

The second edition will continue to be essential reading for all students and scholars of International Relations, Political Science and Philosophy of Science.

Patrick Thaddeus Jackson is Professor of International Relations and Associate Dean for Curriculum and Learning in the School of International Service at the American University in Washington, DC. He is the author of *Civilizing the Enemy* (2006) and the co-editor of *Civilizational Identity* (2007).

In this nicely revised edition, Patrick Jackson makes a significant contribution to IR meta-theory with an impressive range of knowledge and a reassuring depth of understanding on important philosophical issues.

Hidemi Suganami, Emeritus Professor of International Politics,
Aberystwyth University, UK

Praise for the first edition

The Conduct of Inquiry in International Relations outlines a constructive and convincing path for getting beyond unproductive debates about the relative merits of the various methodologies that inform IR. Calling for a post-foundational IR that rests on a more expansive definition of science than that which is conventionally accepted by the field, Patrick Jackson makes a compelling case for an engaged pluralism that is respectful of the different philosophical groundings that inform a variety of equally valid scientific traditions, each of which can usefully contribute to a more comprehensive and informed understanding of world politics.

J. Ann Tickner, School of International Relations,
University of Southern California, USA

This is a book that will have a deep and lasting impact on the field. It displays impressive and sophisticated scholarship, but lightly worn and presented in an engaging manner, student-friendly but never patronising or afraid to challenge the reader. I know no better account of the various ways by which one can study IR scientifically and I am confident that this is a text that will be very widely adopted.

Chris Brown, Professor of International Relations,
London School of Economics, UK

Neatly framed, balanced, informed, lucid and, yes, important, this is the rare book I wish I had written myself. Not that I could have done it nearly as well.

Nick Onuf, Professor Emeritus of International Relations,
Florida International University, USA

In this vigorously argued, incisive and important book P.T. Jackson liberates us from the misplaced polarity between "hard, scientific" and "soft, interpretive" approaches that has bedeviled international relations scholarship for half a century. Neither approach has any grounding among philosophers of science with their insistence on the irreducibly pluralist nature of science. The immense value of this book is its accessibility and the intimate connections it builds between theories of international relations and their philosophical foundations—or lack thereof. Neo-positivist, reflexivist, critical realist and analytical stances can now engage in ecumenical dialogue rather than shouting matches or with silent scorn. If you are accustomed to worship only in your favorite chapel, here is an invitation to visit a magnificent cathedral. Graduate field seminars in international relations now have access to a first rate text.

Peter J. Katzenstein, Walter S. Carpenter, Jr. Professor of
International Studies, Cornell Universtiy, USA

Not only is *The Conduct of Inquiry in International Relations* a breathtakingly original and rigorous analysis of the scholarly work in the field, it is also an excellent teaching tool for graduate and upper level undergraduate students. By showing how ontological starting points lead to a variety of methodological options, Patrick Jackson opens up a broad toolkit for the production of knowledge in IR. His use of philosophy of science is both rich and accessible to the unacquainted reader, and brings to the light numerous misunderstandings, false argumentations, and incorrect presumptions that have become common to the field. As a result, *The Conduct of Inquiry* is both revealing and instructive, and a must-read to all who have an interest in reflecting on what's actually being done in IR.

Gerard van der Ree, Universiteit Utrecht, The Netherlands

The New International Relations

Edited by Richard Little, *University of Bristol*,
Iver B. Neumann, *Norwegian Institute of International Affairs (NUPI)*,
and Jutta Weldes, *University of Bristol*.

The field of international relations has changed dramatically in recent years. This new series will cover the major issues that have emerged and reflect the latest academic thinking in this particular dynamic area.

The Conduct of Inquiry in International Relations

Philosophy of science and its implications for the study of world politics

Second edition

Patrick Thaddeus Jackson

Routledge
Taylor & Francis Group

LONDON AND NEW YORK

Second edition published 2016
by Routledge
First edition published 2011
by Routledge
2 Park Square, Milton Park, Abingdon, Oxon OX14 4RN

and by Routledge
711 Third Avenue, New York, NY 10017

Routledge is an imprint of the Taylor & Francis Group, an informa business

British Library Cataloguing in Publication Data
A catalogue record for this book is available from the British Library

Library of Congress Cataloging in Publication Data
Names: Jackson, Patrick Thaddeus, 1972– author.
Title: The conduct of inquiry in international relations : philosophy of
science and its implications for the study of world politics / Patrick
Thaddeus Jackson.
Description: Milton Park, Abingdon, Oxon ; New York, NY : Routledge,
2016. |
Series: New international relations | Includes bibliographical references
and index.
Identifiers: LCCN 2015046320| ISBN 9781138842649 (hardback) |
ISBN 9781138842670 (pbk.) | ISBN 9781315731360 (ebook)
Subjects: LCSH: International relations--Philosophy. | International
relations--Methodology. | International relations--Research. | World
politics.
Classification: LCC JZ1305 .J318 2016 | DDC 327.101--dc23
LC record available at http://lccn.loc.gov/2015046320

ISBN: 978-1-138-84264-9 (hbk)
ISBN: 978-1-138-84267-0 (pbk)
ISBN: 978-1-315-73136-0 (ebk)

Typeset in Times New Roman
by HWA Text and Data Management, London

Printed and bound by CPI Group (UK) Ltd, Croydon, CR0 4YY

This book is dedicated to the memory of
Hayward Alker
and
Charles Tilly
in the hope that something of their pluralist spirit
lives on in its pages
and in its readers.

There is *only* a perspective seeing, *only* a perspective "knowing;" and the *more* affects we allow to speak about a thing, the *more* eyes, different eyes, we know ourselves to apply to the same thing, the more complete will our "concept" of this thing, our "objectivity," be.

—Friedrich Nietzsche

As we approach the third millennium, our needs are different, and the ways of meeting them must be correspondingly rethought. Now, our concern can no longer be to guarantee the *stability and uniformity* of Science or the State alone: instead, it must be to provide the elbowroom we need in order to protect *diversity and adaptability*.

—Stephen Toulmin

Contents

Series editor's preface

Things should be made as simple as possible—not simpler. So, if this is not exactly philosophy of science made easy, it is definitely highly accessible philosophy for social scientists. It is also the most accomplished attempt to date at linking debates internal to International Relations (IR) to the history and philosophy of science generally. In Chapter 1, Professor Jackson reviews the normative debate on how to delimit science. For Jackson, science is defined by its goals, and not by its methods or theories. It is systematic, communal, and empirical production of knowledge. Social science is the systematic production of empirical, factual knowledge about political and social arrangements. Since the discipline is defined by its empirical object of study, it stands to reason that it should also take care of non-scientific tasks, such as evaluating political orders normatively or forging political arguments. Jackson is skeptical of prescribing more rigorous standards to practicing scholars, preferring instead to celebrate a broad church and pushing ecumenical dialogue. He defines philosophy of science as reflection on how we produce knowledge. Its tasks are to defuse indefensible claims about knowledge and truth, warrant specific ways of producing knowledge, and clarify implications of specific assumptions.

Chapter 2 discusses what these different ways of doing science are. For Jackson, this is first and foremost a question of philosophical ontology—that is, our hook-up to the world, how we are able to produce knowledge in the first place. There is also scientific ontology, questions concerning what kind of stuff the world consists of (individuals? theories? practices? witches?), but that is secondary. The key fissures in overall debates about science concern, first, what kind of hook-up the scholar has to the world. Am I a constitutive part of the world, or do I follow Descartes in thinking about my mind as radically cut off from the (rest of the) world? In the former case, I am a mind–world monist. In the latter case, I am a mind–world dualist. There is a choice to be made here, one consequence of which is what kind of methodology is suitable for doing research. Methodology—the logical structure and procedure of scientific inquiry—must necessarily follow the scholar's type of hook-up to the world. Jackson sees the key problem of the discipline in the doxic status accorded to mind–world dualism. The only places in the book where Jackson is scathing of his colleagues are the ones where he dissects how scholars who had their heyday in the 1970s spent the 1980s and

1990s attempting to discipline younger colleagues who attempted to enrich the discipline by trying out other ways of doing science:

> Putatively radical insurgencies have their critical edges blunted by the seemingly reasonable offer of being taken seriously by the rest of the field as long as they formulate testable hypotheses and join the search for systematic cross-case correlations arranged so as to approximate covering-laws.
>
> (p. 60)

The fissure between monists and dualists is not alone in dividing the discipline, however. A second key fissure turns on another question of philosophical ontology—namely, what kind of status our theories are given. Are they transfactual, meaning that they are based on the real existence of structures that generate observable stuff that we may then study, or are they phenomenalist, meaning that they are based on the scholar's experiences (and not rooted in any further claim about something really existing outside of those experiences)?

Note that Jackson privileges these two fissures at the cost of a number of other candidates, such as positivist versus interpretivist and qualitative versus quantitative. Such fissures easily degenerate into questions of methods—techniques for gathering and analyzing bits of data—questions that are less foundational than the questions of ontology and methodology singled out for discussion here. Note also the lack of interest in debates about epistemology. If philosophical ontology concerns the choice of how to hook up to the world and methodology how to order the proceedings of doing it, then epistemology may be safely occluded.

Depending on what philosophical wagers scholars place regarding the two key fissures, they place themselves in one of four cells in a two-by-two matrix. Chapters 3 through 6 give the historical preconditions for the emergence of the ensuing four positions—neopositivism, critical realism, analyticism, and reflexivity—and discuss their internal debates and aporias. Here we have a neat ideal-typical heuristic device for presenting ongoing research in IR in terms of philosophy of science orientations. Each cell gives a different answer to the problem with which we have wrestled since Descartes, namely how to overcome the mind/world split when we hook our inquiry up with the world. Neopositivist workhorses find the answer in falsification. Critical realist ones find it in the best approximation between abduced dispositional properties and the object under study. To analyticists and reflexivists, the answer is not to put Descartes before the horse, however, but to put the horse before the cart. Rather than let the old Cartesian legacy drag them along, they try to dissolve Descartes' question, either by drawing up an ideal-typical analytic, or by using themselves as effects of structures, structures that may be found by looking at one of its effects: me and my social relations.

Neopositivism is "neo" because of Popper's insistence that falsification, and not verification, should be our guiding star of hooking up to the externally given world. A key point in Chapter 3 is, however, that IR neopositivism is not particularly "neo," inasmuch as its methodology usually comes down to "tossing hypothetical conjectures against the mind-independent world, in the hope that at least some of them will survive repeated attempts to refute them" (p. 82) The joy seems to be in evading falsification, not in actually locating it. Inasmuch as neopositivism remains the wholesaler of IR theory, far outstripping other providers, from a mainstream point of view, any other way of doing research remains controversial. For this second edition of the book, Jackson has consolidated the argument by elaborating on how US positivism battens down the hatches.

Among the small subset of IR scholars who preoccupy themselves with philosophy of science questions, critical realism seems to be almost all the rage. The underlying theme in Chapter 4 is the continuity from Marxist to critical realist methodologies. In order to get from the postulation of really existing transfactuals to the inquiry into observables, critical realists avail themselves of abduction, the act of positing or conjecturing the existence of some process, entity, or property that accounts for observable data. The ultimate point of the exercise seems to be to delineate "the real limits of the possible, in the hope that a politically savvy agent will take advantage of them in transformative ways," as Jackson puts it.

The hero of Chapter 5 is Max Weber, whose ideal-type procedure is paradigmatic of the mind–world monist phenomenalist approach. Jackson stresses that constructivism is "the generic term for non-dualist approaches to the production of knowledge that limit themselves to the empirical realm," but that since that term is already in use within the discipline with another address, analyticism will have to do. This is the home of IR theorists such as the Weberian Morgenthau and the structural-functionalist Waltz, who stresses how theories may only be overtaken by another theory (since there simply does not exist for him an independent world against which to "test" the theory). Practice theory of a Wittgensteinian kind, which is now finally reaching IR, does also belong here.

Most practice theory would, however, end up with the reflexivists, who are discussed in Chapter 6. Where analyticists stick to the empirical realm, inspired by a tradition stirring in Kant, fleshed out by Hegel, and coming into its own in Karl Mannheim's sociology of knowledge, as well as in the work of sundry continental philosophies, reflexivists go further in one (or more) of three ways. They postulate further knowledge claims to round out accounts of social worlds; they claim to be able to approximate knowledge that is constitutive of a certain social group (and so is not necessarily there to be experienced directly, but must be postulated to exist transfactually); and/or they "make space for ... [a social] group's perspective to contribute to a potentially broader grasp of things." Jackson draws his argument to a close with a blistering defense of pluralism.

In the preface to the first edition, I hazarded the guess that there would be an interesting reception in store for this book, not least because young scholars would be wont to find different ways to hook up their research to the world. It gives me professional and personal pleasure to report that, since the publication of the first edition five years ago, *The Conduct of Inquiry* has gone on to become the new gold standard for philosophy of science debates within the discipline.

Iver B. Neumann

1 Playing with fire

Although an innovative astronomer and an important contributor to the development of planetary science, the late Carl Sagan is probably best remembered among the general public for two of his other activities: his popularization of contemporary natural science (especially astrophysics), and his highly public and unapologetic condemnation of "pseudoscience" concerning crystals, ESP, and alien abductions. The two activities fit together quite well, as they are united by a commitment to spreading a particular sensibility out beyond professional specialists and into the wider community. In a collection of essays entitled *The demon-haunted world*, Sagan borrows a metaphor from Thomas Ady's seventeenth-century tract condemning witch-hunts, to describe his public and popular work as an effort to shine an illuminating light into the dark corners of the contemporary world: to light a candle in the hopes of banishing the shadows. The candle he sought to light and to wield against the darkness was what he called *science*:

> In science we may start with experimental results, data, observations, measurements, "facts." We invent, if we can, a rich array of possible explanations and systematically confront each explanation with the facts. In the course of their training, scientists are equipped with a baloney detection kit. The kit is brought out as a matter of course whenever new ideas are offered for consideration. If the new idea survives examination by the tools in our kit, we grant it warm, although tentative, acceptance. If you're so inclined, if you don't want to buy baloney even when it's reassuring to do so, there are precautions that can be taken.
>
> (Sagan 1997, 209–210)

Sagan's account of the mechanics of science is probably fairly familiar to us, as it tracks quite closely with the notion of "falsification" famously propounded by Karl Popper (1992): science, in Popper's formulation, proceeds and progresses through successive efforts to *dis*prove conjectures, rather than through efforts to verify or justify them. But Sagan's metaphor—science as a candle in the darkness—should be scarcely less familiar, drawing as it does on a longstanding tradition in the philosophy of knowledge that equates knowing with seeing, and reason—often exemplified by science—with a source of light. Famously, John

Locke drew on this metaphor in his *An Essay Concerning Human Understanding*, admonishing his readers to use their natural faculties of reason to the best of their ability:

> It will be no excuse to an idle and untoward servant, who would not attend his business by candle light, to plead that he had not broad sunshine. The Candle that is set up in us shines bright enough for all our purposes.
>
> (Locke 1959a, 30)

Further, Locke deployed the notion of reason as a defense against popular deception in a manner quite reminiscent of Sagan's stance:

> Reason is natural revelation, whereby the eternal Father of light and fountain of all knowledge, communicates to mankind that portion of truth which he has laid within the reach of their natural faculties: revelation is natural reason enlarged by a new set of discoveries communicated by God immediately; which reason vouches the truth of, by the testimony and proofs it gives that they come from God. So that he that takes away reason to make way for revelation, puts out the light of both, and does muchwhat the same as if he would persuade a man to put out his eyes, the better to receive the remote light of an invisible star by a telescope.
>
> (Locke 1959b, 431)

Setting aside the language of divinity for a moment, we can see a clear continuity between Locke and Sagan. Both point to a natural faculty that can be developed and deployed against error, and both symbolically equate that faculty with "light"—and oppose it to the "darkness" of misconception and superstition. Similarly, both privilege science as a superior way of gaining and evaluating knowledge—Sagan uses the term "science," while Locke, preferring the term "reason," explicitly associates himself and his argument with great scientists of the day such as Newton and Boyle. Whatever else it is good for, science appears in their conception as our best defense against error.

Of course, such arguments are not only advanced by philosophers and astronomers. Closer to home, as it were, David Laitin (2003, 169) advances a very similar image of science—including social science—as containing "ample procedures for figuring out if our best judgments are misplaced" and hence serving as "the surest hope for valid inference." Laitin pairs this declaration with a denunciation of Bent Flyvbjerg's *Making Social Science Matter* (2001) for allegedly violating the strictures of science and opening the door to a kind of anything-goes relativism—the ultimate nightmare about what the abandonment of the ground of "science" might mean in practice.[1] In their popular and oft-cited methods handbook, Gary King, Robert Keohane, and Sidney Verba flatly declare: "research designed to help us understand social reality can only succeed

---

1   Quite a debate ensued; see the papers collected in Schram and Caterino (2006).

if it follows the logic of scientific inference" (King, Keohane, and Verba 1994, 229). And King, in a triumphalist article about his Institute for Quantitative Social Science at Harvard University, declares that "areas of scholarship dedicated to understanding, or improving the well-being of, human populations" are well served by the construction of an infrastructure explicitly modeled on the organization of research in the natural sciences (King 2014). The juxtaposition of science and (potential) error, therefore, seems just as prominent in our field as it is in other domains.

Arguments such as these pose extremely fundamental questions about the character of our scholarly enterprise. Scholars of politics who advance such claims are quite clearly drawing on the cultural prestige associated with the notion of "science" in the contemporary age (Litfin 1994) as part of an effort to shape the practices of their colleagues involved in the effort to produce knowledge about the social world. To invoke "science" is to call to mind a panoply of notions connected with truth, progress, reason, and the like—and, perhaps more importantly, to implicitly reference a record of demonstrated empirical success. These sorts of appeals function this way particularly in internal debates among scholars of the social world, as tossing an appeal to "science" into such debates is like playing a very valuable trump-card that implicitly, if not explicitly, calls the entire status of the scholarly field into question. Within the field of International Relations (IR)[2] in particular, the "science question" has long vexed scholars, coming to a head in the field's second "great debate" between self-identified traditionalists and scientists (Knorr and Rosenau 1969) but never really getting resolved or losing its scholarly resonance (see the discussion in Kratochwil 2006). Especially under such circumstances, it is impossible to invoke the notion of "science"—let alone to propose turning to either the practice or the philosophy of science in an effort to clarify or improve our own scholarship!—in any kind of neutrally descriptive manner. Playing the science card raises the stakes.

The science question in IR

It is important to note at the outset that the role played by "science" in our field is at least conditionally, if not completely, independent of any detailed philosophical or conceptual sense afforded to the term. In debates about the proper conduct of IR scholarship, we typically operate with caricatures and generalities rather than precise specifications, speaking loosely of "*the* scientific method" or "*the* philosophy of science" as though either of those two things actually existed. Although there have been some notable exceptions in recent years, most references to and invocations of "science" in the field seem to operate with

---

2 I follow conventional scholarly usage in distinguishing between "international relations" (or "international affairs") as an object of analysis and "International Relations" or "IR" as a scholarly enterprise. Although increasingly my thinking prefers "international studies" to "International Relations / IR" as a way of naming the scholarly field, I adhere to common usage throughout the text.

an image of knowledge-production that is a curious amalgamation of Sagan's skeptical "baloney detection kit," an embrace of mathematical formalism, and a desire for law-like generalizations that hold true across cases (given appropriate scope conditions, of course). This is a curious amalgam because the first defines a skeptical *attitude*, the second defines a formalist *method*, and the third defines an epistemic *goal*—and none of these are perfectly characteristic of any actually existing scientific practice. In debates about knowledge-production in our field, what is most often in play is not a specific account of science, but a vague and general sensibility.

Of course, this is in no way just a comment on the present state of the field. Throughout the history of IR, the term "science" has been flung around in extremely cavalier ways, serving most often as the positive pole of a contrast that an author wishes to draw between her or his approach to generating and evaluating claims about international affairs and some reviled alternative. For example:

> This book has two purposes. The first is to detect and understand the forces that determine political relations among nations, and to comprehend the ways in which those forces act upon one another and upon international political relations and institutions. In most other branches of the social sciences this purpose would be taken for granted, because the natural aim of all scientific undertakings is to discover the forces underlying social phenomena and the mode of their operation.
>
> (Morgenthau 1985, 18)

Thus Hans Morgenthau claimed early in his textbook *Politics among nations*, characterizing his approach as a "scientific undertaking" with little more than a vague gesture in the direction of "forces underlying social phenomena." There is no more specific discussion of the character or value of science in the book, although Morgenthau generally takes it for granted that only a scientific study can provide the basis for a responsible pursuit of a peaceful world; that, indeed, is the second "purpose" of his book (ibid., 20). The general notion or idea of "science," and the cultural prestige associated with it, suffices to legitimate Morgenthau's enterprise.

Morgenthau was very aware of this cultural prestige, having railed at length against the over-scientizing of the contemporary age in his 1946 masterpiece *Scientific man vs. power politics*:

> Politics is an art and not a science, and what is required for its mastery is not the rationality of the engineer but the wisdom and the moral strength of the statesman ... The age has tried to make politics a science. By doing so, it has demonstrated its intellectual confusion, moral blindness, and political decay.
>
> (Morgenthau 1946, 10)

The problem, Morgenthau argued then, is that we put too *much* stock in science, and thus overlook the distinctiveness of the political and social world.

In his typically Weberian fashion, Morgenthau argued that we make a category mistake when we expect science to solve our political problems; instead, we should respect the limits of human knowing, and keep science in its place. "For the liberal, science is a prophecy confirmed by reason; for the conservative, it is the revelation of the past confirmed by experience" (Morgenthau 1946, 32). Casting himself on the "conservative" side of the ledger, Morgenthau engaged in a very interesting double intellectual operation: on one hand, criticizing the over-reliance on science, but on the other hand, claiming some of its cultural prestige for his own project of knowledge-production. The result, whether by accident or by design, is the simultaneous preservation of the notion that we ought to have "scientific" knowledge of international affairs, along with a good deal of ambiguity about precisely what that might mean in practice.

In pursuing this line of argument, Morgenthau was in a way simply following the precedent laid down by E.H. Carr in *his* announcement of a scientific study of international affairs.[3] Carr talked about science, but never precisely defined the term except to contrast science with both unchecked idealism and unchecked realism (Carr 2001, 87). The science Carr announced would avoid both of those partisan-political stances, instead aiming for a more comprehensive view. But the scientific study of international affairs, Carr acknowledged, would not be a simple transplantation of procedures from the natural sciences:

> The laboratory worker engaged in investigating the causes of cancer may have been originally inspired by the purpose of eradicating the disease. But this purpose is, in the strictest sense, irrelevant to the investigation and separable from it. His conclusion can be nothing more than a true report on facts. It cannot help to make the facts other than they are; for the facts exist independently of what anyone thinks about them. In the political sciences, which are concerned with human behavior, there are no such facts. The investigator is inspired by the desire to cure some ill of the body politic. Among the causes of the trouble, he diagnoses the fact that human beings normally react to certain conditions in a certain way. But this is not a fact comparable with the fact that human bodies react in a certain way to certain drugs. It is a fact which may be changed by the desire to change it ... The purpose is not, as in the physical sciences, irrelevant to the investigation and separable from it: it is itself one of the facts.
>
> (Carr 2001, 4–5)

This does not tell us much about what it *means* for something to be a science. Indeed, Carr's claim is quite difficult to elucidate, because it is unclear just what is "scientific" about *both* a report on facts that are independent of human recognition *and* a report on facts that can be changed by the desire to change them—and Carr

---

3 Of course, the U.S. context within which Morgenthau's claim was advanced also decisively affected both his strategy and the eventual—unintended—outcome of that strategy. For an extended discussion, see Guilhot (2011).

gave his readers little explicit guidance on this issue. Neither did Morgenthau, who similarly claimed that "social conditions" are more closely interwoven with scientific inquiry in the social sciences (Morgenthau 1946, 162). Both of these seminal IR scholars were quite confident that the study of international affairs can and should be a "scientific" one, but it was not a central concern of either author to spell out precisely what it means for a study to be scientific. Instead, both were content simply to invoke the notion of "science" in the course of justifying their approaches.

Matters became more specific with the next of the field's "great debates"—a controversy "over the merits of the traditional and scientific approaches to the study of international politics," in which the main protagonists were Hedley Bull, arguing for tradition, and a diverse cast of characters arguing for science (Knorr and Rosenau 1969, iii). Bull characterized the opposition between these two approaches as mostly a matter of style and technique, with the traditional approach emphasizing "judgment" derived from an intimate experience with the history and philosophy of politics, and the scientific approach aspiring "to a theory of international relations whose propositions are based either upon logical or mathematical proof, or upon strict, empirical procedures of verification" (Bull 1969, 20–21). That this was largely a tactical difference became clear with Bull's declaration that:

> The theory of international relations should undoubtedly attempt to be scientific in the sense of being a coherent, precise, and orderly body of knowledge, and in the sense of being consistent with the philosophical foundations of modern science. Insofar as the scientific approach is a protest against slipshod thinking and dogmatism, or against a residual providentialism, there is everything to be said for it.
>
> (Ibid., 36)

In this broad sense, Bull's definition of science was strikingly similar to that of Carr or Morgenthau. What he objected to were quantitative and formal techniques, and the drive towards generalization—precisely the features privileged and defended by self-identified "scientists" such as J. David Singer and Marion Levy. Levy was quite clear that "a generalized system of theory … hopefully with deductive interdependencies among the members of the set" (Levy 1969, 92) is the ultimate goal of any science, and he agreed with Singer that "we will never build much of a theory, no matter how high and wide we stack our *beliefs*" (ibid., 71)— the conduct of science means moving beyond beliefs and evaluating those beliefs in the light of systematic empirical evidence. In this debate, scientists took traditionalists to task for simply resting, content with their intuitions; traditionalists took scientists to task for their remoteness from the subject-matter.

But all sides of the debate agreed that the point of studying international affairs is to produce empirically grounded and justified claims. This made the controversy a disagreement about the relative contribution of general propositions and hypothetical models, on one hand, and detailed historical reconstructions, on the other, to the understanding of international affairs. Read in this way, the debate featured much less of an unbridgeable divide than might have at first appeared: everyone wanted to be "scientific" in the broad sense, and to produce coherent and orderly knowledge, but they disagreed as to which techniques were actually "scientific" in the relevant way. However, it is significant that this was *not* Bull's rhetorical strategy; instead of defining and defending a broad account of science against the more elaborate and specific account advanced by his (largely American) opponents, Bull in effect *conceded* the notion of "science" to his opponents and took his stand elsewhere. The fact that Bull's broad definition of science is buried within the sixth of his seven critiques of formalist quantification and the quest for general propositions indicates something of how far it was away from the main thrust of his argumentative strategy.

Thus, the actual, if unintended, result of the "second great debate" in IR was to link "science" with quantification, formal models, and general propositions, replacing Carr and Morgenthau's vague notion of science with something more precise, while retaining the cultural prestige of the notion. Singer, Levy, and other self-identified "scientists" made numerous references to the successes of physics and economics, holding out hope that IR could enjoy similar successes by becoming equally "scientific." The editors of the volume containing many of the important essays constituting the controversy even pioneered a strategy of reconciling the two approaches under a common banner, a strategy that further reinforced the equating of "science" with the formulation of general propositions:

> [W]hy could not the traditionalists take on the burden of casting their conclusions in the form of hypotheses testable in other situations? This would not undermine their inquiries, but it would maximize their possible contribution to the work of their more scientific colleagues. Likewise, why could not the scientists append summaries to their studies that straightforwardly identify their major propositions and findings? Such additions would not jeopardize their procedures, but they would make the products of their research more accessible to those who prefer nonscientific modes of inquiry.
>
> (Knorr and Rosenau 1969, 18)

Notice that, in this passage, the main "burden" falls on the traditionalists, who have to adopt a form of presentation that makes their claims ready for evaluation by the techniques preferred by self-identified "scientists." The only thing that the "scientists" have to do, apparently, is to produce a plain-English account of their study—a communicative, rather than a methodological, modification. Testable hypotheses and general claims are thus portrayed as almost unquestionable goals of IR scholarship, hardly even needing the label "science" to distinguish them from alternatives. But the label continues to serve a useful function in reaffirming the status of those fundamental assumptions—as when, a quarter-century later, King, Keohane, and Verba declared that "the social science we espouse seeks to make descriptive and causal inferences about the world" (King, Keohane, and Verba 1994, 7) and passed quite seamlessly from that claim to a series of discussions about strategies for testing hypothetical generalizations.

In fact, "science," in IR, has come to mean more or less precisely what Bull's opponents asserted that it meant, and the historical controversy between the traditionalists and the scientists has been recoded or reconceptualized as a dispute about styles of presentation or argumentation. "'Science' versus 'tradition'" has morphed into "'quantitative' versus 'qualitative'," a characterization that effectively strips any fundamental philosophical or conceptual issues out of the disagreement (Yanow and Schwartz-Shea 2006, xv–xix). Knorr and Rosenau noted this at the time of the initial debate:

> Why, then, could not the traditionalists employ rather than deplore the quantitative findings of the scientists, refining them as seems suitable to their own way of thinking? And why could not the scientist use rather than abuse the qualitative insights of the traditionalists, subjecting them to the rigors of their procedures in the same way they do their own ideas?
>
> (Knorr and Rosenau 1969, 18)

While it remains a bit unclear how traditionalists uninterested in general propositions might "employ" quantitative findings, the idea that a "scientist" could take a traditionalist's conclusion or insight and subject it to procedures of hypothesis testing (especially if the traditionalist had followed their advice to state the insight in the *form* of a testable hypothesis, thus relieving the "scientist" of any conceptual labor of translation) is both a well-defined intellectual operation and a clear example of the priority accorded to "science" understood as the quest for generalized theoretical knowledge. The persistence of this priority of general propositions over insight based on intimate familiarity with particular situations can be seen in King, Keohane, and Verba's suggestion that "nonstatistical research will produce more reliable results if researchers pay attention to the rules of scientific inference—rules that are sometimes more clearly stated in the style of quantitative research" (King, Keohane, and Verba 1994, 6). This applies above all to "qualitative" studies, where researchers can only guarantee their "scientific" status by seeking to distinguish systematic from nonsystematic components of a situation even in their descriptions of that situation (ibid., 56). Every scholarly practice, then, is to be subordinated to the specific notion of "science" established as dominant in the discipline during the debate with Hedley Bull.

Of course, this outcome was somewhat foreshadowed by Bull's own confused position about science (Kratochwil 2006, 9). Because Bull failed to articulate a clear *alternative* to systematic generalization across historical cases, for example, he opened his position up to the rejoinder that there was no compelling reason *not* to subject the results of a detailed empirical-historical account to broader evaluation. Especially since this technique seemed to have proven so helpful in other fields of inquiry, the argument in favor of the "scientists" appeared almost unassailable. In practice, the most prominent dissenters focused more on pointing out the shortcomings of the "scientific" position than on elucidating a concrete alternative, calling for greater reflexivity among scholars (Lapid 1989) or affecting a whole-scale turn towards political and normative theory (Connolly 1989). Critics of generalized theoretical systems, such as Richard Ashley (1983; 1984), followed in Bull's footsteps by leaving the notion of "science" itself untouched in the field and permitting the self-proclaimed "scientists" to continue their monopoly on defining the term.

This strategy was evident even in the most successful effort to garner some "thinking space" (George and Campbell 1990) in the field for empirical scholarship not particularly interested in the formulation and evaluation of theoretical generalizations. Martin Hollis and Steve Smith's *Explaining and understanding international relations* was one of the first books to elucidate cogently a form of empirical knowledge-production that was not simply a deficient or low-tech version of the hypothesis testing/generalization approach. Hollis and Smith began with the delineation of two "intellectual traditions" animating the production of empirical knowledge in the social sciences: one derived from the natural sciences and the other derived from nineteenth-century hermeneutics. "Explaining" designates the first approach; "understanding," the other. Hollis and Smith then quickly proceeded to draw a series of other distinctions that map onto this same basic division: "outsider" versus "insider" accounts, causes versus meanings, and preferences versus rules (Hollis and Smith 1990, 1–7). The authors argued that these two bundles—causal outsider accounts using preferences to explain what actors do in international affairs, and meaningful insider accounts using social rules to understand what actors do in international affairs—were virtually incommensurable, leaving us with a situation in which there are always two separate stories to tell about any given empirical situation. The authors were also meticulous in avoiding any kind of comparative analysis of the two approaches, concluding the book with a dialogue between themselves that highlights the strengths and shortcomings of each approach in terms of the other (ibid., 203–214).

The clear implication of the Hollis and Smith depiction of empirical inquiry in IR was that "scientists" did not have a monopoly on knowledge-construction; there was an established, vibrant tradition operating with very different assumptions about how knowledge ought to be produced, and it was in some sense equal in value to its "scientific" alternative. The argument established a diversity of modes of inquiry, but at a fairly significant cost. "Explanation," rooted in "the attempt to apply the methods of natural science to the world of international relations" (ibid., 45), received causation and preferences, while "understanding" was left with the explication of social rules and the delineation of the motives of actors[4]—a stance that, incidentally, left many understanding-accounts vulnerable to critiques that they were actor-reductionist or perhaps even idealist.[5] More to the

---

4 Understanding might also have received constitutive explanation, but that is a more complex issue, which I will defer discussion of until Chapter 4.

5 "Motives lead to outcomes" is, in fact, the classic statement of reductionism criticized by Waltz (1979) and Singer (1961). And "social rules help us understand outcomes" is only a small step away from "ideas and beliefs cause outcomes," which is how IR "scientists" typically misunderstood idealism (Ashworth 2006).

point, the Hollis and Smith strategy allowed the self-proclaimed "scientists" to continue to claim both the centuries-old tradition of the natural sciences *and* the cultural prestige associated with that tradition. Practitioners of "understanding" had no such proud parentage to claim, but instead had to be content with a bevy of German philosophers and British anthropologists.

From this potted history of some key debates in the field of IR, I would like to draw two conclusions. First, "science" has been a notion in play in IR debates since the very beginning of the scholarly study of international affairs. Indeed, we could easily go back *before* the establishment of the study of international affairs as a distinct scholarly endeavor and find "science" playing an important role in debates about the status of international law (Schmidt 1998, 104–106; Orford 2014) and in the efforts of scholars of politics to distinguish themselves and their work from purely partisan-political activity in the very early part of the twentieth century (Adcock 2003, 501–506)—to say nothing of the continuing role played by "science" in the shaping of the discipline of Political Science, within which so much of Anglophone IR scholarship is located (Gunnell 1993). For the moment, it is sufficient to note that the shapers of the field of IR have been concerned about the scientific status of their scholarship for a very long time. Because of this long-standing history, "science" remains a notion to conjure with in the field of IR; it is a veritable "rhetorical commonplace" (Jackson 2006, 27–32), which is available for deployment within all kinds of controversies. And a powerful resource it is, too: charging that a piece of work is not "scientific" carries immensely negative connotations, both because of the field-specific history I have sketched here and because of the broader cultural prestige enjoyed by "science" (Moses and Knutsen 2007, 155–156).

This leads to my second conclusion: the *function* of the commonplace "science" within IR is primarily a *disciplining* function. When "science" makes an appearance, it is a pretty good bet that the text in which the term is invoked is more or less explicitly trying to reshape how inquiry is conducted, and doing so by drawing on the rhetorical power of "science" in order to privilege some modes of inquiry at the expense of others. If "science" is a good and valuable thing, then non-"science" cannot be as worthwhile an endeavor. Simply rejecting "science," or elaborating an alternative such as "understanding," leaves the whole discursive arrangement intact, and does not really offer a reasonable or effective rejoinder to the charge that the non-"scientific" work that one is doing is not somehow of lesser value. There is no effective way around this unless the whole field abandons any claims to or aspirations of being scientific. Absent this unlikely possibility, the question of science remains almost unavoidable for IR scholarship.

The demarcation problem

Philosophers of science sometimes refer to the "science question" as the *demarcation problem*: the quest for a set of criteria that can adequately demarcate science from non-science. "Adequately" here generally means something more profound than the disciplining deployment I have been discussing; philosophers working on the demarcation problem are looking for defensible logical or conceptual criteria, powerful enough that their application to a given scholarly controversy will yield a philosophically valuable determination of the scientific status of a given claim or position or approach, and help to explain the success of that science. Such philosophical work does, of course, draw on the cultural prestige of the commonplace "science," but seeks to give content to that label such that the claim to be "scientific" might rest on firm foundations rather than on a vague appreciation for modern technological marvels such as the computer or the airplane.

Inasmuch as philosophical elaborations of demarcation criteria are based on detailed study of successful (and sometimes unsuccessful) sciences, a philosophical solution to the demarcation problem would provide an answer to the question of how IR ought to proceed as a scientific field. In fact, the most prominent use of philosophy of science in IR has been precisely along these lines and has featured efforts to spell out concrete steps that need to be undertaken in order to make IR more, or more properly, scientific. The basic structure of the argument is quite simple: according to some philosopher, successful science S engages in scientific practices $sp_1 \ldots sp_n$; we want IR to be a science too; ergo, we ought to engage in $sp_1 \ldots sp_n$ in IR. Elaborating such sets of practices by referring to something that is rather uncontroversially a science, such as evolutionary biology (Bernstein et al. 2000) or paleontology (Van Belle 2006), implicitly invokes a set of demarcation criteria that both define the science in question as a science, and encompass the subject matter of IR in such a way that practices the author identifies in one domain can be easily transported into the other domain. The uncontroversial identification of the "scientific" domain *as a science* spares the person making the argument from having to spell out explicitly just what it is that defines something as a science: we know it when we see it, after all, and if something works in physics or in paleontology it ought to work in IR, right?

The problem, of course, is that without a clear explication of the criteria that make a given practice of knowledge-production scientific, we have no good way to answer that question. Maybe there is something specific about, say, the empirical domain of physics that enables it to be uniquely scientific in a way that simply will not work if applied to the study of human beings and their social relations.[6] Or maybe different approaches to knowledge-production have their own internal standards and practices, such that trying to apply techniques and procedures from one domain to another is nonsensical at best and harmful at worst. It is impossible to make a decision about matters such as this without a much clearer and more precise elaboration of what a science *is*, which is where philosophers of science might enter the picture. If philosophers agreed on a set of criteria that served to demarcate science from non-science, then we would have a defensible basis on

---

6 Elizabeth Anscombe suggests that this may just be the case with the motion of planets in the solar system, which erroneously gave rise to the notion that Newton's laws provided a paradigm for scientific explanation *per se* (1993, 99).

which to examine claims about particular ways in which knowledge-production practices in IR ought to be disciplined.

Unfortunately, philosophers have come to no global consensus about what defines a field of inquiry as a "science" or a practice of knowledge-production as "scientific." Even worse, different attempts to determine such criteria proceed in wildly divergent directions and elucidate incompatible or contradictory positions on the importance of logical consistency, empirical observability, and predictive accuracy (among other criteria) to a compelling definition of science. Under these circumstances, a turn to the philosophy of science is unlikely to be able to put an end to the science question in IR, precisely because philosophers of science have not themselves reached a consensus about these issues.

The roots of the traditional demarcation problem in the philosophy of science go back to the early twentieth-century "logical positivists" of the Vienna Circle. Confronted with Marx, Freud, Einstein, and a whole slew of theories about racial and national "destinies," the logical positivists sought to elucidate a foolproof way to distinguish between a scientific and a non-scientific statement. Besides being an interesting intellectual puzzle, the scientific status of a claim was also a pressing political and social problem: it mattered a great deal whether a denunciation of the received wisdom about sexuality, time, space, or governmental authority should be considered "scientific" and thus worthy of respect, or unscientific and hence intellectually valueless (Moses and Knutsen 2007, 38–39; Lakatos 2000, 22–24). The logical positivists' major criterion for distinguishing a scientific from a non-scientific claim was *verifiability*, which maintained that a claim could only be scientific if all of its terms could be checked or confirmed through an examination of the empirical world (Ayer 1952, 38).[7] The verifiability criterion would rule out claims involving "'entelechy' in biology, 'historical destiny of a race' or 'self-unfolding of absolute reason' in history," because they were not verifiable—but were instead "mere metaphors without cognitive content" (Hempel 1965b, 237).

However, the verifiability criterion also raised problems for notions such as "force" or "cause," which had long been staples of natural-scientific work. Indeed, a sensibility in many ways quite akin to that of the Vienna Circle led Ludwig Wittgenstein to banish causality from the scientific lexicon altogether: "There is no compulsion making one thing happen because another has happened. The only necessity that exists is *logical* necessity" (Wittgenstein 1961, §6.37). In general, logical positivists preferred to speak of a nomological explanation of an event, "showing that its occurrence could have been inferred ... by applying certain laws of universal or of statistical form to specified antecedent circumstances" (Hempel 1965c, 302). Causality was thus redefined to mean a law-like relationship between phenomena. But this only displaced the problem, because *law-like claims are not verifiable*. All that exists, empirically, are specific objects and entities inhabiting particular situations, and if we were to confine ourselves strictly to what we can

---

7 However, not all of the members of the Vienna Circle were content with the verifiability criterion, and many of them moved beyond it in their own subsequent thinking. See the discussion in Chapter 2, below.

verify we could not say with certainty that, for instance, "books fall to the floor when dropped." All that we could say would be that *this* book fell to the floor when dropped, and *that* book fell to the floor when dropped, and so on ... and we would never reach a law-like statement about books and floors *in general*, no matter how many books we dropped. Rewriting the law-like statement so that it was only probabilistic would not solve the problem, inasmuch as a gap would still remain between "books have been observed quite often to fall to the floor when dropped" and "books quite often fall to the floor when dropped."

Of course, this was a known issue. David Hume had made a similar point over a century earlier:

> All inferences from experience suppose, as their foundation, that the future will resemble the past, and that similar powers will be conjoined with similar sensible qualities. If there be any suspicion, that the course of nature may change, and that the past may be no rule for the future, all experience becomes useless ... In vain do you pretend to have learned the nature of bodies from your past experience. Their secret nature, and consequently, all their effects and influence, may change, without any change in their sensible qualities. This happens sometimes, and with regard to some objects: Why may it not happen always, and with regard to all objects? What logic, what process of argument secures you against this supposition?
>
> (Hume 1977, 24)

Logical positivists worried extensively about this problem and designed increasingly sophisticated ways to try to get around it,[8] but they all floundered on the same basic conceptual gap between particular observations and law-like claims. And this, in turn, would mean that no law-like claim was scientific, because no means could be found for verifying it.

Karl Popper's famous solution to these logical problems involved an inversion of the basic stance of the logical positivists: since law-like claims could never be verified, and since scientific claims were phrased in law-like—often universal—terms, perhaps it made sense to stop asking whether a claim could be proven *true* and instead ask whether a claim could be proven *false* (Popper 1992, 92). If a law-like claim were treated as a hypothetical conjecture instead of being regarded as the logical endpoint of a process of empirical observation and inductive reasoning, the conceptual gap between general laws and particular observations could be subsumed under the procedure of *falsification*: instead of vainly trying to assemble enough particulars to ground a law, a researcher could instead toss a law-like conjecture out into the world and then use particular observations

---

8 Because of their understanding of the relationship between language and the world, the logical positivists could not adopt Hume's own solution: there might not be a logical way to connect past and future events, but there was certainly a link in practical everyday experience (Hume 1977, 17–19). That may have been good enough for Hume, but it was in no way good enough for the Vienna Circle.

to try to disprove it (Popper 1979, 29–30). This, in turn, suggested a different demarcation criterion for scientific claims: instead of being verifiable, they should be falsifiable. Indeed, Popper even added the requirement that the conditions under which a claim would be disproven should be stated in advance of conducting any empirical research; if one could not state such criteria, then one did not have a scientific claim.

The Popperian criterion of falsifiability enjoys a great deal of support, especially among practicing scientists—charges that some claim or piece of research is "unfalsifiable" are often used in a transparently disciplining manner, to exclude that claim or piece of research from serious consideration (Taylor 1996, 30–31). The idea that claims must be testable through the collection of empirical evidence has, to some extent, become commonsensical in many discussions of science, taken for granted to the point that an explicit defense of the idea is not considered to be necessary. For example, in debates about evolution and "creation science," one regularly sees each side accusing the other of holding onto their core assumption in defiance of the available evidence, and thus not adhering to the principle of falsifiability (Beil 2008); but nowhere in those debates will one find a *defense* of falsifiability as a criterion demarcating science from non-science. Instead, debate using the Popperian criterion revolves around the two behavioral implications of the falsifiability principle: researchers should be actively trying to falsify their conjectural claims, and only tentatively and provisionally accepting claims that survive a more or less rigorous series of tests; and researchers should abandon claims that have been falsified, because knowledge only expands if discredited propositions are discarded. Hence the focus of evaluation shifts from claims themselves (as long as they are falsifiable) to the behavior of the communities of researchers working with them, and science ceases to be a purely logical endeavor—it is, rather, a *practical* one.

One problem with falsifiability, however, is that it does not appear to work very well even when applied to established sciences such as physics. That was the chief empirical argument advanced by Thomas Kuhn, who spent a lot of time observing the actual history and practice of science when writing his classic book *The structure of scientific revolutions* (Kuhn 1970b). He discovered that practicing physicists do not, in fact, spend a lot of time attempting to falsify foundational claims about the world. In fact, they seem to take a lot of claims for granted in the conduct of their everyday research work, and when confronted with results that would appear to call into question those foundational claims, they were more likely to creatively reinterpret the results (for instance, by postulating an exogenous intervening factor) than simply to abandon their claims. Kuhn argued that acceptance of these foundational claims was, in fact, the precondition of scientific work:

> When engaged with a normal research problem, the scientist must *premise* current theory as the rules of his game. His object is to solve a puzzle, preferably one at which others have failed, and current theory is required to

define that puzzle and to guarantee that, given sufficient brilliance, it can be solved.

(Kuhn 1970a, 4–5)

"Normal science," as Kuhn defined it, was characterized by puzzle-solving, not by ongoing efforts to falsify any and all conjectures and claims. Actual scientists did not, in practice, adhere to the behavioral implications of falsifiability; hence there was either something wrong with the principle of falsifiability, or with the practice of science itself. Kuhn preferred the former; Popper, in a rather striking contrast to his own principle of falsifiability, stuck to his claim in defiance of the empirical evidence about scientific practice, claiming that Kuhn's normal scientist "has been badly taught" and "is a victim of indoctrination" rather than possessing a properly critical intellect (Popper 1970, 53).

In a way, the disagreement between Kuhn and Popper about what constitutes science illustrates another difficulty involved in attempting to implement the principle of falsifiability in the first place. Take a (Popperian) statement such as "science is characterized by the making of bold conjectures and the attempt to falsify them," and confront it with evidence that practicing scientists do not, in fact, behave in this way; what is the result? Perhaps the statement is rejected because of the discrepant evidence, but perhaps the statement's author questions the accuracy of the potentially falsifying empirical claim, or the definitions involved in the collection of that data, or the meaning of the phrase "science is," or any one of dozens of other things that might be done to call into question the precise relationship between the statement and the evidence. The point is that falsifying a statement is a very complex endeavor, and some philosophers (notably Quine 1961) have argued that one can in principle *always* preserve a theoretical statement by adjusting various background assumptions: the meanings of key terms, the scope of the claim, or the theory built into the way that the empirical data was collected and organized in the first place (Chernoff 2005, 183–184). All of these considerations mean that it is almost impossible to determine when and whether a claim has been falsified, making falsifiability a deeply problematic way to demarcate science from non-science (Hay 2002, 83–84).

It is important to note that the disagreement between Kuhn and Popper about falsifiability as a demarcation criterion is not merely an empirical dispute. Instead, falsifiability versus normal science rests on profoundly divergent views about how knowledgeable actors—scientists, to be sure, but also people in general—relate to one another and to the world that they are studying. For all of his criticisms of logical positivism, Popper retains one of the key Vienna Circle presumptions throughout his work: the presumption that it is always possible to translate claims from one conceptual vocabulary into another one. To the extent that there are "frameworks" of assumptions standing behind our statements, Popper suggests, if we want to be intellectually honest and critical we have to break through those frameworks, lest we allow "ourselves to be caught in a mental prison" (Popper 1996, 53). Falsifiability, like verifiability, depends on the idea that a statement and the pieces of empirical evidence used to evaluate it must all be expressible in ways that would make them clear to any competent observer. Both falsifiability and verifiability would fall apart if they were relativized to a specific conceptual vocabulary, because that would make any statement's scientific status dependent on the language used to express it—and render the principle in question not a very useful demarcation criterion.

However, in many ways, this is precisely what Kuhn's argument *does*. Kuhn embeds scientific statements in the "paradigmatic" framework within which they occur and are evaluated, making it virtually impossible for anyone not working in a given paradigm to determine whether any particular statement is or is not falsifiable or verifiable—or whether the statement presents a viable puzzle to be solved. In this way Kuhn disrupts the very idea of "science" as a single unified field of endeavor, replacing that image with one of islands of incommensurable research. Needless to say, a science made up of incommensurable islands need not have, and most likely does not have, any common standards or criteria for the production of knowledge; nor does it have a single measurement of progress (Kuhn 2000, 85–86).[9] The unity of science—the assumption of perfect translatability that underpinned both logical positivism and Popperian falsifiability—is disrupted by Kuhn's suggestion that science is instead marked by radical discontinuity. Needless to say, the Popperian demarcation criterion drops out of contention too.

In an effort to get around these problems, Imre Lakatos famously proposed that analysts shift away from the evaluation of the scientific status of individual statements, and instead examine a series of statements—a "research programme"— in order to ascertain whether it is progressing or degenerating over time. Lakatos accepted much of Kuhn's account of science, including the idea that one cannot simply subject hypothetical statements to empirical testing in order to ascertain whether the statement is close to the truth. Although Lakatos rejected Kuhn's strong claims about the incommensurability of rival scientific theories (Lakatos 1978, 112), he retained the idea that direct comparison of rival claims—either with one another or with the empirical world—is impossible. This necessitated the formulation of a second-order conceptual language, revolving around the rational reconstruction of scientific controversies *after the fact*, which would permit the comparison of research programmes in terms of their "progressive" or "degenerative" character (Lakatos 1970). Were scientific theories directly testable, this conceptual architecture would not be needed, as one could more or less straightforwardly seek to falsify them by adducing the appropriate evidence (Jackson and Nexon 2009). Hence Lakatos' efforts should be seen as an effort to retain certain elements of the traditional definition of science while

---

9 Note that Kuhn does, however, pull back from a full-blown "relativism" about the value of scientific statements: "There are shared and justifiable, although not necessarily permanent, standards that scientific communities use when choosing between theories" (Kuhn 2000, 76). But those standards are themselves tied to particular scientific communities in a way that Popper would likely find unacceptable. I return to this issue in Chapter 5.

acknowledging the weakness (or, less charitably, the failure) of the Popperian account on methodological and empirical grounds.

All of this philosophical controversy about the definition of "science"—and I have only scratched the surface here, referencing mainly authors whose names have been commonly invoked in existing demarcation debates within the field of IR—makes it deeply problematic to claim, as IR scholars often do, that there are *any* criteria for the definition of "science" that are "standard in philosophy of science" (Vasquez 1995, 230). Instead, we are confronted with a situation in which a variety of standards and criteria present themselves, and absent a widespread consensus about these issues in the philosophy of science the door is opened for IR scholars to, in effect, reach into an alien field of study and pull out something that fits their immediate aims, while retaining the cultural prestige of "science" as a rhetorical warrant for their disciplining maneuver. Far from solving the science question, this kind of intellectual instrumentalism simply muddies the conceptual waters even further.

Even worse, in staging these opportunistic raids into foreign scholarly territory, IR scholars routinely ignore the fact that demarcation debates among philosophers of science are generally concerned with shoring up or preserving notions such as "progress" and "truth" in the face of what might at first seem like discrepant evidence about how actual scientists do their empirical work. Philosophers engaged in demarcating science from non-science are thus, and necessarily, engaged in something of a *normative* enterprise (Laudan 1996, 217–218; Lakatos 1978, 118–121). IR scholars also ignore the fact that philosophers of science engaging in these discussions are working in a *transcendental* mode, and are faced with obviously successful knowledge-producing endeavors, the success of which they are trying to account for in terms of their "scientific" character. No such obvious successes exist in IR, which changes the terms of the debate quite radically (Chernoff 2005, 54–55). Indeed, IR scholars routinely ignore Lakatos' firm division between the "*methodological* appraisal of a programme" and "firm *heuristic* advice about what to do" (Lakatos 1978, 117)—a division that renders deeply problematic any effort to learn what science is from the study of other sciences, with intent to apply those lessons elsewhere. Finally, IR scholars ignore the fact that many contemporary philosophers of science would agree with Larry Laudan's observation that "the problem of demarcation ... is spurious" because even a cursory examination of how various scientific endeavors proceed indicates that they are "not all cut from the same epistemic cloth" (Laudan 1996, 221). By simply taking what we like from the philosophical literature, we miss the context of, and the controversy surrounding, discussions about demarcation among philosophers.

All of this means that it is futile to look to the philosophy of science expecting a simple and clear answer to the question of how we ought to produce knowledge about international affairs, because no such consensus answer is even remotely in evidence. Philosophers of science simply do not speak with one voice when it comes to demarcating and analyzing scientific practice.

Science, broadly understood

Faced with the impossibility of putting an end to the science question within IR by invoking a consensus in the philosophy of science, what should we do? One option is to become philosophers of science ourselves, and to spend our time and our scholarly efforts trying to resolve thorny and abstract issues about the status of theory and evidence and the limits of epistemic certainty. But this is an unappealing option for a scholarly field defined, if loosely, by its empirical focus (international affairs), and it would be roughly akin to advising physicists to become philosophers of physics in order to resolve the question of what physics was and whether it was a science. This also mis-states the relationship between philosophical debates and scientific practice; practicing scientists have a pretty good working definition of what it means for something to be "scientific," but this "is less a matter of strategy than of ongoing evaluative practice," conducted in the course of everyday knowledge-producing activities (Taylor 1996, 133). We do not expect physicists to give philosophical answers to questions about the scientific status of their scholarship; we expect them to produce knowledge of the physical world. Similarly, we should not expect IR scholars to engage in "philosophy of IR" to the detriment of generating knowledge about international affairs; the latter, not the former, is our main vocational task.

If we should not all become philosophers of science, perhaps we should simply continue what we have been doing: deploying philosophical snippets in the course of our "ongoing evaluative practice" of one another's scholarship about international affairs. After all, we are not philosophers of science, so why should it matter whether we are taking philosophical claims out of context? This option is equally unappealing, but for different reasons. For one thing, the rhetorical power of an appeal to "science" within IR, as within other scholarly fields that have inherited a "science question" from their forebears (Steinmetz 2005a), depends on a claim—perhaps implicit—that the criteria identified as "scientific" *are in fact* the kinds of knowledge-production practices that, if adopted, will establish IR as a science. In principle, at least, this is a claim that can be evaluated, and more importantly, it is a claim that can be true or false. Whether it is true or whether it is false has enormous implications for whether we ought to engage in the specified course of action. While the lack of consensus among philosophers of science should put to rest the idea that any given knowledge-production practices are *uniquely* scientific, it is still entirely possible to ground claims to scientific status in firmer philosophical arguments, and thus to move beyond the merely tactical use of a term such as "science."

Besides this logical reason, there is also an ethical reason why we should stop taking philosophical claims about "science" out of context and using them to shore up our positions within disciplinary debates: when we invoke "science," we are in a very practical sense playing with fire. The cultural prestige of "science" is such that tapping that commonplace in a debate is really akin to bringing out the big guns, raising the temperature of the controversy to the point where one wonders how far we are from an accusation of "relativism" and an accompanying violation of Godwin's Law.[10] Under such circumstances, it is even more important to ask whether the appeal to "science" is philosophically appropriate.

A third option would be simply to de-escalate our controversies about research practices and refrain from invoking "science" in such discussions at all. Larry Laudan suggests that philosophers of science ought to do just this, shifting their attention to "the question of reliable knowledge" and giving up any attempt to define the boundaries of scientific practice (Laudan 1996, 222). But Laudan's proposal, I would argue, is only feasible within a scholarly field not as dominated by the science question as IR has historically been. Whether the philosophy of science is itself a science remains a much less pressing question than the question of whether the study of international affairs is or can be a science. The cultural prestige of "science" makes the notion a very appealing rhetorical weapon; a simple promise not to use it is probably not credible, and as long as "science" retains its broader appeal, it will likely be too tempting for one party of a debate to reach for the commonplace in the course of discussion. Simply removing the claim to "science" from IR discussions is, therefore, probably quite a futile endeavor.

Hence, the best response to the fact that the science question cannot be simply resolved by a turn to philosophy is to *replace* the narrow definition(s) of "science" circulating in the field with a definition that simply cannot be deployed by partisans of any single approach to the study of international affairs as part of an effort to render their opponents' claims unworthy of serious consideration. What we should be avoiding, as a field, are derisive caricatures of one another's work as "storytelling," "mindless number-crunching," or "philosophical mumbo-jumbo," and the accompanying characterization of those approaches as "unscientific" and hence not worthy of intellectual engagement. Similarly, we ought to be avoiding caricatures of self-proclaimed "scientific" work as being out of touch with the actual world, incapable of appreciating the complexity of social life, or necessarily wedded to the preservation of the status quo. Instead, a principle of charity (Blackburn 1994, 62) is called for: treat other arguments about international affairs as serious attempts to generate knowledge. But as long as "science" remains in circulation in the field in the vague form in which it presently exists, such charitable readings are unlikely to survive, as it is too tempting simply to wield "science" as an excuse for not engaging claims at odds with one's own.

In order to craft a sufficiently broad definition of science, it is important not to replicate the errors and weaknesses associated with the disciplining deployments I have been criticizing. As such, it is unlikely that an acceptable definition of science can be produced by looking for fundamental "rules of inference on which" the "validity" of "scientific research ... depends" (King, Keohane, and Verba 1994, 9). The reason is simple: different kinds of empirical research in IR adhere to

---

10 Godwin's Law (http://en.wikipedia.org/wiki/Godwin's_law) is a principle of online discussion forums that attempts to regulate inappropriate references to Hitler (or, in some variants, the Holocaust) during heated controversies. It is simply astonishing how many claims about "relativism" in demarcation debates are closely followed by accusations that an abandonment of the ground of "science" or "reason" leads directly to Hitler and the Holocaust.

different "rules of inference," and some reject inference itself in favor of (for example) thick description or structural overdetermination or discourse analysis. Hence, making some set of "rules of inference" the criterion for scientific status simply replicates the same disciplining move under the guise of advancing a putatively neutral set of methods and techniques. Arguably, *any* attempt to specify universal rules and procedures is doomed to collapse into a disciplining move, since there are no rules so universally agreed upon that their adoption would be uncontroversial. The commonality of "science" in IR, then, cannot be sought in rules or procedures for handling evidence or evaluating claims.

Perhaps the common element animating a field-wide definition of science can be found not in the supposed methods of science, but in the *goals* of science. Colin Wight suggests that "what distinguishes scientific knowledge is not the method of knowledge acquisition, nor the immutable nature of the knowledge produced, but the aim of the knowledge itself," which he takes to be the "explanatory content" of scientific knowledge (Wight 2006, 61). Defining science in this way seems promising, as long as the precise definition of "explanatory" is allowed to vary so as to encompass a variety of approaches to explaining phenomena in international affairs. Unfortunately, Wight promptly goes further in specifying a sense of "explanatory" that excludes more than a few ways of studying international affairs:

> What marks scientific knowledge out from other forms of knowledge is that it attempts to go beyond appearances and provide explanations at a deeper level of understanding. This implies that the scientist believes that there is a world beyond the appearances that helps explain those appearances.
>
> (Ibid., 18)

Thus Wight offers a unity of *ontology*—the belief in a mind-independent reality to which our concrete researches should be directed (as in Wendt 1999, 52–53)—as the crucial element in science. But this locking down of a precise meaning of "explanatory" drives us right back into the disciplining move of accepting one philosophically controversial account of science and shaping our empirical work in IR in accord with it—and dismissing other kinds of work as not sufficiently "scientific."[11] Absent a universal consensus about the validity of presuming the existence of a "world beyond ... appearances," this is not a solution to our problem.

Indeed, perhaps the only solution that does not presume a non-existent philosophical consensus about the definition of "science" would be an account of science that, in effect, equated science with empirical inquiry designed to produce knowledge. Such an account would not give a lot of specific guidance as to how empirical research should be conducted, but it would serve to differentiate

---

11 In point of fact, the strategy of critical realists such as Wight is more often to argue that everyone in the field is already a critical realist, at least implicitly (Wight 2006, 26). I take up the problems with this claim in Chapter 4.

the production of knowledge about international affairs from other things that one might do with respect to international affairs—other things that might be valuable in their own way, but which would not be reducible or equivalent to knowledge-production. Such an account would also allow the criteria for *good* knowledge about international affairs to vary between approaches; designating all empirical inquiry designed to produce knowledge as science in no way says that all knowledge-claims are equally good ones. It simply shifts the question—along the lines of both Laudan's and Lakatos' criticisms of the demarcation problem— from "Is this piece of work scientific?" to "Is this piece of work a good piece of work?" Naturally, *answering* that question in any particular situation will require us to elaborate and specify standards for good work, but by getting the rhetorical trump-card "science" out of the mix, a broad definition allows us to focus on the knowledge-production techniques in our own field instead of focusing on what we think other fields are doing.

This may be the most important contribution of a broad and pluralistic definition of science: to cure IR of its perennial envy of other fields of scholarly inquiry by highlighting the important conceptual work on the matter of science that has already been done *within the social sciences themselves*. Almost four decades ago, Albert O. Hirschman called for precisely this kind of self-assertion by practitioners of the study of politics, arguing (as an economist!) that political scientists need not accept the colonization of their field by economists:

> [R]eciprocity has been lacking in recent interdisciplinary work as economists have claimed that concepts developed for the purpose of analyzing phenomena of scarcity and resource allocation can be successfully used for explaining political phenomena as diverse as power, democracy, and nationalism. They have thus succeeded in occupying large portions of the neighboring discipline while political scientists—whose inferiority complex vis-à-vis the tool-rich economist is equaled only by that of the economist vis-à-vis the physicist—have shown themselves quite eager to be colonized and have often actively joined the invaders. Perhaps it takes an economist to reawaken feelings of identity and pride among our oppressed colleagues and to give them a sense of confidence that their concepts too have not only *grandeur*, but *rayonnement* as well?
>
> (Hirschman 1970a, 19–20)

What Hirschman claims about *substantive* concepts, I mean to suggest, is equally true of *methodological* concepts: those of us engaged in the scholarly study of social and political life have our own proud tradition of reflection on the science question, and the broad definition of science I want to propose comes directly from the seminal reflections of Max Weber on this topic. Adoption of this broadly Weberian account of science, I suggest, can quite neatly resolve the problems I have been discussing, and take the science card out of the hands of anyone looking to deploy it in a disciplining fashion while retaining key elements of the specificity of science.

Weberian science

For Weber, what defines "science" is not its manner or its method, but its goal—a goal that, in the first instance, differentiates it from partisan politics:

> The taking of practical-political positions and the scientific analysis of political structures and party positions are two very different things. If you are speaking about democracy in a popular meeting, you do not need to make a mystery of your personal position; instead, clearly taking a recognizable position is your damned duty and responsibility. The words you use are not tools of scientific analysis, but political advertisements against the positions of others. They are not ploughshares for the loosening of the soil of contemplative thought, but swords for use against your opponents: weapons.
>
> (Weber 1917, 14–15)

The distinction that Weber is drawing here is a *logical* distinction between two different ways of using words and concepts, and a distinction of *intention* between the goals of such usage. In the realm of practical politics, the key goal is the achieving of results; the clarity or defensibility of those words and concepts is of decidedly secondary importance. But in the realm of scientific analysis, the order is inverted: what matters most of all is the systematic application of a set of theories and concepts so as to produce a "thoughtful ordering of empirical actuality" (Weber 1999a, 160). Weber elaborates:

> The social science that we want to concern ourselves with is a *science of actuality*. We want to understand *in its particularity* the encompassing actuality of the life in which we are placed—on one hand, the coherence and cultural *significance* of individual occurrences in their contemporary configuration, and on the other hand, the reasons for those occurrences being historically so and not otherwise.
>
> (Weber 1999a, 170–171)

For Weber, then, there is no fundamental opposition between "explaining" and "understanding," as both are equally scientific. Instead of reading Weber as advocating one or another specific *kind* of social science, as Hollis and Smith (1990, 72–82) do, we should understand Weber's project as the attempt to define a basic and broad notion of "social science" *within which* we might then discuss or debate (for example) the extent to which we ought to take an actor's description of her or his action as a point of departure for our analysis. Thus Weber's encompassing definition of science, which we might think of as "systematic empirical analysis that aims to produce knowledge rather than aiming to produce innerworldly effects," provides a big enough tent to put out the fires associated with accusations that someone is being "unscientific" by not conducting her or his research in the way we would prefer, but to simultaneously preserve the difference between (social) science and other forms of human action.

Another way to put this is that Weber's definition is that science, including social science, should be concerned with empirical *facts* rather than with evaluative *judgments*.[12] For example, Weber distinguishes between an abstract concept of "Christianity" that might be used to generate factual knowledge about some particular sect or arrangement, and an evaluative definition of "Christianity" that might provide a basis on which to judge whether some particular doctrine or arrangement was or was not actually *Christian*:

> Here it is *no longer* a matter of a purely theoretical process of *referring* to values empirically, but instead of value-*judgments* which have been taken over into the "concept" of Christianity. *Because* the ideal-type claims empirical *validity*, it towers into the region of the evaluative *interpretation* of Christianity. The ground of empirical science is forsaken; before us stands a profession of faith, and *not* an ideal-typical *conceptual* construct.
>
> (Weber 1999a, 199)

In IR terms, we might think of this as an admonition that we ought not to confuse a concept such as "sovereignty" or "human rights" that we might use in generating empirical facts about international affairs with a normative standard that we might use to judge or evaluate international affairs. For Hedley Bull, the distinction between "order" and "justice" illustrated this nicely: Bull treated order primarily as "an actual or possible condition or state of affairs in world politics," and thus as an instrument for generating factual knowledge of social relations, while arguing that justice "belongs to the class of moral ideas, ideas which treat human actions as right in themselves" (Bull 1977, 77–78). Justice, for Bull, is therefore a concept useful for a normative evaluation of those same social relations: an evaluative commentary on the facts, rather than the production of factual knowledge. These are logically distinct endeavors.[13]

However, it does not follow from the dictum that science ought to be focused on the production of factual knowledge that the practice of academic analysis is somehow devoid of values. Indeed, Weber argues:

---

12 Note that although Weber uses the notion of an "ideal-type" in making this distinction, the argument itself, logically speaking, does not depend on the abstract concept being ideal-typical in a strict sense I will discuss in Chapter 5 below. Rather, the important point here is the difference between the intent to generate factual knowledge and the intent to judge and evaluate what exists.

13 I am well aware that some scholars, especially critical realists, may try to reject this distinction on the grounds that "if ... one is in possession of a theory which explains why false consciousness is necessary, one can pass immediately, without the addition of any extraneous value judgments, to a negative evaluation of the object ... that makes that consciousness necessary" (Bhaskar 1998, 63). However, the fact that even such scholars argue that there is a *necessary connection* between empirical analysis and subsequent normative critique, and refrain from arguing that there is *no difference* between empirical analysis and normative critique, helps to support my claim that the two activities are conceptually distinct—even for those who argue that they ought to be tightly connected.

There is simply no "objective" scientific analysis of cultural life—or, put perhaps somewhat more narrowly but certainly not essentially differently for our purposes—of a "social phenomenon" *independent* of special and "one-sided" points of view, according to which—explicitly or tacitly, consciously or unconsciously—they are selected, analyzed, and representationally organized as an object of research.

(Weber 1999a, 170)

The inescapability of value-commitments does not mean that "*research* can only have *results* which are 'subjective' in the sense that they are *valid* for one person and not for others" (ibid., 183–184). Indeed, as I have been arguing, the distinctiveness of science for Weber is not that it embodies no value-commitments, but that it does something distinctive with those commitments. Value-commitments place a specific duty on the practicing (social) scientist:

A systematically correct scientific demonstration in the social sciences, if it wants to achieve its goal, must be recognized as correct even by a Chinese (or, more accurately, it must constantly *strive* to attain this goal, although it may not be completely reachable due to a dearth of documentation). Further, if the *logical* analysis of the content of an ideal and of its ultimate axioms, and the demonstration of the consequences that arise from pursuing it logically and practically, wants to be valid and successful, it must be valid for someone who lacks the "sense" of our ethical imperative and who would (and often will) refuse our ideal and the concrete *valuations* that flow from it. None of these refusals come anywhere near the scientific value of the *analysis*.

(Ibid., 155–156)

The basic point here is that even someone who rejects our values should be able to acknowledge the validity of our empirical results within the context of our perspective. The fact that we have a perspective—that our results were produced by the application of concepts and procedures laden with specific sets of values—is philosophically and epistemologically important, but it has little or no bearing on the question of whether a piece of work is "scientific" or not. Instead, the decisive issue is *internal validity*: whether, given our assumptions, our conclusions follow rigorously from the evidence and logical argumentation that we provide.

None of this is to say that normative evaluation of international affairs is not a good and worthwhile activity, or to say that the distinction between science and politics denigrates the actual practice of politics. Nor is the implication here that the scholarly field of IR ought to be exclusively "scientific," even in the broad Weberian sense I have proposed here. It is, rather, to distinguish logically between a number of ends to which we might apply our scholarly efforts. We could engage in the generation of political arguments and commentaries; we could engage in the normative evaluation of actually existing political and social arrangements; or we could engage in the systematic production of factual knowledge about those political and social arrangements.[14] Calling only the third of these "science" preserves the integrity of all of these different orientations and intentions: in order for the claim to scientific status to have any *value* in the political or normative spheres, it is logically necessary for science to be distinct from those endeavors. Otherwise, calling a claim "scientific" is perhaps nothing but shorthand for saying that one agrees or disagrees with it, perhaps on political or normative grounds. Whether a scientific claim ought to trump a political one, or whether normative claims ought to build on scientific ones, are open questions, but they cannot even be *asked* if one does not start from the position that science constitutes a distinct endeavor. Not necessarily a better or worse endeavor, but a *distinct* one.

---

14 Elsewhere (Jackson 2015a) I have argued that the vocational orientation underlying the practice of scientific work should be understood precisely as the intent to generate factual knowledge, and contrasted it with *three* other orientations and intentions: the results-oriented vocation of technical work, the expressive vocation of aesthetic work, and the evaluative vocation of ethical work. There I also made the case that all four of these vocations and intentions belong in the scholarly field of international studies. But as this is a book about the "science question" in IR, I am not going to go into detail about those alternative vocations here.

2 Philosophical wagers

The broad, Weberian definition of science I have sketched in the previous chapter is designed to accomplish two tasks. First, it effectively makes science equivalent to systematic inquiry designed to produce factual knowledge. Second, it differentiates science from other knowledge-laden endeavors, such as practical politics and normative evaluation. As such, this broad definition of science makes it virtually impossible for the charge of being "unscientific" to be used as a way to discredit a piece of scholarship that intends to contribute to our factual knowledge of the world. The only kinds of works against which such a charge could be legitimately deployed—works of normative analysis and works of political advocacy or commentary, along with works of art and summaries of technical practice—would, almost certainly, not be particularly interested in classifying themselves as "scientific." Even critical-theoretical scholarship in the Frankfurt School (Linklater 2007) or neo-Gramscian (Cox 1996b) traditions, which routinely emphasizes the evaluative aspects of scholarship, relies on factual claims about the empirical world in order to give its critical interventions sufficient force (Geuss 1981, 109). The critical-theoretical argument about scholarship and values is, in the language I have introduced here, an argument that the scientific parts of scholarship ought to be supplemented by normative or even partisan-political parts. As long as Weber's admonition about making it clear "where the analytical researcher becomes silent and the advocating person begins to speak" (Weber 1999a, 167) is adhered to, this poses no special problems for a broad definition of science.

That said, the Weberian definition of science does not tell us very much about precisely what we ought to be doing when we conduct research on international affairs. This is also by design, since linking any *specific* approach to worldly knowledge-production with the label "science" simply re-opens the unproductive disciplining debates so prominent in the field of IR over its history. The only way that such a strategy would be justified would be if there were broad philosophical consensus on the definition of science, but this is simply not the case. Hence, deploying claims derived from, or authors working on, the philosophy of science for the purpose of defining science—and therefore disciplining all empirical research in the field of IR—appears to be an enterprise fraught with peril. If philosophers of science as a group do not agree on what science is, what intellectual warrant do we have to pluck out one or another position on science from within their discussions and place it as a standard in front of our particular campaign to alter the field?

However, the fact that we should not be looking to philosophy of science as a way to resolve definitively the science question does not mean that IR scholars have no use for the philosophy of science. If we stop expecting that philosophy of science contains some kind of master strategy that will, if implemented in IR, make us truly "scientific," perhaps we can start to appreciate the *actual* value of philosophical reflections on knowledge-production: systematically clarifying the implications, especially the methodological implications, of taking a particular stand on how to produce knowledge. A broad definition of science, by design, does not provide us with any standards for good research, or indeed any specific advice for how to go about doing research, beyond its basic admonitions to focus on factual knowledge of the world, and to separate this activity logically and conceptually from the promulgation of normative judgments and from partisan-political stances. But methodological advice and standards are indispensable components of any actually existing line of scientific research; practicing researchers necessarily operate with a wide variety of techniques designed to facilitate and improve their research, and to criticize constructively the research produced by others. Philosophy of science, as a reflection on scientific research practice, can help us to make explicit some of the tacit principles with which researchers in particular traditions are already operating. In other words, philosophy of science can help us to *clarify* IR research practices, with an eye towards making them more coherent and potentially more productive.

This makes the utility of the philosophy of science for IR primarily a *methodological* utility. By "methodology" in this context I mean something quite different than "methods": methods are techniques for gathering and analyzing bits of data, whereas methodology is "a concern with the logical structure and procedure of scientific enquiry" (Sartori 1970, 1,033). Philosophy of science is not going to teach anyone how to run a multivariate regression testing hypotheses about democracy and economic growth, or how to craft an ethnographic account of the activities of the Ministry of Foreign Affairs, but it can help us think through the decision to utilize those methods, and make sure that we are using research methods in ways that complement one another or generally hang together. We do not spend much time in the field wrestling with such methodological questions; instead, we engage in discussion about methods, debating such technical issues as the relative merits of different techniques of case-selection and case-comparison (George and Bennett 2005; McKeown 1999; Mahoney and Goertz 2004; Beach and Pedersen 2013) or how to identify the appropriate documents for use in a discourse analysis (Hansen 2006, 51–54; Bially Mattern 2004, 63–68). These are important questions of method, but they are not questions of methodology, inasmuch as these discussions presume a whole variety of things about the definition of knowledge and the overall goal of empirical research. Indeed, absent at least a broad agreement on strategic questions about the character and status of knowledge, it is unlikely that the tactical debates about how best to achieve those strategic goals could even take place.

That we do not do a lot of this kind of reflection in IR, or in the sciences generally, is quite understandable when one remembers that our primary professional job is the production of knowledge about the world, and our primary specialized training is in specific techniques of data-collection and data-analysis. Philosophy of science is not even a required course in many, if not most, Ph.D. programs in IR (Schwartz-Shea 2003), further contributing to our challenges in engaging in these kinds of conceptual discussions. However, it is tremendously important that we not lose sight of methodological issues as we craft and evaluate pieces of empirical research, both because methods without methodology can be quite myopic in lacking a big picture within which specific techniques might make sense, and because in the absence of explicit methodological reflection there is a not inconsiderable chance that scholars working in various lines of research will continue to consider their way of conducting research to be uniquely "scientific" rather than *a* way of doing scientific research. Methodological reflection, assisted by readings in the philosophy of science, is the cure for both of these ills.

Ontology, philosophical and scientific

By linking philosophy of science to methodology, and foregrounding methodological reflection in thinking about how to do empirical research, I am deliberately breaking with a tradition of denigrating methodology that is common among philosophers and scientists alike. In that tradition, methodological questions come late in the game, after more fundamental issues have been sorted out; hence the proper place of philosophy of science would be *prior* to methodology. Three section-headings from Audie Klotz and Cecelia Lynch's book on research techniques (Klotz and Lynch 2007), and the sequence in which they occur in the book's first chapter, tell the story:

> Ontology: how do researchers conceptualize what they study?
> Epistemology: how do researchers know what they know?
> Methodology: how do researchers select their tools?

The sequence here, which is echoed in numerous contemporary guides to research, runs from ontology (concerning *being*, and what exists in the world) to epistemology (concerning *knowing*, and how observers formulate and evaluate statements about the world) and only then to methodology—here, as elsewhere in the literature, defined as the selection of specific research tools. Colin Wight clarifies this sequence, contrasting an "inclusive" definition of methodology such as the one I have advanced with a "less expansive notion" (such as that presumed by Klotz and Lynch) that equates methodology with "the differing methods of gaining knowledge *relative to the object of inquiry*" (Wight 2006, 258; emphasis added). I have highlighted the crucial clause in Wight's claim, since by linking methodology to "the object of inquiry" he also privileges ontology and epistemology over methodology. Indeed, Wight explicitly claims that "methodologies are always, or at least should be, ontologically specific ... the methods used to study atomic particles, for example, would be wholly inappropriate when applied to the study of social processes" (ibid., 259).[1] Therefore we ought to begin with the world and compose our research strategies accordingly—a position that involves putting ontology first, and maintaining that "it is the nature of objects that determines their cognitive possibilities for us" (Bhaskar 1998, 25).

Wight further argues that a privileging of methodology in the abstract might lead to efforts to define a single "scientific method," and thus act as "a potential barrier to methodological innovation and pluralism" (Wight 2006, 258). His fear seems partially justified when we consider the fact that contemporary efforts to define a universal, categorical scientific approach—especially within the social sciences—stake their claim *precisely* on the distinction between claims about the world and claims about the design and goals of empirical research, as when King, Keohane, and Verba (1994, 20, 29–30) distance themselves from "parsimony" (a claim about the composition of the world) in favor of "leverage" (a principle of hypothesis-construction). Hence, we appear to have a choice between starting with the world and conforming our methodology to that world, or starting with methodology and thus losing the world as we try to articulate universal standards for scientific research—universal standards that I have been claiming *do not exist* in any intellectually defensible way.

On Wight's account, the role of philosophy of science would be to clarify our *ontological* assumptions, not our methodological practices. Philosophy of science has been used to do this in the field of IR, starting with Wendt's seminal paper on the agent-structure problem (Wendt 1987), which drew on critical realist philosophy of science to suggest that unobservable structures, both in the natural and the social worlds, were as real as the objects of sensory experience. Notions of "punctuated equilibrium" (Spruyt 1994) and "complexity" (Hoffmann and Riley 2002) have made their way into the study of international affairs through a similar route: from natural science, through philosophical reflection, and finally into IR. The implicit logic driving such importations seems to be that if natural scientists, or those philosophers who reflect on the natural sciences, have a way of apprehending the world that works well for them, then maybe it will work equally well for us—even if certain technical aspects of empirical research need to be altered so as to take account of the ontological differences between mute natural objects and self-aware human beings (Bhaskar 1998, 159). In any event, ontology comes first.

However, I do not think that putting ontology first is the panacea that many seem to think it is. For one thing, if one puts ontology first then one is, at least provisionally, committed to a particular (if revisable) account of what the world

---

1   There is some—perhaps deliberate—irony in Wight's citation of Alex Wendt at this point in his text, given that one of Wendt's current projects involves *precisely* the effort to explore the implications of the study of (sub)atomic particles to the study of social processes (Wendt 2006; Wendt 2015).

is made up of: co-constituted agents and structures, states interacting under conditions of anarchy, global class relations, or what have you. This is a rather large leap to make on anyone's authority, let alone that of a philosopher of science. Along these lines, it is unclear that we could provide any *warrant* for most ontological claims if ontology in this sense were to always "come first." If someone makes an ontological claim about something existing in the world, then we are faced with an intriguing *epistemological* problem of how possibly to know whether that claim is true, and the equally intriguing problem of selecting the proper *methods* to use in evaluating the claim (Chernoff 2009b, 391). But if epistemology and method are supposed to be fitted to ontology, then we are stuck with techniques and standards designed to respond to the specificity of the object under investigation. This problem is roughly akin to using state-centric measurements of cross-border transactions to determine whether globalization is eroding state borders, because the very object under investigation—"state borders"—is presupposed by the procedures of data-collection, meaning that the answer will always, and necessarily, assert the persistence of the state.

There is also a more fundamental problem with "putting ontology first," which is that ontology in contemporary philosophical usage can refer to two different, but related, components of a way of apprehending the world. On one hand, ontology can refer to a catalog of objects, processes, and factors that a given line of scientific research expects to exist or has evidence for the existence of: ontology as bestiary, so to speak, concerned with what exists, or with the general principles on which such existence might be determined. On the other hand, ontology can refer to the conceptual and philosophical basis on which claims about the world are formulated in the first place: ontology as our "hook-up" to the world, so to speak, concerned with how we as researchers are able to produce knowledge in the first place (Shotter 1993b, 73–79). Patomäki and Wight helpfully distinguish between these two uses of the term "ontology" by designating the former "scientific ontology" and the latter "philosophical ontology" (Patomäki and Wight 2000, 215); they also note that philosophical ontology is logically, and necessarily, prior to the construction of any scientific ontology, since we cannot make defensible claims about what exists until the basis on which we are doing so has been clarified.

So when we talk about putting ontology first, which kind of ontology do we mean? Since philosophical ontology takes logical and conceptual priority, one would think that philosophical ontology ought to come first. However, most advocates of putting ontology first seem more concerned with elaborating their particular scientific ontology, and putting *that* first: before epistemology, methodology, or concrete research methods. For Wight, this scientific ontology involves agents and structures as irreducible objects of "interdependent nature," meaning that they never occur separately but nonetheless remain essentially distinct from one another (Wight 2006, 296). For Wendt, this scientific ontology involves states as the actually-existing persons of international society interacting so as to produce and sustain a variety of "cultures of anarchy" (Wendt 1999, 246–250). In that way, the call to put ontology first seems to mean approximately the same thing as having a clear definition of the entities and factors with which one is concerned: states (Nettl 1968), firms (Williamson 1998), transnational social movements (Keck and Sikkink 1998), and so forth. What it means to produce knowledge and how we produce knowledge could then be customized to the particular features of the entities and factors under investigation.

This pull away from philosophical ontology towards scientific ontology is so strong as to affect even works overtly concerned with ways of producing knowledge rather than with the objects of knowledge. A most prominent example of this is Hollis and Smith's widely read book *Explaining and understanding international relations* (Hollis and Smith 1990), which begins with some claims about philosophical ontology proper but then mixes in claims about objects and entities—elements of scientific ontology—in seeking to elaborate what it might mean to study international affairs from different theoretical and conceptual standpoints. Hollis and Smith begin by contrasting "explaining" and "understanding" as separate "traditions" yielding different kinds of accounts of international affairs, with an "explaining" story working from an outsider's perspective "in the manner of a natural scientist seeking to explain the workings of nature and treating the human realm as part of nature," while an "understanding" story works from the inside, "told so as to make us understand what the events mean, in a sense distinct from any meaning found in unearthing the laws of nature" (ibid., 1).[2] At the outset, then, we are in the realm of philosophical ontology, since what is at stake in the contrast between "explaining" and "understanding" is not the character of the world, but rather how we observers are hooked up to it. That this is the case can be easily glimpsed by asking whether it would make sense to generate both kinds of stories about any given situation, social or natural; to do this we need not look far to find both insider and outsider accounts of both the natural and social worlds.[3] Insider "understanding" and outsider "explaining" accounts can, in principle, be used to generate knowledge of *any* kind of object; as philosophical ontologies, they logically precede any possible scientific ontology or catalog of entities and factors.

Hollis and Smith, however, quickly slip into enumerating characteristics of objects, linking those enumerations to the two traditions with which they are concerned. Insider and outsider accounts, we quickly learn, conceptualize individual human beings quite differently:

> X is an actor conceived in the spirit of the scientific ["explaining"] tradition, Y the counterpart in the spirit of the interpretative ["understanding"] tradition … Being part of the natural world and a proper object of scientific study, X is predictable on the basis of X's preferences and information, which are in

2   Although in the previous chapter I have discussed the explaining/understanding contrast and criticized the equating of "science" with the "explaining" tradition, I am setting that issue aside for the moment and focusing more directly on the content of Hollis and Smith's contrast itself.

3   For a fascinating study of the issues involved in dueling "insider" and "outsider" accounts, see Corbey (2005).

turn the result of *X*'s nature and nurture ... The fabric of *Y*'s social world is woven from rules and meanings, which define relationships among the inhabitants and give interpretations their purpose ... *Y* is expected to pick an intelligent course through a variety of social engagements, to which actors bring something of themselves in exercising their social capacities.

(Ibid., 4–6)

We are no longer in the realm of philosophical ontology, and "explaining" and "understanding" now name substantive conceptions of things in the world rather than ways in which the researcher is connected to the world. The shift here is subtle, but important: in the space of a few pages we have gone from different ways of encountering objects (from the outside or from the inside) to different conceptions of existing objects (*homo economicus* and *homo sociologicus*, so to speak).[4] Indeed, it would not be too much of a stretch to say that Hollis and Smith's argument that "explaining" and "understanding" accounts cannot be reconciled rests on the fact that, substantively speaking, the world envisioned by "explaining" and the world envisioned by "understanding" are *not the same world*, as the explaining-world is a world of structural constraints where people's social capacities have to be explained in terms of broader social forces, while the understanding-world is a world of historical endowments that offer possibilities that can only be actualized by playing out a set of social interactions (ibid., 209–212). But that is a disagreement that takes place almost exclusively on the terrain of scientific ontology, and involves "worldviews" rather than ways that the researcher might be connected to the world.

The virtual disappearance of philosophical ontology from IR debates—and its ready replacement by sets of substantive considerations—carries with it a set of costs for IR scholarship. Chief among these is that every substantive disagreement is transformed into an empirical dispute, but without any clear guidelines for how such disputes are supposed to be resolved. That such empirical disputes are difficult to resolve is evidenced by a quick glance at the ongoing debates surrounding the question of whether "balancing" or "bandwagoning" behavior among states predominates at the level of the international system (Kaufman, Little, and Wohlforth 2007), or whether "ideas" or "material factors" were the most important cause of the end of the Cold War (Brooks and Wohlforth 2001; English 2002; Brooks and Wohlforth 2002). Further, what comes up in these debates on a regular basis are questions of methodology and research design: what kind of knowledge of the world we can and should produce, and how to go about producing such knowledge. However, in the absence of any sustained attention to philosophical ontology, *such questions are almost certainly irresolvable*, as

---

4   Oddly, however, Hollis and Smith treat the "rational actor model" as a type of insider "understanding" account (Hollis and Smith 1990, 74–77). But anyone who has ever read a technically sophisticated rational-choice account of *anything* knows full well that such analysis is not about increasing insider "understanding" at all, but is almost wholly concerned with subsuming behavior under analytically general principles of decision-making and thus "explaining" it.

any scholar can at almost any time retreat behind the safety of their particular view of the world—their scientific ontology—and the sets of research techniques designed to work in and with that world. Thus, realists read international affairs as characterized by a struggle for power among independent political units ("international politics," as in Waltz 1979), neoliberal institutionalists read international affairs as characterized by a competitive set of mixed-motive games under conditions of interdependence (the "partially globalized world" of Keohane 2002), and when confronted by evidence emanating from the other camp, partisans of each worldview simply reassert their central postulates and go on reading the world in their own way.[5]

Of course, one way to resolve this fragmentation would be to impose a set of common standards—one might even call them "scientific" standards—on the field as a whole, and then subject every worldview to the same procedures of systematic evaluation. But the very idea of empirically adjudicating between scientific ontologies *presumes a certain philosophical ontology*—a philosophical ontology that implicitly animates both calls to put ontology before epistemology (Wendt 1999, 52) and calls to dispense with "meta-theory" in favor of a focus on substantive claims (for example, Friedman and Starr 1997). In both cases, scholars are enjoined to stop worrying about their "hook-up" to the world and simply focus on the world itself and the entities and factors in it, whether those are sovereign territorial states or patterns of global class domination or whatever. The philosophical ontology underlying all of these claims, the grounds on which a claim advocating a focus on the world rather than on our hook-up to the world can be sensibly articulated, is the apparently innocuous notion of "independently existing reality" (Patomäki and Wight 2000, 217)—the notion that there is a world "out there," beyond all of our knowledge-making practices, to which our claims refer and with which those claims can be compared in order to assess their veracity. This *mind–world dualism* is the philosophical ontology that makes meaningful the proposition that we can empirically evaluate scientific ontologies, because if there is a world existing "out there" in a mind-independent way, we can in principle compare any given scientific ontology to that world and see if it in some sense "matches."[6]

In fact, mind–world dualism also underpins the very distinction with which I began this discussion of types of ontology: the separation between ontological concerns on the one hand, and epistemological and methodological concerns on the other. In order to coherently argue that knowledge-production is separate from and subordinate to the way that the world is, it is necessary to argue that the world

---

5　Accompanying this procedure of reasserting one's strongly held views on world politics by out-of-context citations from Thomas Kuhn or Imre Lakatos does not make the procedure any more logically defensible. I provide a more explicit consideration of Kuhn and Lakatos and their (mis)use among IR scholars in Chapter 3; see also Jackson and Nexon (2009).

6　Note that the phrase "in some sense" here encompasses a wide variety of philosophical and methodological controversies, some of which will be surveyed in subsequent chapters. Likewise the notion of "matches."

exists independently of our knowledge of it, and that the world places limits on how we may produce knowledge of it. Epistemology as a separate philosophical focus only emerged after the early Enlightenment redefinition of the situation of human beings as individual minds facing an external world, and from Descartes onward largely concerned itself with trying to bridge the gap between the mind and the world in a robust and defensible manner, asking whether we could trust sensory impressions, whether ideas were innate or arose from observation, and whether and in what sense generalizations could be considered valid (Taylor 1995, 3–5). I will unpack some of these controversies below; for the moment, my point is simply that *all of these issues presume mind–world dualism*. In the absence of a firm separation between the mind and the world, there would be no mind–world gap to bridge and, indeed, no "epistemology" as such. If "mind" and "world" are not two separate and distinct things, then it literally makes no sense to speak of the world as independently existing, since mind would be always and already intertwined with the world; nor would it make sense to subordinate epistemological and methodological concerns to the specific features of the world, since those features cannot be sensibly referred to outside of the context of the practices of knowledge-production that we employ when investigating them.

So perhaps the most significant implication of the disappearance of an explicit consideration of philosophical ontology within IR debates, and the consequent rush to elaborate scientific ontologies and to design research techniques and approaches, is that mind–world dualism goes largely unnoticed and largely uncriticized. This would not present any particular problems or challenges, except for the fact that mind–world dualism is far from uncontroversial in philosophical circles, where it has been contested under a banner that should be very familiar to contemporary IR scholars: social construction. This is more than a mere coincidence of labels, as IR constructivists have been leveling challenges at mind–world dualism for at least two decades (Onuf 1989; Kratochwil 1989), but have often been charged by critics with failing to elucidate empirically testable propositions about international affairs. In other words, constructivists are charged with failing to subject their scientific ontologies of rules and norms and transactional social practices to the kinds of evaluation procedures that are only meaningful *within* a philosophical ontology of mind–world dualism, procedures involving efforts to compare expected outcomes with observed outcomes, and so to test (for example) the relative causal weight of social identities versus structurally induced preferences (Fischer 1992; Schweller and Wohlforth 2000). We persistently fail to notice the logical absurdity of the situation—obviously it makes no sense to evaluate a claim *opposing* mind–world dualism by *presuming* mind–world dualism—in part because we do not think enough in IR about philosophical ontology and its implications for research practice.[7]

---

7   That there is a debate between IR constructivists about whether to articulate constructivist claims as testable hypotheses or not (Price and Reus-Smit 1998; Adler 1997) simply reinforces my point about the power of the mind–world dualist

Philosophy of science can help us to think more clearly about these issues, not by providing us with solutions but by elaborating the logical consequences of adopting particular positions on issues such as mind–world dualism. In order to realize that potential, we have to affix philosophy of science not merely to scientific ontology, and not merely to epistemology or the choice of methods, but first and foremost to methodology broadly understood: methodology as philosophical ontology, setting the context within which particular practices of knowledge-production might make sense. Wight (2006, 258) is entirely correct that this account minimizes the "difference between methodology and philosophy of science," but I do not think that the dire consequences that he foresees for "innovation and pluralism" necessarily follow because I am not proposing new restrictive methodological or philosophical standards for "science." Indeed, the important thing about the philosophy of science for IR scholars and scholarship is precisely that there is a *diversity* of claims about our hook-up to the world, and thus a variety of philosophical ontologies, each of which holds different implications for how we should go about producing factual knowledge about international affairs. "Putting ontology first" in this philosophical sense means embracing pluralism (Shotter 1993a, 77–78). As long as we recognize the diversity of philosophical ontologies, there is no danger that a connection between philosophy of science and methodology broadly understood will lead to anything like a new orthodoxy.[8]

Core wagers

How should we organize that diversity so as to bring out the most salient points of agreement and disagreement? In order to produce a mapping of philosophical ontologies that will be of use to IR scholars, we are faced with the challenge of specifying a set of distinctions between approaches to the philosophy of inquiry that might enable something similar to an informed discussion between aficionados of various perspectives. But philosophy of science as a field does not have a widely accepted organizational scheme dividing authors and positions into distinct schools of thought, and to the extent that particular authors self-identify with a tradition of inquiry, they generally do not do so in terms of philosophical ontology per se. Getting a grasp on the disputes among philosophers of science is a tricky business.

Indeed, surveys of work in the philosophy of science—and I am setting aside those putative "surveys" that have as their not-so-hidden aim the vindication of the

---

philosophical ontology in the field and underscores the need to bring it out into the open so as to subject it to a full and thorough scholarly discussion.

8   In this way, my foregrounding of philosophical ontology to the detriment of epistemology is in broad agreement with Charles Taylor's (1995, 11–17) call to overcome the "epistemological construal" of knowledge—although I am more sympathetic to what he calls the "neo-Nietzschean" critique of epistemology than to his own philosophical project of replacing the epistemological construal of knowledge with something less illusory and more transcendentally warranted. This should be apparent in what follows.

author's own particular standpoint—adopt one of two strategies of presentation: they either proceed historically, describing authors and debates more or less chronologically (for example, Godfrey-Smith 2003), or they proceed topically, organizing the discussion around issues such as justification or perception (for example, O'Brien 2006, or Cartwright and Montuschi 2015). Along the way, we sometimes hear of more or less coherent positions such as "realism," or supposedly coherent positions such as "positivism,"[9] but such positions encompass a wide variety of stances and claims that frequently overlap with one another in a way that makes it difficult to summarize the core commitments of each. Add to this the fact that certain positions are quite intimately connected to the work of a particular author—such as Duhem and conventionalism, or Quine and naturalism—and the task of enumerating a general overview starts to look quite daunting.

A clue about how to proceed might be found by redirecting our attention to the purpose of the exercise: to make the systematic reflections found in the philosophy of science accessible to IR scholars, and to do so in a way that foregrounds salient points of distinction. It is therefore not necessary to capture every debate in the philosophy of science; it is only necessary to produce a set of categories that helps to illuminate discussions within and issues pertinent to IR, and perhaps other social sciences. Such a set of distinctions—such a classification scheme—should, in John Dewey's terminology, be evaluated "functionally, not structurally and statically": the central issue should be whether the classification permits and promotes the particular end to which it is directed (Dewey 1920, 150). In the present case, the end to be promoted is a robust contrast between perspectives, and this carries two consequences for the scheme: distinctions must be drawn sharply enough to clarify disagreements, but the resulting positions have to resemble one another sufficiently that scholars can meaningfully elaborate the consequences of adopting one or another of the positions. This certainly does not mean that positions and perspectives on the philosophy of science have to be made *commensurable* in a way that would permit some kind of direct empirical test between them; indeed, because of the nature of the philosophical issues under discussion, no such empirical testing is even *conceivable* (Smith 1989, 21). But it does mean that we have to construct positions that are susceptible to comparison and contrast, because they are at the very least trying to occupy the same conceptual terrain.

Dewey also gives some helpful advice for the construction of such a classification scheme:

> The teleological theory of classification does not therefore commit us to the notion that classes are purely verbal or purely mental. Organization is no more merely nominal or mental in any art, including the art of inquiry,

---

9   "Positivism" is a term that, at least in contemporary parlance, often simply means a position with which one disagrees (Patomäki and Wight 2000, 216). Indeed, a number of opposing views on the nature and status of knowledge are often subsumed under this term, which is why I have argued for dividing it into more precise categories such as "neopositivism" and "logical positivism" (Jackson 2008). See below.

than it is in a department store or railway system. The necessity of execution supplies objective criteria. Things have to be sorted out and arranged so that their grouping will promote successful action for ends.

(Dewey 1920, 154)

Two important procedural suggestions emanate from this observation. First, and in line with calls to bring *practice* back in to the analysis of social action (Neumann 2002), analysts neither should nor need to invent a classification scheme from scratch. Instead, analysts can and should take their bearings from extant classificatory practices, seeking only to bring some abstract order to the sorts of things that are already and empirically going on in the social domain under investigation. Applied to the present task, this means that we should take our bearings for a classification of positions in the philosophy of science with relevance to IR scholarship from the existing contrasts and distinctions that active IR scholars in fact draw in their work. But second, analysts need not be bound simply to reproduce or redescribe extant social practices; instead, and much like the skilled craftsperson in any other field of activity, scholarly analysts can and should abstract from particular practices in order to forge more useful tools for accomplishing specific purposes (Dewey 1920, 55). Hence the challenge is not simply to get various positions in the philosophy of social inquiry "right" (whatever *that* might mean operationally). Instead, the challenge is to abstract from existing controversies so as to focus them and ultimately make them more productive, and to do so in a pluralistic way that highlights a diversity of approaches to "science" rather than seeking imperialistically to foreclose discussion by promulgating a narrow and uniform definition.

With that by way of prelude, let me now offer a methodological principle followed by a provisional set of distinctions that, when combined, form what I believe is a useful typology for the discussion of the philosophy of science in IR. The methodological principle is that we should regard positions on the character and conduct of science as resting on provisional commitments—*wagers*—about matters of philosophical ontology that can really never be settled definitively.[10] "What is the nature of Being?" and "What is the purpose of human existence?", to give two of the best-known examples, are the sorts of ontological/theological/ ethical questions to which particular scholars give answers that depend, in the final analysis, on a measure of *faith*, precisely because they cannot be resolved empirically or rationally. But commitments of this sort undergird every instance of scientific research, implicitly shaping what the goals of such research are

---

10 By referring to these commitments as "wagers"—a term that emerged in conversations between Dan Nexon and myself as we engaged in our ongoing work on the character of theoretical debate in IR—I am deliberately remaining agnostic about the question of whether any particular scholar can or should subject their basic commitments to criticism and possible alteration in the course of debate and discussion. In principle, IR scholars ought to change their wagers when appropriate, but in practice, few do. Whether this constitutes evidence for the immature character of IR as a field of scholarship, or simply reflects a sociological fact about the organization of the field into an academic discipline, is a matter that I will leave for the reader to ponder.

thought to be and how the research goes about trying to accomplish those goals. Even the most flat-footed empiricist has implicitly decided that reality is made up of tangible, measurable stuff and that true knowledge consists in discovering how that stuff is related so that knowledgeable humans can conform their expectations to those relations. It is a measure of the conceptual and philosophical poverty of the field that we rarely if ever acknowledge, let alone *discuss*, such commitments. Instead, we focus on technical application, obscuring the wagers that animate those technical procedures.

Wagers constitute worlds, in that they quite literally set the stage for the kinds of empirical and theoretical puzzles and challenges that a scholar takes to be meaningful and important. For example, if one does not believe that the purpose of social science is to contribute to human emancipation, then the deplorable living conditions of much of the world's population at the present time, or the impacts on daily life wrought by the increasing interconnectedness of global financial markets, look very different than they do to a scholar who believes—as, for example, James Bohman does—that "the social sciences play a special role in not only reconstructing ... communicative capabilities, but also in developing reflexivity sufficient to allow speakers to make manifest the limitations of existing discursive practices" (Bohman 2002, 507).[11] At a minimum, a wager locates and specifies three things: the researcher, the world to be researched, and the character of the relationship between them. Bohman's critical-theoretical stance, for example, separates researcher from social actors to the extent that the researcher is empowered to introduce or induce, through the practice of social science, changes in existing practices that are intended to disclose the deficiencies of those practices as ways of approximating a broad and subtle notion of democracy. It also upholds the researcher's privileged—because social-scientific—grasp on the normative goal of democracy, even if the actual working-out of that ideal in practice depends on collaboration with social actors and even if that normative ideal is transcendentally related to the actual practices of social actors rather than being handed down from some ideal realm *á la* Plato.

To put this a slightly different way, Bohman's position combines two analytically distinct wagers. The first involves the relationship between the researcher and the world, and speaks to the question of whether the objects of study have a more or less determinate character that is separate from the researcher's activity, or whether the process of research in some sense constitutes the object of study *en passant*, in the course of gathering and assembling data. Critical evaluation of a set of social practices seems to call for the first answer rather than the second one, as it is difficult to conceptualize the standpoint from which a social-scientific researcher could possibly critique existing practices without some detached ground from which to

---

11   Although I could have chosen another philosophically inclined IR scholar, I chose Bohman here as an example of an IR scholar who is unusually forthcoming about his philosophical-ontological commitments. Thus, the issues that Bohman brings up explicitly are also implicitly present in the work of others in the field.

launch such critiques.[12] The second wager involves the kind of knowledge to which the social scientist is thought to have access, which in this case is super-empirical or transcendental (albeit, in Bohman's case, in the complex and Habermasian sense of that term) rather than confined to the empirical or experiential sphere. Together, these two wagers produce an image of knowledge-production and an account of scholarly social-scientific practice that make possible the kind of critical emancipatory activity that Bohman argues should characterize more of IR scholarship.

Not by accident, these two wagers seem to me to constitute two of the most important commitments of philosophical ontology made by IR scholars, and suitably abstracted they provide a useful way of clarifying debates about the philosophy of science in the field. As I have suggested above, the first wager—concerning the relationship or connection between the researcher and the researched world— presents an idealized choice between *mind–world dualism* and its opposite, which I will call *mind–world monism*.[13] The former option maintains a separation between researcher and world such that research has to be directed toward properly crossing that gap, and valid knowledge must in the end be related to some sort of accurate correspondence between empirical and theoretical propositions on the one hand and the actual character of a mind-independent world[14] on the other. The latter, on the other hand, maintains that the researcher is a part of the world in such a way that speaking of "the world" as divorced from the activities of making sense of the world is literally nonsensical: "world" is endogenous to social practices of knowledge-production, including (but not limited to) scholarly practices, and hence scholarly knowledge-production is in no sense a simple description or recording of already-existing stable worldly objects. But mind–world monism is no more "idealist" (in the sense of privileging ideas about the world) than mind–world dualism is "realist" (in the sense of privileging the world); it is not the privileging of one or the other side of a mind–world dichotomy that makes a position monistic, but the rejection of the very distinction in the first place.[15]

The fact that the mind–world dualist position has often been characterized as "positivist" (Wendt 1999, 39–40) while the mind–world monist position is often characterized as "interpretivist" (Yanow and Schwartz-Shea 2006) is one of those

---

12 Indeed, efforts to solve this problem have animated fierce debates among critical theorists for decades—at least as far back as Horkheimer and Adorno's *Dialectic of enlightenment* (1947). See Chapter 6.

13 In an earlier paper (Jackson 2008) I referred to these commitments simply as "dualism" and "monism." The addition of the modifier "mind–world" clarifies the intent rather than changing the substance of the argument.

14 Note that "mind-independent" here means "independent from the mind of the researcher," and should not be confused with the principle of scientific materialism, which maintains that the only things that are real are those things that exist independent of *all* minds. There is no conceptual or philosophical problem with maintaining a mind–world dualist stance on a set of social relations, since this simply means that those social relations are thought to exist in a more or less determinate way separate from the investigator's scholarly research activity. See Chapter 4.

15 For a nice discussion of the issues involved, see Schiff (2008, 368–371). See also Chapter 5.

examples of a less-than-useful classificatory scheme that does not really clarify the issues at stake in the philosophical distinction. Despite the best intentions of many who use this distinction, the result of contrasting "positivist" and "interpretivist" scholarship seems to be the kind of faux "synthesis" advocated by David Laitin (2003) in which participant-observation and other experience-near modes of data collection are assigned the role of gathering raw materials for the testing of covering-law hypotheses (see also King, Keohane, and Verba 1994, 36–41). When used in this sense, "positivist" versus "interpretivist," like "quantitative" versus "qualitative," collapses all too easily into a difference of *method*, rather than a difference of *methodology*, and the key wager about our hook-up to the world made in more anthropological modes of knowledge-production is obscured. The only way to avoid this is to clarify the terms of the distinction more clearly, something that my terminological shift is designed to do, both by avoiding the "interpretivism-as-raw-materials-gathering" misunderstanding presently operative in large parts of the field and by refocusing attention on the issues of philosophical ontology at the heart of the distinction properly understood.

The mind–world dualism/mind–world monism wager, however, is not the only core wager that we need in hand in order to order contemporary IR debates about social inquiry usefully. After all, both hypothesis-testers such as King, Keohane, and Verba (in common with the majority of American IR scholars and political scientists, protestations about mechanisms and "qualitative" strategies of inference to the contrary) and critical realists such as Wight and Bohman are mind–world dualists inasmuch as they posit an external world to which knowledge in some sense approximates. But there are clearly important differences between hypothesis-testers and critical realists, issues that critical realists indicate by critiquing the restriction of knowledge to those aspects of reality that can be more or less directly observed, experienced, and measured (Patomäki and Wight 2000, 218–219; Wight 2006, 25–26). The key issue here is whether knowledge is purely related to things that can be experienced and empirically observed, or whether it is possible to generate knowledge of in-principle unobservable objects.

Following language introduced by Roy Bhaskar (1975), I will refer to the position that maintains the possibility of knowing things about in-principle unobservables *transfactualism*, since it holds out the possibility of going beyond the facts to grasp the deeper processes and factors that generate those facts (Wight 2006, 18). The opposite position, *phenomenalism* (Harré 1985, 68–86),[16] maintains, to the contrary, that it is neither necessary nor possible for researchers to "transcend experience by some organ of unique character that carries [them] into the super-empirical"

---

16   In earlier versions of this chapter, I referred to this position as "experientialism," so as to stress its connection to experience in the pragmatic sense. I have adopted the term "phenomenalism" instead because the connection to experience is itself contested within the relevant philosophical debates, and because the term "phenomenalism" is as unfamiliar to IR scholars as "transfactualism" is, thus helping to highlight the distinction and to distinguish it from other distinctions already operative in the field. Also, I was getting tired of people reading "experientialism" as "experimentalism," a slippage that itself says something very interesting about our field.

(Dewey 1920, 77)—that knowledge, to the contrary, is a matter of organizing past experiences so as to forge useful tools for the investigation of future, as-yet-unknown situations (Dewey 1910, 126–127). Between them, transfactualism and phenomenalism define the parameters of this second wager.

Putting these two wagers together generates the following 2 × 2 table of commitments in philosophical ontology and the methodologies that arise from those commitments:

		Relationship between knowledge and observation	
		phenomenalism	*transfactualism*
Relationship between the knower and the known	mind–world dualism	neopositivism	critical realism
	mind–world monism	analyticism	reflexivity

Fleshing out the specifics of the four cells of this table—both explaining what each of these philosophical-ontological commitments entail in greater detail, and clarifying the methodological implications of each for IR scholarship—will be the task of the remainder of this book.

The European Enlightenment and its problem of knowledge

But before turning to that task, I will note that all four of the methodologies in my table represent mid- to late twentieth-century responses to a specific philosophical tradition: the tradition of the European Enlightenment, and in particular, the part of that tradition that sought to ground knowledge on a purely secular source and thus break away from ecclesiastical hierarchy and the authority of divine revelation (Hollis 1994, Chapter 2). Beginning with Rene Descartes' meditations in the seventeenth century, philosophers in this tradition wrestled with the relationship between the knower and the known in ways that generally privileged some blend of reason and observation as part of the recipe for secure knowledge. In the main, this tradition, dominant in European philosophy of knowledge up until the early twentieth century, took the mind-world dualist and phenomenalist wagers. That said, the "neopositivist" position that occupies the upper left-hand box in my typology, and will occupy center stage in Chapter 3, is not simply the continuation of that older tradition; it is, rather, an updating and remixing of that tradition in the light of some of the very same deficiencies that prompted other thinkers to move more radically away from it. At roughly the same time as neopositivism arrived on the scene, other combinations of wagers began to make their appearance. So the historical story here involves the *in*ability of the European Enlightenment philosophical tradition to solve the problem that it set for itself, which thus set the stage for the four methodologies that I will discuss in the core of this book.[17]

---

17 I hope that it is clear that by focusing on the European philosophical tradition here I am not making a claim that this tradition has any special claim to worth or validity when it comes to thinking about the problems of knowledge. I am instead engaged in

It may prove helpful to begin, then, with a sketch of that philosophical tradition.

The Cartesian problem

Any discussion of the European Enlightenment problem of knowledge must, of necessity, end up focusing significant attention on the writings of the seventeenth-century philosopher René Descartes, and in particular on his *Meditations on first philosophy* (Descartes 1993). Although Descartes is not the first of the "modern" philosophers whose work sought to break with the classical and medieval traditions of natural philosophy—that title probably belongs to Sir Francis Bacon (Moses and Knutsen 2007, 21–24)—he is arguably the most important, in that his is a particularly thoroughgoing effort to reject both the procedure and the results of those older traditions. Classical Greek natural philosophy revolved around a concern with the proper ordering of empirical phenomena, including human beings and their social and political relations, by applying reason to those phenomena in order to grasp their metaphysical essences. In Plato's terms, reason was the part of the soul that ought to be in control of other capacities in order to enable a person to penetrate past mere appearance and grasp the metaphysical forms that lay behind and gave rise to them (Plato 1992, Book 7). Like his student Aristotle, Plato argued that such a use of reason was to be sharply distinguished from the merely technical use of crafts to achieve some practical end, and should remain purely contemplative. Medieval scholastics added the notion that the basic categories into which empirical phenomena should be ordered were best derived from the study of authoritative texts, including sacred scriptures (Dear 2008, 9–10); here again, the basic concern was with putting everything together to form a seamless whole, within which human knowledge played a specific and limited part.

Descartes upended all of this, beginning with the assumption that grounding arguments about the world—and, in particular, arguments about the existence of God and the immortality of the soul, which according to Descartes were the two most pressing issues to be addressed by philosophy—in the authority of a text was insufficient:

> Although it suffices for us believers to believe by faith that the human soul does not die with the body, and that God exists, certainly no unbelievers seem capable of being persuaded of any religion or even of almost any moral virtue, until these two are first proven to them by natural reason.
>
> (Descartes 1993, 47)

---

a little conceptual archaeology (after Foucault 1972): the debates and discussions that inform methodological distinctions in contemporary international studies scholarship derive from this very particular and provincial soil, and if we are to understand and reorder those debates and discussions, we need to first understand the intellectual context from which they come. Maybe we all should have started someplace else, but the fact is that we as a scholarly field did not.

Referring to sacred scriptures to buttress these points would be inadequate, since the primary reason for trusting those scriptures was a belief in their divine origin, and "this reasoning cannot be proposed to unbelievers because they would judge it to be circular" (Descartes 1993, 47). Hence a different ground for arguments must be sought, a ground that did not presuppose assent to the authority of traditional texts but rested purely on natural reason—a ground which, not incidentally, could be shared by any reasonable person, whether or not they were schooled in Aristotle and the Bible.

To seek this ground, Descartes argued, it was necessary to doubt everything that could be doubted.

> I had to raze everything to the ground and build again from the original foundations, if I wanted to establish anything firm and lasting in the sciences ... I will not need to show that all my opinions are false, which is perhaps something I could never accomplish. But reason now persuades me that I should withhold my assent no less carefully from opinions that are not completely certain and indubitable than I would from those that are patently false ... It will suffice for the rejection of all of these opinions, if I find in each of them some reason for doubt.
>
> (Ibid., 59)

This refusal to assent to anything that is questionable meant that Descartes could immediately reject texts and other carriers of received wisdom, since their authors might have been in error. He could also reject information provided by his senses, because they were sometimes deceptive, especially when he was dreaming—and how did he *know* that he was not dreaming at any particular moment? Finally, he could also reject non-empirical apparent truths, such as those of pure mathematics, on the suspicion that some supremely powerful and clever "evil genius[18] ... has directed his entire effort at deceiving me" and making things *appear* self-evidently true when they were, in fact, not true (ibid., 62).

This line of argumentation led Descartes to a situation in which there was only one thing that he could not doubt: his own existence. Even if there were an evil genius deceiving him about everything, Descartes reasoned, he himself would still have to be around to be deceived; hence, the evident fact of his own existence was actually secure enough not to be doubted. But this thing that exists could not be a body, since he might be mistaken about his having a body—remember that sensory information was already rejected because it can sometimes mislead—and so Descartes concluded that the absolute certainty of his own existence extended only as far as his mental processes. "I am therefore precisely nothing but a thinking thing; that is, a mind, or intellect, or understanding, or reason—words of whose meanings I was previously ignorant. Yet I am a true thing and

---

18 Implicitly, Descartes is referring to the Devil, or to some other supernatural evil being. This becomes clear when we see that the *opposite* of an "evil genius" is none other than God; see below.

am truly existing; but what kind of thing? I have said it already: a thinking thing" (ibid., 65). Descartes thus established the centrality of the autonomous mind—the thinking subject—to systematic reflections on any subject.

In so doing, and in particular in conceptually isolating the mind from the rest of the world (including the physical body in which the mind appears to be somehow enclosed), Descartes set up a problem of knowledge-production that would dominate the next several centuries of European philosophical reflection: how does a world-independent mind gain reliable knowledge of a mind-independent world? Descartes had little problem arguing that the mind can know things about itself by simply examining what it does, but knowing anything outside of the mind presented the problem that even though sensory impressions often *appear* to deliver reliable information about the outside world, and even though pure speculation *appears* to deliver mathematical and geometrical ideas such as the conclusion that the angles of a triangle add up to 180 degrees, there was still a possibility that an evil genius might be responsible for perpetrating a deception in both of these realms. Descartes therefore devoted much of the text of his *Meditations* to putting to rest the idea that such an evil genius might exist. His vehicle for doing so involved establishing the existence of God, primarily by arguing that Descartes himself, a finite and imperfect being, would not have been able to conceive of the idea of God (an infinite and perfect substance) unless God actually existed to serve as the objective source of the ideas of infinity and perfection.[19] And the existence of such a God underpinned the confidence Descartes could then have in clear and distinct perceptions:

> Often the memory of a previously made judgment may return when I am no longer attending to the arguments on account of which I made such a judgment. Thus, other arguments can be brought forward that would easily make me change my opinion, were I ignorant of God. And thus I would never have true and certain knowledge about anything, but merely fickle and changeable opinions ... But once I perceived that there is a God, and also understood at the same time that everything else depends on him, *and that he*

---

19 Descartes' metaphysics is complicated, and rests on a subtle distinction between "formal" and "objective" reality: objects have formal reality, which is how they exert their effects in the world, where ideas have objective reality, which refers to their content (that is, the thing with which they are concerned). But ideas, for Descartes, are also objects, which means that they too have formal reality and as such have to be caused by something with the power to make them have the objective reality that they in fact have. This leads to the following rather dense formulation: "there can be in me no idea of heat, or of a stone, unless it is placed in me by some cause that has as least much reality as I conceive to be in the heat or in the stone ... that a particular idea contains this as opposed to that objective reality is surely owing to some cause in which there is at least as much formal reality as there is objective reality contained in the idea" (Descartes 1993, 74). Hence there could be no idea with the objective reality "perfection" unless it were caused by something with the formal reality of perfection; that formal source cannot be Descartes himself, since he is an imperfect being, so the formal source has to be an actual perfect being, that is, God.

is not a deceiver, I then concluded that everything that I clearly and distinctly perceive is necessarily true.

(ibid., 92; emphasis added)

This argument sufficed for Descartes to establish the incontrovertibility of clearly perceived ideas. The validity of sensory impressions, and the actual existence of those things that we sense, follows from a similar appeal to the fact that God is not a deceiver: "consequently, corporeal things exist" (ibid., 98).

I have explicated Descartes' argument in some detail because, although somewhat remote from the subject-matter of any particular empirical science, Descartes' formulation of the problem of knowledge has been absolutely decisive for subsequent thinkers down to the present day, and the inadequacy of Descartes' solution to the problem he formulated has prompted numerous attempts to improve on it (McCulloch 1995, 9–11). Both the positing of absolute certainty as the sole grounds for accepting a claim to knowledge, and the delineation of a gulf between the mind and the world that somehow has to be bridged in order for knowledge-claims to be produced in the first place, continue to haunt and trouble subsequent thinkers. "Cartesian anxiety," a term coined by Richard Bernstein (1983), very neatly encapsulates the challenging inheritance that Descartes' embrace of mind-world dualism provided: a desire for absolute certainty along with a gnawing sense that such certainty is impossible to achieve without some kind of super-human facilitation.

Cartesian anxiety, I would argue, emerges from mind-world dualism in two distinct but related ways. First, mind–world dualism intensifies the need for absolute certainty, because the alternative to absolute certainty, under a dualist account, is a subjective flight of fancy—which *anything* might be if it is not firmly founded on something outside of the mind.[20] Second, mind–world dualism makes it virtually impossible to achieve such certainty in any universally compelling way, because a skeptical response that re-opens the gap between the mind's knowledge-claims and the world is almost always possible. This is perhaps most especially demonstrated when the widespread use of God in philosophical arguments began to decline, and Descartes' own solution to the problem of knowledge started to look woefully inadequate—opening up the kind of despair that Descartes himself reported near the outset of his investigation, before he had articulated his answer:

Yesterday's meditation has thrown me into such doubts that I can no longer ignore them, yet I fail to see how they are to be resolved. It is as if I had

---

20 In this connection, note how mind–world dualism informs the everyday way of speaking that equates "subjective" with "arbitrary," as when a "subjective opinion" is contrasted to an "objective fact." This is an expression of Cartesian anxiety and the fear that one's supposed knowledge might not be founded on anything but one's own whims.

suddenly fallen into a deep whirlpool; I am so tossed about that I can neither
touch bottom with my foot, nor swim up to the top.

(Descartes 1993, 63)

Efforts to ameliorate Cartesian anxiety provided much of the impetus for
subsequent philosophical reflections on knowledge in general, and on science in
particular. For the next several centuries, these reflections followed Descartes in
generally remaining within the ambit of dualism, but tried to reduce anxiety either
by stressing sensory experience or by stressing the power of reason. None of
these attempted solutions actually worked, even though they provided the context
within which later efforts—efforts of more direct consequence to contemporary
IR—were articulated.

Solving the Cartesian problem

The first effort to brush aside the problem that Descartes had identified involved
the "empiricist" effort to ground all knowledge on sensory impressions. Thomas
Hobbes announced such an orientation in the opening pages of *Leviathan*,
declaring empirical sensation to be the origin of all thinking; he dispensed with
Cartesian anxiety by simply observing that, upon reflection, "I am well satisfied,
that being awake, I know I dreame not; though when I dreame, I think my
self awake" (Hobbes 1601, 14). However, it is John Locke who built the first
consistent empiricist effort to account for knowledge in general, arguing that even
the most complex ideas could be disentangled and traced back to basic sensory
impressions. Unlike Descartes, Locke rejected the notion that it was possible
to know anything "innately"—that is, through the mind simply reflecting in
isolation; hence Locke's empiricism contained nothing like Descartes' elaborate
metaphysics of substance to support the notion of God's existence, but confined
its efforts to deciphering the simple ideas of basic sense-impressions that had
been joined together to produce more abstract notions (Locke 1959b, sec. II,
xii, 8). However, inasmuch as empiricism continued to labor within the basic
parameters of mind–world dualism, it could not insulate itself against the kind of
skepticism characteristic of Cartesian anxiety: how does a self-contained world-
independent mind actually gain reliable knowledge of the world presumptively
outside of it? No amount of observation can ever make us *sure* that we have
properly apprehended the world, especially since we regularly use our minds to
amend sense-impressions that we know to be misleading, such as the appearance
of a round globe as a flat circle (McCulloch 1995, 51–53).

David Hume, an empiricist himself, posed a more radical solution to the
Cartesian problem of knowledge: accept that there is no way to solve the
problem rationally, and move on to ask what difference this made in practice.
"The mind has never any thing present to it but the perceptions, and cannot
possibly reach any experience of their connexion with objects," Hume admitted;
"The supposition of such a connexion is, therefore, without any foundation in
reasoning" (Hume 1977, 105). But Hume immediately went on to suggest that

this lack of a foundation in reason was only troubling to an overblown universal skepticism that is subverted by:

> [A]ction, and employment, and the occupations of common life. These [skeptical] principles may flourish and triumph in the schools; where it is, indeed, difficult, if not impossible, to refute them. But as soon as they leave the shade, and by the presence of the real objects, which actuate our passions and sentiments, are put in opposition to the more powerful principles of our nature, they vanish like smoke, and leave the most determined skeptic in the same condition as other mortals.
>
> (ibid., 109–110)

Hume thus inverted Descartes' position, suggesting that the certainty Descartes sought was precisely *not* available where Descartes was looking for it: namely, in the rational operation of the mind. But conveniently, the *content* of those things about which Hume could be certain turned out to be pretty reassuring to anyone concerned, much as Descartes had been, with finding solid ground on which to place arguments about the world and objects within it: things in the world were knowable, claims about them could be founded on observations rather than on traditional authority, and the world itself existed in a mind-independent way. Too conveniently, a skeptic might respond: a gulf remains between the claim that people *speak and act* as though their knowledge corresponded to an external world, and the claim that such knowledge *actually does* correspond. Hence the lingering doubt that all Hume was doing was re-stating common sense and not actually solving the problem.[21]

Among those deeply troubled by Hume's claims was Immanuel Kant, who quickly realized that an abandonment of the quest to put knowledge on absolutely secure rational foundations—that is, foundations that did not themselves rely on contingent empirical observations about what people do and did in their everyday lives—would leave open the logical possibility that our highest ideals and most significant judgments were not based on anything known *a priori*, or before experience, but might instead be based on "whim or chance" (Kant 1999, 204). Against this possibility, Kant sought to erect a firmly rational edifice that would solve Descartes' problem through what Kant referred to as a "Copernican revolution": instead of trying to determine how cognitions corresponded to objects, Kant would explicate the preconditions of cognition that were rationally and transcendentally presupposed by the very operation of cognition itself (ibid., 110–111). Those preconditions, which Kant conceptualized as forming the "sensibility" through which objects are given to us, would in turn form an absolutely certain basis on which to erect claims that would be valid at least for

---

21 There is a way of recasting some of Hume's claims in a way that does not so much *solve* the Cartesian problem as *dis-solve* it, in the sense of making it disappear by removing the ways that the problem was set up in the first place. Such a radicalization of Hume starts to sound a lot like Ludwig Wittgenstein, as I argue in Chapter 5.

all human beings, and perhaps for all rational beings (ibid., 191). In so doing, both Cartesian anxiety and the recourse to contingent empirical observations could be simultaneously avoided.

Unfortunately for Kant, his ambitious effort did not quite succeed in vanquishing either of his foes. Subsequent developments, both in philosophy and in the natural sciences, illustrated that a great many of the supposedly *a priori* notions that Kant sought to explicate seemed, instead, to reflect a very time-bound and historically contingent set of ideas about individuality, freedom, and—most damagingly from the perspective of the philosophy of science—material substance itself. General and special relativity, in particular, would eventually overturn a good many of Kant's transcendental principles about space and causation about a century after Kant lived, illustrating that what he thought to be universal was rather less solid than that even though it was very well grounded in the mathematics and physics of his time (Friedman 1992). As for Cartesian anxiety, so many readers of Kant's *Critique of Pure Reason* took him for an Idealist who denied that an external world existed at all[22] that he had to add several new sections to the book's second edition specifically designed to refute the charge. Even those defenses could not address the underlying problem, which was that Kant *did*, in fact, deny the possibility of knowing anything about objects as they were in themselves, while retaining the notion that objects did actually exist in themselves.[23] Kant's whole approach was premised on the notion that human knowledge was limited by human sensibility (Friedman 2000, 27–28). While that may have turned skeptical claims about the gap between knowledge and the world into the kinds of "transcendental illusions" that philosophers ought to combat, it did little to address the perception that, like Hume's solution, Kant's solution to the Cartesian problem simply meant ignoring the problem—and, perhaps, losing sight of the world itself!—and moving on (Patomäki and Wight 2000, 220–221).

Logical positivism

In terms of the philosophy of science, the next major effort to solve the Cartesian problem involved the Vienna Circle of logical positivists, whom I have already had occasion to mention in connection with the "demarcation problem" of

---

22 Idealists accepted a differentiation between mind and world, and *then* claimed that only mind existed. James Boswell's famous recording of Johnson's "refutation" of Berkeley's Idealism—Johnson firmly kicked a rock—should provide a sense of the argument, and its absurdity.

23 Kant did this by firmly dividing objects into "phenomenal" and "noumenal" objects, with only the former accessible to the senses. Noumenal objects were only accessible by the understanding, which tells us what the objects must be in themselves. However, Kant also claimed that even the understanding only had access to the principles defining how "objects must be represented as objects of experience … and not how they might be outside of the relation to possible experience and consequently to sense in general" (Kant 1999, 364). Whether this actually is a mind-world dualist conception remains a matter of some dispute; sufficiently developed, it might to the contrary be monistic—a suggestion I take up in Chapter 5.

differentiating science from non-science.[24] The Vienna Circle thinkers took pieces from several of the earlier efforts as they worked to provide a solution that would also respond to the exciting cultural and scientific developments going on in and around early twentieth-century Vienna, especially in physics and psychology (Godfrey-Smith 2003, 22–24, Janik and Toulmin 1996, 211–219). From the empiricist tradition, they took the idea that meaningful statements about the world were grounded in experience rather than speculation; the gulf between knowing minds and the known world was bridged by the apparent fact that people experienced things. But the logical positivists avoided the problems of Locke and Hume's empiricism by taking from Kant the idea that there could also be claims founded not in experience, but in pure reason: *analytic* truths, devoid of factual content but firmly grounded in systematic (by which the logical positivists generally meant "formal") argumentation and elaboration. This allowed them, in effect, to avoid the charge directed against traditional empiricism that its advocates could not properly distinguish between sensory impressions and rational deductions from (and even corrections of) those sensory impressions: logical positivists could retain mathematics and logic, but rigorously separate them from knowledge about the empirical world.[25]

Instead, the job of generating knowledge about the empirical world, the logical positivists held, was performed by experimental science. Science systematically examined empirical patterns and how they were related to one another; the contribution of philosophy to this process was in logically evaluating language to see what kinds of claims were susceptible to this sort of systematic empirical investigation, and which were not (Ayer 1952, 48–51, 57–59).[26] Claims that were susceptible to scientific evaluation were considered "verifiable." Other apparently empirical claims were, strictly speaking, meaningless, unless they were analytic claims such as those of pure, formal logic (Hempel 1965b, 236–238).

In this way, the logical positivists proposed what was in effect a two-pronged solution to the Cartesian problem: first, the elimination of meaningless phrases via logical analysis, and second, the evaluation of the remaining sensible claims through systematic empirical investigation. Descartes' skepticism about sensory impressions was avoided both through the reductionist move of relating complex claims to more basic "observation statements" that were incontrovertibly true, and through the logical move of rigorously pruning language of statements that went beyond strict empirical reference:

> It is a just demand that Science should have not merely subjective interpretation but sense and validity for all subjects who participate in it.

24 See Chapter 1.
25 The precise placement of mathematics in this scheme is a matter of no small controversy between the Vienna Circle thinkers and their interlocutors, but this need not concern us here. For an insightful account, see Carus (2010).
26 Although Ayer's account of logical positivism differs in important ways from the actual complexity of Vienna Circle thinking, on this point he is fairly accurate (Reisch 2005, 4).

Science is the system of *intersubjectively valid statements*. If our contention
that the physical language is alone in being intersubjective is correct, it
follows that *the physical language is the language of Science*.

(Carnap 2012, 66–67)

The logical positivist position, although in many ways a more compelling
solution to the Cartesian problem than its predecessors, suffered from a basic
problem in that its central criterion for an empirical claim—"verifiability"—
turned out to be a lot less easy to evaluate in practice than it was to state in
principle. To be verifiable, a claim had to be able to have its truth-value decided
by experiment, but determining the criteria under which this would be the case
presented a rather vexing puzzle (Lakatos 2000, 53–56). One difficulty was that
it was almost always possible to take a claim—even a claim about one of the
pieces of putatively metaphysical nonsense that so incensed the members of the
Vienna Circle—and bring it into the sphere of verifiability by conjoining it to
an observation statement. For example, a claim such as: "It is the destiny of our
people to repossess this piece of territory."—which is precisely the kind of claim
that the logical positivists would have wanted to exclude from verifiability on the
grounds that "the destiny of our people" is a nonsensical piece of metaphysics[27]—
can be made verifiable if we posit an observable implication—*any* observable
implication, even an absurd one—of the claim (for example: "If it is the destiny
of our people to repossess this piece of territory, then our leader is male."). Then
we have a claim and an implication that precisely follow the form of a classic
syllogism (X; X → Y; therefore Y), and is therefore supposed to be experimentally
verifiable. With no reliable way to exclude claims from being verifiable, however,
the logical positivist position ran the danger of being unable to sustain the firm
distinction between sense and nonsense, and thus not escaping Cartesian anxiety.

From empiricism to phenomenalism

In important ways, the Vienna Circle take on empiricism transformed the
approach well beyond the classic version of the doctrine. Empiricism, as I have
noted above, is the notion (first systematically elaborated by Locke) that sensory
impressions are the only and sufficient grounding for empirical knowledge. In the
empiricist conception, the senses bring us information about the outside world,
and then our understanding and reason go to work on that sensory data to produce
ideas that represent the world to our minds (McCulloch 1995, 44–46). As such,
every complex idea has to be reduced to an original bundle of sensory impressions
if we want to make sure that it is properly connected to the world, and no higher-
order abstraction can ever be sufficient knowledge in itself.

However compelling a solution to the Cartesian problem this seems to be,
the argument runs into serious difficulties once we move away from the direct

---

27   The *political* valence of such an apparently technical claim in the German-speaking
world of the 1920s and 1930s should not be underestimated (Galison 1990, 736).

perception of objects and into any form of *mediated* perception, such as the use of a telescope or a microscope. Quite obviously, the natural science going on at the time of the Vienna Circle had become more or less dependent on a whole slew of technical instruments, and had left direct perception far behind. The major philosophical difficulty this raises for classical empiricism is that microscopes and telescopes, and other pieces of scientific equipment, are material instantiations of theories about sensation—theories that have to be tacitly, if only provisionally, accepted in order for a researcher to use the equipment (Lakatos 1970, 98; Feyerabend 1993, 63–64, 103–105). Thus, mediated perception presents a problem that classical empiricism has a hard time dealing with.

This is, however, only the beginning of the problem, because the empiricist idea of "immediate perception"—that is, pure sensation delivered by the senses to a blank slate of a mind—has been quite roundly demolished by philosophers and psychologists alike. Whether Kant's argument that the senses only perceive objects insofar as those objects are given to us by a sensibility that is structured by *a priori* principles (Kant 1999, 155–156), Karl Popper's notion of theory-laden observation and his "searchlight theory" of the mind whereby observation becomes an active rather than a passive process (Popper 1979, 341–346), or the more recent Gibsonian view of direct perception as an exploration of a ceaseless flow of stimulation (Grene 1990), research on the mind provides little support for the older empiricist notion of immediate—or, better, *unmediated*—perception. When we walk into a room, we are not met with a bundle of sensory impressions that we somehow have to arrange in order to figure out that this object over here is a chair and this one is a desk; instead, we walk in and sit at the desk, perhaps due to our prior expectation that this room is an office, combined with our prior desire to get some work done. It is as though seeing with the eyes is quite similar to seeing through a telescope: there is no pure sensation on which we might ground our observations, but only a series of mediated perceptions—mediated by language, by social conventions, by hypothetical conjectures, and so forth.

However, far from spelling the end of empiricism, the generally accepted proposition that all perception is mediated and active rather than unmediated and passive provides precisely the necessary ingredient to produce *phenomenalism*, which we can regard as a more robust and compelling descendant of empiricism. Although the Vienna Circle thinkers did not use this term, preferring instead to refer to the role of "experience" and the "empirical" in grounding scientific theories and scientific philosophy, the way that they deployed those notions marked a clearly modernist break with older usages (Galison 1990, 749–750). The classic empiricist tradition was almost entirely wrapped up with outmoded ideas about how the senses work, but by removing that restriction we can speak in broader terms about a focus on perception that bases itself not on unaided sensory impressions but instead on *the experiences that we have*. Thus we need not say that worldly knowledge is grounded in our seeing or hearing, but can say instead that our knowledge of some object is grounded in our experience of it, whether that experience involves touching it with our bare hand or peering at it through a telescope. This more robust descendant of empiricism would, much like classic empiricism, say that we cannot know anything about something that we cannot experience; in order to know about something we have to be able to experience it, in order to prevent our thoughts and speculations from simply wandering off into the metaphysical ether. Such was the "empiricism" of the Vienna Circle.

By terming this more robust descendant of empiricism "phenomenalism," I also want to suggest a link to the phenomenological tradition inaugurated by Edmund Husserl around the same time as the Vienna Circle was active, and subsequently developed by subsequent philosophers, psychologists, and anthropologists. The phenomenological approach emphasizes the adoption of a first-person point of view, so that specific experiences can be foregrounded and analyzed; like logical positivism, it announced itself as a newly "scientific" approach to the traditional problems of philosophy (Friedman 2000, 42–44). David Carr's *Time, narrative, and history*, is illustrative of the productivity of the approach, as he seeks to develop an account of historical memory that is firmly grounded in our everyday experiences of time. A close look at that experience, Carr suggests, reveals similarities between events and melodies:

> What counts about the melody as an example of an event is that it is heard *as* beginning, and each of its phrases is heard in anticipation (whether correct or not) of an ending ... Insofar as the event consists of unfolding and distinguishable phases, each of these is experienced either as a beginning or as an end, or as an intervening phase which gets its sense and its place by its reference backward and forward to beginning and end.
>
> (Carr 1986, 47–48)

The focus in Carr's analysis is not on anything having to do with the melody or event "itself," but rather on our typical *experience* of melodies and events. Phenomenology seeks to disclose the structures of those typical experiences, steadfastly refusing to speculate on objects or entities outside of experience.

Phenomenalism is not necessarily phenomenology, however. Rather, phenomenalism as a category incorporates both updated empiricism *and* phenomenology in order to emphasize what they have in common: a shared reluctance to go beyond experience in the construction of knowledge, and a shared desire to ground knowledge in the experience of concrete phenomena. Vienna Circle logical positivism is thus clearly a phenomenalist approach; its members "sought nothing less than to specify and to help fulfill" the European Enlightenment project of setting everything on a firmly rational basis "while taking full advantage of twentieth-century developments in science, logic, social thought, and politics" (Reisch 2005, 3). For this reason, among others, the category of phenomenalism serves a useful purpose in allowing us to clearly see the connections between earlier efforts to solve the Cartesian problem and the modernist update to those efforts present in early twentieth-century Vienna.

However, given that most of the thinkers I have discussed thus far were concerned with the status of our knowledge of *physical* objects, one possible objection to the category of phenomenalism has to be dealt with before moving on. Even if it is clear that phenomenalism, as a robust descendant of empiricism, can accommodate perceptions and experiences in the *natural* world, what does this mean for the study of the *social* world? Telescopes and microscopes extend our ability to see physical objects, and hence to experience them: I can neither see the planet Neptune nor an individual red blood cell with the unaided eye, but an appropriate arrangement of lenses allows me to see them in what we might call a "non-epistemic" sense: I can pick the objects out of my general visual field, even if I have no idea precisely what I am looking at (Chernoff 2005, 71–73). But because there is a theory of optics woven into the apparatus through which I am seeing Neptune and the red blood cell, it is certainly not the case that my experience of those objects is theory-independent, even though it is more or less neutral with respect to particular explanatory theories about Neptune and red blood cells. This in turn means that the evidence generated by my optical-theory-laden observations can, as long as I provisionally accept the relevant optical theory, be treated in pretty much the same way as evidence generated by my unaided senses (Gifford 1991).[28]

Is the situation really so different when dealing with social objects? While it is true that one cannot simply see "democracy" or "the gross domestic product" or "the illegitimate use of force" with the unaided eye—this is the point of Donald Moon's (1975, 161–166) famous demonstration that a physical description of the movements involved in voting would not yield a meaningful definition or account of the action called "voting," and of Clifford Geertz's (1973, 6–7) equally famous differentiation between a wink, a twitch, and a burlesque of a wink—it does not necessarily follow that this makes these social objects categorically and constitutively different from physical objects. Indeed, one might argue that social objects are in fact quite similar to red blood cells and the planet Neptune, in that they cannot even be perceived in the absence of the right kind of equipment, but that with the right kind of equipment they can be perceived and experienced in a more or less ordinary non-epistemic way. This is the operational sense of the claim that some social objects are "concept-dependent" (Wight 2006, 55–56): they are literally *invisible* in the absence of the correct equipment.

An appropriate conceptual apparatus, in other words, allows one to pick voting or democracy or the illegitimate use of force out of the general hustle and bustle of the social world, and to do so in a way that does not necessarily prefigure any particular explanatory theory that we might subsequently attach to those objects.[29] The existence of pronounced and ongoing debate about precisely what

---

28 I am deliberately postponing any discussion of the tricky issue of how a detection apparatus is joined to the objects purportedly detected by it, since it matters quite a bit whether the objects in question are understood to be merely unobserved or in-principle unobservable. See Chapter 4.

29 Of course, it is often possible to construct one's operational measures of a phenomenon in such a way that a particular explanatory theory *is* in fact prefigured in the data collection itself, such as when one engages in an evaluation of the proposition that globalization is eroding state boundaries by collecting *state-level data* and concludes, not surprisingly, that state boundaries are surviving globalization quite nicely

the "appropriate conceptual apparatus" is, and therefore precisely what should count as a "democracy" or "the GDP" or an "illegitimate use of force," raises no special problems beyond those faced by physicists trying to determine the appropriate physical equipment to use in detecting subatomic events, or whether particular observable physical traces in a measurement apparatus actually count as evidence of something.[30] For phenomenalists, the important point is that the extension of the range of the senses through physical and conceptual equipment poses no special conceptual problems and demands no special philosophical grounding, and indeed part of the phenomenalist story of the expansion of human knowledge involves the construction of better and better equipment for enlarging the range of human experience.

Hence: when contemplating the problems of knowledge, the European philosophical tradition from Descartes through the Vienna Circle tended towards the upper left-hand side of my matrix, generally working to elucidate a variety of answers to the challenge of obtaining secure knowledge of a mind-independent external world while rejecting knowledge of things that went beyond experience. Mind–world dualism and phenomenalism thus dominate and enframe the work of empiricists, rationalists, and logical positivists alike. This dominance was not absolute, of course; in subsequent chapters I will consider other thinkers who are clearly part of this tradition although they are skeptical of either mind–world dualism or phenomenalism or both, and I will also endeavor to bring to the surface some contrary aspects in the writings of even the mainstays of the dominant tradition: Hobbes, Hume, and Kant in particular are complex thinkers whose work does not always fit neatly into the category of "mind–world dualist phenomenalism." But my point is that the four methodologies on offer in the remainder of this book are inextricably connected to the historical tradition with which they wrestle and out of which they come—and that tradition was, for the most part, both mind–world dualist and phenomenalist.

A practical typology

In the rest of the present chapter I want to sketch out, in a preliminary way, the discussion of the four methodologies that will unfold over the next four chapters. Before I do that, however, I want to make the *status* of the typology absolutely clear. This typology is not an exhaustive account of debates in the philosophy of science; it is not even articulated in terms that philosophers of science would necessarily use to describe their own positions. It is not an intervention into

---

(Keohane and Milner 1996). But this kind of tautological reasoning is not necessitated by the role of conceptualization in the "seeing" of social objects.

30   There *are* issues about whether the debate about the proper measurement of social objects has a different effect on those social objects than the debate about the proper measurement of physical objects has on those physical objects. That, however, is a discussion best postponed until later, because we need to address issues of unobservability (Chapter 4) and social construction (Chapter 5) in order to flesh out the relevant issues.

debates in the philosophy of science; indeed, by conceptually placing these four philosophical-ontological combinations on something of a level playing field, I am likely to be annoying the partisans of each camp. The typology is also focused on those positions within the philosophy of science that are concerned to clarify the implications that a particular combination of ontological commitments has on the actual practice of knowledge-production, and as such more or less completely ignores thoroughgoing skepticism of the sort that would call the very possibility of knowledge-production into question (for example, Williams 1995).

In addition, the typology is a deliberate oversimplification of a complex set of philosophical disagreements for the purpose of highlighting certain themes or aspects. In this way, my procedure shares something with Imre Lakatos' approach to the characterization of debates and controversies:

> The history of science is always richer than its rational reconstruction. But rational construction or internal history is primary, external history only secondary, since the most important problems of external history are defined by internal history ... Internal history is not just a selection of methodologically improved facts: it may be, on occasions, their radically improved version.
>
> (Lakatos 1978, 118–119)

"A selection of methodologically improved facts" strikes me as a very good summary of what my typology contains: not detailed nuances of specific positions taken by specific people (that would be "external history"), but a purposeful summary of the conceptual and philosophical *content* of those positions. However, unlike Lakatos, whose rational reconstructions are designed for use in retrospectively evaluating whether a given scientific research programme has been progressive or has degenerated, I am not primarily concerned with *evaluating* any of the four philosophical-ontological combinations in my typology. Instead, I hope to provoke two things: a clarification of the issues involved in, and the concrete research implications of, taking up any one of these positions; and a general sense of the importance of getting our philosophical ontology straight when making and evaluating factual claims about international affairs. In other words, I want to *foreground* philosophical-ontological concerns, not *re-ground* the field on some particular ontological basis.

Hence, the test of my typology is ultimately a practical one. First, how useful is thinking about mind–world dualism/mind–world monism and phenomenalism/transfactualism for clarifying the relevant philosophical issues? The four methodologies discussed in this book, each of which occupies one of the cells of the typology, certainly have identifiable analogues within the contemporary philosophy of science. Neopositivism, arising from the conjunction of mind–world dualism and phenomenalism, points towards hypothesis testing and the attempt to falsify general claims against empirical evidence; none of that would make much sense without the presumptions of an externally existing world against which to test claims and the limitation of the objects of knowledge to those things we can observe and measure. Broadly speaking, this is the post-Popperian tradition in the philosophy of science. Similarly, critical realism, which departs from the classical tradition (and from neopositivism) by pushing the limits of knowledge into the realm of the in-principle unobservable,[31] stands with the neopositivists in presuming that the world exists independently—otherwise, no sense could be given to the notion of objects and relations that were "real but unobservable," disclosed through abductive inference and other similar techniques. Analyticists[32] also differ from neopositivism, but not in the same way that critical realists do. Analyticists reject the notion that in-principle unobservable relations and objects are anything but instrumental devices used to make sense of the world that we *can* observe, whether with our unaided senses or with specialized detection equipment. Thus, for analyticists, knowledge is a useful ordering of experience, and it makes little sense to formulate and test hypotheses because the idea of an externally existing world against which to test them is literally nonsensical. And those committed to reflexivity reject both the notion of an externally existing world and the notion that knowledge is limited to experience; instead, they ground knowledge in the social situation of the researcher, arguing that what we know is inseparable from where we are situated when we produce knowledge. This is the province of critical theory, social studies of science, and certain types of feminist and post-colonial scholarship.

However, even if the typology clarifies philosophical and ontological issues, does it do so in a way that is useful *for IR*? In order to answer this second, and ultimately more important question, it is necessary to consider the alternative ways of dividing up the field so as to clarify debates and controversies. One of the most curious things about IR from a philosophical perspective is that we do not generally organize the field along conceptual or philosophical lines at all; rather, we divide into schools and research communities based on substantive topics and preferred causal factors. Thus "international security" and "international political economy" name subfields in IR, subfields that are not in any meaningful way characterized by common ways of analyzing particular topics. Similarly, we have a set of "isms" that often seem, in practice, to be little more than groups of scholars who maintain that military, economic, or ideational factors exercise the most influence over the course of international affairs. Then we also have lines of research united by techniques and tools: rational-choice modeling, large-n statistical analysis, qualitative case studies. In the midst of all of this chaos, we lack any good and defensible way to make choices, or to evaluate the choices that other scholars make, about how research is conducted.

We might think of this as a good thing for the diversity of the field as a whole, but we should not lose sight of the fact that global diversity is quite compatible with enforced local homogeneity, whether we are talking about cultures (Inayatullah and Blaney 2004, 124–125) or methodologies. Thus one possible result of field-

---

31   The phrase "in-principle unobservable"—or "undetectable"—is critically important, for reasons I will take up in Chapter 4.

32   I elaborate my reasons for not calling advocates of this philosophical-ontological stance "constructivists" in Chapter 5.

wide diversity is not a freewheeling and problem-driven eclecticism (Sil 2
Sil and Katzenstein 2010), but instead an archipelago of small groups of schola
doing their own thing in blithe disregard of the rest of the field. The first step
towards avoiding that fate, I think, is to highlight the extent to which the various
methodological commitments that scholars make are, ultimately, composed of
the kind of philosophical-ontological wagers I have sketched here—wagers
about which there is no simple final resolution. In addition, a philosophical-
ontological typology ordering different methodologies has the merit of placing
commitments in a common conceptual space, so that when we disagree we are at
least disagreeing about the same or similar things. At least in principle, having a
commonplace about which to disagree fosters conversation, not isolation.

Finally, one might ask whether this typology actually captures any debates
that are actually going on within the field of IR, or whether this whole exercise
represents yet another attempt to import a set of concerns derived from outside
the field in an effort to press the field in some specific direction. It would
be disingenuous of me to deny that I for one would greatly prefer a more
philosophically self-aware IR, a field characterized by a broader consideration
of the fundamental philosophical issues that are intimately intertwined with *any*
effort to generate factual knowledge. It would be equally disingenuous of me to
deny that the two axes of debate that I have ideal-typically isolated in my typology
are also the issues that I think we ought to be having more debates about in the
field; of course they are, and anyone who claims anything different about *any*
conceptual typology or distinction is most likely not being entirely forthcoming.
But I do not think that this kind of objection suffices to disqualify any substantive
claim; instead, what matters is how well the claim does what it is supposed to do
in practice, whether that is to reflect accurately an externally existing reality, or to
order lived experience usefully, or what have you.

The typology I have sketched here—and have organized the remainder of this
book around—does, I think, capture current controversies within IR, even though
it remains true that most Anglophone IR scholars are probably located in the upper
left-hand quadrant and practice some form of neopositivism (which also helps to
contribute to the continued absence of debate about the philosophical ontologies I
am sketching, since those IR scholars already *share* a philosophical ontology, and
what is understood need not be discussed). But IR certainly also features critical
realists, analyticists, and scholars pressing for increased reflexivity. If my typology
helps place such scholarship on more of an equal footing with neopositivism, it
will have accomplished perhaps its most pressing task.

Ontological commitments, whether philosophical or scientific, logically precede substantive claims, and serve as the often-unacknowledged basis on which empirical claims are founded. In this sense, ontological commitments are "foundational"—not in the sense that they provide unshakable grounds that universally guarantee the validity of claims that are founded on them, but "foundational" in the sense that they provide the conditions of intelligibility for those claims. In that way, ontological commitments are *world-disclosing*, since they make a particular kind of tangible world available to a researcher (Habermas 1990, 321). A claim such as "democratic states do not go to war with one another" implicitly makes a number of ontological presuppositions. The claim makes scientific-ontological presuppositions that a state's "democracy-ness" is a conceptually separable attribute of that state, and most likely also presupposes that a state's standing as a democracy is something that is visible to external scholarly observers and specifiable in an abstract fashion.[1] The claim also makes philosophical-ontological presuppositions, although these are somewhat further removed from the individual claim and pertain more to the overall intellectual context within which the claim makes sense; hence one needs to know something about the broader body of scholarly literature within which a claim has standing in order to explicate the philosophical-ontological commitments that it tacitly presumes.

The academic study of the democratic peace has been almost completely dominated by a *neopositivist* methodology. Neopositivism, although neutral with respect to the truth-value of specific empirical propositions, sets the contours of the research design within which claims about the democratic peace—and, quite frankly, claims about many of the other empirical phenomena regularly studied within academic IR—are evaluated. Before scholars can engage in debates about whether the democratic peace is best measured and assessed as a dyadic or as a

---

1   Of course, the speaker advancing this claim might be following Ido Oren's (1995) suggestion that what matters is not whether a state "really is" democratic, but whether participants in the interaction regard the state to be democratic. But in that case, they would be more likely to modify the claim to something like "states that regard one another as being democratic do not go to war with one another."

monadic phenomenon (for example, Rousseau et al. 1996), it is first necessary for those scholars to agree on some basic methodological principles, such as the notion that a causal connection shows itself in systematic cross-case correlations between specific factors (in this case, variable attributes such as "being a democracy" and "going to war with another democracy"), and the notion that knowledge is constructed through the successive proposing and testing of hypothetical guesses about the character of the world.

The fact that these assumptions are so widely shared, both within the democratic peace research community and within the field of IR more generally, does not make them any less philosophical—or any less philosophically contentious. Hypothesis testing and covariation-causality[2] are more or less direct consequences of the pair of philosophical-ontological commitments on which neopositivism stands: mind–world dualism and phenomenalism. Mind–world dualism enables hypothesis testing, inasmuch as testing a hypothetical guess to see whether it corresponds to the world makes little sense in the absence of a mind-independent world against which to test that hypothesis. Phenomenalism enables covariation-causality, since the limitation of knowledge to those aspects of the world that can be empirically grasped and directly experienced implies that the only confidence that observers can have about a causal relationship—which must be *inferred* rather than abduced or counterfactually ideal-typified—must be founded on its systematicity.[3] In the absence of these philosophical-ontological commitments, testing hypotheses in order to arrive at reliable statements about robust covariations would make little sense, and if we were interested in knowing about how democracy was connected to questions of war and peace, we would have to engage in some other kinds of knowledge-production procedures.

In this chapter I will expand on these claims with an eye to fleshing out the profound interconnections between these two wagers in philosophical ontology and the neopositivist methodological procedures to which they give rise.[4] This is somewhat more challenging to do in the case of neopositivism than it is in the other methodologies in my typology, simply because neopositivism is in many

---

2   When describing this conception of causation, I use the more general term "covariation" instead of the term "correlation," primarily because "correlation" in contemporary statistical parlance makes a number of assumptions about linearity that covariance does not.

3   Abduction is the methodological procedure preferred by critical realists, especially for dealing with causality; I discuss this further in Chapter 4. Similarly, ideal-typification and the analysis of counterfactuals are the methodological procedures preferred by analyticists; I discuss this further in Chapter 5.

4   While it is in principle the case that some other methodology could inhabit the quadrant of my typology formed by the intersection of mind–world dualism and phenomenalism, in practice neopositivism seems to have cornered that market nowadays—at least in IR. The same could be said of the other three quadrants: the methodology that I have chosen to discuss in each is the methodology that most clearly illustrates what a particular combination of philosophical-ontological wagers means in contemporary IR research, in part because there is actual IR scholarship utilizing that methodology.

ways more *commonsensical* in IR at the present time than the other philosophical ontologies I am discussing. What is understood among the parties to a conversation need not be explicitly discussed in the course of that conversation—indeed, its not being discussed is a large part of what enables it to work, to use John Searle's (1995) terminology, in the background of our efforts to make sense of the world— but it does *not* follow that any particular set of commonsensical presumptions is therefore justified or justifiable. Common sense is by no means conceptually neutral; nor is the content of common sense constant over time. What we, both as a scholarly field and as inhabitants of the planet at the present time, take for granted in conducting our knowledge-producing activities has both a history and a future, and the fact that our history has brought us here does not necessitate, or even prescriptively mandate, that our future look the same way.

Regardless, the fact is that the dominant Anglophone mainstream of the field of IR, in common with the dominant mainstreams of many of the other fields in the human sciences (Steinmetz 2005a), operates nowadays with and in terms of a neopositivism so widely circulated and so firmly encoded into scholarly practices of researching, writing, reviewing, and, perhaps most importantly, the training of graduate students, that it is difficult to raise systematic questions about it and receive much of a hearing. Indeed, this commonsensical consensus is so potent that sustained attempts to question it within IR—most recently by constructivists and feminists—have, for the most part, resulted in what Steve Smith (1994) once referred to in a slightly different context as rearranging the deckchairs on the epistemological *Titanic*: moving from a thoroughgoing critique and rejection of neopositivism to a straightforward expansion of the neopositivist research agenda to incorporate novel cases and causal factors. Thus, constructivism becomes a call to pay attention to ideational or subjective causal factors (Price and Reus-Smit 1998), and feminism becomes a call to measure the difference that gender makes (Keohane 1998; Carpenter 2002), leaving the more fundamental philosophical and methodological issues untouched. Putatively radical insurgencies have their critical edges blunted by the seemingly reasonable offer of being taken seriously by the rest of the field as long as they formulate testable hypotheses and join the search for systematic cross-case covariations arranged so as to approximate covering-laws. This offer seems reasonable, in turn, because of the too-little-theorized dominance of neopositivism and its component commitments in philosophical ontology. Thus, dominance reproduces itself, without the advocates of a neopositivist approach having to provide much, if any, explicit defense or justification of their position.

By working to make neopositivism *visible* in this chapter, my aim is not to reject it out of hand. Rather, I aim to open it up for robust scholarly debate and discussion. The unacknowledged and virtually unquestioned dominance of *any* methodology, I would submit, is a precarious situation for a scholarly field, as it amounts to a tacit placing of all of one's philosophical-ontological eggs in a single basket, or betting everything on a single turn of the roulette wheel: unless you are *completely* sure that you will be vindicated in the end, such a move is extremely risky. Given the voluminous scholarly attention in the philosophy of science dedicated to questioning both of the constituent philosophical-ontological assumptions that inform a neopositivist approach, the move seems even riskier. None of which is to say that neopositivist methodological procedures might not be the most appropriate way to answer certain kinds of empirical questions. The problem is with the assumption that neopositivist methodological procedures are the only ("scientifically") acceptable procedures for producing ("scientific") knowledge. But inasmuch as neopositivism is widely commonsensical in the field, the equation of neopositivism and scientific acceptability per se is difficult to avoid without challenging the very commonsensicality of neopositivism—no matter how much that may look like a criticism of neopositivism itself.

I undertake this task through a combination of textual explication and disciplinary history. Through such a genealogical procedure—what Foucault (1979, 30–31) might call a "history of the present"—conjoining texts and contexts in an effort to explicate the power exercised by the promulgation and defense of particular methodological claims, I aim to provide both a sense of what neopositivism and its philosophical ontology entails, and a sense of how these became so firmly established in the field. Neopositivists themselves would undoubtedly explain this dominance in neopositivist terms and claim that empirical work proceeding on neopositivist methodological lines has successfully accumulated a body of statements that have stubbornly resisted falsification and can be provisionally accepted as valid, and hence that neopositivism *itself* can be at least provisionally accepted as valid. This is clearly, however, a circular argument, unlikely to be compelling to anyone who is not already a neopositivist! That said, the fact that the argument is often taken to be compelling is an interesting sociological observation about the production of knowledge in our field, and deserves some attention. Hence my combination—in this chapter, as in the next three—of disciplinary history and textual explication.

Mind–world dualism

I begin with the philosophical-ontological presupposition of mind–world dualism, largely because it has a longer and richer philosophical history behind it, but also because it is arguably the more significant of the two wagers informing a neopositivist approach. What distinguishes neopositivism from the other methodologies in my typology is its wholehearted embrace of the Cartesian split between the knowing subject and the known object—a split that made it necessary to find ingenious ways to cross the gap between the mind and the world, and to avoid error when so doing. Valid claims, for a neopositivist, *correspond* to the (mind-independent) world, and hypothesis testing is the key neopositivist procedure for evaluating claims to see whether they do in fact so correspond. Phenomenalism—the reliance on empirical observation and directly apprehendable data—rounds out a neopositivist approach by telling the neopositivist what to focus on, but mind–world dualism sets the overarching context within which this takes place.

Logical positivism in exile

In the previous chapter I discussed some of the philosophical views of the Vienna Circle of logical positivists, which exemplified a commitment to mind–world dualism and phenomenalism through the turbulent scientific findings of the early part of the twentieth century. Indeed, it would not be an exaggeration to characterize the Vienna Circle as part of a general anti-metaphysical movement aiming to re-ground most aspects of life on a firmly rational and scientific basis: "in place of traditional philosophy the Circle wanted to erect a unified structure of science in which all knowledge…would be built up from logical strings of basic experiential propositions" (Galison 1990, 713). The wide-ranging scope of the Vienna Circle project is perhaps best exemplified in the Circle's 1929 pamphlet *Wissenschaftliche Weltauffassung* [The Scientific Conception of the World]:

> The goal ahead is *unified science*. The endeavor is to link and harmonize the achievements of individual investigators in their various fields of science. From this aim follows the emphasis on *collective efforts*, and also the emphasis on what can be grasped intersubjectively; from this springs the search for a neutral system of formulae, for a symbolism freed from the slag of historical languages; and also the search for a total system of concepts. Neatness and clarity are striven for, and dark distances and unfathomable depths rejected…. The scientific world-conception knows *no unsolvable riddle*. Clarification of the traditional philosophical problems leads us partly to unmask them as pseudo-problems, and partly to transform them into empirical problems and thereby subject them to the judgment of experimental science.
>
> (Neurath 1973, 306)

For Rudolf Carnap, one of the central members of the Vienna Circle, the "enthusiastic missionary spirit" of the Circle's proclamation of its new approach to the traditional problems of philosophy was connected to the responsibility of intellectuals to influence general cultural norms, particularly in the German-speaking world where so much traditional philosophy "was more of a hindrance than a help" in bringing scientific knowledge to bear on social problems (Carus 2010, 155–156). Because traditional philosophy did not sufficiently foreground the distinctiveness of empirical science, it made the task of reforming society and solving social problems more difficult, cordoning off topics like individual psychology and making them appear to be not amenable to scientific investigation. So cutting through metaphysics was a highly politically charged task, bearing some resemblance to the Marxist campaign for a scientific socialism founded on an analysis of the actual conditions of classes in society.[5] Indeed many, if not

---

5   Such similarities only count for so much, of course, and the denunciations of the Vienna Circle's campaign against metaphysics by critical Marxists of the Frankfurt School—particularly Marcuse and Horkheimer—are legendary in their vitriol (Reisch 2005, 121–123). In fact, this difference turns out to revolve around the phenomenalism/transfactualism divide, as will become apparent in subsequent chapters.

most, of the members of the Vienna Circle, including Carnap and Otto Neurath, were avowed socialists; the "Unity of Science" movement in which Neurath was extremely active "was not about revolutionary politics in any direct sense, but it was directly about goals and concerns—modernity, education, and the place of science in society—that were unmistakably linked to liberal and socialistic progressivism" (Reisch 2005, 35).

I emphasize this political aspect of the Vienna Circle because it helps to explain why events in the German-speaking world in the early 1930s pushed members of the Circle into exile as surely as they pushed other left-leaning intellectuals. We do not nowadays think much about the *politics* of logical positivism; instead, we often think of logical positivism as a *rejection* of political engagement in favor of a more pristine and detached approach to the production of knowledge, particularly scholarly knowledge. But Vienna Circle thinkers had high ambitions for the application of the scientific conception of the world to the problems of social life, and suggested that the same "process of elimination of metaphysical admixtures" that was operating in the fields of physics and mathematics should be encouraged in economics and history (Neurath 1973, 315). Theirs was no quietist approach, which is precisely what made it impossible for them to remain in Vienna as fascist parties became ever more prominent; many members of the Circle ended up in exile in the United States (Feigl 1969). But after arriving in the United States, many of these exiles steadily backed away from the very political involvement that had led to their exile in the first place, choosing instead to emphasize the technical aspects of their philosophical work. After the Second World War, this trend intensified, as the emphasis on the unity of science that had been a hallmark of Vienna Circle logical positivism began to appear suspiciously out of step with the black-and-white cultural logic of the Cold War: the scientific conception of the world had no room for unquestionable moral truths. In order to avoid being accused of harboring Communist sympathies, logical positivists moderated their pronouncements (Reisch 2005, 343–345).

In consequence, logical positivism became an approach to the philosophy of science that emphasized semantics, worried endlessly about problems of representation, and spent most of its energy in formal logical constructs. What had been a manifestation of an effort to complete the project of the European Enlightenment by applying scientific reasoning everywhere became increasingly detached from the actual practice of science, and increasingly uninterested in anything but technical solutions to the problems of knowledge. Mind–world dualism continued to frame these efforts, as the core concern was still to have language accurately convey knowledge of the external world, but the anti-metaphysical critical edge of the movement was blunted.

Falsification

Into this situation came Karl Popper, a uniquely important figure in the philosophy of science in that elements of his account of science have become, in effect, the operative self-understanding of many practicing scientists (Godfrey-Smith 2003,

57). Popper's criticism of Vienna Circle logical positivism, and his inversion of the Cartesian problem, signals such a profound reorientation of the philosophical discussion that it is sometimes difficult to recover or even remember the earlier positions—especially in IR, where core Popperian ideas have become largely synonymous with "science" per se. Popper's chief contribution to the discussion, and the one that has exercised enormous influence ever since, was to replace "verifiability" with an alternative criterion: *falsifiability*. What made a claim susceptible to scientific evaluation, Popper suggested, was whether the claim could be *dis*proven, not simply whether it could be evaluated empirically. That required not only that the claim be stated in such a way that its observable implications were clearly spelled out in advance (Popper 1992, 119–121), it also required that the distinction between the mind and the world be positively *solidified*, instead of eroded or circumvented along the lines of many previous attempts to solve the Cartesian problem.

Thus, Popper's solution to Cartesian anxiety was quite novel in that he embraced dualism and instead attacked the drive for certainty. Popper argued that the central problem was the conflation of knowledge with justified belief that a claim is absolutely certain; these were different things, he claimed, inasmuch as "there is nothing like absolute certainty in the whole field of our knowledge" and that if we continued looking for such certainty we would end up rejecting almost all of science (Popper 1979, 76–77). Instead, we should celebrate the conjectural character of scientific knowledge and strive to make and falsify conjectures in an effort to improve our picture of the world (ibid., 81). In this way, humans can make progress in the realm of knowledge, knowing more now than they did before, and with reasonable confidence that their knowledge is at least provisionally good because it only contains those conjectures that have survived repeated attempts to falsify them. Of course, not even those provisionally accepted conjectures are secure from future falsification: "*all theories are hypotheses*; all *may* be overthrown" (ibid., 29).

It should be fairly obvious how much of Popper's position depends on an embrace of mind–world dualism. A mind-independent world is a necessary presupposition of the idea that theoretical conjectures are falsified by not having their implications realized; the only way to determine whether a given set of implications actually obtains is to look and see, unless the implications were simply logical consequences—in which case they would not be the kinds of empirical implications required by Popper's account of science. Popper's embrace of dualism even extends into his understanding of observation itself: unlike the way in which observation serves both empiricists and logical positivists as a privileged source of knowledge, in Popper's conception, observation is basically theoretical, wrapped up with notions and ideas that cannot be directly derived from experience or observation: "*we approach everything in the light of a preconceived theory*" (Popper 1970, 52; see also Popper 1979, 71–72). This means that even observations are falsifiable, because seeing something in a particular way does not mean seeing into the heart of the object itself as much as it means tendering a hypothesis about what an object is. Subsequent investigation might lead to the modification of that hypothesis, and that would constitute scientific progress as well. Of course, none of this would make any sense without the notion that there were real, mind-independent objects "out there" someplace, against which such hypotheses could be tested. In this way, for Popper as much as for Descartes, dualism sets the parameters within which valid knowledge can be produced.

Ambiguities of falsification

The Popperian position is quite commonplace within IR, and the idea that one should build empirical knowledge by looking for "evidence that is inconsistent with our ideas" (Sprinz and Wolinsky-Nahmias 2004, 312) in an effort to falsify our conjectures has become quite conventional. It was not always this way, however. In fact, the first sustained attempts to "scientize" IR were scarcely Popperian at all, but were rather more influenced by logical positivism's concern with technical issues of language use. The main concern was to "operationalize" the concepts that scholars were using to make sense of international affairs, and to do so in formal and/or quantitative ways that often made use of data analysis tools or modes of conceptualization that had been developed in the 1950s. Morton Kaplan's systems theorizing provides a clear example of this kind of operationalization, which involved defining systems of interconnection between different attributes of states and states systems, in order to allow "past history [to] be examined in a way that illuminates the hypotheses" (Kaplan 1969, 47). Note that the aim here is not to *test* these "hypotheses," but— as is proper for systems theory—to use them as a starting-point for empirical investigation and see if they demonstrate their instrumental worth in the course of that investigation. As in logical positivism, the methodology here is more about deductively building up a system of propositions than it is about tossing out conjectural guesses and then setting out to disprove them.

Similarly, the quantification approach of the early IR scientizers was not particularly Popperian. David Singer, while admitting in a footnote (Singer 1969, 65) that he agreed with "Popper's logical argument" about falsification versus verification, put this philosophical nuance aside when designing and executing research projects that were designed to produce knowledge through data aggregation, "converting … traditional insights into operational language and gathering data on all relevant cases" in order to disclose systematic patterns of association among variables (ibid., 69–70). Likewise, Karl Deutsch and his collaborators (Deutsch 1954) set out to gather systematic and quantitative data on transactional flows across state borders, and on a number of other attributes of actually existing interstate "security communities"; they then reasoned backwards to come up with necessary, but not sufficient, conditions for the production of such communities at the international level. Such inductive procedures have considerably more in common with logical positivist verification than they do with Popperian falsification. This point is underscored by Hayward Alker's heroic effort to introduce complexity and nonlinearity into IR statistical methods, not for the purpose of conducting better hypothesis tests, but for the purpose of better modeling and operationalizing the sense shared by many scholars that world politics cannot be neatly divided up into discrete causal factors acting independently so as to produce outcomes (Alker 1966). A more logical positivist use of mathematics can scarcely be imagined.

The change from logical positivism to a more hypothesis-testing approach to knowledge-production did not, in fact, happen through any sudden upsurge of Popperians in IR. Instead, it was the work of two of Popper's philosophical critics—Thomas Kuhn and Imre Lakatos—that brought "falsification" into the IR lexicon: Kuhn by denying that falsification was how science progressed, and Lakatos by arguing on behalf of "sophisticated methodological falsification" as a way of understanding science. As with many methodological developments in IR, the centrality of Popper (along with Kuhn and Lakatos) was midwived by a set of developments within American Political Science, which—along with many of the other social sciences in the United States—quickly seized on these philosophers and historians of natural science as though they were providing a template that the social sciences could use to make themselves more scientific (Barnes 1982). This transpired despite the fact that all three thinkers were quite dismissive of the "scientific" status of the social sciences; Popper had devoted a significant number of writings to demolishing the scientific status of Marxism, which had been claiming to be a science ever since its nineteenth-century struggles with "utopian socialism," and Lakatos was hardly less dismissive of both Marx *and* Freud:

> [Marxism and Freudianism] are, no doubt, "unified," [and] give a major sketch of the sort of auxiliary theories they are going to use in absorbing anomalies, but [they] unfailingly devise their actual auxiliary theories in the wake of facts without, at the same time, anticipating others. (What *novel* fact has Marxism *predicted* since, say, 1917?)
>
> (Lakatos 1970, 176–177)

More importantly, both Kuhn and Lakatos were abundantly clear in their writings that they were in no way trying to provide a template along which any science *ought to* proceed. As previously noted, Lakatos (1978, 117) declared categorically that one should never "conflate *methodological* appraisal of a programme with firm *heuristic* advice about what to do" and associated himself firmly with the former option, while Kuhn (2000, 139) claimed that social scientists looking for prescriptions in his work were "badly misconstruing" his point.

Of course, none of this prevented the flourishing of quite a cottage industry within various social science disciplines, dedicated to implementing basic principles derived from Popper, Kuhn, and Lakatos in order to make themselves more scientific. The basic structure of the "lore" (Ashley 1984, 230) linking these three names was established (perhaps unintentionally) by Terence Ball in a 1976 article calling for a "post-Kuhnian political science" (Ball 1976). The story goes something like this: Popper slayed the dragon of logical positivism by calling for falsifiable theories; Kuhn called all of science into question by arguing that major changes in scientific knowledge and scientific theories were not the result of rational deliberation, but that the history of science showed more than a few discontinuous jumps in basic notions instead of the steady empirical progress envisioned by Popper; and Lakatos rode to the rescue, both of science and of Popper, by providing a way to make discontinuous jumps rational, and to let falsification proceed.

While not precisely *wrong*, Ball's summary ignores two tremendously important facts. First, all three of these thinkers were writing about the natural sciences, and in particular about physics, which has an unquestioned record of empirical success; as such, all three were trying to account for a success that no one denied. It is unclear that any of the social sciences, and IR in particular, has anything like this empirical record, so the Popper/Kuhn/Lakatos triumvirate may have little to say to IR (Chernoff 2005, 54–55; see also Jackson and Nexon 2009). Second, and related, Ball's summary detaches Popper and his critics from the actual context within which they were writing, and as such obscures both the broader philosophical and the more narrow philosophy of science issues that they were trying to resolve. As I have suggested, the central philosophical context animating Popper's advocacy of falsification was approximately three centuries of failure to satisfactorily or definitively ameliorate the Cartesian anxiety provoked by mind–world dualism; Popper was trying to explain how knowledge and science were *possible*, and whether it was reasonable to accept—even if only provisionally—the findings of science. More narrowly, Popper was engaged in replacing the logical positivist account of science, within which the central connection between knowledge and the world occurred at the level of *basic observation*, with an account in which conjectural claims—formulated by world-independent minds and directed towards the mind-independent world—only encountered the world at the level of *theoretical implication*. Logical positivism understood knowledge as being constructed from axiomatic grounds upwards, with those axioms in turn being derived from empirical observation; Popperian falsification inverted this, and Popper was famously unconcerned with where a claim came from as long as it was formulated in a falsifiable manner (Popper 1979, 104).

It is in this context that Kuhn's and Lakatos' work raised the most problems for Popper's position. In order for falsification to correct our knowledge over time, we would have to be clear when something had been falsified and when it had not been falsified; in order for falsification to account for the progress of science, it would have to be the case that practicing scientists actually engaged in the systematic effort to refute their conjectures and those of others. But Kuhn, based on direct empirical studies of modern physicists as well as historical studies of physics and chemistry, concluded that falsification did not explain very much about how day-to-day science worked. Instead, Kuhn (1970b)[6] famously argued that normal scientific practice involved a kind of "puzzle-solving" in which the

---

6   Note that what I am briefly summarizing for the remainder of this paragraph is the
     view that Kuhn expressed in his most (in)famous book—*The structure of scientific
     revolutions*—and not his later views on scientific knowledge. On these later views,
     see Chapter 5.

scientist treated most of her or his explanatory framework as an unproblematic background that was not subject to direct test, let alone to falsification. Normal science therefore meant coming up with solutions to puzzles that did not directly challenge the parameters of the currently dominant "paradigm." This meant, however, that falsification could not operate so as to guarantee the provisional validity of a commonly accepted scientific claim; if Kuhn was right, many scientific claims persisted not because they had survived and continued to survive robust attempts to prove them wrong, but because they had been embedded in institutions of scientific training (such as textbooks) and techniques of professional socialization. Indeed, these claims had become part of the very perceptual equipment that scientists used to view the world, so absent a "gestalt switch," the scientists would not even *perceive* a solution to the lingering anomalies that accompanied every paradigm.

Kuhn's account of science, unlike Popper's,[7] featured discontinuous jumps between paradigms: moments where an old paradigm, the worth of which has been called into question by a plethora of unresolved puzzles, is replaced wholesale by a radically different set of assumptions. According to Kuhn, these revolutionary jumps do not happen very often, and when they do happen it is not entirely clear that a successor paradigm always preserves everything associated with its predecessor, either in terms of specific contents (Kuhn 2000, 161) or in terms of its ability to explain the world (Kuhn 1970a, 20–21). Kuhn's position was no less dualist than Popper's, however, despite Kuhn's claim in the second edition of his most famous book that "the notion of a match between the ontology of a theory and its 'real' counterpart in nature now seems to me illusive in principle" (Kuhn 1970b, 206); the decisive fact about a theory or paradigm is its ability to generate and solve puzzles, and that ability depends on an interaction between the theory or paradigm and a world that remains independent of it. However, Kuhn's account provided no way to ascertain whether successive scientific theories and paradigms were producing "better" representations of the world over time, and this raised problems for the Popperian claim that scientific progress takes the form of a change of theories rather than by logical deduction from secure premises.

Lakatos, often misunderstood in IR as a *defender* of the Popperian position, was in fact almost as severe a critic of Popper as Kuhn was (Kadvany 2001, 12–13). Indeed, Lakatos only retained one important idea from Popper—the idea that progress could occur through a process of learning from errors—and basically rejected everything else that was specific to Popper's position. In fact, Lakatos' position was a lot closer to Kuhn's in at least two important ways: Lakatos accepted Kuhn's picture of actual science as characterized by discontinuous jumps, and Lakatos also agreed with Kuhn that it was never clear whether something had

---

7   Popper did, however, acknowledge the value of a dogmatic refusal to abandon immediately an apparently falsified theory, because only a vigorous defense of the theory could help scientists sort out the strengths of the theory from its weaknesses, and thus contribute to the growth of knowledge (for example, Popper 1979, 30, 266). This would of course mean that transitions between theories might not be completely seamless, but this is a far cry from Kuhn's understanding of such transitions.

been falsified as definitively as was required for the Popperian procedure to work as advertised. The latter point lay at the heart of Lakatos' rejection of the notion of a "crucial experiment" that could decide between two rival scientific theories; instead, Lakatos argued that it was only "when one research programme suffers defeat and is superseded by another one" that scientists (or philosophers and historians of science) might designate some experimental result to be a definitive refutation of the older approach (Lakatos 1970, 173). Definitive experimental falsification, then, is only claimed *after* scientists have rejected an approach, and falsification cannot therefore explain why that rejection took place to begin with.

As for discontinuous jumps in the history of science, note that the entire apparatus of Lakatos' "methodology of scientific research programmes"—the conceptual equipment of hard-core assumptions, negative and positive heuristics, and evaluations of "progressive" and "degenerating" problem-shifts that has been endlessly elaborated (Elman and Elman 2002) and applied (Elman and Elman 2003b) in the field—would *not be necessary* if Lakatos agreed with Popper rather than with Kuhn about moments of discontinuity in science (Jackson and Nexon 2009, 911–914). Although Lakatos rejected Kuhn's claim that such discontinuous moments were "incommensurable" and hence that there was no way to evaluate rationally how science developed at those moments, the *terms* of Lakatos' rejection of incommensurability are significant:

> Incommensurable theories are neither inconsistent with each other, nor comparable for content. But we can *make* them, by a dictionary, inconsistent and their content comparable. If we want to eliminate a programme, we need some methodological determination. This determination is the heart of methodological falsificationism.
>
> (Lakatos 1970, 179)

The important point here is that Lakatos sought to accept Kuhn's basic account while avoiding the problematic implications of that account for rationality and scientific progress. Lakatos' conceptual equipment was intended to portray—in retrospect—different scientific theories and theoretical aggregates ("research programmes") as belonging to one essentially continuous conversation, over the course of which claims were replaced by other claims that appeared to do a better job at explaining the world. The methodology of scientific research programmes was to be the "dictionary" that would allow the historical-comparative evaluation of different schools of thought and research in terms of whether they were progressing or degenerating over time—in a sense, giving Kuhn's scientific revolutions a chance to be rational, and hence, to contribute to scientific progress.

So in this sense, Lakatos does rescue Popper from Kuhn, in that Lakatos provides a way to talk about scientific progress in the face of evidence that science does not work through the steady falsification of conjectural claims. However, Lakatos' rescue operation comes with a significant cost: scientific progress only appears *in retrospect*, through the "rational reconstruction" of actual controversies in a way that differentiates between the "internal history" of science-as-rational-progress and the "external history" of science-as-arbitrary-accident, and then plays these accounts off against one another in an effort to make sense of those controversies (Lakatos 1978, 118–120). In other words, Lakatos' entire effort—as with Kuhn's—has to be seen as a methodology for writing a philosophically informed history of science that rejects logical positivist claims about verifiability. Such a history would provide important empirical support for the Popperian "post-positivist"—that is, post *logical* positivist, not "post-positivist" in the philosophically misleading IR sense of that term[8]—solution to the Cartesian problem.

Ironies of importation

So how did a set of discussions about the historical and philosophical preservation of scientific progress make its way into IR as a template for the conduct of empirical research? The basic pathway involves precisely the kind of opportunistic deployment of "science" that I criticized in Chapter 1: IR scholars looking to delegitimate a substantive theory that they thought inaccurate, or to set their own theories on a more solid footing, reached into the philosophy of science and pulled out decontextualized notions such as "falsification" and "research programme" that they could utilize within IR debates. Kuhn was received almost as a prophet who would show the way to true science, and was appealed to as a sanction for an imposed homogeneity of basic assumptions within an IR school of thought—which then became known as a "paradigm," despite the absence of any assumptions that would preclude simple empirical testing. So at the same time as Kuhnian language was introduced, scholars sought to test their theories against empirical evidence, despite the fact that the whole point of a Kuhnian paradigm is precisely that it *cannot* be directly tested, and hence cannot be falsified in the Popperian fashion. Thus was born the "inter-paradigm debate" that dominated the field during the 1980s and into the 1990s (Banks 1985; Wæver 1996): a strange hybrid of Kuhn and Popper in which rival "paradigms" (usually realism, liberalism/pluralism, and Marxism/radicalism) squared off against one another in a variety of empirical contests that no one ever won because the advocates of the "losing" position claimed both Popperian and Kuhnian sanction for sticking to their position in order to develop it further.

Lakatos enjoys a similarly odd career in IR. John Vasquez (1997; 1999) used an inventive, if somewhat philosophically incoherent, combination of Lakatos and Kuhn[9] to argue that the realist school of IR theory was not making sufficient

---

8   On the philosophically misleading nature of IR "post-positivism"—popularized in the course of Yosef Lapid's otherwise insightful article on the "third debate" in IR (Lapid 1989)—see Jackson (2008).

9   Combinations of Kuhn and Lakatos are philosophically incoherent largely because of the differences between the two authors concerning the implications of discontinuity for progress. One might plausibly argue that Lakatos *met* Kuhn's challenge, or that Kuhn *resists* Lakatos' solution, but in neither of those cases is there any ground for combining the two authors. Indeed, it is only in a philosophically impoverished field

scientific progress and therefore ought to be abandoned. IR realists responded (Elman and Elman 1997; Wohlforth 1999), kicking off a wide-ranging and ultimately inconclusive debate about precisely which propositions of IR realism constituted the "hard core" of the putative research programme.[10] Lakatos was also utilized in the evaluation of other schools of thought in IR (for example, Moravcsik 2003; Ray 2003); the notion of a research programme, sometimes without any explicit reference to Lakatos, also showed up in more general discussions of research methodology (for example, King, Keohane, and Verba 1995, 477–478), serving largely as a warrant for the proposition that scientific theories should be evaluated in a group rather than singly. Lakatos' elaborate conceptual architecture, detached from its historical and philosophical context, became a weapon in a disciplinary legitimation game: a way of demonstrating that a particular research endeavor was "scientific" and therefore should be taken seriously.

Perhaps the greatest irony of this instrumental, decontextualized importation of "falsification" and its critics into IR is the way that an entire line of thought that privileged disconfirmation and refutation—no matter how complicated that disconfirmation and refutation was in practice—has been transformed into a license to worry endlessly about foundational assumptions, in an almost logical positivist manner. At the very beginning of the effort to bring terms such as "paradigm" to bear on the study of politics, Albert O. Hirschman (1970b, 338) noted this very danger, suggesting that without "a little more 'reverence for life' and a little less straightjacketing of the future," the focus on producing internally consistent packages of assumptions instead of actually examining complex empirical situations would result in scholarly paralysis. Here as elsewhere, Hirschman appears to have been quite prescient, inasmuch as the major effect of paradigm and research programme language in IR seems to have been a series of debates and discussions about whether the fundamentals of a given school of thought were sufficiently "scientific" in their construction. Thus we have debates about how to evaluate scientific progress, and attempts to propose one or another set of research design principles as uniquely scientific, and inventive, "reconstructions" of IR schools, such as Patrick James' "elaborated structural realism," supposedly for the purpose of placing them on a firmer scientific footing by making sure that they have all of the required elements of a basically Lakatosian[11] model of science (James 2002, 67, 98–103).

---

like IR that a decontextualized deployment of Kuhnian and Lakatosian notions in conjunction with one another would even make sense.

10 That this debate would be inconclusive is quite understandable if we keep in mind that for Lakatos, the "hard core" of a research programme—like the research programme's other elements—is only visible *in retrospect*, once the relevant scientific community has reached consensus about core propositions and commitments. Debates about what is truly essential to a research programme might play an important role in the formation of that consensus, but they cannot be prematurely resolved by an analyst wielding Lakatosian criteria! Instead, we simply have to wait and see what happens: "One can be 'wise' only after the event" (Lakatos 1978, 113).

11 James modifies Lakatos with the addition of some concepts drawn from Larry Laudan. While nowhere near as prima facie incoherent as a Kuhn/Lakatos blend, there is

The bet with all of this scholarly activity seems to be that if we can just get the fundamentals right, then scientific progress will inevitably ensue … even though this is the *precise opposite* of what Popper and Kuhn and Lakatos argued! In fact, all of this obsessive interest in foundations and starting-points is, in form if not in content, a lot closer to logical positivism than it is to the concerns of the falsificationist philosophers, despite the prominence of language about "hypothesis testing" and the concern to formulate testable hypotheses among IR scholars engaged in these endeavors. That, above all, is why I have labeled this methodology of scholarship *neopositivist*. While it takes much of its self-justification as a science from criticisms of logical positivism, in overall sensibility it still operates in a visibly positivist way, attempting to construct knowledge from the ground up by getting its foundations in logical order *before* concentrating on how claims encounter the world in terms of their theoretical implications. This is by no means to say that neopositivism is not interested in hypothesis testing; on the contrary, neopositivists are extremely concerned with testing hypotheses, but only after the fundamentals have been soundly established. Certainty, not conjectural provisionality, seems to be the goal—a goal that, ironically, Popper and Kuhn and Lakatos would *all* reject.

Phenomenalism

Mind–world dualism is certainly the most important philosophical-ontological commitment made by neopositivists. Dualism informs the overall design of neopositivist research projects, both by setting up a particular epistemic situation—the gap between the world-independent mind and the mind-independent world has to be bridged somehow—and by introducing a characteristic fear: the fear that our elaborate intellectual constructs might be, in whole or in part, nothing more than the fanciful products of our own imaginations. Neopositivist research is designed to meet both of these challenges by seeking to be "scientific," which for a neopositivist means both having the proper "back end" logical preparation and structure and making sure to formulate falsifiable claims on the "front end" of the research project, where conceptualization directly confronts the world. The ultimate goal is to construct on the "mind" side of the mind–world gap a theoretical edifice that captures, mirrors, or at any rate somehow corresponds to the world on the other side of that gap; this correspondence, demonstrated through the accurate and compelling explanations generated by the theoretical edifice, can put Cartesian anxiety to rest by demonstrating that our knowledge is actually in touch with the world.

That said, there are a number of different ways to go about trying to implement this correspondence. Does *every* element of a theory have to correspond directly to something in the world, or is it acceptable if only some elements correspond?

---

something a little unsatisfying about using a prominent critic of Lakatos (and Popper, and Kuhn) in conjunction with his object of criticism without first establishing their compatibility on a philosophical level.

Does an accurate explanation mean systematically connecting inputs and outputs in a given situation, or is it also necessary to provide an account of precisely how inputs bring about outputs? Is predicting an outcome given a set of initial conditions the same thing as explaining that outcome? Finally, what kind of evidence is required to accomplish any of these tasks? Answers to these and related questions are what differentiate neopositivism from other forms of mind–world dualism. Although all dualist procedures are arrayed against Cartesian anxiety, there are at least two very different ways of tackling the problem: the neopositivist way under consideration here and the critical realist way that I will take up in the next chapter. What differentiates the neopositivist solution from the critical realist solution is the relationship each approach has to observability, and therefore, the kind of causality each seeks to establish.

Constant conjunctions

Near the beginning of the classical empiricist tradition, David Hume realized that founding knowledge solely on the experiences of phenomena posed some particular challenges. Chief among these was the difficulty of finding a rational basis for extending past and present experience into the future, and for anticipating that the past would serve as a reliable guide to the future. Such an extension seemed necessary in order to craft an explanation of anything—to go beyond simply describing what one saw. The difficulty stemmed from the fact that experience gave an observer "only the knowledge of a few superficial qualities of objects," and not a knowledge of the "secret powers" that produced those superficial qualities; hence learning from experience that *this* rock hurts when dropped on my foot does not give me rational grounds to suppose that *that* rock will hurt also. Or, to use Hume's own example:

> The bread, which I formerly eat, nourished me; that is, a body of such sensible qualities, was, at that time, endowed with such secret powers: But does it follow, that other bread must also nourish me at another time, and that like sensible qualities must always be attended with like secret powers? The consequence seems nowise necessary.
>
> (Hume 1977, 21)

At this point in the argument it seems necessary to clear up a potential misunderstanding that may arise from Hume's reliance on the unaided senses to provide experiences of phenomena. In the contemporary world, we have an explanation for the nourishing qualities of bread that does not simply depend on our observation that bread nourishes us; to the contrary, we have an entire panoply of nutritional studies based on the bread's chemical composition and its interaction with the body's digestive processes, studies made possible by pieces of physical and conceptual equipment that Hume could scarcely have imagined. So we *have* ascertained something about what Hume called the "secret powers" of bread and do not have to ground our knowledge exclusively on our experience of being nourished by bread in the past. Despite this, Hume's more fundamental philosophical point still holds, inasmuch as shifting our attention from the bread to the chemicals that compose it simply *displaces* the problem instead of solving it. Explanation still involves some notion of causality, and the route from experience to a causal claim remains opaque:

> These two propositions are far from being the same, *I have found that such an object has always been attended with such an effect*, and *I foresee, that other objects, which are, in appearance, similar, will be attended with similar effects.* I shall allow, if you please, that the one proposition may justly be inferred from the other: I know in fact, that it always is inferred. But if you insist, that the inference is made by a chain of reasoning, I desire you to produce that reasoning. The connexion between these propositions is not intuitive.
>
> (ibid., 22)

Whether we are talking about bread or about chemical components—or for that matter about rocks or planets or people—the problem remains: the presumption of continuity over time, or the presumption of a causal relationship, does not itself arise from the experience of the object, but is somehow added onto the experience by the mind. Hume argued that this presumption, or belief, whereby we pass easily from the past experience of two objects or qualities that are repeatedly conjoined (bread and nourishment—or a certain level of GDP and a democratic form of government) to the expectation that such a conjoining will persist among future objects and qualities, is "a species of natural instinct," and arises naturally—even *necessarily*—when the mind observes and experiences that repeated conjoining (ibid., 30). The more frequently the conjoining is observed to take place, the stronger the belief (ibid., 39). On this basis, Hume suggested that when we talk about a causal connection between two things, we are actually referring to our experience of a constant conjunction between the two things, and nothing more:

> We say, for instance, that the vibration of this string is the cause of this particular sound. But what do we mean by that affirmation? We either mean, *that this vibration is followed by this sound, and that all similar vibrations have been followed by similar sounds*: Or, *that this vibration is followed by this sound, and that upon the appearance of one, the mind anticipates the senses, and forms immediately an idea of the other*. We may consider the relation of cause and effect in either of these two lights; but beyond these, we have no idea of it.
>
> (ibid., 51–52)

So for Hume, the only thing that experience gives us is a pattern whereby two things keep occurring together. It is then through a natural instinct, or custom, that we build on this pattern and infer a causal relationship. What gives us the confidence to expect that the pattern will persist into the future is simply the natural feeling that we have, based on our experience of a constant conjunction of interest to us, that this cause and this effect go together. For Hume this kind of instrumental knowledge of causality was not only sufficient, but it was in fact all that we could hope to know anything about (Kurki 2008, 151). Reason and understanding, he suggested, should limit "itself to common life, and to such subjects as fall under daily practice and experience, leaving the more sublime topics to the embellishment of poets and orators" (Hume 1977, 112). Mind–world dualism and phenomenalism combine here to demarcate the boundaries of secure knowledge: the only way to be sure that the gap between mind and world has been safely crossed is to look for repeated experiences of objects, or qualities, or factors, co-occurring, and then being content with the natural instinct that inclines us to believe that these things will recur together in the future.

In essence, Hume's outline of the limits of explanatory knowledge set the agenda for the philosophy of causation for most of the next two centuries. Kant's quest to set knowledge on firmer—which for Kant meant *a priori*—grounds than mere observation, while in many ways a reaction to Hume, ended up in a strikingly similar place with respect to causality, which for Kant was both a speculative connection between objects and occurrences that was drawn by the mind, and a logical principle of temporal contiguity and succession: to say that a relation is causal is to say that a particular effect always follows a particular cause (Kant 1999, 222–223, 304–305). Causal explanation, for Kant as much as for Hume, is thus squarely on the "mind" side of the mind–world gap, and the mark of a causal connection is co-occurrence.

This basic notion of causal explanation is then handed down essentially unaltered through generations of philosophers and scientists, until it was formalized by Carl Hempel of the Vienna Circle into the scheme of "deductive subsumption under general laws, or briefly, *deductive-nomological explanation*":

> Any explanatory argument ... falls into two parts, which will be called the *explanans* and the *explanandum*. The latter is the statement, or set of statements, describing the phenomenon to be explained; the former is the statement, or set of statements, adduced to provide an explanation ... The explanatory import of the whole argument lies in showing that the outcome described in the explanandum was to be expected in view of the antecedent circumstances and the general laws listed in the explanans.
>
> (Hempel 1965c, 298–299)

Hempel's definition, although more elaborate, differs in no essential respect from Hume's. This is even clearer if we ask what Hempel means by a "general law"; this turns out to be a statement that asserts

> a regularity of the following type: In every case where an event of a specified kind *C* occurs at a certain place and time, an event of a specified kind *E* will occur at a place and time which is related in a specified manner to the place and time of the occurrence of the first event.
>
> (Hempel 1965b, 232)

In other words, for Hempel a "general law" is *nothing but* a statement of an empirical regularity, much as for Hume a causal relationship was *nothing but* a natural inference based on empirical regularity (Kurki 2008, 49). Thus explanation, for both Hume and Hempel, consists of bringing prior observations of empirical regularities together with specific information about a particular situation and demonstrating that the outcome was to be expected. Hempel was clearer than Hume that there is no significant problem posed by probabilistic rather than deterministic laws; the overall *form* of the explanation remains the same, and Hempel even suggested that probabilistic laws may be more appropriate for the explanation of historical events (Hempel 1965b, 237). In any case, we still have the same intellectual operation involved in explanation: observation of an empirical regularity, observation of a particular situation, and the mental combination of the two to create an account that corresponds to the mind-independent world.[12]

The only significant difference between these empiricist and logical positivist accounts of causal explanation and the contemporary neopositivist account is the introduction of Popperian falsifiability. This changes the epistemic status of a general law from an observationally verified constant conjunction—or, in more contemporary language, a *covariation*—to a hypothetical claim about a covariation. Not surprisingly, this claim can be empirically tested against appropriate data and provisionally retained for use in explanations if, and only if, it survives repeated attempts to refute it. In almost every other respect, neopositivist notions of causality and causal explanation, which are widespread throughout contemporary IR scholarship (Kurki 2008, 116), remain essentially continuous with Hume and Hempel. Neopositivist causality is inevitably marked by "constant conjunctions," and neopositivist causal explanation necessarily follows a logic of subsumption that makes outcomes rationally expectable in the light of a general law (Fetzer 2000, 120–121).

By way of example, consider King, Keohane, and Verba's widely read handbook of small-n statistical methods, which defines causality "as a *theoretical* concept independent of the data used to learn about it" (King, Keohane, and Verba 1994, 76; see also Kurki 2008, 103–105). As with Hume and Hempel, King, Keohane, and Verba place causality on the "mind" side of the mind–world gap. The parallel continues as the authors define a causal effect as the difference between an observed outcome in a given situation and the posited alternative outcome that *would* be observed in that same situation if a particular causal factor were changed: if it were absent instead of present, for example, or if its intensity were increased. This poses a challenge that the authors, following Paul Holland, term the "fundamental problem of causal inference":

No matter how perfect the research design, no matter how much data we collect, no matter how perceptive the observers, no matter how diligent the

---

12   One interesting implication of Hempel's formulation is that prediction and explanation are logically equivalent. This equivalence is bitterly contested by critical realists, and so I will postpone discussion of it until Chapter 4.

research assistants, and no matter how much experimental control we have, we will never know a causal inference for certain.

(King, Keohane, and Verba 1994, 79)

The sources of this uncertainty lie in two places.[13] The first involves a mind–world split: if we observe a situation in which two democracies do not go to war with one another, we do not have any reliable way to turn back the clock, make one of the countries a non-democracy, and observe what happens. The mind-independent world simply does what it does, leaving us and our world-independent minds to observe it. The second involves phenomenalism: if all that we have access to are our experiences and observations of the world, then we have no reliable way to go beyond those experiences—particularly experiences of constant conjunction—and therefore no completely solid basis on which to place a conjecture about what would happen if things had been different. We cannot observe the counterfactual situation in which one of the two countries was not a democracy, so we do not actually *know* what would have happened, although we can tender a hypothetical guess. These two sources of uncertainty combine to produce a situation in which we can never directly perceive a causal effect, and are limited to inferring it from our observations—much the way that Hume argued that we could never get behind our experiences to directly perceive the "secret powers" that brought about effects.[14] Neopositivist research techniques—most centrally the technique of case comparison, which I will discuss in a moment—are designed to work around this fundamental problem of inference and deliver as reliable a grasp of causal relations as can be expected.

It is important to note that this conception of causality and causal explanation is not idiosyncratic to King, Keohane, and Verba, but is almost universally shared by large-n "quantitative" IR researchers and small-n "qualitative" IR researchers alike. I place the terms "quantitative" and "qualitative" in scare-quotes here largely to underscore the extent to which I think the "quantitative"/"qualitative" divide to be a distinction without a difference—a distinction of *method* without a difference of *methodology*. Whether one uses numerical or non-numerical data, or whether one considers a small or a large number of empirical cases, is either a technical consideration or an aesthetic preference: either the relevant data is not

---

13 Note that this derivation of the neopositivist emphasis on cross-case covariation roots causation firmly in philosophical ontology, not in scientific ontology. Cross-case covariation as the mark of a causal relationship is *not optional* for a neopositivist, as it is more than simply an empirical conjecture about the world: in the absence of observed cross-case covariation, a neopositivist would have no grounds for believing that any two factors were causally related in the first place.

14 I am glossing over one important difference of method or technique between Hume and King, Keohane, and Verba, which is the latter's adoption of Paul Holland's (1986) conception of causation in terms of treatment and control groups, and the resulting quasi-experimental notions to which it gives rise (see also Goldthorpe 2001, 4–8). This does not change the situation in any fundamental philosophical way, as criticisms of the classical Humean notion of causation are equally applicable to experimental and quasi-experimental settings.

available in a quantitative form, or the researcher finds words more compelling than numbers, or vice versa. Such considerations pale in importance beside genuinely methodological issues of the sort that I have been discussing: questions about the "hook-up" between the mind and the world, including the relationship between knowledge and experience. In this respect, *large-n "quantitative" and small-n "qualitative" research in IR are fundamentally the same*, in that it is basically all neopositivist in approach. In saying this I do not mean that King, Keohane, and Verba are correct that "all good research can be understood— indeed, is best understood—to derive from the same underlying logic of inference" (King, Keohane, and Verba 1994, 4); but I *do* mean that if they had said "all good *neopositivist* research can be understood—indeed, is best understood—to derive from the same underlying logic of inference," then they would have been correct. It is the authors' failure to admit the existence of non-neopositivist methodologies that is the primary methodological weakness of their book—and the primary methodological weakness of the entire debate about "qualitative methods" in IR and in Political Science more generally.

In fact, for all of their protestations to the contrary, the most prominent "qualitative" critics of King, Keohane, and Verba are fundamentally, *methodologically*, on exactly the same page as the work they are criticizing. Alexander George and Andrew Bennett are basically correct[15] when they differentiate between the "logic of deriving testable implications from alternative theories, testing these implications against quantitative or case study data, and modifying theories or our confidence in them in accordance with the results" on one hand, and "specific methodological injunctions on such issues as the value of single-case studies, the procedures for choosing which cases to study, the role of process-tracing," and so forth on the other, and recognize that although they disagree with King, Keohane and Verba on the latter, they basically agree on the former (George and Bennett 2005, 11). Almost the entire debate sparked by King, Keohane, and Verba's book takes place on the level of tools and techniques and not on the level of fundamental goals and purposes of inquiry. Timothy McKeown's critique of the "statistical world-view" (McKeown 1999) basically boils down to a plea to use a more Bayesian logic of case-selection—studying cases that are least likely to display a hypothesized causal relationship—instead of simply looking to maximize variance when choosing cases to study (see also Beach and Pedersen 2013). Charles Ragin's "case-oriented" Qualitative Comparative Analysis (QCA) technique (Ragin 2000) allows the researcher to identify and analyze complex situations in which a causal effect is realized only in the presence of a diverse set of facilitating conditions, but this does not change the basic presupposition that

---

15 I would argue that George and Bennett are incorrect by regarding the deriving of testable implications from alternative theories to be solely an *epistemological* matter; I would also argue that the "methodological injunctions" that they mention are actually *method* injunctions. But their conceptual vocabulary is quite typical of neopositivists, for whom hypothesis testing appears to be a purely epistemological issue because the philosophical ontology of mind–world dualism is unreflectively presupposed. For much the same reason, neopositivists typically collapse methodology into method.

to say a factor is the cause of an outcome means that the factor is systematically associated—constantly conjuncted, or covaried—with it.[16] James Mahoney and Gary Goertz's effort to identify different "cultures" of qualitative and quantitative research (Mahoney and Goertz 2006) likewise operates almost entirely at the level of technical minutia—leaving unquestioned a fundamental methodological similarity that Mahoney subsequently (Mahoney 2008; see also Mahoney, Kimball, and Koivu 2009) foregrounds as a unified neopositivist methodological agenda of testing hypothesized causal factors to ascertain systematic and generalized connections between inputs and outputs.

Finally, the editors of a volume of essays intended to engage critically with King, Keohane, and Verba can find no stronger statement of the differences between their views and those they are criticizing than to distinguish between "data-set observations," which use data collected from a number of cases in order to gain insight into causal relationships, and "causal-process observations," which use data specific to a single case as a way of exploring or illustrating a hypothesized causal relationship (Brady and Collier 2004, 252). Interestingly, what the authors appear to have in mind, judging by the three examples of causal-process observation they provide (ibid., 256–257), is one of two things. Either causal-process observation means searching within a case for additional observable implications of a hypothesized causal relationship, or it means treating causal processes—in accord with both George and Bennett (2005, 140–141) *and* King, Keohane, and Verba (1994, 85–86)—as intervening factors that can and should be studied in the same manner as any other causal factor.[17] In that case, causal-process observation is a way to "motivate the systematic collection of new data" (Brady and Collier 2004, 253) in order to test a hypothesis in the conventional neopositivist way.

I have deliberately descended down into the level of subtle technical discussions for a moment in order to illustrate a basic point: the overwhelming majority of so-called "methodological" discussion within IR, as within Political Science more

---

16 To be fair, Ragin's QCA techniques also allow for the inductive disclosure of complex and even idiosyncratic patterns of causal influence, and the inductive delineation of a universe of cases, in ways that press the boundaries of a neopositivist methodology. In the end, however, causation for Ragin remains a matter of a systematic cross-case association between variables, albeit a complex one.

17 Along these lines, Mahoney, Kimball, and Koivu's (2009) effort to incorporate a diversity of conceptual definitions of causation into a single unified procedure—the "method of sequence elaboration"—stands as perhaps the most intricately elaborated form of neopositivist methodological subsumption. That Mahoney and his co-authors argue that it makes sense to supplement claims of necessity and sufficiency with claims about the relative importance of those causal factors already designated necessary and sufficient (ibid., 118–123), and that they regard a cause "both necessary and sufficient for an outcome" to be the "gold standard" for a cause's importance (ibid., 141), illustrate quite clearly that the underlying methodological strategy here involves causal inputs independently exercising an effect on an outcome—precisely as neopositivists expect. John Gerring's (2012) "unified" framework proceeds along much the same lines.

generally, is actually discussion about methods—and *discussion about methods for achieving neopositivist goals*. Constructing a theoretical edifice on the "mind" side of a mind–world gap, and evaluating that edifice by testing hypotheses against empirical observations of the world on the other side of the gap, are procedures that only make sense in a philosophical-ontological space jointly characterized by mind–world dualism and phenomenalism. Mind–world dualism tells researchers to test hypotheses; phenomenalism tells researchers to seek indicators of causal relations in constant conjunctions of objects or factors or qualities, and not to go beyond the evidence of experience in seeking those indicators. Everything else is, quite literally, just details: important details for a neopositivist actually engaging in the systematic production of empirical knowledge, but of decidedly secondary importance for getting a handle on how philosophical ontology shapes different modes of scientific research.

Neopositivist comparison

That said, I would like to conclude this chapter with a brief discussion of a method—the comparison of multiple cases—that shows up in the technical toolkits of social scientists occupying all four boxes in my organizing typology of philosophical-ontological commitments. Studying single, or multiple, cases does not place a scholar in any particular methodological box any more than the use of numbers places one in any particular methodological box; technical tools are compatible with different philosophical ontologies.[18] Having said that, the *way* that a particular technical tool works in practice obviously depends a great deal on the kinds of philosophical assumptions that underpin and guide its deployment and use in a particular piece of research, and thus on how that research project is designed and executed. There are thus as many ways of comparing multiple cases, methodologically speaking, as there are methodological commitments, and we should not conclude from the mere presence of case-comparison that a researcher is engaged in any particular kind of knowledge-production.

Neopositivist case comparison[19] is a more or less direct logical derivation from the covariation definition of causality, combined with the evident success of the experimental natural sciences. Because the covariation notion of causality depends on the systematic observation of some set of objects or factors co-occurring in order to conclude that a causal relationship exists, it follows that (as Hume had already claimed) the more clearly and frequently one observes that covariation, the stronger a case one has to infer a causal relationship. It would be even better if one could observe that covariation in isolation from other factors that might be causing the outcome, so that (for example) one could be sure that

---

18 Many technical tools are compatible with different *scientific* ontologies as well, but that is not my concern here.

19 The account I am sketching here is necessarily brief and focuses on philosophical issues rather than operational challenges and how to meet them. Excellent accounts of how actually to *do* neopositivist case-comparison include Ragin (1989); George and Bennett (2005); and Chapter 5 of Moses and Knutsen (2007).

poverty was caused by an inefficient system of property rights rather than by governmental mismanagement of the economy. On the neopositivist account, this kind of separation of causal factors from one another so that their effects can be observed independently is what takes place in a laboratory setting, and this in turn contributes to the extraordinary success of the natural sciences: working within Hume's strictures, experimental researchers manipulated physical objects so as to test hypotheses about which of their qualities produced which effects, and what kinds of outcomes were generated by various combinations of objects and factors.

Hence, neopositivist case comparison is an attempt by social scientists to emulate the success of the experimental natural sciences by replicating, as much as possible, the circumstances that permitted scientists to identify causes and their effects precisely. Because of the absence of a laboratory into which neopositivist social scientists could place governments or societies or the international system as a whole, they have to use multiple cases as proxies for deliberately engineered "control" and "experimental" groups. For instance, one can ascertain the effect of radiation on a given chemical compound by subjecting some of the compound to radiation and then comparing the result with some un-irradiated compound, but one cannot inject "democracy" into a given inter-state dyad and then compare it with the same dyad absent democracy. (Recall that this is what King, Keohane, and Verba called the fundamental problem of causal inference.) So instead, one takes a democratic dyad and compares it to *another* dyad, preferably one that is as similar to the democratic dyad as possible except for not being democratic. In that way, the causal effect of democracy could be isolated, allowing for the testing of various hypotheses about what democracy in a dyad might produce.

This kind of case comparison, similar to many others conventionally deployed in the social sciences, derives from the work of John Stuart Mill (1874), who elaborated the logic of four (and possibly five, depending on how one understands the Indirect Method of Difference) experimental methods commonly used in laboratory sciences. Somewhat ironically, since Mill devoted an entire section of the book to contesting the idea that any of these experimental methods could be used in the study of social life (Tilly 1997, 43–45), Mill's methods have been widely adopted as ways of producing neopositivist knowledge. The method that attempts to compare cases that are as similar to one another as possible except in the causal factor of interest is known as the Method of Difference. Mill also identified a Method of Agreement in which cases are as different from one another as possible except in the causal factor of interest; a Method of Residues in which a known causal effect is subtracted from a case so that the impact of the remaining antecedent conditions can be ascertained; and a Method of Concomitant Variation in which associated changes in two factors, especially across multiple cases, provided evidence of their causal connection.[20] It should be fairly obvious how all

---

20 Mill's Indirect Method of Difference is a kind of hybrid method, or a derivative case of the Method of Agreement, in which a total of four cases are compared: two that are unlike except for sharing the hypothetical causal factor in common, and two that are unlike except for sharing the *absence* of the hypothetical causal factor in common.

of these methods are designed to allow an observer to perceive directly systematic cross-case covariations—just what a neopositivist researcher needs in order to substantiate a causal claim.

What may be less obvious is that there is no significant philosophical or methodological difference between this kind of case comparison and the use of large-n quantitative data to calculate systematic cross-case covariations on a much broader scale. A finding that the democratic character of a inter-state dyad is significantly correlated with the absence of war, or even a finding that democratic inter-state dyads *never* go to war with one another, is no more or no less justified, philosophically speaking, than any other constant conjunction. Of course there are measures of statistical significance that can render such a finding more robust than a finding that is based on the small-n comparison of a few cases, and of course sophisticated quantitative techniques can simultaneously evaluate the independent impact of multiple independent variables, but from the point of view of philosophical ontology, those are not particularly relevant considerations. What matters is that the evidence supporting a causal inference is evidence of systematic cross-case covariation.

In fact, whether large-n or small-n, neopositivist comparison has precisely *one* ultimate goal, and that is to disclose cross-case covariations so that hypotheses about general causal relationships may be evaluated. Everything in neopositivist research inclines towards this end, because without the evidence of cross-case covariation, Cartesian anxiety rears its head once again and insinuates that these fine mental and theoretical constructs are subjective and arbitrary. Against this possibility neopositivism has only one answer, and that is to keep tossing hypothetical conjectures against the mind-independent world, in the hope that at least some of them will survive repeated attempts to refute them. That, and only that, constitutes scientific progress for a neopositivist.

4   Critical realism

The last few years have seen a marked upsurge in philosophical discussions within the field of IR. This was in large part a reaction to a particular kind of bifurcation that gripped the field in the 1980s and into the early 1990s: on the one hand, the dominance of the neorealist–neoliberal debate and its emphasis on technical, as opposed to conceptual, questions (Powell 1994; Niou and Ordeshook 1994), and on the other hand, a variety of efforts to introduce social-theoretical and philosophical considerations so as to move the field in a radically different direction (Kratochwil and Ruggie 1986; George and Campbell 1990). This bifurcation—christened the "Third Debate" by Yosef Lapid (1989)—produced a rather unfortunate situation in which the "debate" was largely a dialogue of the deaf, with most of the social and philosophical theory on the side of the dissidents while most of the empirical propositions were on the side of the fairly unreflective neopositivists. The field appeared to be heading for some kind of profound fissure.

One of the first efforts to address this situation was Alexander Wendt's attempt to forge a common ground that would unify what he called "'strong' liberals" and constructivists interested in "the issue of identity- and interest-formation" (Wendt 1992, 393). Wendt sought to do this by crafting a model of state action that took its inspiration from symbolic interactionist accounts of social structure, and thus incorporated some of the substantive critiques that had been leveled at the rationalist approach to state action shared by neorealists and neoliberals alike. Wendt also argued that IR scholars should stop spending so much time with issues related to "the epistemological status of social science," and should instead concentrate on making and evaluating empirical claims about world politics: "Neither positivism, nor scientific realism, nor poststructuralism tells us about the structure and dynamics of international life. Philosophies of science are not theories of international relations" (ibid., 425). In subsequent work, however, Wendt explicitly recognized that it was not possible simply to proceed directly to the evaluation of empirical claims without *some* philosophical common ground—especially since the neopositivist ground generally preferred by neorealists and neoliberals ruled out the kind of thickly constitutive account of social structure that he and other constructivists[1] called for.

---

1   In the *IR* sense. Wendt, as will become clear throughout this discussion, is not and has never been a constructivist in the philosophical-ontological sense. See also Chapter 5.

Considerations of this sort prompted Wendt's explicit advocacy of a critical realist philosophy of science, which he offered as a way to move the IR debate away from epistemological questions about science and toward a concern with the kinds of things that exist in world politics. Wendt sought to distinguish between ontological questions (primarily, whether the international-political realm was made up solely of material objects, or whether independent ideational factors also existed) and epistemological questions (which largely involved the issue of "naturalism," or whether the techniques of the natural sciences could be validly applied to social reality), and then argued that the ontological questions took precedence:

> I do not think an idealist ontology implies a post-positivist[2] epistemology ... I hope to find a "via media" through the Third Debate by reconciling what many take to be incompatible ontological and epistemological positions ... Some will say that no via media exists. They may be right, but I nevertheless press two arguments: (1) that what really matters is what there is rather than how we know it, and (2) that science should be question-driven rather than method-driven, and the importance of constitutive questions creates an essential role in social science for interpretive methods.
>
> (Wendt 1999, 40)

Wendt therefore offered an intriguing compromise position: the substantive interests of dissident scholars could be incorporated, at the cost of some fairly abstract epistemological commitments. The key to making this work was the acceptance of critical realism—and in particular, its twin presuppositions that knowledge reaches out to a mind-independent world and that knowledge can go beyond experience to grasp deeper levels of reality—by orthodox and dissident scholars alike.

Wendt's interventions, and the ensuing debate about the philosophical presuppositions of scientific inquiry in IR, have had a profound effect on scholarly debate in the field, particularly by opening up new philosophical vistas for many in the field and exploring their implications for world politics. But this opening has come with two related costs: the widespread promulgation of terms such as "ontology" and "epistemology" with conceptually specific definitions that preclude other alternatives, and the virtual disappearance of *philosophical* ontology from IR debates. Much like the promised benefits, both of these costs stem from Wendt's adoption and advocacy of critical realism, since it is a critical realist sensibility about ontology that informs the very ways that Wendt defines "epistemological" and "ontological" questions—and that, in turn, makes it difficult to raise questions about philosophical ontology that do not end up giving a critical realist answer. Critical realism *is itself a philosophical ontology* first

---

2   Note that Wendt is here using the conventional IR vocabulary that calls neopositivism "positivism" and refers to rejections of neopositivism as "post-positivist." When Wendt occasionally refers to himself as a "positivist," what he actually means is that he is a dualist committed to "hypothesis testing and objective reality" (Wendt 1999, 39), although he is not a neopositivist in the terms I defined in Chapter 3 since he decisively rejects phenomenalism.

and foremost, and so the conceptual terminology to which it gives rise is, not surprisingly, critical realist in orientation.

Consider, for a moment, Wendt's separation of ontology (concerning what things are made of) and epistemology (concerning how we ought to generate knowledge of those things), which goes hand-in-hand with a privileging of ontology over epistemology—because "epistemology will take care of itself in the hurly-burly of scientific debate" (ibid., 373). Although seemingly abstract or innocuous, this separation carries enormous implications for how we might think about the production of knowledge. For one thing, defining "ontology" in this way directs our scholarly attention towards scientific rather than philosophical ontology; if ontology is about what things are made of (as it also is in, for example, Dessler 1989, 445) and epistemology is about ensuring the correspondence between knowledge and things, where is there even conceptual *space* to talk about the "hook-up" between the mind and the world? Further, this disappearance of the category of philosophical ontology is not innocent, because defining and arranging ontology and epistemology in this way virtually ensures that knowing about things necessarily becomes a matter of making sure our propositions about things correspond to the innermost essence of those things. In other words, the separation of ontology and epistemology presupposes the kind of philosophical ontology I have called "mind–world dualism"—but this is a *presupposition*, not an *argument*.

Nothing I have said thus far should be construed as a dismissal of critical realism. Instead, what I want to call attention to here is the way that the very *terms* of conceptual debates in IR about the relationship of ontology and epistemology have been set by critical realists starting with Wendt, and as such, they tend to privilege a critical realist answer to certain fundamental questions. Separating ontology and epistemology, and privileging ontology over epistemology, are moves that only make sense within a mind–world dualist conception—and once we have decided that minds face a mind-independent world and strive to represent it to themselves as faithfully as possible, we have already foreclosed half of the available philosophical-ontological positions. From that point critical realists only have to demonstrate—as many of the authors drawn on by neopositivists eventually came to recognize themselves—that experience cannot exhaust mind-independent reality, and then critical realism emerges as the only viable contender. However clever and efficacious this strategy is at making inroads in a disciplinary debate, it is slightly disingenuous inasmuch as critical realism has not demonstrated its worth against the full range of philosophical-ontological alternatives.[3]

---

3   It is not even just critical realists who advance this project. Consider Nuno Monteiro and Kevin Ruby's claim (Monteiro and Ruby 2009, 16) that of the positions in the philosophy of science, only critical realism "prioritizes ontology over epistemology"—and that rival positions invert the order. Although Monteiro and Ruby do not themselves advocate a critical realist resolution to the issues of methodological foundations for IR, preferring a deflationary attitude towards foundational claims of all sorts, locutions such as this certainly indicate that the basic stance they are deflating is, in important respects, *already* a critical realist one. Where one starts thinking about these issues *matters*.

Considerations such as this have prompted my decision not to adopt the ontology/ epistemology split as a way of organizing this book and my firm desire to confine the discussion to the very commitments in philosophical ontology that are so often presumed rather than explicitly defended by critical realists. As I have suggested, there are two such commitments informing critical realism. One is a commitment to mind–world dualism, which critical realism shares with neopositivism. The other is a rejection of phenomenalism in favor of *transfactualism*: the notion that valid knowledge-claims reach beyond experiences to grasp the deeper generative causal properties that give rise to those experiences. Transfactualism is what makes it possible to go beyond correlations and start talking about causal powers, and thus avoid the perils associated with the Hume-Hempel kind of covariation-causality upheld by neopositivists: instead of simply noting that democracies do not tend to go to war with one another, transfactualism holds out the promise that researchers can identify those dispositional features of democratic states that incline them not to go to war with one another, and thus have knowledge that is more secure than knowledge simply based on systematic associations and more or less reliable predictions and retrodictions. To put this another way, transfactualism would allow for the possibility of going beyond the observation that seeds grow when watered and determining precisely *why* this constant conjunction is observed as frequently as it is.[4] Together, these two philosophical-ontological commitments shape a critical realist approach to social science.

To be fair, critical realists have in fact spent quite a lot of effort defining and defending transfactualism. But because they are operating from within a dualist frame of reference, critical realists often mis-state transfactualism as if it were a claim about the character of the objects under investigation rather than a claim about the "hook-up" between the mind and the world. Thus, for example, we have Patomäki and Wight's discussion of the "ontological stratification" of the social world, and their contention that going beyond empirical observations and elucidating structural contexts can produce a more holistic analysis of social life that can encompass "actors, actions, rules, resources, and practices" all together (Patomäki and Wight 2000, 232–233). Here as elsewhere, Patomäki and Wight conflate a scientific-ontological claim about social objects with a philosophical-ontological claim about how minds connect to the world. There is precisely *no* necessary connection between a scientific ontology that includes particular layers and levels of social relations, and a philosophical ontology that claims that these various levels and layers are in a mind-independent sense *real things*. One might, in principle, accept Patomäki and Wight's conceptual picture of the social world while rejecting their claim that this picture in some sense corresponds to how the world "really is"; likewise, one need not reach their specific conceptual picture of the social world by starting with their philosophical ontology, as there is no

---

4   While it is also possible to go beyond constant conjunctions without leaving the terrain of neopositivism—through the elaboration of increasingly fine-grained chains of intervening variables between an input and an output—this is not what critical realists recommend. See below.

necessary reason why what lies behind experience needs to look like the world that they have described. But here again, the internal structure of critical realist arguments obscures rather than clarifies the issue, since a largely unquestioned mind–world dualism prompts critical realists to freely intermingle claims about the specific character of a mind-independent world with claims about how observing minds are connected to that world.

To avoid accidentally presuming the truth of critical realist arguments in the course of explicating the critical realist position, I am going to be more careful about the distinction between philosophical and scientific ontology than critical realists themselves typically are. Much as in the previous chapter, my presentation here is intended to de-naturalize the critical realist position so as to make it available as one option among others. The difference here is that unlike with neopositivism, I do not have to call into question a commonsensical position that is widespread in IR. Instead, I have to call into question an *emerging* commonsensical account of the relationship between epistemology and ontology—a commonsensical account that derives at least part of its appeal, I would argue, from the fact that it shares with neopositivism the important presumptions of a mind-independent world and a gap that has to be crossed in order to connect minds to that world through valid knowledge-claims.

Accordingly, I will begin this chapter with a discussion in which I endeavor to foreground transfactualism as a philosophical-ontological commitment. For critical realists, transfactualism underpins the inferential strategy of "abduction," a form of reasoning that works from observed phenomena to underlying principles and factors that give rise to those observed phenomena. Although critical realists share a presumption of mind–world dualism with neopositivists, the fact that critical realists believe that knowledge can go beyond phenomenal experience decisively colors how their dualism plays out in practice; I will take up mind–world dualism in the second section of the chapter and illustrate the differences between the neopositivist focus on cross-case covariation as the mark of causality and the critical realist focus on dispositional causal properties. As in the previous chapter, I will conclude with some reflections on what case comparison might look like if practiced in a critical realist way.

Two further definitional caveats. First, in this chapter I am largely focusing on *critical* realism, which is a subset of a larger set of claims in the philosophy of science generally called "scientific realism" or just "realism." Scientific realism comprises a number of specific lines of argument loosely clustered around a particular "doctrine about the truth of scientific theories and the reality of the entities those theories postulate" (Chernoff 2009b, 388), and is thus locked in contention with various alternative ("anti-realist") accounts of scientific theories, including constructive empiricism, instrumentalism, skepticism, idealism, constructivism, and pragmatism (Chakravartty 2007, 9–13). Critical realism, as a subset of the broader tradition of realism in the philosophy of science,[5] shares

---

5   To say nothing of the broader realist tradition in philosophy writ large—a tradition that, of course, intersects with IR as a kind of anti-utopian sensibility about the

certain commitments in common with other strands of scientific realism, but specifically focuses on elaborating those claims in the context of the study of the social world. Given the philosophical continuities, however, I will expand the discussion to scientific-but-not-critical realists as appropriate in order to elucidate broadly realist philosophical-ontological claims and commitments.

Second, it often goes unremarked in IR that critical realism's main philosophical advocates—Roy Bhaskar, Margaret Archer, Mario Bunge—have virtually *no* presence in philosophy of science debates narrowly construed, where the mantle of realism is borne these days by authors such as Richard Boyd, Ilkka Niiniluoto, and Stathis Psillos. I mention this not to in any way discredit or disparage Bhaskar et al., but simply to point out that the project in which critical realist philosophers are engaged is somewhat broader than the more orthodox philosophy of science project of accounting for the success of science. Through institutes such as the Centre for Critical Realism and organizations such as the International Association for Critical Realism, critical realist scholars are often directly involved in political advocacy that is explicitly linked to their methodological commitments. Critical realism also has profound links to debates within Marxist thought about the scientific status of a critique of society, and while this does not automatically equate critical realism with Marxism, it does suggest the need for some caution when explicating critical realist thought—caution that the focus remain on critical realism as a philosophy of (social) science, and not on critical realism as a program of political advocacy.[6] The inclusion of scientific-but-not-critical realism in the discussion is one way to address this concern. Inasmuch as most scientific realist philosophy is about the practice of the natural sciences, particularly physics, some of what follows will begin someplace quite distant from IR before returning to substantive ground that is more familiar to IR scholars.

Transfactualism

Historically speaking, critical realism as a philosophy of science comes from a series of efforts to resolve a vexing if technical problem within the antecedent traditions feeding into neopositivism: the problem of unobservables. For decades, natural scientists had been positing unobservable quantities and factors—such as "mass," "inertia," and even "force"—as part of their equations and theories for explaining basic phenomena such as motion. The atomic theory of matter, which made use of the idea that physical objects were mostly made up of empty space, also proposed minute unobservable particles as the fundamental constituents of actually existing things; such an approach led to significant advances, such as the ideal gas law, which related temperature, pressure, and volume in a precise

---

inescapability of power struggles (Williams 2005; Jackson and Nexon 2004). Needless to say, critical realism has very little to do with IR realism, or indeed with the broader tradition of realism in political philosophy.

6   I am fully aware that this is a distinction that critical realists would reject. For a defense of the separation, see Weber (2004); Jackson and Kaufman (2007); and Chapter 1.

mathematical way (Harré 1985, 26–27). Subatomic physics posed an even more bizarre set of puzzles, positing fundamental limits to observation *itself*. The problem, from a phenomenalist perspective, was that all of these evidently useful scientific theories contained terms that seemed to refer to things that could not be directly perceived, and therefore could not be known as directly as the objects of everyday experience. This led to a fierce debate about how to regard such terms: were they purely instrumental conveniences, or did they actually indicate the existence of things that existed beyond our ability to perceive them?

The status of unobservables posed such a significant problem because it called into question the whole basis on which efforts to bridge the gap between the mind and the world were based. Logical positivism was threatened by unobservable theoretical terms because such terms could not be related to basic observation statements; hence they appeared anomalous within scientific theories. Falsificationists, on the other hand, had argued that scientific knowledge progressed towards a more complete and accurate correspondence with the actual world, but it was difficult to give any sense to the notion of "correspondence" for theoretical terms lacking empirical referents. For many, solving the problem while retaining a commitment to mind–world dualism turned out to mean abandoning a commitment to phenomenal experience as the limit of knowledge. Instead, these philosophers sought to theorize "real but unobservable" objects: properties and entities that we could not perceive, but that exercised important effects in that part of the world we could perceive.

While the ensuing transfactualism has significant implications for thinking about the reality of subatomic particles such as electrons and quarks, it has perhaps even greater implications in the social sciences, where terms referring to unobservable factors—such as "social structure"—are even more prominent than they are in the contemporary physical sciences. No small part of the initial introduction of critical realism into IR, and Political Science more generally, came about because of a perceived inadequacy in the dominant ways of conceptualizing social structure, because "the social relations which constitute states as states will be potentially unobservable" and would thus require a "non-empiricist understanding of system structures and structural analysis" (Wendt 1987, 344; see also Isaac 1987). The critical realist answer opened the door to real but unobservable structures that could "generate agents and their behavior (in the sense that they make the latter possible)" (Wendt 1987, 357). The reality of unobservable objects is thus at the heart of many of the most important efforts to draw on realist philosophy of science in order to enable a distinct form of social-scientific practice.

The invisible dragon

To give a clearer example of what is at stake in this debate over the status of unobservables, consider this story that Carl Sagan once told about an invisible dragon. Suppose that someone comes to you and tells you that they have a fire-breathing dragon in their garage, but when you ask to see it, you are shown a garage that looks empty and are told that the dragon is invisible. So you propose a series of ingenious physical tests—the use of an infrared sensor to detect heat, the application of spray paint to show the outline of a corporeal mass, and so on—but are met every time with some reason why that test will fail to show the existence of the dragon. Speaking as a fairly orthodox neopositivist, Sagan concludes:

> Now, what's the difference between an invisible, incorporeal, floating dragon who spits heatless fire and no dragon at all? If there's no way to disprove my contention, no conceivable experiment that would count against it, what does it mean to say that my dragon exists? Your inability to invalidate my hypothesis is not at all the same thing as proving it true. Claims that cannot be tested, assertions immune to disproof, are veridically worthless, whatever value they may have in inspiring us or in exciting our sense of wonder. What I'm asking you to do comes down to believing, in the absence of evidence, on my say-so.
>
> (Sagan 1997, 171)

The crucial issue here is that Sagan's invisible dragon is *completely* unobservable: it is impervious to any conceivable physical test of its existence. But further, the dragon in question does not *do* anything in Sagan's account; it is unclear why anyone would claim to have such a dragon in their garage in the first place, unless the claim did some kind of explanatory work for them.[7] Hence, we should tweak the account just a bit (as Sagan himself does subsequently) and start not with the claim that an invisible dragon inhabits a garage, but with the claim that an invisible and otherwise undetectable dragon inhabiting the garage is the best explanation for various puzzling things that we *can* see. Then we have a setting that more closely parallels the epistemic situation of a scientific investigation, where an unobservable factor is utilized as part of the explanation for some observable phenomenon.

Sagan's invisible dragon raises challenges when used in a scientific explanation precisely because there is no way to directly verify or falsify directly claims about its existence. These challenges depend on the dragon's unobservability *in principle*, and not simply on the dragon's not having been observed or on its not having been observed because we have not yet constructed the appropriate kind of dragon-viewing apparatus. The issue in Sagan's story is that the dragon cannot *possibly* be observed by any conceivable observational apparatus that we might construct. Something in the nature of the dragon itself prevents it from becoming manifest in the world; it is, so to speak, permanently unavailable, even to our augmented senses, and so cannot be directly experienced. In the case of an invisible dragon in the garage, this may not make much of a difference, but if the invisible dragon starts showing up in explanations for why livestock is vanishing from

---

7   Of course, the claim might also be understood as doing some psychological work for those making the claim; this is, roughly, Sagan's understanding of theological claims, which are more than likely his actual target with this story.

nearby farms, we have a slightly different situation: an explanation that posits that something we cannot possibly see directly is playing a causally significant role.

Invisible dragons may seem a bit contrived as an example, but modern physics provides a bestiary scarcely less strange: "de-localized" fundamental particles, entangled quantum states, vibrating strings existing in part in higher-order dimensions, and so on.[8] The fundamental problem posed by these unusual objects is much the same, epistemically speaking, as the problem of the invisible dragon: theories that incorporate these unobservable objects seem to do a reasonably good job accounting for otherwise puzzling observable phenomena, and there is not any easy way to dispense with those unobservables and still retain explanatory power. Hence the problem: what sense do we make of those theoretical terms referring to unobservables, and in particular, how do we know whether such terms are accurate? Terms that refer to observable entities and their attributes— weight, length, angular momentum—are relatively easy to evaluate, since they can be more or less straightforwardly compared with observational data, but there is no such straightforward way to evaluate a proposition about the "spin" of an electron—especially since the spin of a subatomic particle is explicitly formulated "without reference to any classical visualizable model" (Arabatzis 2006, 228). Making sense of *those* invisible dragons is every bit as challenging as dealing with those in Sagan's original story.

To oversimplify a bit, theoretical terms referring to in-principle unobservable entities and properties can be handled one of three ways. First, they can be treated *instrumentally*, as not truly referring to anything but instead as playing important roles in enabling theories to cohere and to generate sensible explanations and predictions. Familiar to many social scientists from Milton Friedman's oft-cited essay on "positive economics" (Friedman 1979), an instrumental construal of theoretical terms referring to in-principle unobservables avoids the necessity to evaluate such terms directly at all, and focuses instead on the operational results delivered by the theory as a whole. Bas van Fraassen's "constructive empiricist" stance (van Fraassen 2004a) is perhaps the most important exemplar of this approach in the contemporary philosophy of science; van Fraassen maintains that the goal of science is to improve the empirical adequacy of our theories, and such adequacy in no way requires that every single term in the theory correspond to some externally existing, mind-independent reality.[9]

A second way of dealing with unobservables, which like instrumentalism sidesteps the specific question about the status of unobservables by arguing in favor of a focus on a slightly different issue, would treat terms referring to unobservables as *provisional* placeholders, destined to be replaced as scientific

---

8 Indeed, Wendt's most recent book is an exploration of the implications of this strange bestiary for theories in the social sciences (Wendt 2015).

9 As I will discuss in the next chapter, an instrumentalist view of theoretical terms lends itself more or less directly to an analyticist philosophical-ontological stance on the production of scientific knowledge—despite the fact that the most common references in IR to theoretical terms as instrumental conveniences can be found among self-proclaimed "positivists."

knowledge advances. The various attempts to understand quantum mechanics—which is riddled with in-principle unobservables and irreducibly statistical discontinuities, such as particles popping in and out of existence in a vacuum state[10]—in terms of yet-to-be-discovered hidden variables or unities beyond our present perceptual grasp provide the clearest example. David Bohm's work on "implicate orders" (Bohm 2002) is probably the best-known of these approaches in the philosophy of physics, and it is possible to read certain accounts of social and cognitive evolution (for example, Teilhard de Chardin 2008) in this way.[11]

Both the instrumental and the provisional construal of theoretical terms referring to unobservables, however, raise problems for the logical coherence of the theories containing such terms. In particular, it is difficult to explain why such terms should not simply be dispensed with in favor of more conventional terms referring to observables. Carl Hempel (1965a, 185–186) referred to this as the theoretician's dilemma: if theoretical terms referring to unobservables served their proper function and linked an observable input with an observable output, they could be replaced with a law-like statement simply connecting the input and the output—thus rendering the theory itself unnecessary. Therefore, either massive amounts of contemporary scientific theory were irrelevant and unnecessary, or there was something wrong with the phenomenalist limitation of knowledge to the realm of experience. After much formal logical argumentation, Hempel concluded the latter, arguing that if a theory was to do anything other than "establish deductive connections among observation sentences" it had to go beyond observables (ibid., 222). Going beyond the establishment of deductive connections, in turn, was essential even to simple operations such as determining whether some object was a magnet: it was impossible to use a purely observable definition of a magnet—it "attracts every iron object in its vicinity" (ibid., 197)—to ever identify a magnet successfully, because one would need an infinite number of observations in order to do so. The solution, therefore, was to handle unobservables in the same way one handled observables, and to derive "observable symptoms of their presence in certain specified circumstances" (ibid., 220) as a way of evaluating whether they existed.

Karl Popper, usually an inveterate opponent of logical positivists like Hempel, reached a similar conclusion by a different route. In fact, Popper had never been in favor of strictly limiting knowledge to observable objects and properties; in his *Logic of Scientific Discovery*, originally published in 1934, he had argued in favor of moving the burden of scientific explanation away from observed empirical

---

10   Quantum field theory indicates that there is a distinct statistical likelihood that particles will spontaneously appear and disappear in a vacuum, giving rise to (among other things) the "Casimir effect" whereby metal plates in close proximity are attracted to one another (Mohideen and Roy 1998), and "Hawking radiation" produced around the event horizon of a black hole when one half of a spontaneously created particle/antiparticle pair falls into the black hole, leaving the other to radiate out into the universe (Shapiro and Teukolsky 1983).

11   This kind of "provisional realism" is arguably compatible with a phenomenalist limitation of knowledge to the objects of experience; see below.

regularities, because "the connections between our various experiences are explicable, and deducible, in terms of *theories* which we are engaged in testing" (Popper 1992, 107). This was part of Popper's overall shift away from the notion that scientific explanations could be built up by induction from basic observations, and although the specific issue of unobservable entities and theoretical terms referring to them was not a major component of his strategy, the notion that knowledge went beyond experience was a fairly unproblematic consequence of his position:

> Universal laws transcend experience, if only because they are universal and thus transcend any finite number of their observable instances; and singular statements transcend experience because the universal terms which normally occur in them entail dispositions to behave in a law-like manner, so that they entail universal laws.
>
> (ibid., 425)

Hence, Popperian falsification strongly suggested that universal terms were not different in kind from other theoretical terms and presented no special challenges to the scientist or to the philosopher of science: all such terms were equally conjectural and had to demonstrate their merit by surviving repeated attempts to falsify them.

Thus we see that under certain circumstances, logical positivists and falsificationists were not opposed to adopting an approach to unobservables that was neither instrumental nor provisional: as long as terms referring to such entities and properties and laws played an important explanatory function in scientific theories, there was no reason to declare that those entities and properties did not exist merely because they could not be directly observed. From here it is only a small step to the realist position about unobservables, which is that if terms referring to such entities and properties play an important explanatory function in scientific theories, then we *should* believe that those entities and properties actually exist, despite the fact that we cannot directly observe them (Wight 2006, 24; Chakravartty 2007, 4–5). The realist position about unobservables is, then, a logical elaboration of two of the streams of philosophical thinking feeding into neopositivism, even though neopositivists themselves have generally refrained from taking that step.

Abduction and unobservables

In order to understand better both why neopositivists are able to maintain their anti-realist stance even though their own philosophical forebears often point towards its abandonment, and what difference the embrace of real-but-unobservable objects makes to empirical scientific practice, it is necessary to be somewhat more precise about what it means for some object to be "unobservable" (and, for that matter, what it means for some object to be "observable"). It is also necessary to say a bit more about why scientists—chiefly physicists—utilize unobservable objects in their explanations in the first place, because this utilization serves as a template or exemplar for the critical realist practice of positing unobservable objects in order to explain events in the social world. Proceeding carefully through this conceptual thicket is particularly important given the tendency of critical realist scholars to speak loosely about what it means for an object to be real but unobservable. To get a better sense of critical realism's methodological consequences, these ambiguities need to be addressed.

Why would scientists feel the need to posit unobservable objects—entities, properties, or processes that cannot be directly perceived with *Homo sapiens-*normal senses—in the course of their explanatory accounts? Ideally, the need to do so arises not from some kind of prior conceptual or even ideological/ theological commitment by the scientist, but rather from the ways in which the world resists the efforts of scientists to capture it successfully with models and machines (Pickering 1995, 21–22). The orbits of the planets were calculated, and some discrepancies in the orbit of Uranus were observed; astronomers seeking to explain those discrepancies hypothesized the existence of a planet beyond Uranus, and calculated its mass and orbit based on Newton's laws of motion; telescopes trained on the appropriate area of the sky detected a new planet— subsequently named Neptune—right where it was supposed to be (Baum and Sheehan 1997, 104–106). Physicists smashing particles together at higher and higher energy levels kept on finding novel particles being produced, and order was only brought to this particle zoo by the formulation of the "Standard Model" in which particles were taken to be composed of even more fundamental entities called "quarks"— but quarks never appear singly, only in combination, so they cannot ever be directly detected (Gell-Mann 1995). Despite this strangeness at its core, the Standard Model has been quite successful at predicting novel particles, and has informed the construction of ever more powerful particle accelerators designed to produce the most exotic particles envisioned by the theory (Lederman and Teresi 2006).

Both of these examples point to a particular strategy for generating hypothetical conjectures—the strategy of *abductive inference.* Unlike the more familiar processes of deductive inference (which reasons from general claims to particular conclusions) and inductive inference (which reasons from particular claims to general conclusions), abductive inference works by generating plausible explanations from available data (Wendt 1987, 352–354). Abductive inference is a way of reasoning from some puzzling set of observations to a likely explanation of those observations: we go beyond what we have observed in order to posit something that plausibly accounts for what we have observed, as when astronomers posited a planet beyond the orbit of Uranus as a way of explaining discrepancies between Uranus' predicted orbit and its observed orbit. It is in this sense that abduction relates a whole to another whole (Onuf 1989, 98–100); the whole of our observations are taken to be explained, not by some general law of which they are a specific case, and not by some general system that they suggest, but by a whole conception of the world that includes our observations *along with* the posited explanatory factor(s). The abduction of quarks did not simply bring order to the particle zoo by subsuming it under a general law (which would be deduction) or moving from the plethora of particles to some broader pattern (which would be induction), but by conjecturing a world in which particles were composed of unobservable quarks—a world that would contain all of the detected particles, but would also contain something else that could explain what had already been detected.

Unlike induction and deduction, which are procedures for reaching conclusions, abduction is a procedure for generating conjectures. Charles Sanders Pierce, the philosopher perhaps most responsible for theorizing abductive inference, introduced the notion in part as a way of accounting for the uncanny way that scientists were able to formulate hypotheses for testing that were at least *plausible* (Rescher 1979, 41–42). This suggested to Pierce that scientists were engaging in some kind of process of pre-selection of their conjectures, and only putting forward for evaluation those conjectures that were likely to be true. This pre-selection, rooted in scientists' practical experience with the tools of their trade (which means: their *equipment*, both physical and conceptual), helped to explain why science made progress in understanding the world. Instead of evaluating every potential hypothesis, abductive inference ensured that scientists only had reasonable hypotheses to consider. But "reasonable" hypotheses are not simple linear extrapolations from existing scientific knowledge; strange and discontinuous jumps are always possible, depending on the complicated interplay of theory, apparatus, and the world (as in Pickering 1995, 146–147). To abduce an explanation is a *creative* act, not an automatic one.

The connection between abduction and critical realism is simple: to abduce an explanation is to posit, or conjecture, the existence of some process, entity, or property that accounts for the observational data. In order for this conjectured object to exercise effects in the empirical world, critical realists suggest, it must be taken to be real, to *actually* exist, and thus to be something other than an instrumental theoretical convenience (Wight 2006, 31–32). It cannot be stressed enough that abductive inference is a technique for generating conjectures and is *not* a technique for establishing the truth or falsity of any particular conjecture (Chernoff 2005, 82); abduced explanations (and the abduced objects that they contain) remain purely conjectural until someone finds some additional evidence in their favor (Wendt 1987, 357–358). But in principle, the provision of such additional evidence takes the explanation out of the conjectural realm and allows scientific researchers to solidify the claim that their posited objects really exist.

How that additional evidence is provided, however, differs depending on what kind of object is posited by the scientific researcher in the course of abducing an explanation. First, note that there is nothing intrinsic to the procedure of abductive inference that mandates that an *unobservable* object be conjectured; abduction operates equally well if all of the elements of the conjectured explanation are observable, as when we observe a set of tracks on the ground and infer that they were made by an "unobserved observable" such as a deer (Turner 2007, 165–166). To observe such an unobserved observable is a relatively simple matter of getting oneself into the proper observational position. Providing the evidence needed to evaluate an abduced explanation involving unobserved observables, then, is quite straightforward: simply look and see. This requires no special philosophical doctrine, fitting instead into what we might call a "common sense realism" (Chernoff 2009b, 373) about ordinary, everyday experience. One need not make any strong ontological commitments about the reality of objects outside of experience in order to accept the reality of observable objects that one is not *personally* presently experiencing; such objects *can* be experienced, and that is the important point. Contra Wight (2006, 26) and Wendt (1999, 49), one need not be a philosophical-ontological transfactualist of any sort to refer to objects in the everyday world of experience; common sense realism suffices for such moderate-sized specimens of dry goods.[12]

Matters get more complicated when we turn to objects that even those who conjecture their existence admit cannot be perceived with the unaided senses. The problem is that without direct sensation, we lose our best warrant for claiming that the objects in question are anything other than phantasms of mind—at which point the Cartesian problem rears its head with a vengeance.[13] Here is where the realist position seems to kick in, since it provides an alternate warrant for claiming that an object exists: the explanatory role played by terms referring to that object in a successful scientific theory. At issue, as Wendt put it, is whether it is "*reasonable* to infer the existence of electrons as the cause of certain observable effects, given that electron theory is our best satisfactory explanation for those effects" (Wendt 1999, 62). The fact that Wendt is talking about "electrons" matters here, since subatomic particles such as electrons cannot *possibly* be directly perceived; hence a staunch empiricist would have real trouble admitting their existence. As a solution, critical realists—in common with scientific realists more broadly— offer the suggestion that because successful scientific theories use the notion of the electron, accepting that the term "electron" refers to a real but unobservable object is the most natural conclusion.

Critical realists, then, argue that theoretical terms[14] may be construed as referring to *real* objects when they serve important scientific explanatory functions. But this formulation too contains an important ambiguity. In his discussion of the reality of dinosaurs—entities that we can certainly no longer perceive with our unaided senses—Derek Turner distinguishes between two "species" of scientific realism appropriate to two different kinds of sciences, historical and experimental, and argues that the *way in which* objects are unavailable to the unaided senses matters

---

12   As J. L. Austin (1962) sardonically referred to them.
13   Recall that even though Descartes himself had doubted whether sensation provided a warrant for claiming that an object existed, his neopositivist successors had provisionally resolved (or addressed) that skepticism by making the Popperian move of treating all claims of existence as conjectural and hypothetical. But the complete absence of sensory data about these objects would also eliminate this Popperian resolution/addressing, since it would call into question any effort to directly falsify conjectures about these objects.
14   In conventional scientific realist usage, a "theoretical term" is an explanatory term in a scientific theory that refers to an unobservable object (Wendt 1999, 60).

a great deal for what it means to make knowledge-claims about them (Turner 2007, 66–67). The difference, claims Turner, is that unobservables in historical science serve to "unify" phenomena under a common explanation, while unobservables in experimental science can also serve as "tools for producing new phenomena" (ibid., 70). This is an intriguing contrast, but it does not account for the fact that not all of the work that went into isolating and analyzing the electron, for example, was about manipulating electrons; quite a bit of it was about bringing assorted physical phenomena under a single, electron-based, interpretation (Arabatzis 2006, 173). There are apparently "historical" aspects to "experimental" work, and vice versa.

Therefore, I think it makes sense to distinguish not between the unobservables found in "historical" and "experimental" sciences, but instead to distinguish between two kinds of unobservable that could be found in *any* kind of science: detectables and undetectables (Chakravartty 2007, 14–15). Neither of these kinds of unobservable can be perceived with the unaided senses, but detectables can be indirectly glimpsed—or, perhaps better, perceived at one remove—via the direct traces that they are taken to leave on specialized detection equipment. I cannot perceive that a substance is radioactive, but I can use a Geiger counter to detect its emission of radiation; likewise, I cannot perceive that the interstellar medium around certain kinds of stars contains crystalline silicates of the sort that might have produced complex organic molecules contributing to the evolution of life, but through spectroscopy—the systematic study of the characteristic spectrums produced by raising different elements to higher energy-states—I can detect the presence of such silicates (Hill et al. 2001). In both cases we are dealing with unobservable detectables: objects that can be indirectly perceived through the use of a piece of specialized equipment. Such detection equipment, in a way, extends our unaided senses and opens up new realms of perceivability (Laudan and Leplin 1991, 451–452).

In this typology, electrons fall into the category of detectables. Although scientists cannot perceive electrons, they can be detected in the form of the "Zeeman effect" of magnetic fields on emitted light (Arabatzis 2006, 74–77) and in the form of cathode rays that produce fluorescent spots when directed at certain substances (ibid., 95–104). The construction of such detectors is a complicated process, involving many rounds of the subtle interpenetration of theory and observation: the unobservable entity and its properties have to be conceptualized, an appropriate apparatus has to be constructed, and the data generated by that apparatus has to be interpreted—and in particular, it has to be interpreted by the scientific community as resulting from the direct action of the unobservable entity. This is often a contentious process. To give an example from another branch of physics, Albert Michelson and Edward Morley designed and constructed a device for measuring the speed and intensity of the "luminiferous aether"—in eighteenth- and nineteenth-century physics, this was the medium through which light waves were thought to propagate—and conducted a series of experiments in 1887 using their device, but failed to detect anything like what they had expected to find. Far from simply being accepted as proof that there was no such thing as aether (which is the currently accepted view of the issue), the device and its results became the subject of great controversy among physicists for decades, with Michelson himself continuing to conduct variants of the experiment until 1935 (Lakatos 1970, 159–164). The controversy ran the gamut from the experimental skill of the investigators, to the conception of the aether the device instantiated, to the interpretation of the results; at stake throughout was the *status* of the Michelson–Morley device as a detector for the aether, a status that remained unsettled for years after the initial experiment was conducted.[15]

Even apparently successful attempts to detect the existence and properties of unobservable entities may not be free from controversy. Contrary to how things may appear in retrospect, *after* the scientific community has come to consensus about which observed phenomena to interpret as manifestations of a particular unobservable object, it is often far from clear at the time which laboratory results belong together as common indicators of a single object: it is not sufficient to say that "a long line of experimentalists interacted with the same entity" (contra Chakravartty 2007, 32). Instead, we first have to undertake the "enormous historiographical task of showing the referential continuity" of the relevant theoretical terms (Arabatzis 2006, 34). Referential continuity among scientists, in turn, can help to establish both the detectability of an unobservable object and a more or less reliable means for detecting it, and these can help to underpin a judgment about the unobservable object's reality. But in any case—whether some apparatus is or is not accepted as a reliable piece of detection equipment for ascertaining the existence and properties of a posited unobservable object—a central role must be given to the consensus judgment of the scientific community (as in Chernoff 2005, 106). Successful detection of an unobservable object is not a simple matter of building any old contraption and claiming that it provides evidence of the existence of some real-but-unobservable thing, such as cold fusion or the restless spirits of one's dead ancestors. Rather, claims to have detected an unobservable object need to pass through the public procedures for vetting knowledge-claims that characterize the relevant scientific community before they can be accepted.[16]

This notion of a detectable unobservable captures what Turner means by the unobservability of historical events or entities, such as living dinosaurs. We are

---

15   As even Colin and Miriam Fendius Elman—perhaps the most ardent Lakatosians in the IR field at present—admit, "unambiguous refutations rarely occur" in scientific research (Elman and Elman 2003a, 66).

16   Note that with this formulation I am in no way implying that it is possible, *even in principle*, to provide any kind of abstract or categorical account of what those "public procedures" are or should be, beyond the minimal definition of science that I offered in Chapter 1: science is the systematic production of knowledge about the world. Whether the consensus of the scientific community is achieved through a successful defense of the existing conventional wisdom, a complete revolution in epistemic standards, or something in between, the point is that judgments of whether some apparatus is a reliable detector for a given unobservable object depend on the practice of scientists, and not on some *a priori* or *ex ante* judgment by philosophers or other commentators.

not prevented from directly perceiving living dinosaurs by the same kinds of perceptual limitations as those preventing us from directly perceiving electrons, but in both cases all we have are the observable traces of an object that we cannot now observe with our unaugmented senses. In both cases we also have a reasonably well-stabilized set of procedures for interpreting empirical evidence so as to point to the existence and properties of that object, which suggests a further parallel: just as electrons can be detected and certain of their properties measured with the use of specialized detection equipment, dinosaurs—or at least the fact of their previous existence on Earth—can likewise be detected through an examination of the fossil record, treating that record as itself in part a function of the fossilization processes studied in the discipline of taphonomy (Turner 2007, 24–25, 56–57). Such an account would treat the entire natural history of the planet as, in effect, the record of a very large piece of detection equipment—a record that allows us to draw conclusions about objects that we are unable to perceive directly.

Additionally, the notion of a detectable unobservable can be extended outside the natural sciences with one minor modification: the recognition that detection equipment need not be *physical* equipment, but can also be *conceptual* equipment. Given the tight interrelation of a detection device, the theory it instantiates, and its associated interpretive practices—Geiger counters and scanning tunneling microscopes and bubble chambers for use in particle physics are hardly self-explanatory devices, and require their operators to be specially trained in order to know what they are seeing when they read the generated data (Pickering 1995, 38–39)—the notion of "conceptual detection equipment" should not be much of a stretch. Indeed, physical detection devices are already "conceptual," so subtracting the physical device and replacing it with, say, a set of more or less well-defined data-collection and data-analysis procedures should not make much of a difference. Consider the notion of "public opinion," which although certainly unobservable had been referenced and appealed to in politics and philosophy for centuries before anyone figured out a way to reliably measure it (Ninkovich 1994, 56–62). Some of the requisite effort involved in constructing a detector for public opinion was a reconceptualization of the object itself as a summation of individual mental states (White 2009, 101–102, 105); perhaps equally important was the development of relevant statistical techniques to permit generalization from a small sample of respondents to a much larger population (Desrosières 1998, 210–212). However, with these pieces of conceptual and procedural equipment in hand, and enjoying widespread acceptance by the relevant scientific community, the unobservable object "public opinion" could be and is detected almost daily in modern mass democracies.[17]

---

17 I am setting aside for the moment any consideration of whether the very *conceptualization and measurement* of "public opinion" in this way does something to bring about the phenomenon on which the researchers doing the measurement claim merely to be reporting—whether detection, in other words, might be a subset of construction. As I will argue in the next chapter, precisely this kind of *expressivity of theory* is highlighted and explored by perspectives adopting a monistic stance on the mind–world interface.

Finally, the notion of a detectable unobservable also seems to capture very nicely the status of the planet Neptune, since it too cannot be observed without specialized pieces of perceptual equipment.[18] The trajectory of scientific knowledge about both Neptune and the electron—and, arguably, public opinion— follows the same course: an unobservable object is abductively inferred, a means for detecting it is constructed, and the object's reliable detection puts an end to the necessity of continuing to abduce its existence. Wendt's question about electrons is thus somewhat misleading, because our knowledge of the physical world has moved on from the initial period of controversy about the electron's existence; we no longer *need* to abductively infer electrons, because now we can detect them. Just as in the case of Neptune and public opinion, electrons can only be experienced with technologically extended senses, but given that extension, they can be experienced more or less just like the ordinary objects of everyday life, as anyone who has ever worked in or studied scientists in a laboratory setting can attest (for example, Lynch 1997).

Thus we see that abductive inference participates in roughly the same kind of procedure whether the abduced objects are unobserved observables or detectable unobservables. In both cases, once an object is perceived or detected, there is no longer any need to claim that the warrant for the reality of the object is the explanatory role that references to it play in explanatory theories: electrons and the planet Neptune, or the deer or the dinosaurs whose tracks and traces we are examining, may once have been judged to exist because of their playing such an explanatory role, but the construction of the appropriate sense-extending equipment makes those kinds of inferences unnecessary. The claim that such objects were "real" might have exercised a heuristic effect on the scientific research agenda in urging the construction of appropriately elaborated notions of the relevant concepts, and appropriate detection equipment to go along with those concepts (Wendt 1999, 61; Wight 2006, 121–122), but in cases such as this, any such claim about the reality of an unobservable object based purely on abductive inference should be understood as a provisional claim, *pending direct observation or indirect detection.*

A merely abduced object occupies an ambiguous ontological category, and the development of much scientific knowledge seems to involve getting the object out of that category and either moving it closer to the everyday world of ordinary perceptual experience or determining that it does not, in fact, exist. One need not be a philosophical-ontological transfactualist to go along with this procedure, since any deviation from basing knowledge on experience can be understood as a temporary move intended to expand the range and reach of our experience. This

---

18   The individual red blood cells I referenced in Chapter 2 would also qualify as detectable unobservables in this sense. Although note that an optical microscope or an optical telescope blurs the boundaries between "detection" and "observation"— the eye still receives light reflecting off the object, even if that light is refracted by lenses—in a way that calls attention to the instability of the categories in the first place. This is a primary reason why phenomenalists have little problem with detectable unobservables.

kind of abductive inference is entirely compatible with the kinds of philosophical-ontological assumptions made by neopositivists and other non-realists; there is thus nothing particularly realist about abduction as such (Chernoff 2005, 83–84). Indeed, a non-realist might consider withholding a judgment of reality pending direct observation or detection to be the safer bet, given the impressive list of unobservable objects once believed in by scientists but rejected today (Chakravartty 2007, 28–29). Limiting oneself to observables and detectables does not guarantee the avoidance of error, but it might be a more risk-averse strategy.

Transfactualism and undetectables

All of which is to say that the value of critical realism, and its transfactualist presumption that it is possible to have and generate knowledge of objects that we cannot experience, is mainly on display once we get past both observables (whether or not they are actually being observed at any given moment) and detectable unobservables (which can be perceived with technologically augmented senses). Critical realism's methodological implications are best demonstrated when turning to the reality of *undetectables*, defined precisely as entities and properties that cannot, even in principle, be observed or detected either with unaided or with augmented senses. Any knowledge that we could have of such objects would have to remain conjectural, since there would be no way to make irrelevant the abductive inference that the object existed by replacing it with direct observation or detection of the object; hence we would have to infer on an ongoing basis its existence from other, indirect evidence. Quarks—widely accepted by physicists as among the basic building-blocks of matter, but also theoretically undetectable because they only occur in combinations that form other detectable particles (Feynman 1988, 139)—occupy this strange and unsettled status of irreducibly conjectural objects that also give rise to the entire visible world. Accepting the reality of quarks requires something like a commitment to transfactualism, since our best theories about them indicate than we will never be able to observe or even detect them directly.[19]

However, outside of theoretical physics, do we have any *need* for such transfactualism? Critical realists have argued that we do, both because of real but undetectable entities and processes that exercise a causal effect in everyday life, and because of the undetectable properties of both observable *and* unobservable

---

19 Granted, these theories might be altered in the future, changing something once regarded as undetectable into a detectable unobservable. As the scientific community achieves consensus about the evidence for a particular particle's existence, the line between the detection of a particular particle and the detection of other particles whose existence and properties provide the basis for inferring the existence for that particular particle gets increasingly blurred in practice (Grupen 1999). But such a change would only eliminate the need for transfactualism once the theoretical change had occurred. In the present, we need the transfactual commitment in order to regard the undetectable object as "real." Thanks to Morten Andersen for pointing out this ambiguity in an earlier draft.

objects that account for their manifest behavior. The two usual candidate objects in such arguments are the state and social structure, although the argument is most compelling when applied to social structure.

Consider the state. Wendt argues[20] that we know that states are real both because we would lose explanatory power in our best theories if we treated states as unreal fictions reducible to something more basic, and because the observable pattern by which actions are authorized and constituted as the actions of a collectivity supports an abductive inference to the reality of the collective actor—the state— in the name of which such actions are performed (Wendt 1999, 216–221). But it is unclear why Wendt's abductive inference about the state's existence cannot simply fuel the same kind of procedure that led to the detection of electrons and the planet Neptune: a conjecture about the state's existence that would lead to the creation and refining of (conceptual) detection equipment, which in turn would make the abductive inference irrelevant once direct evidence was obtained. "Do states exist?" would thus be converted into a tractable empirical question; there seems to be no insurmountable obstacle to doing just this. States are not quarks, prevented in principle from ever showing themselves, and in fact there is evidence of the state virtually everywhere one looks in world politics. Why not treat the public diplomatic record, and the patterns of economic and military transactional flows, as evidence generated by an enormous detector, and examine the evidence to see what, if anything, is being detected?[21]

Now consider social structure: "an irreducible entity that 'generates' its elements and their possible transformations" (Wendt 1987, 358). David Dessler (1989, 452–453) likens social structure to the grammatical rules of a language, since they condition and make possible but do not precisely determine the particular actions of those inhabiting them: just as the rules of English do not make me write this sentence, social structure does not make me exercise my academic vocation in a specific way. As Bhaskar (1989, 78) puts it, a social actor within a social structure is a "cognitive bricoleur," with "the paradigm being that of a sculptor at work, fashioning a product out of the material and with the tools available to him or her." But in order to play this kind of enabling[22] role, critical realists argue, social structure must be an *actually existing* unobservable, and not just a hypothetical or instrumental abstraction.

Although it might be possible to treat social structure as the same kind of detectable unobservable as the state, and thus to initiate a scientific quest for ways of detecting it, the transfactualist account of social structure contains a thread

---

20   Or, at any rate, he *argued*. In more recent work (Wendt 2006) he has moved away from the argument that states exist as anything other than emergent patterns of individual activity.

21   Of course, if one were to do so, it is far from clear that one would in fact identify states as the relevant detectable objects (Chase-Dunn and Hall 1997; Ferguson and Mansbach 1996). However, this is an empirical question of scientific ontology, and thus not of direct concern to the methodological matters under consideration here.

22   And constraining, in the sense that one cannot say what is not grammatically permissible—at least if one hopes to make sense to one's listeners.

that would almost certainly be lost if structure could be precisely detected and measured. That thread is *capacity*, in the sense of a potential that may or may not be in fact actualized. Social structures, on this account, are not simply defined by the observable patterns of action to which they give rise; they are, rather, defined in terms of a range of possibilities that might or might not be observed, much as the capacity to engage in repressive action against dissenters cannot be equated with the actual repressing of dissent (Wight 2006, 54). This is the sense in which critical realism is "critical": "it requires a critique and penetration of observable forms to the underlying social structures which generate them" (Wendt 1987, 370). But those underlying social structures have to be not just unobservable but *undetectable* in order to avoid being reduced to their observable manifestations. A detectable object would, in a sense, only be capable of bringing about those things that it actually brought about, without any extra capacity left over (Cartwright 1999, 64–70). This extra capacity—the latent potential that underpins the variety of occurrences and properties actually displayed by the structure in question— ensures that the social structure could have been, but was not, involved in bringing about some other outcome.

In fact, capacities—or what critical realists often refer to as "causal properties" (Chakravartty 2007, 85, 113) or "causal powers" (Kurki 2008, 167)—are also part of the critical realist conception of ordinary observable and detectable objects. The worldly activities of *all* objects are explained by their causal powers:

> [E]ven the simplest seeming property concept is internally complex. To say that something is heavy is not only to refer to experiences or the responses of instruments should we or they encounter it, but it is to ascribe to that entity some permanent state which, if the thing interacts (were to interact) with people or instruments, will (would) manifest itself as weight.
>
> (Aronson, Harré, and Way 1995, 176)

The observed or detected property—weight, in this case—is explained by the interaction of an unobservable, but detectable, property—"mass"—that manifests itself as weight under the appropriate circumstances (such as the presence of a gravitational field). Mass was first theorized by Isaac Newton and describes a range of possibilities for objects by factoring into explanations of their behavior; once abduced, it entered the now-familiar sequence that terminated with such reliable detection-equipment that measuring mass is now a commonplace activity in high school physics courses. However, just as with any detectable unobservable, mass is a record of an interaction between an object and a piece of equipment, or what we might call an "apparatus-world ensemble" (ibid., 181). This in turn suggests that an object displaying mass possesses a causal power *in virtue of which* it has a measurable mass and *in virtue of which* a particular apparatus-world ensemble (such as a balance) is able to detect that property.

It is this causal power—abductively inferred, rather than observed or detected— to which the critical realist presumption of transfactualism most strongly pertains. There is no need for transfactualism when we are dealing with ordinary observable or detectable objects and properties of objects, because we have experience of those objects and properties that is either direct (in the case of ordinary observables) or reliably indirect (in the case of detectable observables). And there is no need for *ongoing* transfactualism about objects and properties which one can in principle validate the existence of; we can stop being transfactualists about Neptune, or about the state, once we have a reliable way of detecting it.[23] But in order to speak meaningfully about unactualized potentials, underpinned by causal powers that we can only ever have abduced, conjectural knowledge of something like the transfactualist wager is required.[24]

Mind-independence

The critical realist commitment to transfactualism decisively affects what it means for a critical realist to say that the world is mind-independent. Because causal powers are undetectable properties the existence of which has to be established outside of the context of observation with unaided or augmented senses, accounts utilizing causal powers are inextricably theoretical in ways that neopositivist hypotheses and data analyses need not be. And because our theories are clearly not mind-independent in the same way that the world is thought to be, critical (and scientific) realism has to be concerned with problems of *reference* in ways that neopositivism is not: the neopositivist focus on observable and experienceable objects and properties ensures that their terms and claims always refer to something other than a phantasm or illusion, but no such confidence can be affixed to terms and conjectures about undetectable causal properties. Like neopositivists, critical realists have to figure out how to bridge the gap between the mind and the world, but they have to do so under very different philosophical conditions.

It is important not to conflate the kind of mind-independence that is required in order to sustain an account of the causal powers of objects with two other kinds of mind-independence. The notion that the world is independent of mind may be justly considered a "starting point for all versions of scientific realism," but it does not follow from such a notion that "the world is ultimately made up of the subatomic particles studied by particle physicists" (Wendt 1999, 52). Nor does it follow from the evident fact that scholars describe and theorize the same empirical phenomenon in different ways (Kurki 2008, 203–204)—or from

---

23   Indeed, we could, in principle, stop being transfactualists about the causal power in virtue of which objects have mass if ongoing investigations into the Higgs boson continue to bear fruit; even though most of the mass of ordinary objects is not theorized to come from the Higgs field, that field's being non-zero on average is held to be responsible for elementary particles having mass—and as a result making it possible for atoms to cohere. The line between detectables and undetectables is not fixed for all time, but continually renegotiated by scientists in the course of their ongoing investigations.

24   Note that unactualized potentials in the critical realist sense differ from counterfactual outcomes in the analyticist sense, in that an unactualized potential is thought to be *real* while a counterfactual outcome is, by definition, *not real*. I return to this point in Chapter 5, below.

the fact that students and scholars easily learn to switch between theory-laden descriptions of the same phenomenon (Wight 2006, 42)—that the phenomenon in question is in the appropriate sense mind-independent. The culprit in both of these cases is an ambiguous and imprecise concept of "mind," which allows scholars to slip between subjective consciousness, intersubjective consensus, and a materially emergent sense of self. A coherent critical realism, I will argue, demands something stronger than the claim that the world exists outside of subjective consciousness, but does not demand something as strong as the notion that the mind-independent world is in any sense reducible to material objects and their properties.

As before in this chapter, I ask the reader's patience in veering quite far from the ordinary topics and subjects of IR scholarship in order briefly to work through these issues. The meaning of "mind" is perhaps an even more abstract topic than the reality of unobservables, but has similarly profound methodological implications for the study of world politics—in addition to the substantive implications it holds for the study of "ideas."[25] If the mind-independence of the world meant that the world was really only composed of subatomic particles and other material objects then we would face a philosophically intractable problem whenever we tried to explain anything other than subatomic particles, which would seem to rule out the study of world politics pretty profoundly. But if the mind-independence of the world only meant that objects in the world were independent of our personal apprehension of them, we would not be able to talk about the reality of the undetectable objects and properties that are the mainstay of any realist account. The value—in terms of methodological implications—of critical realism lies in the notion that the causal powers of objects are just as mind-independently real as their concrete empirical manifestations *despite* being unable to be directly or indirectly perceived, and this in turn demands something stronger than reference-independence but not as strong as a reduction of reality to the physical. Rather, critical realism demands a *stratification* of reality, and a commitment to the notion that the external world exists in such a way that we only have access to part of it.

Reference-independence and the causal closure of the physical

However, to reach this conclusion, it is first necessary to dispense with the two misleading notions of world-independence that often crop up in these discussions. Both claims are, at least implicitly, directed at the Cartesian anxiety that we remain trapped in an illusion of our own (subjective) making, and seek to provide a warrant

---

25 Because those substantive implications take us far afield from my declared topic of *philosophical* ontology, I will just briefly point out that if one maintained that the world was reducible to purely material objects then there would be little point in studying ideas and beliefs and other mental factors (Wendt 1999, 93–95), and if one thought that reference-independence were sufficient grounds to establish the reality of the referred-to object then many of our empirical studies of phenomena such as religion would have to spend a lot more time coming to grips with the reality of God (as in Polkinghorne 2006).

for the actual existence of objects in the world, but they go about this task in very different ways. The first claim, which depends on reference-independence, is too weak to support critical realist claims, since reference-independence is compatible (as I will briefly illustrate) with a whole variety of positions in philosophical ontology, including the position that the world is not appropriately mind-independent at all. The second claim, that only physical things actually exist—which implies, as an immediate consequence, that the physical world is causally closed such that only physical factors can cause physical outcomes—would not only make *social* science a dicey proposition, but it would also propel us back towards the very kind of problematic logical positivism that prompted the neopositivist turn to falsification decades ago. The causal closure of the physical is thus too strong a claim for critical realism, even as reference-independence is too weak a claim.

The argument about reference-independence purports to demonstrate, as Wight (2006, 26) puts it, that "the question is not whether to be a realist, but of what kind." The basic logic is that because we successfully refer to an object, it therefore follows that there must be *some* object to which we are referring, even if our theories about that object change over time. Sometimes called "entity realism" (Chakravartty 2007, 30–31), the argument suggests that it is possible to infer the existence of objects from instances of successful reference, where "successful" means that we have causal contact with the objects in question: we interact with the objects, bringing about alterations in the state of the world in a reliable and replicable manner (Putnam 1979). This causal contact underpins our ability, both in ordinary conversation and in scholarly debate, to refer to objects in such a way that other people can recognize what we are talking about. Indeed, realists claim, such references are necessary for anyone to disagree sensibly about anything—say, the causes of a given war (Kurki 2008, 160–161; see also Wight 1996). Unless all parties to the dispute were referring to the same things (in this case, the war and the different theoretical explanations of the causes of the war), then there would be no way for them to disagree in the first place; hence the things referred to must really exist.

For realists, reference-independence suggests not only that there are mind-independent objects in the mind-independent world, but that there are mind-independent *facts* about those objects. Although determining whether some object counts as a "cat" or a "mountain" involves some measure of arbitrariness, since we have to "fix the application of our terms," once we agree on a set of rules for correctly applying a term, whether the term fits a given object depends on features of the object itself and is not reducible to our descriptions of the object (Searle 1995, 166). The alternative, realists claim, is that "ways of talking ... can't be said to be truer than one another, or more faithful to the way things are in and of themselves than one another" (Boghossian 2007, 44), which would lead to a complete collapse of our notions of knowledge into a thoroughgoing global relativism.[26] So from the fact that we successfully refer to objects in the

---

26   I would be remiss in not thanking Will Schlickenmaier for alerting me to the need to deal with Boghossian's anti-constructivist arguments.

world using grammatical forms that imply true/false distinctions—and even from the fact that we disagree about the truth-value of particular statements—realists conclude that the conditions under which our statements are judged to be true or false cannot be purely arbitrary exercises, but must be instead a function of the actual features of objects in the world. Otherwise there is no sensible way of making sense of our claims.

There are a variety of difficulties with this argument, many of which stem from the fact that it equivocates between two similar but distinct claims:

> *Weak claim*: An object to which we successfully refer exists independently of *my* mind and *your* mind.

and

> *Strong claim*: An object to which we successfully refer exists independently of *all of our* minds.

While many realists argue as if reference-independence established the strong claim, it does not in fact do so. If anything, reference-independence only establishes the weak claim, and the weak claim is insufficient to dispel Cartesian anxiety since it does not firmly ground our knowledge-claims in a mind-independent external world.

This equivocation is quite easy to understand, because the strong claim, if true, would indeed put an end to Cartesian doubts. In the scenario portrayed by the strong claim, an object—such as a mountain—to which we successfully refer would have existed even if there had never been minds to refer to it and would have had the same properties in that hypothetical world without minds as it does in ours.[27] But this argument, as I have pointed out elsewhere (Jackson 2008, 141–2), engages in some subtle philosophical sleight of hand, imagining that a statement such as "there is snow and ice near the summit of Mount Everest" does not imply the covert presence of an observer to make the observation in the first place. But smuggling in an observer means undercutting the putative philosophical point, which was to demonstrate that there are mind-independent facts about mind-independent objects in the world. In any event, there is no simple route from successful reference to strong mind-independence.

As for the weaker claim, while the fact that both you and I can refer to an object might be taken to demonstrate that neither of us is making up the object— a discussion in which we both refer to the international system, or to the amount of money in my wallet, presupposes that those objects are figments of neither of our individual imaginations—it does not follow that in successfully referring we have made contact with something that exists external to and autonomously from us. In fact, all that follows is "common sense realism" and an abandonment of

---

27   It is significant that this example—which comes from Searle (1995, 183–194)—deals with a physical object, and not a social object. See below.

solipsism. In the case of money in my wallet (which is an unobserved observable as long as I keep my wallet closed), reference-independence merely establishes that the amount of money in my wallet is not a matter of my whim or desire, but is instead subject to the constraints of shared everyday experience, including the conventional rules governing the calculation of an amount of money. There is no need to make any kind of a leap from shared experience to a claim that something exists outside of experience; nor is there any compelling evidential warrant for doing so.

The same is true of detectable unobservables such as the international system, but the issue is even more pronounced. When scientists refer to a detectable unobservable, realists argue, they look at certain pieces of evidence and bring them together in a conventional manner. The object itself is built up of those pieces of evidence, with each piece of evidence conventionally thought to illustrate or reveal a *property* of the object. Detectable objects, and classifications of such objects, are thus "distributions of causal properties," and new classifications of properties can (and do) arise when useful (Chakravartty 2007, 179). A detectable object is therefore not a permanent feature of the world. Indeed, the history of science reveals many examples of situations in which researchers have abandoned older groupings of properties because they have found other, more useful, ways of grouping properties together, and have therefore rewritten the contents of their bestiary of unobservable-but-detectable things. At any given point in time, any given detectable object is therefore in part a product of convention and scientific consensus, which is clearly not enough of a warrant to claim that the object exists in a mind-independent way.

In any case, reference-independence only establishes that objects and properties are not subjective whims; it does not establish that those objects and properties exist outside of our conventional practices of referring to them. In fact, both the weak and the strong claims systematically fail to distinguish between the existence of a set of conventional epistemic practices and the validity of those practices, reasoning instead from the observation that some group of speakers—even if that group includes some implicit account of "all human beings"—*do in fact* refer to certain objects in the world in a particular way, to the conclusion that *those objects exist* outside of all of our referential practices. However, this is always an unwarranted conclusion, inasmuch as it is incapable of distinguishing between the correct use of conventional procedures and actual contact with a mind-independent world. From the fact that a group of IR scholars refers to "the international system" follows precisely nothing at all about the mind-independent reality of the international system; the most that could be said is that "the international system" has a conventional meaning among that group of IR scholars. And while a stable conventional meaning for a term *might* be a consequence of the reality of the object to which the term refers, the reverse is not necessarily true: realism is not a consequence of referential continuity (Arabatzis 2006, 262–264). Other factors, including sociological factors, can explain referential continuity just as well.

Even the defenders of the implications of reference-independence implicitly acknowledge these difficulties by refraining from arguing that reference-independence *proves* the existence of an external world. Instead, they suggest that "the price of the abandonment of realism is the abandonment of normal understanding" (Searle 1995, 189) or that the notion that the world and the objects in it exist independently of mind is logically presupposed by normal and scientific discourse (ibid., 181–183). Some defenders even classify the proposition that a mind-independent world exists as an "*intrinsically* credible or self-evident" belief, such that if someone denied it our reaction would be to think that we had misunderstood them (Boghossian 2007, 116). All of this may be true, but it does nothing to increase the plausibility of the inference to the reality of the external world. The specter of Cartesian anxiety lingers: we might, in fact, be deluding ourselves that our knowledge points to a mind-independent reality, and we can never know for sure. All that follows from reference-independence is that observable and detectable objects exist outside of my subjective apprehension of them, a common-sensical claim that no empirical (social) scientist would deny. Critical realism requires a stronger notion of mind-independence than this.

However, critical realism does not require a notion of mind-independence that is so strong that it questions whether anything other than physical objects actually exists. The turn to some kind of physicalism or strong materialism is, of course, a tempting option for anyone attempting to validate the status of our knowledge of an external world (Wendt 1999, 72–73). At least as conventionally understood, the physical world exists outside of our minds, existed before there were minds, and would go on existing if all minds were to disappear—or even if no minds had ever existed in the first place (Boghossian 2007, 38). Our knowledge of the physical world appears to be relatively successful, at least as measured by our demonstrated ability to manipulate it in ways that fulfill our desires and interests; realists claim that this success would be downright miraculous if it were not the case that our scientific knowledge of the physical world more or less accurately represented the world as it is in itself (Boyd 1984). On this account, the relevantly mind-independent world is the physical, material world, and everything else that we experience or study owes its mind-independence to its roots in the physical.

The chief advantage of this claim is that it permits us to use the evident success of the natural sciences—a record of success that the social sciences, including IR, have never amassed—as a way of fending off Cartesian anxiety: airplanes usually fly and our efforts to preserve threatened ecosystems are sometimes successful, so our knowledge of the physical world must be founded on something other than illusion. But the claim that mind-independence is really about physical objects causes more problems than it resolves, particularly when it comes to the study of social life. If we can only be certain that knowledge claims refer to an external world when they are directed at physical objects, then in order to study social objects we have to root those social objects in some kind of physical, material base, and show how those social objects emerge from or supervene on their physical bases; otherwise we remain uncertain that our knowledge is actually referring to anything external. Indeed, for some scientific realists this is precisely why one *cannot* be a realist about *social* objects, because such objects are entirely too dependent on conventions and ongoing referential practices to be meaningfully thought of as mind-independent (Searle 1995, 57, 68–69; Harré 1990, 350–352). In order to remain focused on the reliably mind-independent, the would-be critical realist would thus have to confine her investigations to those properties of social objects that could be understood as manifestations of underlying physical properties.

However, such a focus poses an even more intractable problem: reducing the social to the physical, much like reducing the mental to the physical, inclines towards "epiphenomenalism": the conclusion that everything but the physical is, strictly speaking, irrelevant to any scientific explanation that we might produce. Wendt argues that we can preserve the autonomy of the social and ideational aspects of world politics in our theories by sharply delineating just how much of social life is explained by material factors, so that we can see how much of a difference non-material factors make (Wendt 1999, 135–136), but this strategy is unsustainable if the non-material aspects of world politics are themselves products of material factors! The problem precisely parallels the challenge confronting philosophers of mind who seek to maintain simultaneously that mental phenomena emerge from physical phenomena and—as the natural sciences seem quite unequivocally to maintain—that physical events have physical causes: there is simply no way that mental states emerging from physical arrangements could ever add anything to an explanation that simply linked antecedent physical arrangements to a physical event directly (Baker 1993, 83–86). Analogously, if social arrangements (such as the legitimacy of a territorial border) supervene on physical arrangements (a line on the ground and a set of behavioral patterns—perhaps involving military personnel and equipment—that materially alter when approaching or crossing that line), what does the border's "legitimacy" add to an explanation of what is going on?[28] Why not just explain physical events in terms of the physical arrangements that scientific realism about the natural sciences has already declared can be known without falling into Cartesian anxiety?

It would thus appear that an equation of mind-independence with the physical world preserves reference at the cost of making it almost impossible to study social life per se.[29] Since critical realists clearly want to engage in the study of social life,

---

28 To anticipate a possible objection: one might argue that a border's legitimacy factors into the decisions made by the people responsible for the observed behaviors, or factors into the institutions of which those people are a part. However, this only displaces the problem down one level of aggregation, and does not eliminate it: if mental states supervene on physical states, then a belief in the legitimacy of a border presumably supervenes on some physical state, and an analyst faces exactly the same problem in trying to clarify what the belief adds to the physical state on which it supervenes when it comes to explaining observed behavior. In Chapter 5, I will suggest that one way around this problem without falling into epiphenomenalism is to abandon the mind–world dualism on which this whole problem is premised.

29 Indeed, focusing on the physical world in this reductionist way arguably makes *any* kind of macro-explanation—that is to say, any explanation involving anything but subatomic particles in combination—superfluous and ultimately meaningless (Baker 1993, 89–90). As yet, tossing words like "emergence" and "supervenience" at the problem has not made it go away (see the discussion in Kessler 2007).

it follows that this cannot be what they mean by the "mind-independence" of the world. But reference-independence cannot be what critical realists mean either, since it is entirely possible to accept the reference-independence of observable and detectable objects without making any strong philosophical-ontological commitments concerning the mind-independence of those objects; there is nothing contradictory or even problematic about simultaneously maintaining that the international system exists independent of your and my individual references to it, and that the international system is not independent of our conventional ways of arranging and aggregating observed and detected properties in the first place. Reference-independence, in other words, does not establish that the objects we refer to are actually mind-independent; physicalism does, but at the cost of doing away with everything *but* physical objects.

The stratification of reality

So the question remains: in what sense can social objects—the international system, states, wars, norms about the treatment of non-combatants, and so on—be said to be "mind-independent?" If they cannot be, then there is no sense in adopting a critical realist stance for the study of social life, because the basic realist position is that valid scientific knowledge-claims reach out towards a mind-independent reality. The simple *existence* of social objects is insufficient, because researchers interested in testing hypotheses about the systematic cross-case covariation of factors also acknowledge the existence of the observable and detectable objects and properties they study; such neopositivists are, however, only instrumentally committed to how they characterize those objects and properties and how they arrange them, and need not be philosophical-ontological transfactualists in order to conduct their empirical investigations.

Accordingly, the important issue for critical realists is not whether objects exist, but whether objects of all sorts—observable and unobservable, natural and social—can be conceptualized as possessing real but unrealized capacities. Such a claim could only be sustained if it were possible to have knowledge of objects outside of all possible experience. Otherwise, researchers would be left merely with empirical probabilities, as in Thomas Hobbes' famous definition of the "state of warre":

> For WARRE, consisteth not in Battell onely, or in the act of fighting; but in a tract of time, wherein the Will to contend by Battell is sufficiently known: and therefore the notion of *Time*, is to be considered in the nature of Warre; as it is in the nature of Weather. For as the nature of Foule weather, lyeth not in a shower or two of rain; but in an inclination thereto of many dayes together: So the nature of War, consisteth not in actuall fighting; but in the known disposition thereto, during all the time there is no assurance to the contrary.
> (Hobbes 1601, 70)

The problem with this nominalist definition, from a critical realist perspective, is that it is nothing other than a record of common usage, and gives us no solid warrant for projecting war-proneness (or "foule weather," for that matter) beyond the empirical observations that we have drawn on in order to reach the conclusion in the first place. Cartesian anxiety looms, since we might easily be mistaken in either our observations or in the conclusions that we have drawn from them. The neopositivist response, as we have seen in the previous chapter, is to treat such projections as nothing other than falsifiable hypotheses, and to place no more credence in them than we have to—and, of course, to keep on furiously testing all of our conjectures all the time, as much as possible, on the chance that some of them may turn out to be empirically inaccurate.

The transfactualist commitments of a critical realist provide an alternate way of staving off Cartesian anxiety. Instead of remaining in the realm of probabilities, critical realists engaging in an explanation of some observed phenomenon seek to move to the level of causal properties: "a causal property is one that confers dispositions on the particulars that have it to behave in certain ways when in the presence or absence of other particulars with causal properties of their own" (Chakravartty 2007, 108). Causal properties or causal powers give rise to observed probabilities; they explain *why* occurrences and phenomena are linked, and thus go beyond simply noting that they *are* linked.[30] This makes it possible to refer to, for example, a *tendency* for balances of power to recur under conditions of anarchy, or for democracies to refrain from going to war with one another, or for processes of complex learning to yield institutionalized security communities, and mean by that something other than the existence of a mere *observed probability*.

The challenge with investigating these causal properties is that the actual world is an "open system" in which it is a non-trivial exercise to go from observations of what does or did happen to the identification of the important properties or powers that brought those observed results about (Bhaskar 1998, 46–47; Wight 2006, 51–52; Cartwright 1999, 71–72). This is both because of the sheer number and diversity of factors with varying degrees of importance in bringing about observed phenomena, and because in the complicated course of actual events any number of complications may arise that prevent an object, such as cancer, from realizing its real-but-unrealized potential to end the life of a person who dies in a car crash (as in Elster 1989, 6)—the observation that the cancer does not, in fact, end the person's life does not alter the fact that the cancer had the potential to do so.

In searching for unrealized potentials, critical realists cannot rely on the neopositivists' sophisticated statistical techniques for separating systematic and

---

30   While Wendt (1998, 103) is certainly correct that a focus on causal powers mean that investigations into the constituent parts of a phenomenon are a legitimate kind of scientific research and are something other than mere description, it is going too far to say that the resulting investigations are engaged in something other than causal explanation. After all, the causal powers and properties in virtue of which a thing is what it is are known, on a critical realist account, *precisely* by giving rise to observed tendencies, and are as such causally related to observed outcomes (Sylvan and Majeski 1998, 88). "Causal powers" indicate a different *kind* of causation than that privileged by neopositivists, not a non-causal explanatory alternative.

random variation, because such techniques remain entirely (and, for neopositivists, *deliberately*) within the sphere of the empirically actual. Systematic variation is an *observed* connection between factors that is robust across cases, while random variation is an equally *observed* connection that is just not as robust (as in King, Keohane, and Verba 1994, 95–99), and thus there is no reliable way to infer potential from such empirical observations. Even an apparently robust cross-case covariation, such as the absence of war between democracies, might be a side-effect of special circumstances such as global liberal markets rather than a genuine result of a causal power connected to a democratic regime-type (Kurki 2008, 267–268).[31] Instead, critical realists emphasize the ways that an artificially closed laboratory situation can allow a scientist to formulate and refine a scientific theory involving an undetectable causal power, and to do so in a way that can provide insights into real-world occurrences:

> It is only under closed conditions that there will be a one-to-one relationship between the causal law and the sequence of events. And it is normally only true in the laboratory that these enduring mechanisms of nature, whose operations are described in the statements of causal laws, become actually manifest and empirically accessible to men [*sic*] ... Such mechanisms combine to generate the flux of phenomena that constitute the actual states and happenings of the world. They may be said to be real, though it is rarely that they are actually manifest and rarer still that they are empirically identified by men [*sic*]. They are the intransitive objects of scientific theory.
>
> (Bhaskar 1975, 46–47)

The basic point is that the isolating and theorizing of an object's causal powers under laboratory conditions, together with the transfactual presumption that those powers operate in a similar way outside of the laboratory, provides the relevant procedure for generating an explanation that preserves the notion of unrealized potential (ibid., 132). An artificially oversimplified setting is essential to the process, because it is only in such a setting that an object can be induced to manifest its causal powers in isolation (Cartwright 2007, 222–225).

It is difficult to overemphasize the vital role played by the laboratory setting in such arguments, since this setting prevents the realist argument from becoming "viciously circular" (Turner 2007, 78). In a laboratory, posited causal powers can be subjected to and manipulated in various tests, yielding evidence—in the form of observed and detected properties—that the undetectable causal power does, in fact, give rise to particular results in particular circumstances. That, after all,

---

31 Note that this is different from treating "democratic regime-type" and "global liberal markets" as alternative hypotheses and constructing some ingenious empirical test to adjudicate between them. Instead, the critical realist claim is that there is nothing intrinsic to a democratic regime-type *as such* that inclines a state away from war with other democracies, while there is something intrinsic to global liberal markets that does. Adjudicating this is a matter of properly theorizing the relevant causal powers, not a matter of testing rival empirical hypotheses.

is what a causal power *is*: an undetectable property of an object that endows that object with a disposition to manifest particular behaviors when interacting with other objects (Chakravartty 2007, 129–130), including the laboratory equipment itself (Aronson, Harré, and Way 1995, 179–180). This experimental evidence provides grounds for concluding that the posited power is not just an explanation imposed on the data *post hoc* (see also Hacking 1983; Cartwright 2009). The now-taken-to-exist real-but-undetectable causal power can thus play a role in explanations of events in the wider world.

From these considerations it would seem to follow that critical realist accounts of social life would *have* to be linked to some sort of laboratory setting, such as the experimental cognitive psychology practiced by IR researchers like Philip Tetlock (2006) and Deborah Larson (1985).[32] In this mode of research, human subjects are placed in a variety of experimental situations so as to ascertain the causal powers of the human being as a perceiving creature, such as the phenomenon of "groupthink" (Janis 1982) or the tendency to over-value potential losses and undervalue potential gains when making a risky decision (Kahneman and Tversky 2000). This observed tendency—people making choices at variance with what would be mathematically optimal for them to choose—is taken to be a manifestation of some kind of undetectable causal property lodged in human perception and cognition, a power that manifests itself in the laboratory in the form of a systematic misperception of the opportunities and liabilities specified in the artificially engineered experiment. With a transfactual commitment of philosophical ontology in hand, a researcher could assume that the causal power in question was *real* although undetectable, and as such would persist outside of the laboratory into the open system of the wider world, manifesting itself in some form as long as human beings were involved in making choices. If a choice were suboptimal, this could be attributed to the causal power suggested by laboratory experiments; if a choice were more or less optimal, the researcher would have to look for explanations as to why the causal power did not manifest the same observed property—explanations that would involve the causal powers of other social objects (such as information-processing bureaucracies or strategies for evaluating the potential results of choices before making them) and their interaction.

I mention this possibility not because IR work in cognitive psychology self-identifies as critical realist; in fact, it does not, generally associating itself with neopositivism and treating its cognitive and perceptual patterns as falsifiable hypotheses rather than as abduced causal powers. Much research on the emotional components of decision-making (for example, Mercer 2006) does something similar, seeking to identify discrete, observable indicators of mental states that can then be correlated with observed outcomes as a way of evaluating a hypothetical law-like generalization. Instead of availing itself of the philosophical resources of critical realism, such scholarship forces itself uncomfortably into

---

32 I owe this suggestion that cognitive psychological research in IR could be easily reconstructed as a form of critical realism to Dan Nexon.

a neopositivist box, and thus opens itself up to a potentially damaging line of critique: if posited psychological dispositions fail to be significantly correlated with observed outcomes, this looks like "falsification" rather than like what a critical realist would *expect* in the open system of the real world. Because critical realism eschews the search for law-like generalizations in favor of the abduction of causal powers that may or may not lead to precisely the same manifest expression outside of the laboratory as they do inside of the laboratory, it is philosophically speaking a better place to rest IR scholarship that self-consciously draws on laboratory results.

However, just as cognitive psychology has largely ignored critical realism, critical realism has largely ignored cognitive psychology—which is the only research tradition within IR that regularly engages in the vetting of its posited causal powers in a laboratory setting.[33] Without this vetting, critical realist suggestions of causal powers would start to look uncomfortably similar to falsifiable empirical hypotheses (and thus forego their claim to represent real-but-unrealized potential instead of just realized observations), unless there were another way to evaluate the causal powers that were claimed to be transfactually real. To fulfill this function, critical realists in IR have turned not to the laboratory, but to a series of inferences about social life itself: claims about the necessary presuppositions of global political and economic relations (Patomäki 2001), claims about the deep interconnections between agency and structure even as structures and agents remain ontologically distinct (Wight 1999; Joseph 2008), claims about the ways in which social and material factors presuppose one another (Wendt 1999, 135–136). This makes the critical realist vetting of causal powers subject not to laboratory experimentation, but to *transcendental argument*:

> There are three important features of [transcendental] arguments that require explanation. First, they consist of a string of what one could call indispensability claims. They move from their starting points to their conclusions by showing that the condition stated in the conclusion is indispensable to the feature identified at the start ... The second point is that these indispensability claims are not meant to be empirically grounded, but a priori. They are not merely probably, but apodictic ... The third point is that these claims concern experience. This gives the chain an anchor without which it would not have the significance it does ... The significance of the fact that transcendental arguments deploy indispensability claims about experience is that it gives us an unchallengeable starting point.
>
> (Taylor 1995, 27–28)

As an example, consider the claim that when analyzing wars or other kinds of attacks, we cannot be content with examining "rules, norms, and discourses,"

---

33 In principle, agent-based modeling exercises could be used as laboratories in almost the same way (Hoffmann 2008). But as far as I know, no agent-based modelers in IR have explicitly made this philosophical connection to critical realism.

but must also consider the availability of weapons: "it cannot be ignored that guns have a real material potentiality and real material existence," and that their presence enables certain kinds of combat operations that would not otherwise be possible (Kurki 2008, 237–238). The claim starts with an observation about people using guns to kill one another, and then deploys an indispensability claim about the need to consider the material causal powers of those guns in order to account for the observed combat events.[34] The transcendental argument thus vets the causal power by demonstrating that it is impossible to ignore it.

Transcendental arguments, then, are like abductive inferences with a twist. Unlike the abductive inferences in the natural sciences that I discussed earlier, these critical realist arguments do not ordinarily kick-start a process leading to the manufacturing of detection equipment and a consequent trajectory away from transfactualism. This means that even though critical realist claims about such objects remain conjectural and hence subject to revision and even refutation (Wight 2006, 38–39), such revision and possible refutation cannot take the form of a direct empirical test, but must instead involve a kind of dialectical oscillation back and forth between empirical observation and conceptual refinement: a theorized set of causal powers and their relational dynamics are applied to the study of some phenomenon, and the results of that study might suggest the need for a further development of the theorized causal powers so as to better account for what was empirically manifest. That dialectical oscillation is in turn underpinned and enabled by the bifurcated structure of critical realist arguments: a properly critical realist explanation of some observed worldly phenomenon has to consist of *both* a vetting of posited causal powers either in the laboratory or via transcendental argument *and* an application of those posited causal powers to some concrete occurrence or phenomenon. Either operation alone is insufficient.

At the risk of belaboring the point, consider a famous dispute within Marxist scholarship about the status of the capitalist state and its relationship to the bourgeoisie. Ever since Marx and Engel's (1978, 475) claim that the state in capitalist society was nothing but "a committee for managing the common affairs of the whole bourgeoisie," scholars have been concerned about exactly what that meant—not in the least because an answer to that question would help to determine whether the state could be used as a means of promoting a social revolution (Jessop 1990, 162–166). Matters came somewhat to a head in the scholarly debate when Ralph Miliband (1979) proposed that it would be possible to, in a sense, test the hypothesis that the capitalist state functioned to preserve the bourgeoisie's control over society by looking at the concrete links between the capitalist state and members of that social class. Other Marxists, such as Nicos Poulantzas (2008), reacted strongly against this suggestion, correctly

---

34 The *statistical fact* that being shot with a gun often leads to death is different from the claim that a gun, whether or not it is being fired, has the *capacity* to kill someone. For critical realists, capacity makes observed covariation possible, and cannot be reduced to such covariation. For neopositivists, on the other hand, only the observed covariation is a meaningful object of scientific investigation.

concluding that Miliband's suggestion implied a subtle but important shift in the way that capitalist social structure was being theorized: empirically testing for social structure, in the manner of C. Wright Mills (1967), would reduce structure to its observed manifestations. What was needed was not an empirical test, but a theoretical refinement, because the connection between the bourgeoisie and the capitalist state was a matter of conceptual and transcendental necessity, not a matter of historical accident. In this dispute it is Poulantzas who articulates something close to the critical realist position, while Miliband and Wright appear to instantiate another kind of philosophical ontology.[35]

The dialectical research process enabled by the fact that critical realist causal powers are not simply rooted in empirical observation but are also derived from a complementary procedure (transcendental argument or laboratory experimentation) thus suggests a very different epistemic goal than that prized by neopositivists. Over time, critical realism aims to produce a scientific ontology rich enough to account for the variety of events and phenomena in the social world; empirical observations are not reductively captured by being subsumed under as-yet-unfalsified covering-laws, but are instead analyzed as the more or less contingent products of the real-but-unobservable causal powers of their constituent elements and their relational dynamics. In that sense—and perhaps *only* in that sense—critical realism necessarily demands a correspondence account of knowledge, since the scientific ontology that critical realists evolve through their empirical research has to mirror or accurately represent the causal powers actually possessed by objects in the world. But the transfactual commitments of critical realist scholars ensure that a simple matching of observations and causal powers will never be sufficient; causal powers have to be theorized and vetted outside of their specific explanatory uses, because the empirical is only part of the real world.

In other words, for critical realists, the mind-independent world is *deeper* than our perceptual experiences and technologically augmented detections would suggest. Underneath what we can perceive and detect lies a realm of real-but-undetectable "structures, powers, and tendencies" that give rise to the ordinary empirical sphere (Patomäki and Wight 2000, 223). Analyzing and clarifying that realm is the means by which critical realists seek to construct a more adequate scientific ontology, by refining the "transitive" products of our research endeavors so that they progressively give us knowledge of the "intransitive" objects and properties underlying our observations and detections

---

35   To IR scholars, this dispute might appear to have some parallels with the ongoing debate about Waltz's theorizing of the anarchical structure of the international system: his critics, both sympathetic (Elman 1996) and unsympathetic (Vasquez 1997), call for tests, while he falls back on abstract and almost transcendental claims about the logic of his theory (Waltz 1996; Waltz 1997). But reading Waltz as a critical realist would be *deeply* problematic, given Waltz's own clearly avowed instrumentalist sensibilities about the nature of theory (Goddard and Nexon 2005; Wæver 2009). Accordingly, I will discuss Waltz in Chapter 5, which is where his account belongs in a philosophical-ontological sense.

(Bhaskar 1998, 11–13). That said, it is critically important to separate the philosophical-ontological claim that the world is layered and stratified from any of the various detailed accounts of those layers and that stratification; only the former is intrinsic to critical realism, and not any of the latter. That we have access to real-but-undetectable causal properties is, after all, a statement about our "hook-up" to the world, and as such it logically precedes any particular determinations of *specific* causal properties. In principle, any number of scientific ontologies pertinent to world politics might be elaborated on the basis of laboratory experiments and transcendental arguments, although they would of course have to be carefully evaluated through their application in empirical accounts of specific phenomena. There is nothing mandating that the implications of critical realism for IR must feature particular accounts of the agent-structure relationship or an incorporation of ecological and/or biological factors into our explanations of world politics; such claims are distinct from the philosophical ontology underpinning critical realism, and ought not be conflated with what it means to have a critical realist methodological stance.

Critical realist comparison

The distinction between critical realists and neopositivists comes out most strongly when we turn to a consideration of how critical realists use the technique of case comparison in their empirical work. Recall that neopositivists use case comparison as a way of quasi-experimentally isolating potential causal factors; because neopositivists link causality with systematic cross-case covariation, such a procedure makes sense, as it allows an investigator to determine whether a particular input factor is connected to an output factor when controlling for other potential causes. This is the case whether the factors in question are defined ordinally or nominally (Mahoney 2003), whether the type of systematic connection in question is determinate or probabilistic (Mahoney and Goertz 2004; Adcock 2007), or any one of a hundred other creative technical variations on the same basic methodological theme. Neopositivist case comparison is a technique for ascertaining how robust a law-like generalization linking inputs and outputs actually is in practice, and is as such inextricably bound up with philosophical assumptions not shared by critical realists.

Alexander George and Andrew Bennett's selective appropriation of some of the language of critical realism provides a particularly striking instance of this difference. George and Bennett critique the neopositivist focus on (and satisfaction with) law-like generalizations on two grounds: because a generalization does not easily allow a researcher to differentiate between a causal relationship and a non-causal association—sunspot activity, for example, is correlated with a whole variety of intriguing social phenomena, but probably ought not be considered a cause of those social phenomena—and because the actual world does not seem to display the kind of systematic regularities that a "law-like generalization" would imply (George and Bennett 2005, 132–133). As a solution, they call for a focus on "causal mechanisms":

[U]ltimately unobservable physical, social, or psychological processes through which agents with causal capacities operate, but only in specific contexts or conditions, to transfer energy, information, or matter to other entities. In so doing, the causal agent changes the affected entity's characteristics, capacities or propensities in ways that persist until subsequent causal mechanisms act upon it.

(Ibid.)

So far, so realist: instead of looking to systematic cross-case covariation, George and Bennett look to the enumeration of "ultimately unobservable" factors[36] that are responsible for generating the observed actions or behaviors in question. But George and Bennett then link causal mechanisms to the very law-like generalizations that they urge investigators to move beyond.

If we are able to measure changes in the entity being acted upon after the intervention of the causal mechanism and in temporal or spatial isolation from other mechanisms, then the causal mechanism may be said to have generated the observed change in this entity. The inferential challenge, of course, is to isolate one causal mechanism from another, and more generally, to identify the conditions under which a particular mechanism becomes activated.

(Ibid., 137)

The causal mechanisms that George and Bennett have in mind here are disclosed neither through laboratory experimentation nor through transcendental abduction, but are instead borrowed by the investigator from more "fundamental" micro-level theories and fields of study as a way of filling in the gaps in already-established general laws: "The difference between a law and a mechanism is that between a static correlation ('if X, then Y') and a 'process' ('X leads to Y through steps A, B, C')" (ibid., 141). Those intervening steps, in turn, can be subjected to reliable procedures of data collection ("process-tracing"), thus rendering the general law somewhat less likely to be a spurious correlation.

In other words, George and Bennett's causal mechanisms are *intervening variables* (as in King, Keohane, and Verba 1994, 85–87), not real-but-undetectable causal capacities that can never be fully identified with their observed effects. Such mechanisms "intervene" between the input and output terms of a law stating a systematic cross-case covariation and have little impact or importance in the absence of such a law (Falleti and Lynch 2009, 1146–1147). This is wildly different from the critical realist conception of causality, in terms of which systematic cross-case covariation is, strictly speaking, *irrelevant*

---

36 George and Bennett's conception of "observability" (2005, 143–144) is admirably nuanced, fully accepting the notion that the boundaries of the observable change over time with the construction of more and more refined equipment to augment and extend the senses. But there is little sense in their account that any factor will remain *undetectable*, or that such an undetectable factor could ever serve a meaningful explanatory role.

to a causal claim except under strictly controlled laboratory conditions (Kurki 2008, 198). For critical realists, the actual world is an open system, in which the causal powers of entities might or might not be empirically manifest in any given situation; because critical realists maintain that it is possible to go beyond experience in constructing knowledge, the mere empirical fact that a causal power did not manifest itself neither counts for nor against that power's existence. No general law governs a causal power's manifestation, and no systematic relationship limits a causal power's complicity in the production of an outcome.

Indeed, critical realists are quite skeptical of the whole endeavor of trying to isolate a causal power empirically outside of a laboratory situation. George and Bennett's desire to do so relates more to their basically neopositivist stance on scientific research than it does to the critical realist terminology that they borrow or to the critical realist authors whom they cite. Instead of isolating potential causal factors, critical realists prefer to operate with "causal complexes," each element of which satisfies "INUS conditions": individual factors are Insufficient and Non-redundant components of a complex that is Unnecessary but Sufficient for bringing about the outcome in question (Bhaskar 1998, 129; see also Patomäki 1996).[37] Producing an account of a causal complex preserves all of the elements of the critical realist methodology sketched in previous sections: an initial derivation of elements via transcendental reasoning, the application of a conjectured causal complex to account for a specific event or outcome in all of its specificity, and perhaps a dialectical oscillation back to further conceptual analysis as a way of ensuring that all relevant aspects of the causal complex have been identified. Critical realists prefer a "causal story" that is "holistic" rather than one that seeks to put forward any kind of "ultimate cause"; they "concentrate on accounting for the complex interactions of various causes in specific historical contexts" (Kurki 2008, 286). This causal complexity is an additional reason why it is so important to critical realist accounts that posited causal factors be vetted outside of the explanatory situation itself, and thus be rooted either in a laboratory or in a compelling transcendental argument: simple empirics are insufficient.

So what role can the comparison of empirical cases play in helping to elucidate causal complexes? Given that the complex itself is only sufficient and never necessary for producing the outcome in question, comparing cases in which a complex occurs with cases in which it does not is unlikely to yield much

---

37 Note that Mahoney, Kimball, and Koivu's (2009, 124–126) effort to recast INUS conditions as independent variables presents a good example of what neopositivists typically do with alternatives to covariation-causality: presume that the putative alternative is not actually an alternative, and then subsume it under their own methodological approach. Since the whole point of an INUS conception of causation is that it is the *complex* and not any of the *individual factors* that are meaningfully "causal," the idea that one might discuss which parts of a causal complex are more important than others is, quite frankly, a more or less complete misreading of the critical realist argument.

useful insight; it is only the presence, not the absence, of a causal complex that produces an outcome. By the same token, it would not be very helpful to compare cases in which individual causal factors were present or absent, since nothing follows from a single causal property in isolation; critical realists always seek to circumscribe the possible effect of a factor such as "democracy" or "number of troops available" by investigating the complex and case-specific ways in which factors combine to produce specific outcomes (such as the presence or absence of a war between two states). However, this does not mean that critical realists can only generate idiosyncratic accounts, because the causal factors that they transcendentally abduce and concretely deploy in empirical accounts—factors involving the structural selectivity of the modern state, or the conditions of possibility for successful revolutions (Wight 2006, 221–223, 284–286)—are applicable to situations beyond those from which they are initially derived. But critically, any such factors, in order to be causally relevant, have to be integrated into case-specific narratives that explain how such factors interact with the actions of particular agents to produce social outcomes. The comparison of cases, then, can help to elucidate the variety of ways that causal factors and the complexes into which they are arranged play out in practice—and this in turn can help to clarify the extent of their real-world potential. Critical realists compare not to isolate, but to individuate, and to gain a better sense of just what the limits of the possible actually are.

One final point emerges from this notion of comparing in order to better specify the actualized potentials of transfactually grasped causal properties: the complete and utter impossibility of prediction, either as an epistemic standard or as a scientifically warranted possibility. Neopositivist notions of causation largely equate explanation and prediction, inasmuch as to explain an outcome is to bring it under a law-like generalization linking an antecedent and a consequent, and to predict an outcome is to use a law-like generalization to project a consequent outcome given an antecedent. This is the case whether the generalization in question is categorical, probabilistic, or some hybrid form—the logical structure of explanation and prediction are the same in neopositivist thought and practice, and successful explanation implies successful prediction.[38] This link is shattered in critical realist research, where the open system of the actual world guarantees that prediction is impossible and that explanation is, at best, an account of what *did* happen. The "critical" (transfactual) aspect of critical realism does ensure that through the analysis of actually existing situations, hitherto unrealized potentials might be disclosed, but this is not "prediction" in the same sense. Saying that something *could* happen is not the same as saying that it *will* happen, and critical realism—especially when

---

38 The reverse, of course, need not be true; this is part of George and Bennett's point about the need for "causal mechanisms" (intervening variables) to make a prediction into a genuine explanation. But a neopositivist explanation of this sort would still be predictive, even if it took the highly individuated form "if A, B, C, etc. were to happen again in precisely this sequence, the outcome Y would happen again."

understood as an effort to "play an emancipatory role" (Wight 2006, 51) and not simply as an effort to advance our scientific knowledge—stands firmly on the side of the former. Comparison, just as with every other empirical strategy that critical realists utilize, is always about delineating the real limits of the possible, in the hope that a politically savvy agent will take advantage of them in transformative ways.

5   Analyticism

Although it is one of the most important and most often-cited books in the history of the field of IR, no book in the field has been as profoundly *misunderstood* in essential respects as Kenneth N. Waltz's *Theory of international politics* (1979). There is perhaps no greater indicator of this than the fact that almost all of the debate sparked by Waltz's book has involved a sustained effort to undo what he did in the book, and supplement his deliberately spare formulation of the structure of the international system in ways designed to fashion from Waltz's account an instrument for making falsifiable point-predictions about the behavior of particular state actors. Scholars have added individual-level perceptual factors (Walt 1987), domestic-political factors (Snyder 1991; Schweller 1994; Sterling-Folker 2002), specific characterizations of the incentives facing individual states (Christensen and Snyder 1990; Brooks and Wohlforth 2001), and a whole variety of other things in order to produce theories of foreign policy: theories that would predict what states would do under specific circumstances (Elman 1996). This despite Waltz's strong admonitions against doing any such thing, on the grounds that doing so would conflate theories of different domains and thus make it impossible to explain what was going on in any particular domain in anything other than an idiosyncratic fashion (Waltz 1979, 121–123).

Part of this misunderstanding is undoubtedly related to Waltz's use of a structural-functionalist substantive vocabulary that is somewhat opaque to his successors; the difference between what Waltz meant by "system structure" and what later scholars mean by "structure" (and "state actor") are quite profound (Goddard and Nexon 2005). But equally important—and not unrelated to Waltz's immersion in a social-theoretical tradition greatly at variance from the individualist rationalism of most of his interpreters—is the fact that Waltz, in formulating his balance-of-power theory, was engaged in an endeavor quite distinct from the exercise of formulating hypothetical propositions for comparison with some independently existing real world (Wæver 2009). In a famous, but usually overlooked, statement near the beginning of the book, Waltz declares:

> If a theory is not an edifice of truth and not a reproduction of reality, then what is it? A theory is a picture, mentally formed, of a bounded realm or domain of activity. A theory is a depiction of the organization of a domain and

of the connections among its parts ... The infinite materials of any realm can be organized in endlessly different ways. A theory indicates that some factors are more important than others and specifies relations among them ... Theory isolates one realm from all others in order to deal with it intellectually.

(Waltz 1979, 8)

This is very different than the notion of theory proposed by those of Waltz's critics, like John Vasquez, who want to derive from Waltz's account a "theoretical proposition on balancing" that would take the form of an empirically falsifiable covering-law (Vasquez 1997, 904). Theories, for Waltz, are simply not something that one *compares to* reality; rather, theories "construct *a* reality, but no one can ever say that it is *the* reality," and as such should be evaluated in terms of whether they "convey a sense of the unobservable relations of things" and provide "connections and causes by which sense is made of things observed" (Waltz 1979, 9; see also Waltz 1997).

There is something quite important going on here. Waltz's philosophical stance, a stance that quite obviously and explicitly *rejects* the sharp distinction between theory and empirical reality upheld by neopositivists such as Vasquez, is regularly and systematically misread as though it were in many ways equal to its complete opposite. This persists despite the fact that understanding Waltz's theory in its own philosophical-ontological terms makes sense of Waltz's own statements about how his theory should deal with apparently discrepant evidence—by adducing case-specific factors that interact or interfere with the operation of the structural imperative of balancing power (as in Waltz 1986, 327–328)—in ways that the neopositivist construal of Waltz's theory simply cannot. A dialogue of the deaf, for sure, but a structured and normalized (non-)dialogue made possible by the unquestioned assumption that a neopositivist definition of theory as "a set of interrelated propositions purporting to explain behavior" is "noncontroversial" (Vasquez 1997, 900). Properly understood, the very *existence* of Waltz's work should provide an occasion for controversy on this very point, and the absence of any such sustained controversy is further testimony both to the unreflective dominance of a neopositivist methodology in the field as a whole, and to the costs of such unreflective dominance—in the first instance, a simple failure to communicate.

Waltz's account of theory, and therefore of science and of empirical scientific research, differs quite profoundly from the accounts on offer in the previous two chapters. Unlike critical realists, Waltz maintains a distinctly instrumental view of theoretical constructs; theory does not reveal real-but-undetectable components of the world, but instead provides a set of more or less helpful idealizations or oversimplifications that can be used to order the complex chaos of empirical reality into more comprehensible and manageable forms. This is a far more pragmatic notion of theory than that advanced by critical realists, as Waltz rather sharply limits knowledge to experience and regards theory to be a way of intelligibly ordering and coping with experience. But this phenomenalism is the only commitment of philosophical ontology that he shares with neopositivists, since he rejects the mind–world dualism that neopositivists and critical realists share. The mental constructs of theory do not represent or depict a mind-independent real world in any kind of empirically faithful fashion; rather, theories—and the minds that generate them—are in some sense continuous with the world that they are investigating. Far from dualism, Waltz's account of theory suggests a *mind–world monism* whereby mind is and remains constitutively intertwined with the world in a way that is often baffling to neopositivists and critical realists alike.[1]

In the first section of this chapter I will outline what such a monistic stance on the mind–world interface entails. In philosophical terms, mind–world monism suggests that strategies of falsification or strategies of producing a scientific ontology rich enough to capture the actual constituents of a mind-independent world are, strictly speaking, *non-sensical*, inasmuch as they rest on a presumption that blinds them to the ways in which the production of knowledge is itself also and simultaneously productive of the world. Cashing out this claim requires careful attention to what monists mean by "world," which—in contrast to what dualists ordinarily mean by this term—refers not to a collection of things, but to an assemblage of facts. For a monist, the objects of scientific investigation are not inert and meaningless entities that impress themselves on our (natural or augmented) senses or on our theory-informed awareness, but are instead always and already intermixed with conceptual and intentional content. As such, "world" is in important ways a *component of practical experience*, which does away with any effort to conform mental representations to a mind-independent world.

Instead, analytical monists[2] offer the notion of a disciplined ordering of the facts of experience—what Max Weber, the theorist *par excellence* of this mode of inquiry, called the procedure of "ideal-typification"—as a recipe for engaging in empirical scientific practice. But ideal-typification relies at least as much on the limitation of knowledge to experience as it does on mind–world monism. In the second section of this chapter I will examine the implications of this phenomenalism, particularly when it comes to the making and evaluating of causal claims. Analyticists cannot appeal to the real-but-undetectable causal powers of objects as a way of accounting for the manifest behavior and action of those objects, although they can use such notions instrumentally—that is, without making an ontological commitment to the reality of such deep dispositions and essential properties. At the same time, analyticists are not bound to the kind of covariation-causality that emerges from neopositivist commitments, since for analyticists there simply is no need to distinguish between systematic

---

1   Indeed, the failure to grasp or, in many cases, even to *acknowledge* Waltz's philosophical-ontological monism informs some of the rather odd accusations leveled at Waltz by his critics, such as the critical realist characterization of him as something of a "positivist" because of his instrumentalism about theories (Wight 2006, 130–131; Kurki 2008, 110–112) and neopositivist criticism of him for not recognizing when his theory had been "falsified" (Wohlforth et al. 2007).

2   But not, as I discuss in Chapter 6, all monists. It is logically possible to combine philosophical-ontological monism with a commitment to transfactualism, although this is not a route taken by the analyticists that I discuss in this chapter.

causal relations characteristic of the external world and idiosyncratic relations characteristic of the accidents of specific cases. For analyticists, it is simply meaningless to speak of "the external world" in the first place. So analyticists offer the notion of "singular causal analysis," wherein scientific researchers trace and map how particular configurations of ideal-typified factors come together to generate historically specific outcomes in particular cases. Singular causal analysis, not the evaluation of hypothetical law-like generalizations, is what analyticist science is actually for—despite the fact that many analyticists in IR, laboring under the unquestioned dominance of neopositivist ways of generating knowledge, erroneously persist in using the language of hypothesis-testing and generalization to describe what they are doing while they are in fact crafting case-specific *analytical narratives*.

Mind–world monism

Because mind–world dualism has become quite naturalized in both our everyday lives and the knowledge-production practices into which many of us have been socialized as social scientists, it is particularly important to differentiate mind–world monism from two misleading characterizations frequently emanating from dualist critics. Mind–world dualists, as I have argued over the previous two chapters, are of necessity concerned with making sure that their practices of knowledge-production successfully cross the gap between the mind and the world; the specter of Cartesian anxiety looms, threatening to invalidate any knowledge-claims that cannot adequately demonstrate that they are something other than a figment of subjective imagination. From this point of view, monist claims about the absence of a clear line of demarcation between the mind and the world look suspiciously like either idealism (the claim that only mind exists) or subjectivism (the claim that what exists is a function of individual states of mind), both of which remain quite firmly on the "mind" side of the mind–world gap. These mischaracterizations underpin and give rise to dualist attempts to question or dismiss monist claims by pointing out that material objects exist regardless of whether anyone notices them, and that therefore our ideas can get us into trouble if we do not pay adequate attention to the world beyond them (Mearsheimer 1994, 44–46; Brooks and Wohlforth 2001, 10–12). Wendt provides a particularly extreme example of the trouble that idealism and subjectivism can cause:

> In 1519 Montezuma faced the same kind of epistemological problem facing social scientists today: how to refer to people who, in his case, called themselves Spaniards. Many representations were conceivable, and no doubt the one he chose—that they were gods—drew on the discursive materials available to him. So why was he killed and his empire destroyed by an army hundreds of times smaller than his own? The realist answer is that Montezuma was simply wrong: the Spaniards were not gods, and had come instead to conquer his empire.
>
> (Wendt 1999, 56–57)

Montezuma's incorrect ideas, in other words, prevented him from recognizing what was really going on, just as scientists seeking to explain and understand social phenomena go wrong if they focus too much on their own ideas and not enough on the world. From this, Wendt draws the methodological conclusion that "[T]he external world to which we ostensibly lack access, in other words, often frustrates or penalizes representations. Postmodernism gives us no insight into why this is so, and indeed, *rejects the question altogether*" (ibid., 57; emphasis added). "Postmodernism" here, as elsewhere in Wendt's work, stands for a wide variety of approaches to the production of knowledge, all of which have in common only the fact that they reject the notion that knowledge can be meaningfully thought of as corresponding to or failing to correspond to a mind-independent world.[3] Wendt is quite correct that such monistic approaches "reject the question altogether," in the sense that they are deliberately unconcerned with providing any general answer to why some empirical accounts are successful while others are not, but he, like most critics, does not seem to acknowledge the philosophical argument underpinning this rejection. Monists reject the question of whether and how knowledge corresponds to the world because they reject the dualism implicit in that very formulation itself: for monists, "knowledge" and "world" do not name ontologically discrete or distinct objects that have to be painstakingly related. To accuse monists of focusing on knowledge to the detriment, or the "loss" (Patomäki and Wight 2000, 219), of the world is to (incorrectly) assume that monists are actually dualists, albeit dualists who are deliberately or perversely ignoring the world. This would be a Cartesian nightmare, were it not for the fact that the monistic stance is itself a philosophical strategy of *dis-solving* the very mind–world dichotomy at the heart of such Cartesian anxieties.

Dis-solving Descartes

By my use of the term "dis-solving" I mean to suggest two things simultaneously. First, by claiming that Descartes' problem is a function of his starting-point and his logic rather than a fundamental problem of epistemology, mind–world monist responses to Descartes aim to make the problem simply go away—"dissolve"— by demonstrating that it is, in some sense, a false problem. Second, although monists are not responding to the Cartesian problem in the same sense as dualists are, monist approaches would in a sense constitute a "solving" of the problem in that they would make Cartesian anxiety a non-issue. Mind–world monists are obviously not concerned to demonstrate that knowledge is solidly founded in any mind-independent facts of a mind-independent world, but they are concerned to show how no such solid foundation is required, and how the perceived need for

---

3   On the disciplining/dismissive use of the epithet "postmodern," see Fierke (2003, 69–70). Something of this gesture also informs Emanuel Adler's persistent mischaracterization (Adler 2005, 95; see also Adler 1997) of poststructural and postmodern scholarship as "idealist" because such scholarship denies that it is sensible to speak of a mind-independent external world as constraining the production of knowledge. This only looks "idealist" from a mind–world dualist perspective.

such a foundation is a result of having asked the wrong question(s) in the wrong way at the outset. Instead of wading into a dense philosophical thicket and trying to fight their way through it, monists simply go around what is, for them, a set of non-issues.

Although the mind–world monist approach to knowledge-production does not really get clearly and philosophically articulated until the late nineteenth and early twentieth centuries, antecedent traces of this stance can be found in earlier efforts to grapple with Descartes' formulation of the problem of knowledge—indeed, in the work of the same thinkers forming the root of the orthodox European Enlightenment tradition itself.[4] The first of these traces is a focus on practical experience, together with the notion that knowledge is nothing but a summation of practical lessons learned. Thomas Hobbes, besides inaugurating the empiricist effort that focused on sensory impressions as the necessary foundation of knowledge, also insisted that scientific reasoning was primarily a matter of the logical arrangement of words and symbols. "For *True* and *False* are attributes of Speech, not of Things … *truth* consisteth in the right ordering of names in our affirmations" (Hobbes 1601, 22). Raw experience of particular situations[5] was to be translated into a set of precise definitions, so that logically sound arguments could be produced out of those definitions. The important point here is that Hobbes' conclusions—particularly his conclusions about political authority—derive from conventional definitions rooted in experience, and not from the nature of things themselves:

> These words of Good, Evill, and Contemptible, are ever used with relation to the person that useth them: There being nothing simply and absolutely so; nor any common rule of Good and Evill, to be taken from the nature of the objects themselves; but from the Person of the man (where there is no Common-wealth,) or, (in a Common-wealth,) from the Person that representeth it; or from an Arbitrator or Judge, whom men disagreeing shall by consent set up, and make his sentence the Rule thereof.
>
> (Ibid., 32)

---

4   In fact, there is even a reading of some elements of the Vienna Circle position—particularly the early work of Rudolf Carnap—as similarly rejecting the Cartesian problem altogether, in favor of a more monistic take on the relationship between the mind and the world (Hacking 1999, 42–43, 47–48).

5   As a philosophical nominalist, Hobbes rejected the idea that universals had actual existence. "Of Names, some are *Proper*, and singular to one onely thing; as *Peter, John, This man, this Tree*: and some are *Common* to many things; as *Man, Horse, Tree*; every of which though but one Name, is nevertheless the name of divers particular things; in respect of all which together, it is called an *Universall*; there being nothing in the world Universall but Names; for the things named, are every one of them Individuall and Singular" (Hobbes 1601, 21). This focus on singular situations persists in monist thought up into the present, even though the theories of language preferred by most contemporary mind–world monists are less nominalist than expressive or speech-act performative.

Hobbes thus rejected the notion that any action—and by extension, any object or situation—could be simply and plainly apprehended and evaluated as it is in itself, in the absence of a consensual definition that we might use to reason about it. The proper sphere for human reason and reflection was this space of conventional definition, and the validity of our conclusions depended not on their correspondence to any essential way that things are, but to their logical soundness. Hobbes' argument, therefore, was in many ways an effort to sidestep Descartes' concern with ultimate validity in favor of a focus on more practical utility.

This focus on the conventional character of knowledge, and its roots in practical considerations rather than in a mind-independent world, subsequently became a staple of the empiricist effort to reply to Descartes—but not always with Hobbes' pessimistic conclusions about the need for an overwhelming coercive power to enforce the consistent use of terms and their translation into practical action. John Locke devoted a considerable portion of his magisterial *Essay Concerning Human Understanding* to the problem of how we could be sure that our ideas provided us with accurate knowledge, once we left what Locke took to be the relatively secure domain of original sense-impressions; his eventual answer relied heavily on the notion that it was our practical familiarity with different objects that led to our conventional formulation of ideas referring to them (Locke 1959a, sec. II, i, 7). Thus, the validity of our knowledge of notions such as "murder" depended not on a mind-independent world, but on the practical designation of these actions in particular ways. If people had no need for such notions in the "ordinary occurrence of their affairs," then the terms—and the objects that they specify—would disappear from view (Locke 1959b, sec. III, v, 6–7). As such, grounding knowledge outside of our conventional practices is unnecessary.

Moving further in the direction of the conventionality of knowledge, David Hume suggested that learning from experience was a natural faculty that stood in need of no divine certification. Hume noted that animals, just as human beings, routinely make inferences about the future based on their experience of the past; from this he concluded that experience must be a *direct* source of knowledge, without the need for any intervention of philosophical argument whatsoever.

> Animals, therefore, are not guided in these inferences by reasoning: neither are children: Neither are the generality of mankind [*sic*], in their ordinary actions and conclusions: Neither are philosophers themselves, who, in all the active parts of life, are, in the main, the same with the vulgar, and are governed by the same maxims.
>
> (Hume 1977, 70)

Hume thus radicalized the claims made by Hobbes and Locke about the source of knowledge and stood on the brink of quite profoundly sweeping away the whole problem of Cartesian dualism: knowledge comes not from an abstract operation of mind or process of contemplation, but from participation in the practical activities of daily life.

But this was insufficient for rationalists, who feared that grounding knowledge merely in a practical consensus left open the possibility that the resulting knowledge was nothing but an arbitrary custom, a custom that might diverge quite sharply from how things *really* stood. It was precisely this set of doubts that led Immanuel Kant to look to ground knowledge not in the admittedly conventional character of particular empirical experiences, but in the universal character of the reason that we use to derive claims from the flow of experience. Hence Kant argued that universal reason did not provide knowledge of how things were in themselves, but only knowledge of how they appeared when presented to us by the categories already implicitly structuring our experience.

> That a body is extended is a proposition that is established *a priori*, and is not a judgment of experience. For before I go to experience, I already have all the conditions for my judgment in the concept, from which I merely draw out the predicate in accordance with the principle of contradiction, and can thereby at the same time become conscious of the necessity of the judgment, which experience could never teach me.
>
> (Kant 1999, 142)

Kant thus proposed to sweep away Cartesian anxiety by grounding knowledge not on worldly experience, but on the judgment of pure reason. The *a priori* structuring of our experiences by reason *before* we concretely have any actual experiences makes the world accessible to us, thus producing solid and secure knowledge.

However, the difficulty that this Kantian solution poses is that it looks suspiciously like philosophical Idealism: the doctrine that nothing outside of mind exists, and that there simply *are* no secret powers or physical objects beyond our conceptions of them. To be is to be perceived, as George Berkeley—the most (in)famous Idealist philosopher—put it. Such philosophical Idealism does sweep away any anxiety about our knowledge of objects in the world, but at a fairly extreme cost: if the only things that exist are the ideas produced by mind, how might we explain false or misleading ideas? Why would ideas ever change? For that matter, how would we ever know that the object that I perceive is the same as the object that you perceive? While there may be plausible rejoinders to these objections (for an overview, see Winkler 1989), the important point is that Kant— just as Hume and Locke and Hobbes before him, and in accord with virtually every European philosophical effort to deal with Descartes before the late nineteenth century—vehemently rejected the charge of Idealism, even to the point of providing a fairly complex argument that we can only have the notion of a continuous thinking self if we have consciousness of external objects that persist, and that therefore the existence of mind proves the existence of mind-independent objects (Kant 1999, 326–328).[6] None of these thinkers wanted to be accused of reducing the world to an effect of mind, as this shades uncomfortably

---

6   Dustin McWherter (2012) suggests that these tensions in Kant make him unable to
     escape from the critical realist argument about the ontological stratification of the

into a solipsistic faith in wishful thinking: if only mind and its ideas exist, why can I not simply change the world by altering my thoughts?

Note, however, that this charge—a charge that is continually leveled against mind–world monist accounts of knowledge-production down to the present day— *presupposes dualism*. In fairness, the charge does make sense when applied to philosophers who are trying simultaneously to preserve a separation between mind and world *and* to ground knowledge of the world in some kind of operation of mind, whether that operation involves transcendental reason or a logical derivation from experience. Idealism, as Kant saw, is a symptom of Cartesian dualism; in fact, it would not be going too far to say that Idealism is simply the *inversion* of the Cartesian position. Instead of lamenting the fact that all we have knowledge of is mind, Idealism celebrates this disappearance of the external, material world and revels in the resulting unfettered capacity of mind to do whatever it pleases. Little wonder that philosophers took such pains to distinguish themselves from this position, especially at a time when modern mechanical science was beginning to provide an account of the material world that allowed for considerably more practical manipulation of that world than its predecessors had (McCulloch 1995, 58). In the face of such empirical success, Idealism simply looks implausible.

Indeed, "Idealism" in this form rapidly became something of a dismissive philosophical insult,[7] and it is in this form that Idealism is known to IR scholars, whether in the form of E.H. Carr's utopians (Carr 2001) or Hans Morgenthau's liberal prophets of scientific progress (Morgenthau 1946), or in the numerous contemporary criticisms of "constructivism" for ignoring material factors in world politics (for example, Deudney 2008). Besides the important slippage from philosophical to scientific ontology here—Idealism is more or less converted, by these critics, into an account of what the world is made of, rather than an account of how knowledge of the world is possible (Wendt 1999, 24–25)—it is important to note that these criticisms continue to make sense only in a dualist framework. Only if we *first* commit to a mind–world separation does the privileging of mind equate to a devaluing of world. Of course, dualists have made such a commitment, so it is quite understandable that talk of grounding knowledge in any place but external reality looks to them like Idealism, because on the dualist account there are only two options: either knowledge is a subjective fancy of mind, or knowledge is a solidly established account of the mind-independent world. It is these often-unacknowledged dualist commitments that lend such force to the charge of Idealism; this implies that the charge is only plausibly leveled at thinkers who are

---

world. Be that as it may, there are still sufficient ambiguities in Kant to make a non-realist reading plausible.

7   Note that I mean Idealism *in this form*. Thinkers like Hegel sufficiently reconfigured Idealism—by introducing a dialectical interplay between mind (or Spirit, depending on how one translates the word *Geist* in Hegel's writings) and the world that it contingently constructs for the ultimate purpose of transcending it and propelling itself into a new stage of historical consciousness—that this strain of thought escapes the account I am giving here. The Hegelian dialectic, and its transmutation into various kinds of critical reflexivity, forms part of the subject of Chapter 6.

trying to privilege mind *within a basically Cartesian framework*. But mind–world monists, who reject the Cartesian framework rather than trying to labor within it, are on this account not Idealists, since they are not privileging mind against world so much as denying the separation of mind and world in the first place. Monist thinkers borrow and extend both the notion that knowledge derives from practical experience and the notion that experience itself is in important ways pre-structured, but by doing so outside of the presupposition of mind–world dualism, they push the argument in very different directions.

Nietzsche's overturning of the tradition

Despite these earlier precedents and antecedents, it seems fair to say that the philosophical assault on dualism really did not swing into high gear until Friedrich Nietzsche launched his relentless interrogation of what he diagnosed as the nihilism of the European Enlightenment. For Nietzsche, nihilism—the will to nothingness—was the consequence of how European science and philosophy had moved further and further into the realm of abstraction, leaving behind the actual experience of the world in a desire to penetrate behind appearances and disclose some secret essence that could ground knowledge in a more secure fashion. It is not difficult to see the centrality of Cartesian dualism to that movement, as ever-greater levels of philosophical skepticism were applied to truths that had formerly been taken for granted, in order to see whether they could survive the test; in Nietzsche's diagnosis, it was the quest for philosophical certainty that drove this movement, pushing matters ever closer to a complete philosophical and political crisis. But his solution to nihilism was not to oppose it with yet another attempt to solve the Cartesian problem and posit an unchallengeable ground for knowledge. Instead, Nietzsche advocated pressing nihilistic skepticism as far as it could go, even turning it back on the notion of a knowing or acting subject in the first place.

> Just as the popular mind separates the lightning from its flash and takes the latter for an *action*, for the operation of a subject called lightning, so popular morality also separates strength from expressions of strength, as if there were a neutral substratum behind the strong man, which was *free* to express strength or not to do so. But there is no such substratum; there is no "being" behind doing, effecting, becoming; "the doer" is merely a fiction added to the deed—the deed is everything ... Scientists do no better when they say "force moves," "force causes," and the like—as its coolness, its freedom from emotion notwithstanding, our entire science still lies under the misleading influence of language and has not disposed of that little changeling, the "subject" (the atom, for example, is such a changeling, as is the Kantian "thing-in-itself").
>
> (Nietzsche 1967, 45, my translation)

By extending skepticism in this manner, and thereby questioning the *value* of the Cartesian quest for absolutely secure foundations of knowledge of the subject, Nietzsche sought to free up human potential by eliminating obstacles to creativity; nihilism, he felt, was a phase that had to be passed through in order to reach this higher potential (Nietzsche 1978, 25–27). But the precise details of Nietzsche's broader philosophical project are of less importance to the development of a monist account of knowledge-production than is his understanding of knowledge as a social product to be evaluated less in terms of its correspondence with anything outside of itself and more in terms of its contribution to life. In advancing this account, Nietzsche asked not about whether statements are true or false, but instead about our valuing of truth over falsehood—a valuation that calls for both a philosophical grounding and a cultural history, inasmuch as it is not simply ordained by God or given in the nature of things (Nietzsche 1967, 152–153). Along these lines, Nietzsche proposed a rethinking of practices such as "science" and "history" in terms of their practical ability to help people achieve their ends; while an overzealous focus on details could obscure lessons that might help people achieve their potential, a more instrumental notion of knowledge could open the way for more effective ways of coping with present experiences (Nietzsche 1980, 23).

Indeed, Nietzsche suggested that "truth" and "error" (or "lie") are themselves better understood as social conventions that serve human ends rather than reflections of any way that the world really stands in and of itself:

> Because the human being, out of need and boredom, wants to exist socially and herd-like, he requires a peace pact and he endeavors to banish at least the very crudest *bellum omni contra omnes* from his world. This peace pact brings with it something that looks like the first step toward the acquisition of this puzzling drive for truth. For now *that* is fixed which from this point on will be "truth"; that is, a uniformly valid and binding designation of things is invented, and this legislation of language also establishes the first laws of truth: for here arises for the first time the contrast between truth and lie.
>
> (Nietzsche 1903, 192, my translation)

So far, so Hobbesian, although Nietzsche did not follow Hobbes to the point of claiming that a single identifiable center (or sovereign) is required for the imposition of such a "peace pact." Instead, much as it did for Locke and Hume, a consensus about the correct use of language arises *practically*. Nietzsche noted that the very process of using words to communicate necessitates "equating what is unequal" and overlooking differences between individual cases for the purpose of highlighting relevant similarities—relevant, that is, to specific purposes that we have. In this sense, the very act of communicating implies lying: failing to represent our experiences in all their detail, *mis*-representing them in instrumental ways. It is only by forgetting that we have done so—that our conventional descriptions are intertwined with specific purposes and values at their core—that we can delude ourselves into imagining that our accounts of the world somehow capture the world's essential, mind-independent character:

What, then, is truth? A mobile army of metaphors, metonyms, and anthropomorphisms—in short, a sum of human relations which have been poetically and rhetorically strengthened, transferred, and embellished, and which, after long usage, seem firm, canonical, and binding to a people. Truths are illusions about which one has forgotten that they are illusions: metaphors which are worn out and without sensuous power, coins which have lost their pictures and now are reckoned only as metal, no longer as coins.

(Ibid., 196)

What we actually have in knowledge, Nietzsche argued, is not a firm grasp of the way that the world is in and of itself, but a practical and useful way of organizing our experiences. From the ongoing flow of experience we select different lessons to learn by narrating that experience back to ourselves in terms of the language that we have inherited by being born into particular societies and social groups; that language, itself a product of previous attempts to summarize experience purposefully, shapes how we make meaningful sense of our situations and craft appropriate responses to them. Nietzsche's most elaborate empirical example of how this occurs involves the "ascetic ideal"—the notion that the pursuit of the highest wisdom involves denying the physical world and the sensual experiences of the body—which he traces as originating with priests and Brahmins, but then being utilized by philosophically inclined individuals as a way of making sense of their place in the social world (Nietzsche 1967, 115). In order to make sense of knowledge, then, Nietzsche suggests that we have to recover its function in context, relating particular claims not to some mind-independent external reality, but to their practical utility.

It follows that the worth of any particular set of true-false criteria is what those criteria allow us to accomplish, which in turn depends on the purposes and values that they embody. If a set of knowledge-production practices are designed to allow us to manipulate the physical environment, then within those practices "true" means allowing us to do that while "false" means not doing so; if practices are designed for some other purpose, such as shoring up the dominance of one group of people over another group, then "true" statements advance that end while "false" statements call it into question. Evaluation of any given claim, then, is dependent on a particular set of purposes and values.[8] This in turn suggests that these fundamental purposes and values are not themselves reducible to some overarching consensus, because any such apparent consensus would *itself* be underpinned by values and purposes and rooted in conventional social practices, and thus no more universally valid than any other. There was, for Nietzsche, no

8   Of course, whether the relevant purposes and values for any such evaluation are *our* purposes and values, or the purposes and values of the people making the claim, is a separate issue. The philosophical point (evaluations depend on criteria) should not be conflated with a moral claim (either we ought to evaluate every claim according to our criteria, or we ought to evaluate claims according to (our reconstruction of) the criteria of the claim-makers). See below.

way around this conventionality, least of all through an appeal to any inherent character of the world:

> The overlooking of the individual and the actual gives us the concept, and also gives us the form; whereas nature is acquainted with no forms and no concepts, and likewise with no species, but only with an X which is inaccessible and undefinable for us. For even our contrast between individual and species is something anthropomorphic and does not originate in the essence of things; although we should not presume to claim that this contrast does not correspond to the essence of things: that would of course be a dogmatic assertion and, as such, would be just as indemonstrable as its opposite.
>
> (Nietzsche 1903, 195–196, my translation))

This is the crucially monist move in Nietzsche's position, since it distances knowledge-production from dualism in not one but two respects. First, "the world as it is in itself" becomes a nonsensical notion, because any access that we have to the world is mediated by our conventional practices and values. Nietzsche thus rejected the idea that we could, *even in principle*, learn to see things from a point of view beyond all human experience; we cannot see things from the "outside," as it were. But second, and even more important, was Nietzsche's characterization of our resulting epistemic situation not as an Idealist dreamworld in which we can simply think things however we want them to be, but instead as permanently limited by our inability to answer definitively the question of whether our knowledge is grounded in the sense required by dualism. The fact that our knowledge is rooted in our experiences and in the conceptual ordering of those experiences that produces our operative language does not imply that we can order our experiences according to whim, but instead that we should be extremely wary of characterizing our knowledge as enjoying any privileged relationship— either positive or negative—with some sort of mind-independent reality.

Hence, the implication is that we should *dispense with dualism altogether*, and stop worrying about nonsensical and unanswerable questions of the Cartesian variety. Instead, we should just go about our business, unencumbered by gnawing metaphysical doubts. Mind-world dualism *itself* is the source of Cartesian anxiety, so we should abandon it—which means abandoning all efforts to place knowledge on a securely mind-independent footing. Nietzsche's radicalization of the empiricist claims of his predecessors helped to push him to this point, since experience emerges as a sufficient grounding for knowledge-claims. But there is also something of Kant in Nietzsche's perspective, since our experience never arrives in a raw form, but is always shaped and formed by our purposes and values, institutionalized into the very language that we use to discuss and reflect on our experiences. Nietzsche took the step that Kant did not, and simply gave up the idea of any "thing-in-itself" existing in a mind-independent way; in effect, Nietzsche suggested that since all of the practical work in Kant's philosophy was being done by the categories of reason anyway, losing the "thing-in-itself" would make very little philosophical difference. In this way, what Nietzsche did was to bring together the two central elements of the earlier philosophical efforts to reply to Descartes and think them through to their logical consequences—consequences that suggested the abandonment of Descartes' basic position altogether. If knowledge emerges from experience, and if experience itself is always pre-structured by the categories and values and purposes that we bring to it, Cartesian anxiety vanishes: there is no problem organizing our experiences in more or less useful ways, and no need to ask for anything more than that in evaluating whether our knowledge is good.

Intersubjectivity and the pluralism of knowledge

To put this another way, Nietzsche's dis-solution of Cartesian dualism involved detaching knowledge from the two alternative bases posed by mind–world dualism—mind, or world—and placing it somewhere quite distinct: in the social practices in which people (and scientists are surely people too!) engage as they live their lives and go about their business. In John Dewey's terminology, such a shift makes knowledge "a certain kind of intelligently conducted doing; it ceases to be contemplative and becomes in a true sense practical" (Dewey 1920, 121). Claiming that we know something amounts to claiming that we can do something; judging that a claim is true amounts to judging that a claim gives us helpful advice for achieving some end. The chief contribution of science, or philosophy, or any other systematic manner of thinking to this enterprise is *not* to subject the maxims of everyday practical wisdom to elaborate procedures designed to ascertain their correspondence to some mind-independent reality, but to abstract from those maxims in order to forge tools that can be applied to a wider variety of concrete situations as they arise. Abstraction makes knowledge, as it were, more *portable*:

> Abstraction means that something has been released from one experience for transfer to another. Abstraction is liberation. The more theoretical, the more abstract, an abstraction, or the farther away it is from anything experienced in its concreteness, the better fitted it is to deal with any one of the indefinite variety of things that may later present themselves.
>
> (Ibid., 150)

Dewey's formulation, much as with Nietzsche's, effectively dis-solves Cartesian anxiety by suggesting that Descartes was simply asking the wrong questions about the status of knowledge, and starting in the wrong place. Beginning with a knower concretely embedded in a set of practical activities neatly eliminates any worry about whether that knower is in touch with anything other than idle fancy, simply because practical activities are not meaningfully conceptualized as individual whims. To engage in a practical activity is to participate in an organized set of meaningful behaviors that can be conceptualized as rule-governed, in the sense that engaging in the activity means conforming to the "standards of excellence" characteristic of the activity as such (MacIntyre 1984, 190). To play a game of chess, for example, is not simply to move pieces around on a chessboard, any more than simply moving one's limbs around while standing on a stage is to perform a dance number; what constitutes these practical activities *as* practical activities is the fact that their disparate parts are brought together by a set of rules that are in some sense taken into account by the participants in the activity (Onuf 1989, 52). Playing chess or performing a dance number means entering a domain in which rules specify the means and ends of particular actions, and this in turn provides a basis for practically reasoning one's way to good knowledge about how to engage best in the activity in question.

Two critical ambiguities in this account of knowledge as arising in the course of practical activities cry out, more or less immediately, for resolution. The first such ambiguity involves the question of precisely what it means to take rules into account when engaged in some practical activity; there is a lot packed into the formulation "in some sense" that I used a moment ago, and unpacking it will help clarify why monists do not necessarily agree with the proposition that *subjective assent* to rules is what defines participation in a practical activity. Some monists do maintain the importance of subjective assent, while others do not, and this difference of scientific ontology is quite irrelevant to the broader philosophical-ontological claim that knowledge-production starts with practical activity rather than with minds facing mind-independent worlds. The logical possibility of bracketing subjective assent is particularly important when the practical activity in question is the scientific production of knowledge, because that helps to ensure that the resulting products are something other than arbitrary whims.

The second ambiguity—involving the difference between taking the rules of a practical activity into account while participating in that activity, and analyzing those rules from outside of the activity while participating in scientific inquiry— likewise involves a needless conflation of philosophical and scientific ontology. There is no necessary reason that a philosophical account of knowledge-production has to imply any similarity between how *participants* explain and understand an activity and how *scientists* explain and understand that activity. As a philosophical-ontological wager, monism is about how knowledge is generated; it is not a set of pieces of conceptual equipment for actually generating knowledge, although it of course informs such equipment in profound ways. But throughout the history of anti-dualist interventions in the social sciences, the temptation to reason directly from the situation of the scientific observer to the situation of the individuals under investigation has proved too strong to avoid, leading many monists to reject—explicitly or tacitly—the distinction between scientific inquiry and other forms of human activity, and thus to embrace a global relativism with respect to scientific knowledge. While it is *possible* to reject the distinctiveness of science on a monistic basis, this is certainly not *necessary*. Philosophically speaking, monists accept a diversity of locally valid knowledge-claims that cannot be easily related to one another, but they do not thereby affirm that "anything goes" in the production of valid knowledge, and are therefore not committed to any form of global relativism.

Intersubjectivity, not subjectivity

The charge of subjectivity is a powerful rhetorical weapon, since "subjective" seems to mean at least two distinct but related things in both ordinary and philosophical discussions. To borrow a distinction made by Richard Rorty, we might distinguish between the use of "subjective" to indicate a factor that "has been, or would be, or should be, set aside by rational discussants—one which is seen to be, or should be seen to be, irrelevant to the subject matter," and the use of "subjective" to mean

> [S]omething like "a product only of what is in here" (in the heart, or in the "confused" portion of the mind which does not accurately reflect what is out there). In this sense "subjective" is associated with "emotional" or 'fantastical.'

> (Rorty 1981, 338–339)

To Rorty's list of associations for the second meaning of "subjective," we might add "arbitrary," a notion that often seems especially germane when talking about the production of scientific knowledge: part of the basic package associated with scientific knowledge is precisely that it is *not* arbitrary or dependent on discretion, but solidly warranted and grounded. "Subjective," in either of these senses—and Rorty accurately observes that most actual uses of the charge incorporate all of these ambiguous elements—means detached and divorced from the world.

Properly understood, however, there is little about concrete participation in a practical activity that is "subjective" in *any* of these senses. Practical activities are rule-governed activities, and the rules provide an impersonal standard against which to evaluate particular acts; hence there can be better and worse performances and strategies and productions without reducing such judgments to purely arbitrary acts of will. Such judgments only make sense *within* a given practical activity, but that does not make them subjective as much as it makes them "circumstantial"—which is to say, dependent on circumstances, particularly the circumstances to which the rules relate (Rescher 1997, 12). The impersonality of rules also means that the subjective consciousness of people involved in a practical activity need never come into the picture, further distinguishing the rules and products of any given practical activity from an arbitrary set of ideas. Although rules and the practical activities that they govern are certainly not founded on mind-independent reality in any simple sense, they are also certainly not just phantasms of mind. Hence the most appropriate way to describe them is as *intersubjective*, occupying a public space external to the individual minds of the participants but not therefore independent of all minds in general.[9]

---

9   While it might be possible to follow Pouliot (2007) and refer to these practical activities as "objective" rather than "intersubjective," I am reluctant to do so inasmuch as Pouliot's cashing-out of the term yields a specific kind of research procedure and not a statement of philosophical ontology. Sobjectivist research, we might say, is one way of apprehending intersubjective practical activities.

If we start our thinking about the status of knowledge from those intersubjective practical activities in which we engage when producing knowledge, Cartesian doubts never even arise. Instead, individual minds and the world that they grasp *both* emerge as byproducts of practice, inasmuch as acts—deeds, "doings"— come before either actors or their environments (Onuf 1989, 36). But because of centuries of conceptual confusion about the distinctive role played by abstract reasoning in the production and validation of genuinely *scientific* knowledge, it may be easier to see what starting with intersubjective practical activities actually means by first attending to practical activities other than scientific knowledge-production and then coming back to science once we have a clearer view of the issues involved. Along these lines, consider Martin Heidegger's deceptively simple observation that "when I open the door, for instance, I use the handle" (Heidegger 1927, 96).[10] No cognition or complex reasoning is required, or even appropriate: the door is shut, and in order to open it I extend my hand and turn the handle. I encounter the handle, in this way, as (so to speak) a piece of equipment for opening the door, and not as a mind-independent piece of metal whose purpose and function I first have to ascertain before I can use it. The objects that I encounter in my daily life present themselves to me with functions and purposes *already intact*, and there is no gap between mind and world to be crossed in order to figure out what to do next.

Heidegger suggests that this kind of practical grasping of the objects that we encounter in our daily lives is considerably more fundamental than whatever detached reflection on those objects that we might subsequently engage in.

> Equipment can genuinely show itself only in dealings cut to its own measure (hammering with a hammer, for example); but in such dealings an entity of this kind is not *grasped* thematically as an occurring Thing … The hammering does not simply have knowledge about the hammer's character as equipment, but it has appropriated this equipment in a way which could not possibly be more suitable. In dealings like this, where something is put to use, our concern subordinates itself to the "in-order-to" which is constitutive for the equipment we are employing at the time; the less we just stare at the hammer-Thing, and the more we seize hold of it and use it, the more original does our relationship to it become, and the more undisguisedly is it encountered as that which it is—as equipment. The hammering itself uncovers the specific "manipulability" of the hammer.
>
> (Ibid., 98)

When I pick up a hammer and use it to hammer something, Heidegger is suggesting, it is simply not the case that I have gone through a process of representing a hammer-shaped object to myself as something that might be used

---

10   Here as elsewhere, I have occasionally modified the Heidegger translation in minor ways—the translators used "latch" instead of "handle," but either are appropriate translations of *Klinke*.

for hammering and then acted on that representation. In fact, I have not even encountered the hammer as a simply "occurring Thing," but in using it *as a hammer* I have already entered into a whole series of interrelated functions and purposes in terms of which my activity is guided. Those functions and purposes make my hammering possible, and my prior involvement with their interrelationship is what makes those pieces of equipment available to me in the first place.

> When Dasein[11] directs itself towards something and grasps it, it does not somehow first get out of an inner sphere in which it has been proximally encapsulated, but its primary kind of Being is such that it is always "outside" alongside entities which it encounters and which belong to a world already discovered. Nor is any inner sphere abandoned when Dasein dwells alongside the entity to be known, and determines its character ... the perceiving of what is known is not a process of returning with one's booty to the "cabinet" of consciousness after one has gone out and grasped it.
>
> (Ibid., 89)

In some way, then, we are out in front of ourselves, phenomenologically speaking: our everyday experience of living is not an experience of continually running into inert objects and having to build them into a world of meaningful pieces of useful equipment, but is instead an experience of already having grasped objects as pieces of useful equipment. Any cognitive knowledge we might develop about how to use that equipment—including knowledge about how to use it more effectively or appropriately—is founded on that practical grasping, which is a kind of knowing before we know, or fore-knowledge (ibid., 190–192).

Heidegger's account of the complex phenomenal structure of everyday life has inspired a number of social-psychological accounts of practical consciousness. One of the most famous—recently re-introduced to the social sciences through Bent Flyvbjerg's programmatic *Making social science matter*—is the model of human learning developed by Hubert and Stuart Dreyfus, a model that specifies that conscious rule-based knowledge can only take one so far. In Flyvbjerg's words:

> Intelligent action consists of something other than calculated, analytical rationality ... The best performances within a given area require a qualitatively different expertise based on intuition, experience, and judgment ... Intuition is the ability to draw directly on one's own experience—bodily, emotional, intellectual—and to recognize similarities between these experiences and new situations. Intuition is internalized; it is part of the individual ... Logically based action is replaced by experientially based action.
>
> (Flyvbjerg 2001, 21)

---

11   *Dasein* is Heidegger's term for the basic character of the human being as such. This is not the place to get into the complexities of precisely what he intends with his use of the term; for a good overview, see Dreyfus (1990).

While this model might be taken to have implications for our substantive claims about human social action,[12] its relevance to philosophical ontology lies in the notion that concrete practical involvement logically precedes and implicitly gives rise to any kind of subjective reflection on a given activity. Playing a violin, engaging in medical triage at the site of an accident, performing in a stage production: intersubjectively participating in these activities and developing the relevant practical intuition or expertise comes before any subsequent efforts to represent the activity in words or in thought. This also applies to conversations about the future direction of an organization (Campbell 2000, 92–93) or a community (Shotter 1993b, 192–193), and by extension also applies equally well to efforts to produce scientific knowledge: knowledge is produced *from within* concrete practical activities and is warranted by its stemming from practice rather than from arbitrary operations of individual minds (Michel 2009, 412–414).

Another way of thinking about intersubjective practical activities is to consider the example, much used in twentieth-century philosophical reflection on these matters, of what happens when someone plays a game. Ludwig Wittgenstein, with whose work the game example is perhaps most closely associated, argued that although a game was an activity constituted by its rules, simply knowing those rules in an explicit sense and being able to formulate them consciously was insufficient for actually playing the game.[13] "There is a way of grasping

---

12   The subsequent controversy about Flyvbjerg's argument and its implications for the study of political and social life (White 2002; Schram and Caterino 2006) was almost entirely conducted in the sphere of scientific ontology. In fairness, much of Flyvbjerg's own presentation of the argument occupied that sphere as well, as he suggested that the Dreyfus model meant that there could not be theory in the social sciences, at least not theory of the rational-choice or predictive variety, because the contexts on which human social action depended were not themselves specifiable in a logical manner (Flyvbjerg 2001, 47–48). But as I have argued throughout this book, grounding one's account of a particular subject-matter in the supposed characteristics of that subject-matter, and not in the character of one's "hook-up" to the world—in other words, ignoring method*ology* in order to focus on method—is to proceed in precisely the wrong fashion. *Methodology comes first*, and accounts of practical involvement matter in the first instance insofar as they dis-solve the Cartesian problem faced by dualist scholars and thinkers.

13   Onuf (1989, 44–48) is almost certainly correct when he argues that Wittgenstein does not provide us with a fully fledged social theory beyond a fairly unspectacular conventionalism: the notion that human activity, including the use of language and logic, depends on custom and convention. But Wittgenstein's whole point was that, philosophically speaking, accounts of human activity that fail to acknowledge this conventional background will fail to grasp the phenomenon that they are investigating. Pure logic—pure semantics, or pure logical positivism—thus necessarily fails to deliver a universal metalanguage capable of describing Reality As It Actually Is In Itself, precisely because of its inability to recognize that human activity (including scientific knowledge-production) is founded on convention. But this is a point of *philosophical* ontology, pertaining to the status of and character of knowledge; it is not, or at least not yet, a *scientific* ontology of the sort that Onuf (and other constructivist social theorists) seek to provide as a way of actually generating knowledge about the social world. See below.

a rule which is *not* an *interpretation*, but which is exhibited in what we call 'following the rule' and 'going against it' in actual cases" (Wittgenstein 1953, §201). Elucidating the character of that grasping of the rules—a grasping that somehow enables players to have meaningful discussions about what is essential and inessential to the play of the game (ibid., §562–568)—leads Wittgenstein to conclude that following rules and playing games "are *customs* (uses, institutions)" rather than simply explicit instructions (ibid., §199). The customary character of such activities, in turn, means that they are not meaningfully thought of as subjective, but are irreducibly intersubjective and public.

> Hence "following a rule" is a practice. And to *believe* that one is following a rule is not to follow a rule. And hence one cannot follow a rule "privately," because otherwise believing that one was following a rule would be the same as following it.
>
> (Ibid., §202)[14]

Therefore, playing a game is as little a "subjective" activity as is turning a handle to open a door or using a hammer to drive a nail into a board. The fact that individuals playing a game can be corrected—that it is possible to make a mistake, and to be corrected by other players—illustrates that the rules of the game are certainly something other than phantasms of mind, to be arbitrarily changed at will. In virtue of their function as guides for action, the rules of a game occupy the same intersubjective region as the structures of reference in terms of which hammers can be directly encountered as equipment for driving in nails. Of course it is often possible[15] for people playing a game to agree to change the rules, and thus to change the game, but this does not make the rules "subjective" either (Dewey 1938, 52–53). If we're playing baseball and I suddenly drop the baseball on the ground and start kicking it in the way that I would kick the ball in a game of football,[16] this does not constitute a modification of the rules as much as it constitutes a violation of the already-existing rules of the game we are playing—unless, of course, we subsequently decide to abandon our baseball game in favor of holding a football match, which would make the issue moot anyway.

---

14   Translation slightly modified, since the translator renders *glauben* as "think" (instead of "believe") and *folgen* as "obey" (instead of "follow").

15   But not *always* possible. A group of people playing a game in isolation can almost certainly change the game that they are playing much more easily than can a group of people who are playing a game in front of spectators who have gathered in order to watch a particular game being played; such spectators, in virtue of the expectations that they bring to their witnessing of the game, constitute part of the "team" that is putting on the performance in question (Goffman 1959, 80–82). Changing the game would thus require the assent of the spectators as well as the players, which might be logistically much more difficult to negotiate. But this empirical particularity does not affect the fundamental philosophical point; if anything, it strengthens the point, since the rules of a game with spectators occupy a region intersubjective to both players *and* audience.

16   Or what Americans call "soccer."

As Clifford Geertz (2000, 25) once quipped, "you can't castle in dominoes." The very condition of possibility for meaningfully playing a game is that the individuals involved orient their actions towards the rules, and it is this orientation that renders their actions explicable and evaluable in terms of that game's goals and procedures.

However, note that "orientation toward the rules" neither means that the rules are all stated in clear and unambiguous language, nor that all of the players can state those rules with any degree of specificity.[17] What matters for the playing of a game is practical, not merely intellectual, involvement, inasmuch as the players need not have all of the rules subjectively in mind in order to make a valid move. As Wittgenstein put it:

> Suppose it were asked: When do you *know* how to play chess? All the time? Or just while you are making a move? And during each move, [do you know] the whole of chess?—And how queer that knowing how to play chess takes so short a time, and a game so much longer.
>
> (Wittgenstein 1953, 59)[18]

Subjectively knowing the rules is secondary here. Rather, what is decisive in making a valid move is its conformity, or lack of conformity, to the rules of the game, and this conformity is not a subjective matter. This is easy to see with a game such as chess, in which the fact that a rook can only move horizontally and vertically but not diagonally is simply not open to discussion, but it is equally true of games in which the rules themselves specify room for someone's discretion to play a significant role—as when the rules of baseball permit the plate umpire to determine whether a given pitch was a strike or a ball, or the rules of football permit the referee to make a judgment of misconduct. The existence of such moments of discretion does not make the game "subjective" either; it simply means that as one of the conditions of playing this kind of game, the players have placed the determination of the status of some of their actions in the hands of a duly constituted official.[19] Here again, it is the practical involvement in the game that anchors the determination of the action.

It follows that the act of specifying the rules is itself not necessarily exogenous to the playing of the game. Formalizing the rules—institutionalizing

---

17   Although Pierre Bourdieu's work presents one of the most well-elaborated conceptions of this kind of "logic of practice" that is not itself reducible to an explicitly logical formulation, I am not drawing on him in this chapter because his methodological orientation is decidedly *not* analyticist, but reflexivist. So as to avoid confusion, I will therefore postpone discussion of Bourdieu until Chapter 6.

18   Translation again slightly modified, since Wittgenstein italicizes "*kannst*" (know) in the German, but the translator italicized "When" in the English. "[do you know]" is also my interpolation, in order to clarify the meaning.

19   The fact that such officials can be "second-guessed" only reinforces the point: judgment-calls involve *judgment*, and not every judge will make the same determination—but that's all part of the game.

and codifying tacit conventions in agreed-upon language—can help the rules serve as a more explicit guide for action, defining the expectations for players in a less ambiguous way (Onuf 1989, 85–86). Indeed, the rules of a game are often only formally codified after people have been playing the game for a long while; people were throwing and kicking balls around long before baseball and football were institutionalized, and their institutionalization depends on some of those antecedently agreed-upon conventions that the newly formalized rules designate as officially binding. Explicit rules can certainly introduce new ways of acting, or sometimes even create an entirely new game, but this does not alter the basic situation: stating the rules is a practical activity, and when it is done by a participant in the game it is subject to the (perhaps implicit) evaluation of other actual or potential players. If I claim that the rule in baseball is that a batter gets four strikes before the batter makes an out, *I can be wrong* about this, inasmuch as my statement does not institutionalize the already-existing convention of three strikes making an out. And if I intend the claim as a proposal rather than as a statement of fact, I require assent in order to change the rule. In either case, my statement remains in the region of intersubjectivity.

At the margin, it is possible for any particular statement of the rules to remain completely divorced from *anyone's* subjective awareness, but for the rules still to play a role in the conduct of the game. John Searle offers the following thought-experiment as a way of illustrating the point:

> Suppose there were a tribe where children just grew up playing baseball. They never learn the rules as codified rules but are rewarded or criticized for doing the right thing or the wrong thing ... We can suppose that the children just become very skillful at playing baseball. Now also suppose that a foreign anthropologist tries to describe the culture of the tribe. A good anthropologist might come up with the rules of baseball just by describing the behavior of these people and what they regard as normative in baseball situations. But it does not follow from the accuracy of the anthropological description that the members of this society are consciously or unconsciously following those rules.

(Searle 1995, 145)

Because the rules of a game—or other rule-governed social activity—only specify a set of standards for "external performances" such as the successful scoring of a run in baseball, and do not say anything about the "internal structure" of the participants beyond the open-ended claim that the participants must somehow be capable of delivering those external performances, it is possible to bypass subjective assent altogether when analyzing the play of the game (Turner 1994, 58–59). Playing a game need not involve a subjective grasp of the rules, even though the players of a game would most likely *recognize* a statement of the rules as either capturing or failing to capture the organization of their existing practical activities. Much as with Searle's "foreign anthropologist," players might be able to articulate the rules governing their activities (Giddens 1984, 90–91), but this does not commit either us or them to the proposition that they were "unconsciously" or "tacitly" following those rules beforehand—although they certainly were conforming to the rules.

It should, but might not, go without saying that although the rules of a game are not subjective, they are not objective either, if we mean "objective" in the dualist sense of existing as a mind-independent object in the world. The players of a game first encounter the rules of the game through their practical involvement with the game—that is, through their *playing* of the game, and it is this practical involvement that makes possible any of their subsequent evaluations of statements of the rules. This practical involvement also allows them to make determinations about the relative worth of particular *strategies* for playing the game, and thus to ascertain in an impersonal way that (for instance) a left-handed shortstop is a bad idea in baseball (Gould 2003, 162–163).[20] Such evaluations and determinations are neither individual whims nor mental representations of mind-independent objects, but are instead practical arrangements of experiences that contain within themselves conventional rules. Participation—concrete, practical involvement— makes the production and evaluation of such knowledge possible.

But none of this is to say that participants always have a clearer understanding of their own practical activities than an outside observer might. For answering certain kinds of empirical questions and for investigating certain kinds of empirical phenomena, it might be particularly useful to focus scholarly attention on what kinds of mental and conceptual equipment people use when making sense of their surroundings and situations—to focus not on what people perceive, but on (so to speak) what they perceive *with* (Geertz 2000, 56–58). Something like this is the basic conjecture of a certain kind of IR constructivism, which privileges the ideational and *in this sense* subjective aspects of social life: "people act toward objects, including other actors, on the basis of the meanings that the objects have for them" (Wendt 1992, 396–397) is equivalent to "people's subjective mental representations of objects determine people's behavior," and such a stance would indeed imply the need to ground one's account of some sphere of social life in how actors understand themselves and their situations. However, *this is not a claim of philosophical ontology, but a claim of scientific ontology*. It pertains to a scholar's "model of man" (Moon 1975, sexism in original) and not to a scholar's connection to or interface with the world under investigation. As such, there is no necessary reason why a philosophical-ontological monist need be committed to participant-observation ethnography, qualitative interviewing, or any other "interpretive" research tool or technique (for an overview, see Yanow and Schwartz-Shea 2006).

Instead, the monist claim is that scholarly researchers, like the players of games or in general like people in their everyday lives, do not confront a mind-independent world that they have to make sense of, but that they (as Heidegger might put it) find themselves always and already "thrown" into a world with which they are practically involved (Heidegger 1927, 236–237). Although our

---

20   An elaboration of this claim for the less "baseballically literate" can be found in BBC (2004).

systematized scholarly modes of speaking and theorizing—modes that involve "a reliance upon links with a certain body of *already determined* meanings—a body of special, interpretative resources into which the properly trained professional reader has been 'educated' in making sense of such texts" (Shotter 1993a, 25)— tend to obscure this practical involvement, monists claim that it is always and already there as a condition of possibility for generating knowledge of anything. Scientific knowledge, just as every other kind of knowledge, is practical at its core: it is a way of systematically organizing experience so as to generate useful insights. There is as little that is "subjective" about such knowledge as there is about a game-player's knowledge of rules and strategies, or a carpenter's knowledge of hammering. Intersubjective practical activity, not subjectivity, comes first.

Refuting relativism

However, this account of the situation of the scientific knower leads to a second sort of "scary rhetoric about 'losing touch with the world'" (Rorty 1981, 276). This second set of charges might be thought of as the problem of *bounded knowledge*, and expresses a reservation about any account of knowledge that appears to place boundaries on what we can know. This problem really only arises when we turn our attention away from games and everyday activities and start to focus on scientific knowledge-production. To claim that knowledge of baseball is bounded by the practical activities and rules that constitute the game of baseball is to tender a relatively unproblematic claim, since no one expects that engaging in baseball will yield knowledge of anything *but* baseball.[21] However, engaging in science is supposed, by many commentators, to accomplish something else, which is to deliver reliable knowledge of the world *as a whole* and *as it is in itself*, not merely the world as presented to us through our practical activities. Hence the grounding of scientific knowledge on the practical activities engaged in by scientists looks downright relativist.

This charge of relativism is, however, misdirected on at least two counts. For one thing, the charge of relativism mistakes a set of *logical* claims for *ontological* claims, and misreads monist authors as claiming that no world outside of our ways of referring to and talking about the world actually exists. But the monist claim is not that no such external world exists, but that no sense can be made of the idea of such an external world either as existing or as putting objective limits on our production of knowledge—at least, no sense that would suffice to assuage dualist doubts.[22] For monists, the world in which we live is a world of facts, not of things; each of those facts is what David Easton once called "a particular ordering of

---

21 I am setting aside the numerous pop-psychological books that purport to draw life lessons from the game of baseball—whatever else they do, these books promise *wisdom*, not empirical *knowledge*.

22 Recall Nietzsche's assertion, quoted above, that declaring that our ideas do not correspond to a mind-independent world would be just as unjustified as declaring that they do correspond. The problem is with the very notion of a mind-independent world in the first place.

reality in terms of a theoretical interest" (Easton 1953, 53), and it makes no sense to seek to reach a more basic layer or level of reality than that. Monists therefore prefer simply to stay silent on the whole issue of whether there is or is not an external world, regarding it to be one of those perennial metaphysical questions to which no meaningful answer can be given.

This slippage from logical to ontological claims sets up the charge of relativism. For instance, take the monist claim that knowledge is produced out of a set of concrete practical involvements. Because different societies and historical eras and groups of people, even groups of scientific researchers, have different practical involvements, and because—here is the slippage from logic to ontology—there *is no* external world to place limits on valid knowledge-claims, it appears to follow that it is possible for there to be different, even contradictory, pieces of knowledge.[23] Paul Boghossian (2007, 40) worries that such a situation, if it empirically obtained, would violate the law of non-contradiction ("it is not the case both that P and not-P"): "How could it be the case both that the world is flat (the fact constructed by pre-Aristotelian Greeks) *and* that it is round (the fact constructed by us)?" Because of this absurd consequence, he concludes, it cannot be the case that different communities produce different facts and different knowledge. So maybe they produce factual knowledge that is only *relatively* true?

> Suppose we may never claim that some propositions are simply true but only that they are true relative to this or that way of talking. The ways of talking themselves cannot be said to be truer than one another, or more faithful to the way things are in and of themselves than one another, because there is no way things are in and of themselves. There is just one way of talking as opposed to another ... there is no such thing as reality as it is in itself.
>
> (Ibid., 44–45)

Boghossian goes on to argue that this construal does not make sense either, since in order for something to be true relative to a way of talking or to a theory that we accept, it would have to be a fact that we accept a given theory. But in order to remain consistent, that fact itself can only be a fact relative to some *other* theory that we accept; otherwise, there would be non-relative facts, and thus there would be an external world of the sort that monists are thought to deny the existence of. But if facts about which theories we accept are themselves relative to other theories that we accept, then the cycle repeats over and over *ad infinitum* (ibid., 56). For Boghossian, such absurdity proves that there must be mind-independent facts about a mind-independent world.

However, this conclusion is almost entirely a function of Boghossian's incorrect understanding of the monist claim. When Wittgenstein (1961, §5.6)

---

23   Of course, any such "contradictions" could only arise if the conceptual vocabularies in question were translatable into one another, which would make the apparent conflict between such pieces of knowledge vanish as long as each piece was sufficiently practically warranted. See below.

declares that "*The limits of my language* mean the limits of my world," he does not mean that each of us—or even all of us together—carry around some sort of mind-dependent linguistic bubble that interposes itself between us and the world; still less does he mean that only such a mind-dependent linguistic bubble exists. Instead, Wittgenstein means that it is not *logically possible* to talk about or conceptualize any such situation, and that therefore the mind–world interface has to be more primitive than conscious reflection.

> Logic pervades the world; the limits of the world are also its limits. So we cannot say in logic: the world has this and this in it, but not that. For that would appear to presuppose that we were excluding certain possibilities, and this cannot be the case, since it would require that logic should go beyond the limits of the world: for only in that way could it view those limits from the other side as well.
>
> We cannot think what we cannot think; so we also cannot *say* what we cannot think.
>
> (Ibid., §5.61)

In order for Boghossian to make his claims of relativism, he has to violate Wittgenstein's strictures and "say what we cannot think" by placing himself beyond the boundaries of language but then trying to *speak* from that position. The charge that different groups might construct contradictory pieces of knowledge only has force if there were some conceptual place outside of those groups from which to view and evaluate their claims, and this is precisely what a monist stance denies: any such *apparently* external place is in fact *internal to some other group* with which the speaker is already practically involved, so there is no way for such pieces of knowledge to violate the law of non-contradiction: *from where the speaker is located,* one is correct and the other is not, and the problem dis-solves.[24]

This touches on the second mistake, in which critics take monists to be arguing that knowledge is relative to a conceptual scheme or set of propositions that must be assented to in order for the resulting knowledge to make sense. This is the charge that Karl Popper leveled against (among others) Thomas Kuhn, accusing Kuhn of falling victim to the "myth of the framework," which maintains that agreement on fundamental matters must precede any kind of rational discussion—and that particular frameworks were untranslatable with respect to one another, rendering futile any rational attempt to evaluate frameworks comparatively (Popper 1970, 56–57; see also, generally, Popper 1996). Whether this is what Kuhn was arguing in his most (in)famous book is a complicated question to answer,[25] but in any event it is not what the monist position on knowledge-production actually entails.

---

24   Alternatively, the two communities in question might be saying the same thing with different words, or saying completely different things. In none of these cases does a contradiction arise (Jackson 2015b).

25   For a discussion of the ambiguities of "incommensurability" in Kuhn, see Jackson and Nexon (2009), and the literature cited therein.

The basic problem with the "conceptual scheme" charge is that it is either trivially true or logically incoherent. If "knowledge is relative to a conceptual scheme" simply means that we need to have a basic vocabulary already in hand in order to formulate a claim and determine whether it is valid knowledge, then it means nothing other than the self-evident fact that (as Nicholas Rescher puts it) "all human endeavors are conducted within the setting of place and time ... We cannot extract ourselves from the setting of our history and society and technology and enter into a timeless and acircumstantial realm." But, he continues, so what?

> That two shekels plus two shekels make four shekels is just as true for us as for the Babylonians ... If others have indeed asserted those claims that our *form* of words *conveys*, then they have asserted what is true—and true unqualifiedly rather than "true for us" or "true for them." The fact that the affirmation of a fact must proceed from within a historico-cultural setting does not mean that the correctness and appropriateness of what is said will be restricted to such a setting.
>
> (Rescher 1997, 61)

As long as we can translate the terms of a given "historico-cultural setting" into the terms of our own, then we can in a sense cancel out the empirical specificity of the situation, focusing only on the question of whether the claimed knowledge does or does not do what it is supposed to do in context. And if we cannot translate those terms into our own language, then we are confronted with something rather different: mutual incomprehension, perhaps, or a failure to communicate.[26] In any event, such a situation would not pose any problem of relativism, since there would be no possibility that mutually incomprehensible claims could contradict one another.

While it is therefore the case that the monistic stance very willingly accepts that there can be a diversity of warranted pieces of knowledge, this diversity does not imply "relativism" in the sense feared by dualists.[27] The existence of multiple traditions and vocabularies out of which knowledge is produced does nothing whatsoever to erode or weaken the justifiable claims of our own tradition, or the claims that we can translate into our tradition's terms. Within the way that we do things—which is to say, within our characteristic modes of concrete practical involvement—there are *already* standards and rules and conventional commonplaces, perhaps explicitly articulated, perhaps only implicitly present, so it is never the case that "anything goes" (Shotter 1993b, 97). Our standards and rules and commonplaces are not optional for us, and they form the backdrop against which we evaluate claims whatever their source; thus the specter of

---

26 I return to the challenges posed by such a situation of mutual incomprehensibility in Chapter 7.

27 Although I have derived this conclusion by focusing on translation and conceptual vocabularies, I might also have reached it by following Nelson Goodman (1978) and talking about "versions" and "fit."

relativism recedes. In addition, our standards and rules are not ever exactly equal with their formal expressions; here, too, practical involvement comes first and provides a possible avenue of criticism of *any* effort to make of a living practical tradition a series of ossified formal precepts that could stand in direct contradiction to the precepts of others.[28]

But here again, caution is called for, since many if not most of the social scientists who espouse sentiments such as this treat them as *scientific ontologies*, not as philosophical ontologies. Such scholars argue that because of the tradition-dependent character of particular bodies of knowledge, and their close connection to patterns of concrete practical involvement, it follows that the only valid way to study social life is to adopt an "anti-naturalist" attitude that uses the self-understandings of situated actors as the starting-point for empirical analysis (for example, Bevir and Kedar 2008). In this, they follow along in the line sketched out by philosophers such as Peter Winch, inveterate critic of the naturalist approach to the study of social life:

> In so far as a set of phenomena is being looked at "from the outside," "as experimental facts," it cannot at the same time be described as constituting a "theory" or a set of "propositions." ... For what the sociological observer has presented *to his* [*sic*] *senses* is not at all people holding certain theories, believing in certain propositions, but people making certain movements and sounds. Indeed, even describing them as "people" really goes too far ... To describe what is observed by the sociologist in terms of notions like "proposition" and "theory" is already to have taken the decision to apply a set of concepts incompatible with the "external," "experimental" point of view.
>
> (Winch 1990, 109–110)

I want to be very careful here so that I am not misunderstood as either criticizing or endorsing this "anti-naturalist" position about studying social life by starting with the theories-in-use and other mental and cultural equipment characteristic of a particular social group. IR scholarship in the "constructivist" mode over the past couple of decades has certainly demonstrated the practical utility of social meaning as a starting-place when studying state action (Finnemore 1996; Weldes 1999; Bially Mattern 2004; Jackson 2006), non-governmental organizations (Finnemore and Sikkink 1998), transnational social movements (Klotz 1995; Lynch 1999; Keck and Sikkink 1998), diplomacy (Risse 2000; Neumann 2007), and so on. Many IR constructivists would agree with Onuf's claim that the study of social life ought to concern itself with the "operative paradigms ... constituted by human practices" that animate *both* the social settings that we study *and* the substantive scholarly theories that we produce (Onuf 1989, 15). But whatever

---

28   Thus, instead of sharply defined areas of contradiction and relativistic chaos, the edges of living, practical traditions are better thought of as messy "contact zones" (as in Inayatullah and Blaney 2004, 9–15) within which issues of translation ceaselessly recur. I return to this point in Chapter 7.

the practical utility of this approach, it simply does not follow in any rigorous or necessary sense from the analytical monism that I have been explicating here. There is no logical reason that we should assume a symmetry between our own situation and the situation of the people that we study.

But there is apparently something appealing about the notion that we ought to use the same models of human social action that we use to talk about ourselves as producers of social-scientific knowledge. The claim crops up in an unlikely set of places, ranging from studies of perception and misperception (Jervis 1976, 5–6) to criticisms of the rational actor model (Barnes 1996, 92–95). But the source of that appeal, I would say, is not reducible to the monistic dis-solution of Cartesian anxiety. There is no logical reason why a monist cannot deploy any one of a number of models of human social action and use that model as a way of making intelligible what is going on in the situations or cases that she is studying: rational-choice, network-structural, structural-functionalist, discursive-practical, and other scientific ontologies can be used by a monist researcher without hesitation. Nor does it follow from philosophical-ontological monism that a researcher has to engage in extensive primary-source reading or ethnographic fieldwork; these techniques, although often used by monists, do not in themselves imply *anything* in a philosophical-ontological sense. What is crucial for a monist is that she or he is concretely and practically involved in a research community and tradition, not that she or he is of necessity concretely and practically involved in and with the daily lives of the people inhabiting the social situation under investigation; it is the researcher's involvement in her or his research tradition that provides the rules, resources, procedures, and standards for generating valid social-scientific knowledge. A scientific lexicon need bear no necessary resemblance to the lexicon in use by the objects of study.

This is perhaps easier to see if we leave the social sciences for a moment and consider the natural sciences. Dualists conceptualize natural-scientific knowledge-production as some form of representation of a mind-independent external world; experimentation and theorizing are activities that are directed towards that end, and are understood in terms of their contribution to producing an account that in some way more accurately corresponds to that mind-independent world. Monists reflecting on natural science begin, as monists always begin, from concrete practical involvement, which in this case means the concrete involvement of scientists with their mechanical and conceptual equipment. Out of the complex procedures through which machines for capturing various aspects of the natural world are built and tuned, and theories about their use and the data that they provide are created—procedures that centrally involve concrete, actual, practicing scientists—knowledge is produced through what Andrew Pickering (1995, 17, 97–98) refers to as "interactive stabilization": a complex dance in which scientists and their equipment negotiate locally stable empirical claims. It would be somewhat straining the metaphor to suggest that in doing this the scientists are entering into the cultural lifeworlds of their objects of study when those objects are nonliving bits of matter; the scientists' concrete practical involvement is with their tradition and their tools, and this is sufficient to ground their knowledge-production in a way that dis-solves Cartesian anxiety (ibid., 184).[29]

Now, consider Searle's "foreign anthropologist" whom we met above, trying to make sense of a tribe that played baseball without any subjective knowledge of the rules of the game. That anthropologist is, implicitly (she has been characterized as an "anthropologist," after all), a participant in a research tradition that places great store on mentalities and theories-in-use, and often proceeds as (in Clifford Geertz's famous phrasing) "not an experimental science in search of law but an interpretive one in search of meaning" (Geertz 1973, 5). Her scholarly activities make sense in terms of her concrete practical involvement in that research tradition, and in a very important sense that involvement is what makes her production of knowledge possible: the conceptual vocabulary that she brings with her picks out certain aspects of her experience and helps her arrange them so as to advance the epistemic goals that are also given in the tradition from which that vocabulary stems. We could easily imagine a foreign *economist* producing a somewhat different set of pieces of knowledge, precisely because of the different conceptual vocabulary that she would bring to bear in the process. If we were so inclined, we could probably proliferate examples similar to this quite easily. But in any case, what is decisive for the monist stance is that each of the researchers is capable of producing knowledge as a result of her location in a research tradition, and not necessarily because of her location with respect to the people she is studying. Philosophical ontology determines many things, but it does not generate any substantive expectations.

Phenomenalism

In order to get a better sense of what a philosophical ontology concerned with the mind–world interface *does* generate, however, we have to do as we did in previous chapters and supplement it with a second philosophical-ontological wager. Monism, as with dualism, both affords certain strategies of knowledge-production and rules out others: dualism, for example, more or less necessitates a notion of truth centered around the correspondence between statements and the mind-independent external world, while monism instead equates truth with explanatory utility—with its "cash-value in experiential terms," as William James (1978, 430) once put it. However, this remains an incomplete specification of concrete research methodology, inasmuch as there are a variety of ways to implement correspondence or explanatory utility. With monism, as with dualism, the different potential strategies largely revolve around a posited relationship between knowledge and experience. Although I have used some pragmatist language about experience as a way of sketching out the monistic stance (as do Rytovuori-Apunen 2005 and Kratochwil 2007), it is certainly logically

---

29   But see Karen Barad's (2007) analysis of "entanglement," or Alexandra Horowitz's (2010) discussion of the "umwelt" of a dog. My point is not that such entry into the world of one's research subjects is impossible or unwarranted, only that it is not categorically required by a monist philosophical ontology.

possible to combine mind–world monism with the notion of transfactual truth and obtain a viable research methodology; that combination is the subject of the next chapter. For the moment, I am going to focus on the combination of mind–world monism with a phenomenalist limitation of knowledge to the realm of experience, bearing in mind the important elaborations of phenomenalism tendered over the course of the preceding chapters: phenomenalism is not simple empiricism, because it has no problem incorporating the use of equipment designed to augment the senses, and accordingly it draws its line around knowledge at the boundary of the *potentially experienceable*, whether that experience is afforded by aided or unaided *Homo sapiens*-normal senses.

What to *call* a methodology based in this phenomenalist monism, however, does present a slight problem. In the history, sociology, and philosophy of science, the generic term for non-dualist approaches to the production of knowledge that limit themselves to the realm of experience is a term that we have some familiarity with in IR already: *constructivism*, either "social constructivist" (McArthur 2006) or "constructive empiricism" (van Fraassen 1980). But in IR, "constructivism" names not a philosophical ontology, but a scientific ontology and a set of substantive foci: norms, ideas, culture, and so on. I do not want to unintentionally suggest that phenomenalist monism is somehow inherently linked to the study of culture and ideas, so instead of constructivist, the term I will use for the methodology incorporating these commitments is *analyticism*.[30] By this term and its various derivatives—analytical, analyticist—I mean to pick up several things at once: the dictionary definition of "analyze" as meaning breaking things into smaller parts or, more generally, simplifying for the purpose of increasing comprehension; Talcott Parsons' distinction between concrete and analytical systems (Goddard and Nexon 2005, 15–18; Alexander 1986); a connection to the tradition of analytical philosophy out of which some of the most important monist and phenomenalist thinkers (especially those focusing on language-in-use, following broadly in the footsteps of Ludwig Wittgenstein) come; and the distinction, originally drawn by Kant, between analytic and synthetic statements: analytic statements are true by definition, while synthetic statements stand in need of empirical evaluation.[31] An analytical stance is one that seeks to ground the production of knowledge in the concrete practical involvements of the researcher, and does so through a strategy involving the instrumental oversimplification of complex, actual situations; these deliberate oversimplifications, or *ideal-types*, are then utilized to form case-specific "analytical narratives" that explain particular outcomes. A particular and judicious use of counterfactuals, different from the use of counterfactuals by neopositivists, is an important part of constructing and evaluating such case-specific narratives.

---

30 I could also have called it "worldmaking" (for an overview, see the papers collected in McCormick 1996), but I worry that the very term sounds too much like Idealism to make much sense to dualists.

31 Note that this distinction, untenable in the abstract (as I pointed out during the discussion of logical positivism in Chapter 2), has to be modified in order to be useful; I draw on Weber to accomplish this task in the next section.

This analyticist strategy, which I will elaborate in the next two sections of this chapter by drawing on the seminal, although often misunderstood, work of Max Weber, cashes out phenomenalism and monism in two important respects: by only treating its imaginative analytical constructions as logical instruments, it limits knowledge to the phenomenal sphere; and by grounding its imaginative analytical constructions in the social and cultural world of the researcher, it exemplifies a mind–world monist way of producing knowledge. It should, but probably does not, go without saying that the specific *content* of an ideal-typical explanatory construct is not at issue here. A Waltzian model of the international system is just as ideal-typical, and Waltz's work is just as analytical, as is work that uses rational-choice, discursive-practice, world-system, or any other model of social life. The critical issues are that the model be regarded as ideal-typical—and thus not available for any kind of direct empirical verification or falsification—in virtue of its roots in a set of value-commitments on the part of the concretely embedded researcher.

Ideal-typification

Although I have quoted this passage before,[32] it is worth once more quoting Weber's definition of an ideal-type, as given in his essay establishing an editorial policy for the journal over which he and two colleagues had just assumed control (Ringer 2004, 78–79, 107–108). Rather than "a 'presuppositionless' copy of 'objective' facts," ideal-types are:

> [F]ormed through a one-sided *accentuation* of *one* or *more* points of view and through bringing together a great many diffuse and discrete, more or less present and occasionally absent *concrete individual* events, which are arranged according to these emphatically one-sided points of view in order to construct a unified *analytical construct* [*Gedanken*]. In its conceptual purity, this analytical construct [*Gedankenbild*] is found nowhere in empirical reality; it is a utopia.
>
> (Weber 1999a, 191)

Weber goes on to point out that "whoever accepts the standpoint that knowledge of historical reality should or could be a 'presuppositionless' copy of 'objective' facts will deny any value to ideal-types" (ibid., 192–193). He himself clearly does not accept the notion of a presuppositionless copy, instead placing the human "capacity and the will to deliberately take up a *stance* towards the world and to lend it a *meaning*" at the center of his reflections (ibid., 180). "The quality of a process as a 'socio-economic' event is not something that inheres 'objectively' in the process as such," Weber argues; this is a rather surprising statement to make in the editorial introduction of a journal devoted to what we would now probably call the analysis of political economy. "It is far more conditioned by the direction of our knowledge

---

32   In Chapter 1.

interest as it arises from the specific cultural significance that we attribute pertaining to the process in an individual case" (ibid., 161). In this way, the social sciences are *productive* of the world of facts, beholden not to some externally existing set of objects or their essential dispositional properties but rather to the cultural values that define and orient the investigation from the outset.

As is proper to a monist philosophical ontology, Weber's position—that cultural values shape the ways in which the world appears to the researcher— extends even to the level of the most basic *description* of a phenomenon. There simply is no way to use an apprehendable "world" (or series of externally existing objects) to limit the application of any particular ideal-typical concept, let alone to falsify it by contrasting it to some sort of mind-independent external reality. But it does not follow that theoretical concepts are somehow true by definition and never subject to refinement, as principles of an ideological program would be. As for John Dewey (1920, 145), concepts and theories are for Weber instrumental idealizations of phenomena and relationships rather than representational copies of them—and as such are always provisional rather than final, and are also firmly linked to the specific goals and purposes that animate them. "Idealization" here means that the concept or theory or ideal-typical characterization both simplifies and misrepresents, and does so for pragmatic reasons: an idealization produces a more tractable account of an object or a process by incorporating strictly non-factual notions, such as a perfectly homogenous gravitational force or the concentration of all of the mass in an object at a single point (Jones 2005, 186–188). However, if the resulting simplification and misrepresentation fail to accomplish the pragmatic explanatory goals for which they were crafted, they can be discarded—not for being *false*, but for being *useless*.

It is in this modified sense that ideal-typification produces "analytic" statements about, for example, the relationship between anarchy and the formation of balances of power. In the original Kantian formulation, subsequently adopted and expanded on by the logical positivists, analytic statements were statements where the conclusion was already implicitly contained in the premises and definitions: "all bachelors are unmarried men" is the hackneyed philosophy-textbook example. The idea was that one could evaluate the truth of the conclusion simply by paying proper attention to the propositional content of the statement itself, so that the fact that "bachelor" *means* "unmarried man" would allow one to conclude that the statement was true by definition. However, in a famous paper first published in 1951 (reprinted in Quine 1961), W.V.O. Quine demonstrated that this account of analytic statements and analytic truths was insufficient, because the very act of making sense of a statement implied the use of a vocabulary derived from worldly experience. Hence there could not be any statements that were "true by definition," unless we modified our notion of "definition" such that defining referred to a pragmatically useful way of summarizing experience—which would in turn modify the results of a logical analysis of definitions such that they could never be "true" in any kind of transcendental sense.

Instead, an analytical elaboration of the logical consequences of a particular set of definitions and depictions would provide a frictionless, artificially pure account of objects and processes—what Weber called a "utopia" in the definition above—which is intended less to predict actual concrete outcomes and more to provide a conceptual baseline in terms of which actual outcomes can be comprehended. Ideal-types are useful instruments for achieving this end, but they are not and can never be a way of reaching any kind of stable supra-empirical truth. The only acceptable arena in which to judge whether a piece of scholarship is a good one is in the realm of concrete social experience. A notion such as "class struggle" or "economic rationality" or "state sovereignty" can only be meaningfully evaluated in terms of what kinds of insights into concrete cases it generates, and any purely conceptual or theoretical elaborations of these or any other ideal-typical notions only have scientific merit inasmuch as they help us make sense of actually experienced situations: either situations we experience ourselves or situations for which we have the records of the experiences of others. According to Weber, the value of an ideal-type lies precisely in its being "entirely used as a means for the *comparison* and *measurement* of actuality," and the conceptual error to be avoided involves the slippage from ideal-type to putatively super-experiential standard (Weber 1999a, 199).

Indeed, the whole procedure of ideal-typical analysis is all about the transmutation of cultural values into useful analytical tools.[33] Weber's overall procedure can be summarized in the following diagram, in which three distinct intellectual moves link four elements.

Reading from left to right, the procedure begins in (A) the concrete sphere of values and purposes in which the researcher is concretely located. Ideal-typification begins with that researcher (I) taking a value-laden ethical stand, by which she or he locates himself or herself with respect to the values and norms in circulation in her or his social context. The (B) value-commitment(s) contained in this stance are then (II) formalized and idealized, in part by blending them with empirical observations in order to create limiting-case representations, thus producing an analytical depiction consisting of one or several ideal-types (C). Then that analytic is (III) consistently applied to specific empirical cases in order to produce (D) facts: what we have already seen David Easton, a pronounced analyticist himself, refer to as "particular ordering[s] of reality in terms of a theoretical interest" (Easton 1953, 53). These facts are both dependent on and distinct from the value-commitments that ground the ideal-typical analytic in the first place: "dependent on" because particular factual knowledge-claims are generated by a conceptual apparatus with its roots in specific value-commitments, but "distinct from" because it is possible to evaluate *scientifically* a given piece of research and the facts it produces by focusing our attention on intellectual moves II and III, and essentially ignoring intellectual move I and the specific contents of element B.

Several things are noteworthy in this description of the process. First, ideal-types are nothing like pictorial representations of objects or processes; they are

---

33   For a discussion of this issue that locates Weber even more firmly in the hermeneutic tradition, see Kedar (2007, 327–331).

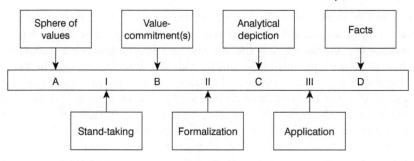

Figure 5.1 The Weberian procedure of ideal-typification

more like partial sketches that focus our scholarly attention on particular aspects of actually existing, phenomenally experienced things to the detriment of other aspects of those same things (Drysdale 2007, 43–44; Gunnell 2007, 67–68). They are less like "lenses" than they are like "caricatures." The value-commitments at the core of an ideal-type ensure that an ideal-type, whether "charismatic authority" or "liberal democracy" or even "public opinion," necessarily functions as a way of expressing values even as it calls attention to specific features of the actual world and gathers them together under one conceptual heading.[34] Second, this deliberate slant is less due to any putatively dispositional characteristics of the object under study, and more to the "emphatic points of view"—what I have labeled "value commitment(s)" (B) in the diagram above—which, in a sense, *direct* us to focus on particular aspects and not others.

From this it follows, third, that a different researcher, formalizing different value-commitments into a different analytical depiction—or even the same value-commitments into a different analytical depiction—might well focus on different aspects of the same entity or object, and as long as useful insights were generated, they would not in any simple sense be "wrong" for doing so (Weber 1999a, 192). Finally, since ideal-types cannot be falsified as one would falsify a hypothesis— comparing an ideal-type to the actual existence of the object the ideal-type was derived from would *invariably* "prove" that the ideal-type was descriptively

---

34 Recall the discussion of "public opinion" in the previous chapter, where I argued that a neopositivist would regard instruments like opinion-polls as a way of detecting an otherwise unobservable object. To this account, an analyticist would add the observation that the decision to conceptualize "public opinion" in one way rather than another could not be grounded on some feature of a mind-independent world, but could instead only be grounded in an irreducible value-commitment—and that therefore it would make little sense to say that opinion-polls were measuring a "real" thing (or, for that matter, to say that opinion-polls were *not* measuring a "real" thing). Instead, the analyticist claim would be that conceptualizing and measuring "public opinion" in the way that most contemporary opinion-polls tacitly conceptualize it is, epistemically speaking, part of the process of constructing the very object itself by blending empirical observations with value-commitments. Here again, in philosophical-ontological terms, analyticism and neopositivism inhabit different worlds.

deficient in some respect[35]—the only meaningful way to evaluate whether an ideal-type is a good one or not is *pragmatically*: that is, to examine whether, once applied, the ideal-type is efficacious in revealing intriguing and useful things about the objects to which it is applied. This last observation might be thought of as the Weberian equivalent of what Dewey called "the pragmatic rule"—"in order to discover the meaning of the idea ask for its consequences" (Dewey 1920, 163)—translated into the sphere of scientific inquiry. A good ideal-type is a useful ideal-type, an appropriate means to the analytical end that animates the scholar's scientific activity. Hence, it is quite literally nonsensical to speak of an ideal-type itself as being "valid" or "invalid," because in the sphere of scientific analysis these terms cannot be applied to analytical constructs—only to applications, and then only in a technical sense.

In this way, ideal-types can be regarded as provisional idealizations of our value-commitments; they are not simply pure types, but remain always and inextricably wrapped up with cultural and moral commitments (Duvall 2001). This monist embeddedness is what allows ideal-typical research to dis-solve any Cartesian anxiety, since ideal-types stem from the researcher's concrete practical involvements instead of remaining on the "mind" side of a putative mind–world gap. But it does not inevitably follow that all researchers inhabiting the same culture or tradition of scientific inquiry will generate or be compelled to use the same set of ideal-typical instruments. Our actual cultures and living traditions are ambiguous and flexible enough to be idealized and formalized in different ways, unless and until homogeneity is *imposed* on them, either from within or from without (Shotter 1993b, 156–159; Joas 1997, 162–163). Rather, it is the act of selecting and formalizing one's value-commitments in the process of forging one's ideal-typical tools that affords the construction of valid scientific knowledge, which means that it is always scientifically appropriate both to inquire after the value-commitments encoded into any given ideal-type and to question the way in which a scholar has idealized her declared value-commitments—to ask about the content of element B and the dynamics of move II in the diagram above. It is *not* scientifically appropriate, however, to question the specific values that a researcher holds, although it is of course ethically and even politically appropriate to do so; such questioning is not, from an analyticist standpoint, a scientific activity. Recognizing and foregrounding value-commitments, and critiquing the way that they are idealized into pieces of conceptual equipment, are logically distinct activities from the enterprise of criticizing someone's values.[36]

---

35   Along these lines, note that every theorist of bureaucracy who begins their analysis with a ritualistic pronouncement that actual bureaucracies do not function like Weberian ideal-typical bureaucracies is, quite bluntly, *missing the point*. Of course real bureaucracies do not look and function precisely like their ideal-typical conceptual limits. It would be quite surprising if they did, and it would most likely also mean that the supposed "ideal-type" was in actuality no such thing.

36   The precise character of the transmutation of value-commitments into ideal-typical analytical depictions also underpins Weber's logical claim that science cannot possibly resolve value-questions. Precisely because there cannot be definitively

Singular causal analysis

An ideal-typical analytical depiction produces not a pictorial representation of any actual situation, but a *model* of it, using categories and terms that a scholar has derived from a set of value-commitments. The distinguishing characteristic of a model is that it is neither true nor false, but is instead an instrumentally useful object that might—or might not!—express some of the relevant features of the object or process under investigation. Hence,

> the question we should ask of a model is whether or not it is similar in certain respects, and for certain uses, to a system in the real world ... "Testing" then becomes a matter not of "confirming a prediction," but assessing whether the degree of similarity between two systems is sufficient for a specific purpose.
> (Clarke and Primo 2007, 742).

In other words, the empirical application of a model is more about *calibrating* the model than about *falsifying* it; the appropriate response to a discrepancy between the model and the data is either to update the model (Johnson 1996, 86–87) or to adduce situationally specific reasons why the observed outcome in that case was not what the model ideal-typically envisions.[37]

The challenge for the phenomenalist monist is that simply constructing a set of ideal-types does little to increase or improve knowledge, because ideal-types are necessarily *general* (analytical) while actual experience is composed of *particular* (concrete) situations. If we are to have a "science of actuality" (*Wirklichkeitswissenschaft*), then we have to use these abstract notions to illuminate the concrete situations in which we are ultimately interested (Weber 1999a, 170–171). Weber's technique for doing this is not well understood, in part

---

correct values or value-commitments, the only things that science can say about any given value-commitment are that a) idealizing it in some particular way is flawed or weak or internally incoherent, and b) an ideal-type stemming from this value-commitment is not useful for comprehending some particular case or set of cases. For Weber, as for analyticists generally, there simply is no super-experiential standard for either the conduct or the scientific evaluation of scholarship, and as such it is simply inappropriate to reject a scientific study on the grounds that one does not agree with its operative values—so long as those values have been properly transmuted into ideal-types, so that the study does not simply devolve into an ideological restatement of its premises in the guise of conclusions.

37 It cannot be emphasized enough that, despite superficial similarities, this procedure has *nothing whatsoever* to do with the Lakatosian division of a scientific research programme into a "hard core" that is retained despite apparent falsifications, and a "protective belt" of auxiliary hypotheses designed to preserve the theory (recall the discussions in Chapters 1 and 3). For Lakatos and for Lakatosians, preserving the "hard core" is a conventional decision of the scientific community, while for analyticists, retaining the core commitments informing a model in the face of discrepant empirical observations is an integral part of the methodology. No amount of out-of-context invocations of Lakatos should be permitted to obscure the fact that calibrating a model and extending a research programme are, philosophically speaking, worlds apart.

because the best-known English translation of the essay where he (tentatively) develops the explanatory procedure[38] is marred by the same terminological ambiguities as most of the other older translations of Weber.[39] In addition, the argumentation is unusually dense and convoluted even for Weber, and makes use of some relatively obscure turn-of-the-last-century criminological writings in developing the argument. But certain key points can be extracted, which when taken jointly point in a more or less definite direction.

The first key point is that a concrete situation is never to be understood as resulting from or consisting of any one factor, but instead from a number of factors coming together in a case-specific way. However, actually existing entities, objects, situations, or sequences:

> [C]an *not* be viewed as the result of a struggle between causes some of which strive towards the concrete result and some of which strive against it. Instead, the totality of *all* conditions back to which the causal chain leads from the "result" had to "act together" just so and in no other way in order to let the concrete result be realized.
>
> (Weber 1999b, 289)

The reference to causal factors struggling against one another is a reference to a notion of John Stuart Mill's that the probability of an event's occurring could be expressed or interpreted as a ratio of those factors working in favor of that occurrence to those factors working against it; if the ratio tilted in one or another direction, the event either would or would not occur (ibid., 288). Mill's idea might sound a bit obscure were it not for the fact that it is *precisely* the causal logic at the core of regression analysis: take an event, decompose it into causal factors by expressing it as a function of some set of independent variables, and then— by examining multiple cases—estimate the coefficients for each independent variable, with each coefficient capturing the independent impact that the particular causal factor has on the outcome. The "struggle," then, is between those variables with positive coefficients and those with negative coefficients, and the probability

---

38   One of the maddening things about Weber's methodological writings is that he never really quite finishes fleshing out what he has in mind, although he lays out a general direction and spends some time criticizing alternatives. Part of this, I think, stems from the fact that Weber did not think of himself as either a philosopher or a methodologist, but as a teacher and researcher: he would rather *engage* in knowledge-production than *talk about* it. Another part, to be sure, stems from the fact that although Weber was many things, unfortunately he was absolutely in no way a gifted prose stylist.

39   This is why I have found it necessary to return to the German original of the "objectivity" essay in my discussion here. A reasonably good English translation of that essay can be found in Whimster (2003). Unfortunately, there is no good English translation of Weber's "Kritische Studien auf dem Gebiet der Kulturwissenschaftlichen Logik," the methodological essay from which I draw here, and the version in the 1949 Shils and Finch collection (Weber 1949) is so hopelessly mired in the terminology of mid-century logical empiricism that it obscures more than it reveals. On the problems with extant Weber translations, see Erdelyi (1992); Baehr (2001); and Jackson (2002).

of the function taking on a particular value is plainly contingent on the summed effect of those coefficients.[40]

Fritz Ringer (1997, 84–90) to the contrary, Weber's approach to causation is *not* the same as that modeled by a regression equation. Indeed, Weber's configurational approach[41] is in many ways the precise *opposite* of the kind of causal analysis so favored by neopositivists. Weber is quite dismissive of the idea that the operation of causality in the actual world (as opposed to, say, in the deliberately contrived situations of rolling dice and drawing colored balls out of urns of which scholars interested in the mathematics of probability are so fond) can be meaningfully captured in quantitative form.

> One isolates those causal components of which the judgment of a "possible" result is composed, as distinct from the totality of all of the other conditions that are *possibly conceivable* as acting together *with* them. Then one asks how the collection[42] of all of those conditions by the presence of which those conceptually isolated components are "suitable" to precipitate the "possible" result relates to the collection of all of those conditions by the presence of which they are *not* "expected" to precipitate it. Naturally, a "numerically" (in any sense) estimable relationship between these two "possibilities" absolutely in no way results from this operation.
>
> (Weber 1999b, 284)

For Weber, the isolation of causal factors does not result from a mathematical operation at all. Rather, Weber advises that researchers begin with "the creation of—let us say it calmly:—*imaginative pictures* through the disregarding of one or more components of 'actuality' that have been factually present in reality, and

---

40 Whether we work with a discrete measurement of the dependent variable in question (for example, "occurrence"/"non-occurrence") or a continuous measurement (which would permit us to talk about *degrees* of occurrence) is quite immaterial. The basic conceptual point remains unaffected.

41 Note that Weber's understanding of a causal configuration is not the same as that recently advanced by Charles Ragin (2008, 112–114), inasmuch as Ragin's procedures for identifying a causal configuration remain linked to notions of empirical generalization. Ragin derives his causal configurations inductively, by examining a large number of cases and looking for "recipes" specifying combinations of variables necessary or sufficient to cause an outcome of interest; for a causal configuration to matter to the outcome, therefore, it has to participate in a law-like generalization linking it to that outcome, since the configuration has no basis in anything but cross-case empirical observation. Ragin's generalizations may be subtle and nuanced, but they remain empirical generalizations—not case-specific combinations of analytically general ideal-types.

42 *Umkreis*, literally, "circumference" or "circle." Weber distinguishes, albeit subtly, between an "Umkreis" of factors making up a particular historical situation and a "Komplex" of ideal-typically isolated factors thought to be causally related to an outcome. The point here is that one takes the ideal-typical *Komplex* and uses it as a way of making sense out of the case-specific contents of the *Umkreis* associated with an actually existing case.

through the mental construction of a course of events altered in reference to one or several 'conditions'" (ibid., 275). In other words, researchers seeking to isolate causal factors should proceed by ideal-typifying processes and causal relations, and then trying to imagine whether the observed result in question would actually occur if things had occurred in a different way, or if factors had been present which were not in fact present. For instance, suppose the model tells us to expect that states in anarchy will seek to balance power; if we do not observe balancing, then we have to ask ourselves what other case-specific factors led to a different outcome in the particular instance.[43]

This imaginative isolation of factors allows an analyst to ascertain which factors are critical to the causal configuration responsible for the outcome in question according to a simple rule: if one can imagine the outcome taking place despite the modification of some factor, then that factor is not part of the causal configuration. It is the analyst's experiential feel for the material and the situation that allows her or him to render such judgments. Weber repeatedly makes reference to *Erfahrungsregeln*, "rules of experience,"[44] as the standard to which the analyst should refer when ascertaining whether some factor is likely to lead to an outcome or not; it is these "rules of experience" that are expressed, in analytically general form, in ideal-types. Weber terms those factors the combined presence of which we think will likely produce an effect regardless of what else transpires "adequate" causes of the effect. He also recognizes that some situations will be decisively influenced by unique, idiosyncratic factors, and terms those factors that were important to the production of an effect in a particular situation but not part of an adequate causal configuration "coincidental" causes of the effect (ibid., 286). In both cases, it is the analyst's experience that allows her or him to determine importance and significance; there is nothing of the mechanical procedure that is associated with the estimation of regression coefficients, but plenty that relates to the systematic organization of experience so as to shed light on novel situations.

The resulting account of a particular situation is, then, a kind of *singular causal analysis*. "Singular" here catches up both the emphasis on concrete, individual cases and the logical independence of a particular causal claim from being subsumed under any generally applicable law-like statements (Nickles 1977; Moore 2009). The basic idea is that using an ideal-type, or several ideal-types in combination, to help comprehend what happened in a particular case—to identify adequate and coincidental causes by referring the complex particularity of the case to various ideal-typical statements of logically general relations—does not suggest any kind of general, necessary-and-sufficient claim about the factors involved. Instead, the kind of causality at issue here involves *counterfactuals*: the researcher must make

---

43   Technically, even if we observe an outcome in accord with the analytical expectations of the model, we still have empirical work to do in order to show just how the ideal-typically isolated causal factor brought about the observed outcome. See below.

44   Frequently mistranslated "empirical rules" by translators desperately trying to make Weber into a neopositivist concerned with nomothetic generalization.

an informed judgment about alternative causal pathways that might have been followed in the particular case in question, by way of illustrating that the outcome that did in fact happen was caused by those factors that did in fact occur. Contrary to the way that neopositivists think about this (for example, Fearon 1991; Tetlock and Belkin 1996; Morgan and Winship 2007), counterfactuals for an analyticist are neither thought-experiments that flesh out the logic of a hypothesized relationship, nor the estimation of the various ways that a set of variables taking on discrete values might condition one another in different experimental or quasi-experimental trials. To the contrary, for an analyticist to claim that some factor is causal is to claim that we cannot imagine the outcome having occurred in its absence—whether these are the adequate causes that we specify in our ideal-types, or the coincidental causes characteristic only of specific cases (Lebow 2010).

Consider, for example, what it means to apply Waltz's ideal-typical model of the international system to a concrete case, such as a specific interaction between the allies within each of the Cold War alliance blocs: say, the Suez Crisis, or the deployment of American nuclear weapons in Germany in the 1980s. We first characterize the situation in terms of the categories specified in the model, which for Waltz means that we have to know the number and relations of the great powers: whether the international system is characterized by bipolarity or multipolarity. The Cold War is of course the paradigmatic example of bipolarity, so this part of the procedure is relatively straightforward. Next, we logically relate that ideal-typical characterization to the observed outcome:

> Disregarding the views of an ally makes sense only if military cooperation is fairly unimportant. This is the case both in the Warsaw Treaty Organization and in the North Atlantic Treaty Organization ... The United States, with a preponderance of nuclear weapons and as many men in uniform as the West European states combined, may be able to protect them; they cannot protect her [*sic*]. *Because of the vast differences in the capabilities of member states, the roughly equal sharing of burdens found in earlier alliance systems is no longer possible.*
>
> (Waltz 1979, 169; emphasis added)

Finally, we use the procedure of disciplined imagination to conduct a singular causal analysis of the situation—for each potentially causal factor, is it:

1   adequately causal (part of an ideal-typically specified causal configuration without which we cannot imagine the outcome having occurred)?
2   coincidentally causal (we cannot imagine the outcome having occurred without it, but it is not part of a systematic ideal-type)?
3   not causal, or incidental (we can imagine the outcome having occurred regardless of whether the factor was involved)?[45]

---

45   It may be helpful to organize our thoughts by elaborating the logical or typological property space associated with each of the relevant combinations (as in Ragin 2000 or

Sorting through these options involves the collective effort of a number of scholars with knowledge of the specific case, as they sift through and evaluate a variety of claims. Would a Democratic president have deployed nuclear weapons to Germany just as a Republican did? Would the United States have been more accommodating to the wishes of its allies if different norms of consultation had been followed in the run-up to the deployment of British and French troops in the Suez region? The first of these claims is a candidate for "coincidental cause" status; the second is a candidate for "adequate cause," although a more elaborate ideal-typical account of how norms relate to state action—an ideal-type that would complement Waltz's ideal-type—would of course have to be provided. And of course, both of these factors would have to be somehow related back to the Waltzian ideal-type wherein bipolarity rules out an equal sharing of burdens: maybe in a specific case a coincidental cause trumps the operation of the logic of bipolarity, or another adequate cause combines with systemic bipolarity to generate a specific outcome.[46]

The point here is that the use of ideal-types is, first and foremost, a way of organizing our scholarly thoughts about a specific case. There are no generally valid rules for evaluating particular counterfactual claims or for determining which ideal-types yield the most insight into specific situations; there are only specific arguments, the value and power of which depend on their empirical plausibility, and not on any kind of elaborate metaphysics about the reality of non-actual worlds or the causal properties of absences (Dowe 2009). As such, there are no transhistorically firm and fixed rules for the scholarly community to follow when making a determination about whether a factor is adequately, coincidentally, or not at all causal. There is (as in Chernoff 2005, 100–106) only the practical sense of the relevant scholars and the limits of their conceptual and empirical imaginations as illustrated and instantiated in the ideal-types that they produce and the use to which these are put (Suganami 1996, 207–209). Indeed, a well-formulated ideal-type will specify a certain amount of room for other causal factors—both adequate and coincidental—to play an explanatory role, as when Waltz suggests that even if states act as his structural ideal-type would expect them to act, a reasonable explanation of their action should involve factors other than systemic pressures (Waltz 1979, 70–72; see also Sterling-Folker 1997). In the Weberian terminology I have proposed here, Waltz has left room for coincidental causes specific to individual cases.[47] Properly understood, this

---

Elman 2005), but in the analyticist approach such property spaces are not rationales for selecting comparative cases, but techniques for clarifying our own thinking about possibilities. This is because analyticist understandings of valid knowledge-claims are logically independent of empirical generalization.

46 Or, of course, maybe the Waltzian ideal-type provides no additional insight into the situation, and it should be replaced by a different—but still equally ideal-typical—depiction of the structure of the international system (Neumann and Sending 2007).

47 See also the discussion in Goddard and Nexon (2005, 23–25). The authors also suggest that another possible response to Waltz is to articulate a parallel systemic ideal-type that incorporates IR constructivist claims about identities and the culture of the international realm (ibid., 42–47); despite Waltz's own dismissals of such

leaves room for subsequent scholarly conversations revolving around how his ideal-typical systemic factors interact with other elements of particular cases to produce specific outcomes.[48]

"Properly understood" is key here, because Waltz's account of the structure of the international system is rarely, if ever, understood in analyticist terms, even by his advocates and students—despite Waltz's own clearly declared allegiance to such a methodology. The problem is much the same with the persistent misunderstanding of rational-choice theory among some of its most outspoken practitioners and defenders, whereby an analyticist research agenda involving the systematic logical elaboration of a set of assumptions is transformed into a machine for generating falsifiable empirical hypotheses (for example, Bueno de Mesquita and Morrow 1999, 57–58; Martin 1999, 75–77; Powell 1999, 100, 104–105). Properly understood, rational-choice modeling—just as ideal-typical modeling in general—is *not about making a direct contribution to empirical generalizations* (Johnson 1996, 84–85; see also Barkin 2004); it is, rather, an exercise in elaborating an analytic based in a set of propositions about rationality, using formal tools to help ensure that no logical mistakes are made. Some of that elaboration takes the form of reinterpreting puzzling situations—situations that seem puzzling from the perspective of the analytic, such as dueling or engaging in ethnonationalist politics (as in Hardin 1995)—from the perspective of the core assumptions of the ideal-type; some of it takes the form of solving or dis-solving conceptual problems posed in other approaches by providing an analytical restatement of them (Johnson 2003).[49]

In other words, properly understood, rational-choice theory and Waltzian structural realism are on the same page, at least when it comes to philosophical ontology. Indeed, they are on the same page as world-systems history (Chase-Dunn and Hall 1997; Denemark et al. 2000), the analysis of language-games (Fierke 1998) and discourses (Weldes 1999; Hansen 2006), the analysis of security communities (Deutsch 1957; Adler and Barnett 1998), network analysis (Hafner-Burton and Montgomery 2006), and in general *any* approach to the study of world politics that proceeds not by proposing falsifiable hypotheses or transcendentally specifying indispensable elements of social and political life, but instead by postulating an ideal-typical account of a process or setting and then utilizing that

---

an enterprise, a second ideal-type would certainly be in keeping with the overall analyticist stance on knowledge-production.

48 It is an open question whether *all* analytical explanations have to include both adequate and coincidental causes, or whether there are situations in which an exclusive focus on analytically general notions expressed in several distinct ideal-types would produce reasonable explanations on its own. In many ways, this relates to a set of disputes about whether causation is a relation between events themselves, the properties of events, or the properties of events only under certain descriptions (see Nanay 2009 for a discussion of the issues involved).

49 That this analytic is grounded in a set of value-commitments is perhaps even easier to see than with the Waltzian analytic, because some rational-choice scholars have been a lot more explicit about the normative basis of their enterprise (for example, Elster 1986, 1–2).

ideal-type to organize empirical observations into systematic facts. The content of these different ideal-types varies widely, of course, as they instantiate different value-commitments, order different experiences, and foreground different objects of analysis: individual people, interpersonal and interstate interactions and transactions, discursive formations, the global political economy as a whole.[50] However, what unifies all of these substantively disparate kinds of scholarship is that they all proceed, methodologically speaking, in a way that is quite distinctive: a set of analytical claims, which frame the subsequent empirical account and so are never exposed to any sort of "testing" within it,[51] provide the framework and the vocabulary for constructing a deliberately and explicitly non-representational case-specific narrative.

Analyticism against comparison

Analyticist science, properly understood, *must* terminate in a case-specific narrative, despite the fact that not all analyticists actually produce such narratives themselves. This division of labor is not a problem, as long as some analyticist work focuses on elaborating the relevant ideal-types and models while other analyticist work focuses on utilizing those ideal-types to analyze specific cases (a point nicely made in Niou and Ordeshook 1999). Because analytical models are ideal-typical, they are of necessity stated in a logically general form and feature broad statements about identity, discourse, economic flows, rationality, and so on. But precisely *because* these are ideal-typical statements, it makes no sense to evaluate them using broad empirics: the analytical claim would almost certainly appear falsified when faced with discrepant observations. It is relatively easy to show that analytical presumptions like rational decision-making or the adherence to discursively established boundaries of action are sometimes violated in practice, but this raises no problems for any ideal-type. Rather, the proof of an ideal-type's worth comes when it is applied to a concrete and specific case, enabling a scholar to discriminate between adequate, coincidental, and incidental factors within it (even if different terminology is used for these categories).[52] Such

---

50 Indeed, sometimes there are different ideal-types at work within a single research tradition, as when the analysis of security communities largely switched from Karl Deutsch's focus on sociological transactions to Adler and Barnett's focus on individual-level mechanisms.

51 This is the case even if the analytical claims are themselves elaborated in the form of quantitative descriptions of a set of data. There is a subtle but methodologically critical difference between testing a hypothesis and analytically organizing a set of observations, in that the latter operation does not necessitate any kind of correspondence between a claim and a putative external world.

52 In fact, it does not even matter whether the scholar in question believes that she or he is actually doing causal analysis. Many, if not most, discourse analysts, for example, would likely agree with Lene Hansen's argument (Hansen 2006, 25–28) that discourse analysis cannot be causal because a) discursively produced identities do not pre-exist their deployment in practice, and hence cannot function as an independent cause of those deployments or mobilizations, and b) the mainstream discourse of causality

discrimination, because it involves a case-specific weighing of counterfactual alternatives, will take the form of a specific discussion of that case, portraying the relevance of various factors by concretely weaving them into a causal account of how an outcome was produced and where things might have gone differently (Hall 2003, 391–395).[53] Generating such case-specific narratives is what ideal-typical analytical models are ultimately for: ideal-types are means for constructing case-specific explanations, and not ends in themselves.

It follows, therefore, that analyticists should set no particular value on case-comparison as a strategy of inquiry. Neopositivists, as we have seen, require the study of multiple cases as a way of testing their hypotheses about the systematic covariation of causal factors; because the goal of neopositivist scientific inquiry is to produce knowledge that is general in that it specifies empirical laws (with appropriate scope conditions, of course, and often probabilistic rather than determinate laws), the only plausible way to evaluate a claim is to see if it holds true across multiple cases. Critical realists, while not needing studies of multiple cases with the same degree of epistemic urgency, can still use case-comparison as a way of refining their conception of the real-but-undetectable causal powers of objects and arrangements, exploring the limits of the possible effects that those underlying dispositions can manifest in the course of actual empirical events. However, analyticists can, for all intents and purposes, take or leave case-comparison without any consternation, and

---

itself purports to escape the discursive constitution of events and actions by identifying relatively immutable systematic relationships among factors. While Hansen is absolutely correct to differentiate between discourse analysis and the (neopositivist) argument that identities cause policies, it does not follow that discourse analysis is of necessity non-causal—especially if we detach "causality" from neopositivism and use the term in its more commonsensical meaning, to identify something that is important for bringing about an outcome (Kurki 2008, 138–141; Kurki and Suganami, 2012; Ruggie 1998, 94–95). Perhaps—although I do not have the space to flesh out this claim fully here—we might say that a discourse-analytical ideal-type begins with the productivity of sense-making activities by the actors involved in a situation and then elaborates a model of the relevant discourses; what is adequately causal in a discourse analysis are the tropes/commonplaces/basic discourses that are implicated in a given situation, and what is coincidentally causal (that is, important but single-case-specific), are the particular deployments and mobilizations that link identity and policy. (Note also that Hansen's objection to the separation of material and discursive factors is, strictly speaking, *not a methodological issue*, but a substantive one, and as such does not have anything to do with the question of whether discourse analysis can be in any sense causal.)

53   Somewhat confusingly, Hall (2003, 397) goes on to suggest a role for case comparisons in elucidating causal processes because "the researcher can investigate causal processes in each" of the small number of cases under consideration "in detail, thereby assessing the relevant theories against especially diverse kinds of observations." Here Hall seems to slip back into a neopositivist hypothesis-testing account of theory, where the value of a theoretical claim is intimately connected to its empirical generality instead of depending on its instrumental utility in making sense out of a *particular* case. Either that, or he is conflating the calibration of an ideal-typical model with the epistemic warrant for that model's status. In either case, linking an analytical model and an empirical generalization is, philosophically speaking, a *non sequitur*.

if a piece of analyticist research does utilize more than one case, it does so only in the pursuit of what Charles Tilly (1989, 82) calls "individualizing comparisons" that are useful for "grasping the peculiarities of each case."[54]

This in turn is because the question of whether an ideal-type is useful for the comprehension of one case or several is epistemically *irrelevant*, since an ideal-type is only an *analytically* general claim. It is critically important not to conflate a logically general claim with an empirical generalization. The "generality" of an analytical claim means that its logical form is devoid of specific references to particular empirical instances, but this emphatically does *not* mean that the relations and characteristics that it instrumentally posits have the same epistemic status as a generally valid empirical law. Keeping these two kinds of claim separate would, for example, clear up the muddled thinking that characterizes the often-heard claim that "interpretive" scholarship cannot "generalize": if this means that interpretive work focused on specific contexts of social meaning cannot produce empirical generalizations, than the statement is quite true, but if this means that such interpretive work cannot utilize or contribute to the formation of analytical ideal-types, then the statement is quite false.[55] Keeping the two types of claims separate would also call attention to the logical *non sequitur* involved in efforts to gather evidence about the frequency of inter-unit balancing across large swaths of world history and to count such evidence either for or against Waltz's analysis (as in Fischer 1992; Kaufman, Little, and Wohlforth 2007); whether or not there were balances of power in feudal Europe or ancient China tells us precisely *nothing* about the utility of Waltz's ideal-type for the analysis of the cases to which he actually applies it. The only thing that would count for or against the use of the Waltzian model would be a concrete, case-specific application of the ideal-type to these and other specific situations—but here again, the case-comparison is incidental to the analysis, as the ideal-type proves or does not prove its worth in a concrete case, and not in general.

None of this is to deny that intimate familiarity with a wide variety of cases can often contribute to the formulation of subtle and powerful ideal-types, by placing a scholar's value-commitments in dialogue with a wider range of concrete situations. Weber certainly drew on his encyclopedic familiarity with legal and economic arrangements throughout history in crafting his ideal-types of legitimate domination—rational-legal, traditional, and charismatic—and in selecting appropriate cases to use in illustrating each of those ideal-types; this historical background also allowed him to identify cases where outcomes were a function of multiple ideal-types in combination. Doug McAdam, Sidney Tarrow, and Charles

---

54   Tilly (2001) outlines a mechanism-based approach to social explanation that follows roughly the same kind of comparative logic.

55   Except for an unfortunate tendency to confuse ideal-types and testable propositions, Malcolm Williams' discussion of this issue (Williams 2000) is quite illuminating. Similarly, except for an unfortunate tendency to equate causal analysis with its neopositivist variant, Asaf Kedar's (2007) accentuation of the hermeneutic aspects of Weberian ideal-typical analysis is tremendously helpful in distinguishing between analytically general claims and empirical generalizations.

Tilly (2001) certainly drew on their similarly encyclopedic familiarity with cases of contentious politics in crafting their ideal-typical social mechanisms—brokerage, certification, and the like—and in identifying cases where these ideal-types might prove explanatorily useful; similarly, Daniel Nexon (2009; see also Nexon and Wright 2007) draws on a variety of empires throughout history in crafting an ideal-typical model of imperial rule emphasizing the segmentation of the imperial periphery, and in identifying a key coincidental cause—the European Reformations—of the collapse of intra-European empire. But all of these ideal-types prove their worth not at the level of empirical generalization, but in the specific cases where they function as components of an *analytical narrative.*[56]

By using the term "analytical narrative" here I mean to suggest that what phenomenalist monists do is to use their ideal-types to organize the empirical material of specific cases into a coherent story that differentiates between analytically general and case-specific factors responsible for bringing about an outcome and details their sequential interaction and concatenation over the time frame of the analysis. This emphatically does *not* mean that one uses a case narrative to "test" the ideal-type in question (contra Büthe 2002, 486–487); because the ideal-type is implicated in the very construction of the narrative itself, there is no way that a narrative that simply provides a concrete illustration of an ideal-type can serve as an evaluation of that ideal-type. Nor is the construction of an analytical narrative a procedure through which scholars "recast" their narratives as explicit models so that their assumptions and conclusions "can be subject to skeptical appraisal" (contra Bates, Greif et al. 1998, 14); such a procedure can certainly reveal a scholar's tacit commitments, but it is in no sense an explanation of the concrete event in question. Simply recoding an empirical account in the terms given by a particular ideal-type (and there is no reason that the ideal-type in question need be based in rational-choice theory: Alexandrova 2009, 13–14) can help to refine or clarify the ideal-type, but it does not constitute a contribution to knowledge about actual situations.

Rather, ideal-types are used to generate knowledge only when we—paradoxical though this may sound—acknowledge their *limitations.* Ideal-types necessarily make "unrealistic" assumptions and lead to "oversimplified" conclusions; they are not designed to capture the whole of actuality, but instead to help us bring some analytical order to our experiences. This means that concern about whether the assumptions of any given ideal-typical model are sufficiently "realistic" in the sense of being reflected in the empirical contours of the situation under investigation (Elster 2000; Alexandrova 2009, 19–20) is, strictly speaking, misplaced: it is simply not necessary that an ideal-type correspond to anything actual in order to serve its proper explanatory function. Ideal-types provide a set of analytical categories in terms of which empirical observations can be generated and sorted, and it is those moments where the messy complexity of actual concrete

---

56 Such analytical narrative would exemplify what Andrew Abbott (2001b) refers to as the explanatory strategy of "narrative positivism," a term I am avoiding at this juncture out of a desire not to confuse the reader even further.

experience *resists* such categorization that an analytical narrative really takes off. It is important to note that the resistance offered by actual experience is a logical consequence not of some inherent essence of a mind-independent real world that we have simply failed to grasp, but from the very procedure of ideal-typical modeling itself (Pickering 1995, 117–119): it is both the idealized character of an analytical claim and the inherent ambiguity of applying an ideal-type to a concrete situation—an ambiguity that permits different scholars to engage in such application differently, and to criticize the ways that their colleagues have applied that ideal-type—that more or less guarantees that an ideal-type will fail to grasp everything of relevance to that concrete situation.

Those moments of limitation or failure are precisely when an analytical narrative can be generated, either by introducing case-specific coincidental factors to help explain why a case does not look exactly like its idealization, or by drawing on multiple ideal-types (and perhaps additional coincidental factors) in order to account for the complexity of the observed outcome. Thus we get depictions of the Catholic Church that emphasize the tensions between rational-legal and charismatic modes of rule (Weber 1976, 142–148, 339–342), depictions of categorical inequality as arising from the concatenation and configuration of social mechanisms such as opportunity-hoarding and exploitation (Tilly 1998), accounts of how governmentality (Neumann and Sending 2010) and networked governance (Abrahamsen and Williams 2009) interact with other features of world politics to produce transformed notions of authority and security, and so on. The resulting narratives explain by relating specific features of the cases that they investigate to ideal-types stemming from our research traditions and the cultural milieu in which they are embedded, and as such contribute to a disciplining of our scholarly imaginations and an expansion in the scope of our practical grasp. Analyticism offers no more than that as a grounding for scientific knowledge, but because of its starting-point in the concrete practical involvements of scholars, it need not do more.

6 Reflexivity

It remains only to fill out the typology of wagers in the realm of philosophical ontology by elucidating a methodological position that is somewhat tension-filled from the outset: the combination of mind–world monism with a transfactual grasp of objects and entities that exceeds the limits of possible experience. This combination is particularly fraught with tension precisely because mind–world monism, as I argued in the previous chapter, denies that it is sensible to refer to a mind-independent world as the ground upon which to place valid knowledge-claims—but if knowledge is internal to concrete practical involvements, it is unclear what it might mean for knowledge to transcend experience. Neopositivism contains no such tension, because neopositivists limit knowledge itself to the realm of perception: although that knowledge refers to a mind-independent world lurking just beyond the reach of our unaided or augmented senses, neopositivists do not claim to have knowledge of that experience-transcending world directly, but limit knowledge to those objects that we can grasp. Likewise, critical realism contains no such tension, because the transfactual character of knowledge of undetectable causal powers is founded on the notion that knowledge refers to a mind-independent world; for realists, mind–world dualism provides a way to get beyond the limitation of knowledge to the phenomenal sphere. And analyticists do not claim transfactual knowledge, so for them, mind–world monism reinforces phenomenalism. The transfactual monist combination, then, looks to be somewhat philosophically fraught.

As with the philosophical-ontological wagers or stances that I have discussed in previous chapters, transfactual monism gives rise to a particular set of conceptual challenges that must be met in order to coherently provide a ground or warrant for knowledge-claims. These methodological implications are what link philosophical-ontological commitments to concrete practices of empirical research. Neopositivists require a way to bridge the gap between the mind and the world while acknowledging the limitation of knowledge to experience; this gives rise to the procedures of hypothesis-testing and empirical generalization based on systematic cross-case covariation, which together serve to ground or warrant particular empirical claims. Critical realists require a way to move knowledge past experience so as to penetrate to the sources of experience; this gives rise to the procedures of laboratory investigation or transcendental reasoning, both of which are designed to bring to light the real-but-undetectable dispositional causal powers of objects and entities, and to ground or warrant particular empirical claims by relating them to those powers. Analyticists require a way to order the experiences arising from their concrete practical involvements in the activity of research; this gives rise to the procedures of ideal-typification and the production of case-specific analytical narratives, which serve to ground or warrant particular empirical claims by relating them to their pragmatic explanatory utility.

By analogy, then, transfactual monism should be thought of as giving rise to particular and distinctive challenges of its own, and methodologies meeting those challenges should provide a ground or warrant for particular empirical claims. The central challenge, in this case, involves reconciling mind–world monism with transfactualism: precisely what can be known transfactually if there is no sense in referring to a mind-independent world that could serve as the ultimate object of knowledge? Logically, the only things that can be known for a monist must stem from the concrete practical involvements of the researcher, and so the only feasible objects of transfactual knowledge would have to be those concrete practical involvements themselves—involvements that give rise to the experiences that analyticists are content to order instrumentally. It therefore follows that the ground or warrant for knowledge generated in this manner would have to be some measure of self-awareness on the part of the researcher when it comes to her or his own research practices and the broader context in which they are embedded: not merely the animating value-commitments that are the subject of analyticist concern, but the broader social and organizational context of the activity of scientific research itself. Transfactual monism thus calls for a certain *reflexivity* of knowledge, by which the tools of knowledge-production are turned back on the situation of the scientist herself or himself; this reflexivity grounds or warrants empirical claims by relating them neither to a mind-independent world nor to a set of cultural values, but to the practices of knowledge-production themselves.

Reflexivity has a long history in the social sciences, as the capacity of human beings to reflect on their own situations has often served as the foundation of arguments for separating the social from the natural sciences. The argument is that because human beings, unlike rocks or plants, have cultures and identities and volition, human beings cannot be studied in the same way that rocks or plants are studied. When studying human beings, researchers are necessarily *internal* to their objects of analysis in a way that they are not when they study non-human objects. In Ian Hacking's (1999, 103–108) helpful terms, the terms and concepts that social scientists use when studying human societies designate "interactive kinds" in that the objects of study can themselves take over or be affected by the way that they are classified, whereas the terms and concepts in the natural sciences are generally taken to designate "indifferent kinds" because the objects of study are unaffected by how they are classified. Classifying someone as a "refugee," for example, can have a direct impact on their actions in a way that classifying a particular piece of rock as "magnetic" does not: the rock is presumably indifferent to its classification in a way that the person is not. A potential axis around which to categorize scientific knowledge, then, would involve the question of whether the objects of knowledge have the capacity for self-reflection, and something similar to this seems to lie at the foundation of the time-honored distinction between the natural and the social sciences—a distinction most familiar to us in IR as the hoary old "explanation" versus "understanding" dichotomy that I have criticized in previous chapters.

However, it is important to notice the critical slippage involved in moving from a refle*xive* science to a human capacity for refle*ction*. The difference between these two formulations is considerably more than semantic; to call a science "reflexive" is to make a claim about the mind–world hook-up characteristic of its practitioners, while a focus on "reflection" changes the question into the rather different substantive issue of the appropriate conception of action to use in generating knowledge about human societies. As such, a lot of important—if tacit—work is done when neopositivists such as Robert Keohane classify a broad swath of scholars of world politics as "reflectivists" because they "emphasize the importance of human reflection for the nature of institutions and ultimately for the character of world politics" (Keohane 1988, 382). In using this kind of characterization, Keohane redirects attention away from almost any claims about the character and status of knowledge, and towards (for example) "hypotheses about why governments create and join international regimes, and the conditions under which these institutions wax or wane" (ibid., 392). Keohane thus defines an emphasis on reflection as, in effect, an alternative hypothesis about state behavior—a hypothesis that must, just as any other hypothesis, be submitted to empirical falsification.

As is usual for neopositivists, Keohane completely bypasses philosophical ontology, reducing the difference that self-reflection might make to a simple empirical proposition.[1] This, in turn, has the effect—tacitly acknowledged, although not explicitly spelled out, by Keohane—of eliminating any constitutive differences between the natural and social sciences, because the claimed distinctiveness of human social actors can only matter if it makes the kind of empirical difference that shows up in the same methodological procedures as we would use to evaluate the empirical distinctiveness of any other natural object. Slipping between reflexivity and reflection, then, is a strategic move: in the absence of any explicit argument to the contrary, a focus on the empirical characteristics of particular objects tacitly upholds the dominant philosophical-ontological wagers of the scholarly field. In the IR context, this means upholding dualism and, to a lesser extent, phenomenalism—thus upholding a unified model of a naturalistic science the rules of which must be obeyed in order for a knowledge-claim to be

---

1   In fact, Keohane (1988, 382) even deploys the traditional logical positivist canard—since the substantive issues that we are studying are so pressing and weighty, we cannot afford the time for "an intellectually derivative and programmatically diversionary philosophical discussion"—as a way of foreclosing the methodologically and philosophically explicit kind of research on world politics that I am seeking to promote throughout this entire book.

valid. Here, as elsewhere, Keohane's apparent olive branch is a philosophical-ontological poisoned pill.[2]

Instead, a focus on reflexivity has to focus on the level of the mind–world hook-up, a level that necessarily precedes any particular empirical observations. Reflexivists take seriously the notion that the very character of knowledge itself is both inseparable from and not in any simple sense reducible to the social position and organizational practices of the scientific researcher. Just as the analyticists discussed in the previous chapter, reflexivists regard knowledge claims as *nonrepresentational*: claims cannot, even in principle, be constrained by the shape of a mind-independent reality, since the notion of "mind-independent reality" is nonsensical within a mind–world monist framework. But scientific knowledge, for a reflexivist, cannot be grounded in just any set of cultural values; instead, it is grounded in and warranted by the researcher's concrete implication (and, perhaps, imbrication) in sets of social relations that are through and through imbued with and marked by race, class, gender, and other logics of distinction. Knowledge either reinforces or challenges these distinctions—simply letting a distinction pass without comment is tantamount to permitting it to flourish uncontested.

In other words, scientific knowledge necessarily fulfills a *function*, if viewed in its full and proper social context—scientific knowledge is not simply an expression of one's class or race or gender or any other categorical or positional attribute, but instead either reinforces or challenges such social distinctions. This function is not an accidental impact of knowledge, but is intimately wrapped up with the very production of knowledge in the first place. Reflexivists are monists in that they do not believe that knowledge corresponds to a mind-independent world, but they are committed to the proposition that a systematic effort to analyze their own role as knowledge-producers and to locate themselves with reference to their broader social contexts will yield knowledge not merely of things experienced, but valid knowledge of the social arrangements that order and give rise to those experiences. Unlike critical realists, who would characterize such arrangements as "real," reflexivist scholars—foremost among them, feminists and critical

---

2   In this way, Keohane has perhaps unintentionally disclosed the chief argumentative weakness of *every* effort to ground the distinctiveness of the social sciences on any particular empirical facts about human beings: such empirical facts have to be known somehow before they can make a methodological difference, and to the extent that knowing what makes human beings distinctive is wrapped up with knowing how their capacity for self-reflection affects their behavior, there is absolutely no compelling reason why the study of human beings and their distinctiveness cannot simply be assimilated to the more general study of empirical objects. "Self-reflection" or even "consciousness" could become just another variable attribute like "charge" or "tensile strength," incorporated into sufficiently detailed equations to allow situationally-specific bounded generalizations and predictions. The argument from the putative empirical distinctiveness of human beings is thus logically unsustainable, and is as such a particularly pernicious option for those trying to argue against neopositivism to utilize. The issues of philosophical ontology that I have endeavored to lay bare throughout this book provide, in my view, considerably more defensible territory.

theorists, including postcolonial scholars—would say that knowledge of social arrangements begins not with the world, but with the self. Explicit, if necessarily incomplete, self-awareness marks the distinctive methodological strategy employed by reflexivist scholars; this is the philosophical-ontological, and not merely substantive, difference that transfactual monism makes.

Transfactual knowledge without a mind-independent world

The key to understanding how a mind–world monist could achieve knowledge of something beyond experience is to recognize that reflexivists, like analyticists, do not claim complete knowledge of any of the things that they discuss. However, unlike analyticists, this incompleteness is not displayed in case-specific narratives of the historical contingencies through which ideal-typically isolated factors concatenate, but in the ways that knowledge can contribute to its own overcoming. For reflexivists, knowledge directs action along pathways that may lead to the invalidation of those knowledge-claims themselves, as when knowledge of gender hierarchies contributes to the practical transformation of those hierarchies both in the social world at large and in the more restricted world of scientific research (Tickner 2006, 21–22). Temporality is important to this process: the overcoming of particular social hierarchies happens in the future, so the reflexivist focuses on bringing things to light in the present, contributing to the reorganization of social arrangements at some future point in time. But precisely how things will turn out is not knowable in advance:

> It is certain that prediction only means seeing the present and the past clearly as movement. Seeing them clearly: in other words, accurately identifying the fundamental and persistent elements of the process. But it is absurd to think of a purely "objective" prediction. Anybody who makes a prediction has in fact a "programme" for whose victory he [*sic*] is working, and his [*sic*] prediction is precisely an element contributing to that victory.
>
> (Gramsci 1971, 170–171)

The transfactual knowledge claimed by a reflexivist is thus not knowledge of specific outcomes; reflexivists identifying the social conditions and distinctions shaping both their situation and the situation of their broader society are not, in this sense, making falsifiable point-predictions about future events. Rather, they are seeking to disclose those historical forces and factors shaping the present, a task that they engage in first and foremost by analyzing the ways that those forces and factors are implicated in their own research practice. Reflexivist scholarship is always historical, but in a specific sense: rather than simply recording what happens, reflexivists seek to bring to light an unfolding pattern that culminates in and clarifies the present. This means that reflexivist scholarship is always *historicist* or *dialectical*, inasmuch as the conceptual vocabulary used to interrogate the social world is continually in the process of emerging from that world and then collapsing back into it as historical change is provoked by the very articulation of that vocabulary. For a reflexivist, knowing the world and changing the world are inseparable.[3]

Dialectical responses to Kant

To elucidate where this notion of knowledge comes from, it is necessary to go back to Kant's attempt to banish Cartesian anxiety by introducing categories of pure reason that would pre-structure experience. As discussed in previous chapters, Kant argued that this pre-structuring, which he called "sensibility" (Kant 1999, 155–156), would guarantee access to a knowable world without any need to worry overmuch about how and whether our minds were able to make contact with the mind-independent world. From this beginning, Kant derived a philosophical account of knowledge that only needed to refer to the operation of the universal principles of disinterested reason in order to validate itself: by attending to the universally necessary preconditions of experience and action, a rational being can bring itself and its actions[4] into accord with securely grounded reasonable laws that it gives itself out of pure reason alone:

> Every rational being as an end in itself[5] must be able to regard itself with reference to all laws to which it may be subject as being at the same time the legislator of universal law... There follows also that its dignity (prerogative) of being taken above all the mere things of nature implies that its maxims must be taken from the viewpoint that regards itself, as well as every other rational being, as being legislative beings (and hence they are called persons) ... every rational being must so act as if it were through its maxim always a legislating member in the universal kingdom of ends.
>
> (Kant 1993, 43)

In the sphere of empirical science, this rational orientation means attending to the rationally necessary presuppositions of practical experience; in the sphere of moral deliberation, this rational orientation means abandoning any particular objects of experience in order to operate in a purely universal frame of reference

---

3   Note that this inseparability comes about not because reflexivists forsake the ground of science by placing practical, worldly effects before the pursuit of knowledge, but because reflexivist knowledge *itself* is inextricable from the concrete practical situation in which it arises. So the pursuit of reflexivist knowledge in accord with the philosophical-ontological principles of transfactual monism produces effects, but this does not alter the scientific status of reflexivist scholarship.

4   Kant explicitly (Kant 1993, 23–24) denies that the abstract principles of universal reason enjoy any special relationship with the particular constitution of human beings, but instead argues that these principles apply to "every rational being as such." Thus my use of the impersonal pronoun.

5   Translation slightly modified, since the translator persists in using "himself" where Kant is very clearly using the impersonal and inhuman term *"vernüftige Wesen"* (rational being) instead of more human/personal terms like *"Mensch"* (human being) or *"Mann"* (man).

(ibid., 47–48). In both cases, however, the overarching principle is that the rational being gives knowledge to itself, either through pure rational deliberation or through the rational and rationally discernible foundations of all possible experiences.

These formulations show Kant at his most unambiguously monistic, operating in a conceptual region where, as John Shotter (1993b, 24–26) might put it, the distinction between "making" and "finding" is not altogether clear: when a rational being formulates knowledge of the world, is that rational being "finding" or "making" the objects to which it refers? As I have noted in the previous chapter, there is certainly ample material in Kant to support a decidedly monistic account of knowledge. Indeed, Ian Hacking (1999, 40–47) refers to the various strains of social constructionist work in disciplines ranging from mathematics to educational psychology as rooms in Kant's house, inasmuch as they all share with Kant the basic position that knowing about anything requires some measure of input on the part of the knowing subject and cannot be simply a reproduction of the external world in thought (see also Adler 2005, 96–97). But Kant, of course, insisted on the *universality* of the reason that works through reasonable beings in constructing the known world—a universality that left essentially no room for any discretion on the part of the knowing subject. To the extent that Kant was a monist, his was a monism every bit as resolutely anti-pluralist as the most orthodox Enlightenment dualism.[6]

Not so Kant's successors, who successively backed away from Kant's demand for universality by calling attention to the historically embedded character of the logical presuppositions of experience in different eras and by different researchers.[7] Certain British empiricists such as William Whewell (Moses and Knutsen 2007, 173–176), along with the leading lights of the German historical

---

6   Kant's anti-pluralism is perhaps nowhere on display more clearly than in an often-neglected footnote in the only one of Kant's essays that regularly gets cited in IR—namely, the essay on "perpetual peace." In the First Supplement to that essay, Kant declares: "*Differences in religion*: an odd expression! Just as if one spoke of different *moralities*. No doubt there can be different kinds of historical *faiths*, though these do not pertain to religion, but only to the history of the means used to promote it, and these are the province of learned investigation; the same holds of different religious *books* (*Zendavesta*, the *Vedas*, *Koran*, and so on). But there is only a single *religion*, valid for all men in all times. Those [faiths and books] can thus be nothing more than the accidental vehicles of religion and can only thereby be different in different times and places" (Kant 1983, 125). Kant may be a liberal humanist, but he is also very clearly a rather pronounced absolutist with little tolerance for political and social ambiguity. On Kant as thereby promoting a kind of anti-politics, see Behnke (2008).
7   No small part of their doing so was related to Kant's failure to accomplish the supreme task that he set for himself and his philosophy: to demonstrate conclusively that the principle of individual autonomy ("freedom") was given by reason alone, and was thus transcendentally grounded rather than simply being a contingent product of historical accidents. Had Kant succeeded in his endeavor, he would have ended philosophy by proving an irrefutable truth from which everything else could be derived. That he, like Descartes, did not succeed is, in fact, a condition of possibility for the fact that we are continuing to grapple with these methodological problems at all.

tradition (Ringer 2004, 18–30), carried this line of thinking to its logical conclusion: the presuppositions of any particular knowledge-producing activity were in important ways *sui generis*, and reached no further than themselves. It was left for Max Weber to push past this kind of historical and cultural relativism and articulate—as we have seen in the previous chapter—the procedure of ideal-typification that would both *accept* the historical and cultural diversity of different value-orientations *and* hold out the possibility of generating knowledge that was not simply relative to a particular set of values. In so doing, Weber both followed and criticized the neo-Kantian thinkers of his intellectual milieu (Bruun 2007, 84–86), draining abstract logical formulations of any pretense to universal validity by treating them instrumentally as conceptual tools, even as he clearly maintained the indispensability of such analytically general formulations for the production of scientific knowledge. By radicalizing and historicizing Kant, Weber—as with other analyticists—replaced universalism with pluralism.

However, pluralism comes with a cost. The urgency of Kant's demand for universality was, of course, integrally linked to the value placed on universal validity by the Enlightenment as a whole: only the claim to universal validity would suffice to ground and warrant the claims of Enlightenment philosophers and activists that traditional ways of doing things needed to be re-evaluated and overturned so as to make them less arbitrary and more in line with something decisively better than the simple weight of existing custom. This critical disruption, with its demand for more secure foundations than were presently in evidence, threatened to collapse into nihilistic anxiety if those foundations were not provided (Bernstein 1992, 16–17). However, the analyticist dis-solution of such anxiety deliberately and decisively refrains from offering anything that can play the role of a new and better foundation for knowledge; living in a pluralistic world means accepting that there simply is no universally compelling way to decide between competing claims about ultimate values and resigning oneself to, in effect, struggles between different gods (Weber 2004, 22–24). The stage is thus set for a certain amount of irreducible mutual incomprehension between different groups of people and their warranted knowledge-claims, and the concomitant inability to claim that any particular claim is transcendentally and universally valid in the sense that Kant (or Descartes before him) required. For those committed to universality, the abyss beckons.

Fortunately, an alternative to existential despair might be found[8] in a different set of extensions of Kant, equally monist but more committed to a reconstitution of universality. Kant himself suggested the way forward in an essay proposing a universal history of reason. Because "the greatest problem for the human species" is "to achieve a universal civil society administered in accord with the right"— a civil society in which "the greatest freedom, and thus a thoroughgoing antagonism

---

8   At least for those interested in studying social life. It is unclear how, if at all, the dialectical extension of Kant I am outlining here would address Cartesian anxiety in the natural sciences; see Plotnitsky (1995) and Barad (2007) for a few preliminary thoughts along these lines.

among its members" is combined with "a precise determination and protection of the boundaries of that freedom, so that it can coexist with the freedom of others" (Kant 1983, 33)—it followed that the correct way to think about human history was as a story of how that civil society had been progressively developed and would continue being developed in the future. If one looked at history this way, Kant suggested,

> one will discover a course of improvement conforming to rules in the constitutions of the nations on our continent (which will in all likelihood eventually give laws to all others) ... one will, I believe, discover a guiding thread that can serve not only to clarify the thoroughly confused play of human affairs, or to aid in the political arc of prophesying future changes in and among nations ... It will also clear the way for ... a comforting view of the future, one in which we represent from afar how the human species finally works its way up to that state where all the seeds nature has planted in it can be developed fully and in which the species' vocation here on earth can be fulfilled.
>
> (Ibid., 39)

However, Kant never developed this project of philosophical history, in effect placing his bets on pure reason rather than on historical development to provide an adequate foundation for universal claims. Instead, it was G.W.F. Hegel who seized on Kant's proposal and developed what might be thought of as an *a priori* philosophical history that would bring "the categories of reason" into the empirical study of world events. For Hegel, philosophy

> proceeds according to the categories of reason, whereby it knows the true value and status of that understanding. But in the process of scientific understanding as well, it is necessary to separate the essential from the so-called inessential, and to give it proper emphasis. For this to be possible, however, one must be acquainted with what is essential. But what is essential in world history, when it is seen as a totality, is the consciousness of freedom, and the determinations of that consciousness in freedom's development. To direct attention toward this category is to direct it at what is truly essential.
>
> (Hegel 1988, 68)

Hegel argued that pure speculative philosophy had concluded that "reason rules the world," and that in regards to world history, this meant "that world history has therefore been rational in its course" (ibid., 12). To reflect philosophically on history was to disclose how reason—which Hegel also refers to as Spirit[9]— had been subtly at work over the ages, driving towards its final goal: "Spirit's

---

9   *Geist*, which can also mean "mind." Hegel deliberately plays on some of the ambiguities of this term in German, blurring the distinction between the rational conclusions of one mind and the conclusions of rational deliberation as such. The

consciousness of its freedom, and hence also the actualization of that very freedom" (ibid., 22). This, and this alone, would give meaning to historical events:

> However, as we contemplate history as this slaughter-bench, upon which the happiness of nations, the wisdom of states, and the virtues of individuals were sacrificed, the question necessarily comes to mind: What was the ultimate goal for which these monstrous sacrifices were made? ... And in this perspective the events that present such a grim picture for our troubled feeling and thoughtful reflection have to be seen as the *means* for what we claim is the substantial definition, the absolute end-goal or, equally, the true *result* of world-history.
>
> (Ibid., 24)

There are two important points here intended to help to address Cartesian anxieties. First, the intimate connection between the concepts with which we interrogate and make sense of history and the historical process itself helps to allay the fear that our knowledge is disconnected from its object. Notions such as "freedom" are, for Hegel, not just moral or political claims, but are equally components of the grand reasonable design of human history. The dominance of reason over the merely empirical world,

> is not just to be taken as a presupposition of our science, but as a summary of the totality—as the *result* of the discussion upon which we are embarking, a result that is known to *me* because I already know that totality.
>
> (Ibid., 13)

The very act of reasoning about history is itself part of the process of Spirit's self-consciousness of its freedom, and not an arbitrary imposition of a pattern where none exists. Thus there is no need to worry about a disjuncture between the world and our knowledge of it, because the unshakable foundation of knowledge is not a grasp of oneself as a thinking thing, but a grasp of reason as animating both the course of events and our reflections on those events.

The second anti-Cartesian point in Hegel's account is a bit more subtle and involves a notion quite foreign to Descartes: the notion that reason *itself* changes and evolves over time, and that what reason gives at one stage of history might not be what reason gives at a subsequent stage. Descartes has no place in his conception for such a notion. Indeed, Descartes' rational knower appears, for all intents and purposes, never to have been a child who would have had to acquire a conceptual vocabulary by being brought up in society, but instead seems to have sprung into existence as a fully formed adult (Elias 1991, 111–113). So neither the knower nor the reason that he uses to create and evaluate knowledge has ever developed or changed—Descartes has no place in his conception for *learning*,

---

German term does not have the ghost-like connotations that the word "spirit" can have in English, so that reading should be avoided when looking into Hegel.

let alone for the improvement of the process of reasoning itself. Hegel, to the contrary, foregrounds just such a process by arguing that Spirit achieves self-consciousness of its own freedom only by setting itself a series of challenges to overcome historically. In this way, Hegel regards world history to be "the exhibition of the Spirit, the working out of the explicit knowledge of what it is potentially" (Hegel 1988, 21). This is not simply a linear manifestation of timeless truths, but is instead the historical emergence of new and better forms from the shells of old forms:

> The process of history thus appears, in its existence, to be an advance from the imperfect to the more perfect, but one in which the imperfect stage is not to be grasped abstractly or *merely* as that which was imperfect, but rather as that which at the same time has its own opposite within itself—i.e., it has what is called "perfect" within it, as a germ or as the source of its drive ... the imperfect, as its own opposite within itself, is the contradiction which certainly exists, but which is, by the same token, negated[10] and resolved. This is the drive, the internal impulse of spiritual life, the drive to break through its own shell of naturalness, sensuality, and self-estrangement, in order to arrive at the light of consciousness, its own selfhood.
>
> (Ibid., 60–61)

To illustrate this process, Hegel outlines the progress of the self-consciousness of freedom throughout world history as stretching across four historical "worlds," each of which knew something partial about freedom that its successor world was able to integrate into its own self-organization. Thus, for Hegel the "Oriental" world is a world in which an absolute despot lords over the masses; the tensions and contradictions between those masses and that absolute ruler are resolved[11] into the individualized ethical culture of Greece and the formal universality of Roman law, both of which put limits on sovereign arbitrariness. But freedom only reaches full realization in the Germanic world, in which individuals as such are free because they are only subordinated to reason, and subordination to reason is no limitation on freedom at all. In this manner, Hegel argues that the conclusion that Kant was trying to reach on the basis of pure reason can instead be reached

---

10 "Negated" here translates *aufgehoben*, which is a form of the word *aufheben*—the word that gives Hegel translators and interpreters most of their frustrations. In ordinary German, *aufheben* simply means "to lift" or "to abolish," but in Hegel's use it also has traces of notions like "preserve" and "transcend." Many translators prefer "negate," but some also use "sublate." In any event, the point here is that Hegel always maintains that newer, more perfect/reasonable forms both improve on and distance themselves from, while retaining links to, the forms that they replace—and that this happens both in history and in philosophy.

11 *Aufheben*, again. Note that for Hegel this historical process does not mean that the "Oriental" world somehow evolves into a place of greater freedom, instead, "history passes over" into another world. It is somewhat unclear precisely what Hegel supposes will happen to the places that history leaves behind; for a somewhat ominous interpretation of what he might have meant, see Blaney and Inayatullah (2010).

by a rational examination of historical practice and a presentation of the ways in which the dilemmas produced by an imperfect realization of universal freedom can be resolved in a future set of concrete political and social arrangements. This dialectic, whereby the principle of freedom in effect calls into being its own opposite through its imperfect realization and thus sets up the need for a subsequent reconciliation of those opposing principles, is for Hegel the motor of history, and is also the guarantor that our own current concepts and principles are securely grounded: rational consideration of our own situation lets us participate in the grand process whereby reason comes to fulfillment in the actually existing world.

It is this basic dialectical movement that provides the reflexivist answer to the problem of producing valid knowledge. Conceptions arise from practical involvements, but not from the practical involvements of a scientific researcher in a world of culturally specific values and traditions of research; instead, the practical involvements in question locate the researcher within a broader historical pattern to which her or his research activity contributes. And not just the individual researcher: the practical involvements of interest to reflexivist scholars are in no way limited to elements of an individual's biography, but encompass the scholarly field to which the researcher belongs, and the wider society in which the researcher participates (Bourdieu 2004, 93–94). Paying attention to the social conditions of possibility for knowledge-production allows the researcher better to locate her or his claims in relation to their presuppositions, and thus contribute to a dialectical process through which those social conditions are transformed—first by being seen clearly, and then perhaps by being more or less deliberately replaced.

In this way, progress, whether conceptualized as freedom, liberation, emancipation, democratization, or some similar notion, is vital to such a dialectical conception of knowledge. The whole wager of a reflexivist approach to knowledge-production is that the actually existing empirical world is *not* simply "one damn thing after another" but that instead history is, in a very real sense, *going somewhere*—and it is going somewhere that the researcher, through the act of producing reflexive knowledge, can contribute to. Where precisely history is headed is a matter of no small controversy among reflexivists, and nowadays almost no one would be quite as brash as Hegel in declaring that they had grasped the inner essence of the logic of history, or that the logic in question involved the idea of freedom coming to realization in practice. Indeed, almost immediately after Hegel's articulation of this dialectical historical logic, scholars fell into a long series of disputes about precisely what the implications of this point of view were for both scholarly and political practice. While the specific content of history's direction were (and remain) open to discussion, the basic notion that reflecting on how knowledge was produced could contribute to some kind of positive social change was not.

One of the central axes of the nineteenth-century debate about these issues involved Hegel's emphasis on ideas as the guiding thread linking history together in a rational way. Those intellectuals interested in upholding the existing order tended to prefer Hegel's form of idealism,[12] while those opposed to the existing order tended to point to other, less ideal forms of historical dialectic that served the same epistemic *function* as Hegel's self-actualizing Spirit (Ringer 1969, 85–87, 109–111; Stern 1961, 277–288; Sieferle 1995, 11–14). Perhaps the most well-known of these critiques, both of Hegel and of the whole social-theoretical tradition involving a focus on ideas, is of course Karl Marx's inversion of Hegel via a "criticism of the speculative philosophy of right" that "leads on to *tasks* which can only be solved by *means of practical activity*" (Marx and Engels 1978, 60). Marx argued that instead of focusing on the dialectic of the idea of freedom and its imperfect realization, scholars ought to focus on the material dialectic produced by the alienation of the laborer from the product of his labor.

> [T]he object which labour produces—labour's product—confronts it as *something alien*, as a *power independent* of the producer. The product of labour is labour which has been congealed in an object, which has become material: it is the *objectification* of labour ... the worker is related to the *product of his labour* as to an *alien* object. For on this premise it is clear that the more the worker spends himself, the more powerful the alien objective world becomes which he creates over-against himself, the poorer he himself— his inner world—becomes, the less belongs to him as his own ... How would the worker come to face the product of his activity as a stranger, were it not that in the very act of production he was estranging himself from himself?
>
> (Ibid., 71–73)

For Marx, it mattered very little whether the labor in question was manual labor or intellectual labor. Much as Hegel took the situation of the *thinker* as his starting-point for self-reflection, Marx took the situation of the *worker* as his starting-point, and both pointed to a dialectical relationship between subject and object that arose from that situation as the subject's effort—intellectual or physical or both—isolated some product and gave it the appearance of self-sufficiency by allowing the social relations that produced it to fade into the background. For Marx, this dialectical relationship led to the alienation of the laborer from himself, an alienation that had to be abolished[13] through a social and political revolution that would restore the social relations of production to the foreground and thus heal the breach between the laborer and the products of her or his labor.

---

12 Note, in the light of the discussion of dualistic idealism in the previous chapter, that Hegel's distinctive reworking of idealism avoids the charges of subjectivism because of its emphasis on how the whole world emerges from the movements of ideational phenomena. For Hegel, as for his successors in this kind of "objective idealist" tradition, ideas do not affect a mind-independent world; rather, apparent mind-independence is one moment in an ongoing dialectical process. On this point, see the discussion of the various forms of post-Hegelian and post-Marxist idealism in Bevir and Rhodes (2006).

13 Again, *aufheben*, as in Marx and Engels (1978, 65).

Notice that although Marx is certainly not talking about "ideas," his account of knowledge-production is *just as monist as Hegel's*. It is not the case that there is a "material" world that somehow pre-exists and confronts laborers, but to the contrary, the externality of the world is produced in the process of labor itself. Any apparent duality of world and worker is, for Marx, secondary to the process of production itself, much the same way that any apparent duality of the idea of freedom and its institutional realization in a particular historical moment is for Hegel secondary to the process of Spirit's self-actualization.[14] The difference between Marx and Hegel, then, involves their substantive starting-point or scientific ontology: Hegel begins with reason, Marx with labor, but both locate their analyses in concrete practical involvements. Both also see their theoretical work as helping to advance the historical dialectic in which they are participating, by theorizing and bringing to consciousness those historical conditions that will allow a proper appreciation of the situation of themselves and their readers in their society at large.[15]

In this way, reflexivist notions of knowledge can be as critical of the existing social order as those advanced by critical realists, but on somewhat different philosophical grounds. For critical realists, the "critical" aspect of their knowledge involves the disclosing of as-yet-unrealized possibilities afforded by the real-but-undetectable causal powers of objects, including human beings and their social relations; in order for those possibilities to be scientifically valid ones, they have to be grounded in some trans-observational technique for isolating and investigating causal powers, such as a laboratory or a set of transcendental arguments. For reflexivists, on the other hand, neither a laboratory nor a transcendental argument is required; what is required instead is a detailed self-examination of the social and historical conditions under which knowledge is produced. The result of this kind of examination—an examination that poses a set of dialectical relationships between a knowledge-producer and her or his own conditions—is not a disclosing of real-but-undetectable causal powers, but a way of helping the members of a given society come to a clearer understanding of their situations:

> A critical theory helps the members of the group to self-knowledge by making explicit for them the epistemic principles they already use (but of which they are not perhaps fully aware) and by giving them knowledge of the implications of these epistemic principles for the rest of their beliefs, i.e. a critical theory gives them knowledge of what changes would result if they were to apply the standards of rationality they tacitly accept in a consistent and thorough-going way to the whole of their beliefs.
>
> (Geuss 1981, 63)

---

14 For a similar argument, gesturing towards the development of this theme in Vico and later in Gramsci, see Cox (1996b, 93–94).

15 Although I have emphasized the direction of European thought that tended in the direction of a revolutionary transformation of society, there was also an evolutionary path, equally monist and transfactual; for a discussion, see Adcock (2009).

Hence, a critical theory in the reflexivist sense is a form of philosophical therapy: it brings to light the actually existing conditions under which knowledge is produced, foregrounding the dialectical relationship between knowledge and its conditions, so that a clearer view of things can be achieved. What warrants such knowledge is less its correspondence to anything external, and more its ability to delineate the relevant social conditions in a way that summarizes the position of the scientist herself with respect to those conditions and allows for the possibility of transcending them.

The problem of the intellectuals

The reflexivist call for self-awareness poses a particularly challenging problem for the products of scientific intellectual endeavor, inasmuch as those products often claim—in their own terms—to be something other than partisan interventions or simple statements on behalf of one or another group in society. Part of the appeal, and part of the very logical structure, of an empirical claim about (for instance) the causes of a given war is that the claim is not just an effort to rally support for a cause; implicit in a claim along the lines of "this war was fought because of the distribution of natural resources such as oil, which they had and we wanted to secure some preferential access to" is the notion that this is a *warranted* claim, a claim in support of which appropriate and compelling evidence can be presented. The dualist approach to such a claim is to look for ways to ascertain its correspondence to the mind-independent world, either by trying to falsify the proposition via evidence about the reasons for war-fighting or by delineating the causal powers of natural resources and the desire for a certain kind of access to them. Such a correspondence would guarantee that the claim was something other than a partisan rallying-cry. The analytical monists discussed in Chapter 5, on the other hand, would cash out such a claim by first reconstructing the claim as consisting of an ideal-type derived from a set of value-commitments, and then asking whether appropriate and sufficient evidence had been presented that would warrant the explanatory claim; in this case the ideal-type would involve a depiction of social action as operating within a set of constraints imposed by the distribution of natural resources, and the evidence required would be an analytical narrative of how the war came about that illustrated how that factor operated in the case in question.[16]

---

16 But the requisite analytical narrative would not actually be able to warrant a monocausal claim along the lines of "this war was fought because of the distribution of natural resources such as oil"; the best it could do would be to demonstrate that the distribution of natural resources was an important part of the story, in the counterfactual sense that absent this factor we cannot plausibly imagine the war as having been fought. As discussed in the previous chapter, analytical monism provides no epistemic resources for ascertaining the relative weight of causal factors in any kind of general sense, and therefore an analytical monist in a punctilious mood would most likely reject the claim as *prima facie* unwarrantable without modification.

Neither of these two options, however, is open to the reflexivist. As monists, reflexivists reject the notion that empirical statements can be warranted by their correspondence to a mind-independent world; instead, mind and world are not separate, and an empirical claim must be value-expressive rather than representational. But as transfactualists, reflexivists are not fully satisfied with the analyticist approach of rooting concepts and theories in a set of value-commitments that are not themselves subject to further scientific critique or dialectical transformation. Instead, the hope is that the tools of reason and science can themselves be turned back on the presuppositions of a given account, opening the possibility of modifying or replacing them in a non-arbitrary manner (Bourdieu 1990, 15–16; see also Alker 1990).

This latter point of differentiation between types of monism requires some brief elaboration. There is more than a trace of an existentialist valorizing of commitment in the analyticist separation of the sphere of values from the sphere of empirical science; although rooted in value-commitments, what makes a given ideal-type scientifically useful is not its conformity to fundamental or universal moral principles, but the consistency and rigor with which a researcher explores the logical implications of a given set of value-commitments sufficiently formalized into an ideal-type. This means that it is quite possible to acknowledge the scientific value of an ideal-type the value-laden basis of which one quite vehemently rejects or, at any rate, does not completely accept, which is arguably Weber's position with respect to the Marxian categories of class analysis (Weber 1976, 531–540). But what cannot be done from an analyticist standpoint is to collapse the scientific and value spheres into one another, and to claim either that the empirical utility of a given ideal-type validates or verifies the value-commitments underlying it, or that there is a way to resolve differences of value-commitment scientifically. Because analyticists limit knowledge to the realm of possible experience, this presents no special problems, as it is sufficient for them that knowledge be a useful account of some empirical case or cases of interest—sufficient in a way that it is *not* sufficient for reflexivists, who call for a more transfactual basis on which to ground their claims.

So it would appear that reflexivists face a particular challenge in trying to maintain simultaneously that their knowledge-claims are something other than partisan political interventions and that they are rooted in the social situations of the scientific researchers advancing those claims. Rootedness must be maintained in order for reflexivist claims not to be mistaken for falsifiable hypotheses or other representational conjectures. Similarly, the distinction from partisan intervention must be maintained in order for reflexivist claims not to be mistaken for impositions of an arbitrary set of values or standards on the audience. The only way to accomplish both of these goals at once is to demonstrate that the investigator and the audience *already* share a set of standards, and that those standards are themselves rooted in the common social situation that both already inhabit. This, as mentioned above, is precisely the critical project of reflexivist theory (Geuss 1981, 63). As such, a reflexive social scientist performs the dual operation of excavating the presuppositions that implicitly inform the designation of certain kinds of worldly claims as knowledge and then presenting them in such a way that they provoke self-examination on the part of those who receive them. The tacit presuppositions in question are not simply plucked at random from some ethereal realm of abstract philosophy, however; they are instead concretely and specifically rooted in an analysis of the role that knowledge plays in society.

In other words, warranting a reflexive scientific claim is intimately intertwined with what has traditionally been called "the problem of the intellectuals": what is it that scientific researchers are doing when they engage in the production of knowledge? Every piece of reflexivist research relies on an answer to this question, whether tacitly or explicitly, and every such answer provides a reply to the charge of raw partisanship by locating the scientific researcher and her or his research with respect to the broader social and intellectual context within which she or he is operating. It is important that this locating—which of course need not be actively accomplished in each individual piece of research, as researchers often rely on the more elaborate analyses of the social conditions of the production of knowledge performed by others, or by themselves in other work—not be regarded as a mere clarification of the researcher's values, but instead as the result of a detailed examination of how society functions. Just as in the case of any other reflexivist knowledge-claim, the locating of a piece of reflexivist research is itself dialectically related to its social conditions of production, both delineating them and potentially contributing to their transformation. Hence location statements are not purely descriptive statements, but are instead provisional articulations that are both grounded in the present and directed from the past towards the future.

Roughly speaking, there are three answers to the problem of the intellectuals, each of which provides different grounds for the distinctiveness of scientific knowledge. Either scientific researchers have a privileged and holistic view of society because of their specific position within it, or their allegiance with a particular group within society affords them an epistemically superior perspective on things, or the promulgation of multiple perspectives can contribute to an enhanced kind of objectivity. While these are oversimplified categories, and in practice researchers often draw on multiple answers, as a rough first cut we might associate the first view with traditional sociology of science, the second with the broadly defined tradition of revolutionary knowledge, and the third with the "standpoint epistemology" articulated by feminist and post-colonial thinkers. Each of these answers can serve as a philosophical basis for reflexivist research.

Intellectuals and the holistic view

Traditionally, the production of scientific knowledge was thought of as the province of specially disinterested thinkers, detached from the demands of everyday life by their location in a laboratory or a university. Conceptualized in this way, intellectuals would be free to formulate accounts of social life unaffected by particular controversies raging within the societies in question, reaching past partisanship to elucidate more general conditions. Hegel's notion (discussed above) of the philosophically inclined historian as able to summarize the rational process of history based on his special position grounded in reason rather than in everyday practical concerns conveys this attitude quite well: by detaching from everyday social life, the rational thinker could better appreciate the universal significance of particular events, without actually having to participate in the wars or conquests under investigation.

It might seem that this kind of social positioning of intellectuals as detached or disinterested would obviate the need for any kind of reflexivity at all. But in the wake of nineteenth-century criticisms of Hegel for ignoring or downplaying the distortions of reason imposed and sustained by social relations of dominance and control, theorists seeking to position intellectuals as disinterested and thus capable of gaining a uniquely clear view of the totality of social life did not rest content with positing that intellectuals were *already* in that position, but instead concerned themselves with elucidating ways that intellectuals—social scientists in particular—could *achieve*, or at least approximate, that kind of disinterestedness. Reaching a disinterested total view became for these thinkers both a normatively desirable goal and the product of a specific historical process: the advent of widespread social mobility. The analysis of that process and its implications, in turn, became one of the first formulations of the task of the sociology of knowledge.

In Karl Mannheim's influential account, the "detached perspective" sought by the theorist of society can be achieved by an intensification and development of the sense of distance from one's own presuppositions brought about by encounters with very different ways of thinking. These encounters were initially provoked either by moving from one social context to another, or by inhabiting the kind of dynamic environment where "two or more socially determined modes of interpretation come into conflict and, in criticizing one another, render one another transparent and establish perspectives with reference to each other" (Mannheim 1936, 282). Mannheim suggested that one is never quite aware of how much one's social location affects one's perceptions and arguments until one is brought into contact with a different way of thinking, an encounter that throws into sharp relief the way that social conditions shape thought. But this is far from the end of the story:

> Every analytical step undertaken in the spirit of the sociology of knowledge arrives at a point where the sociology of knowledge becomes more than a sociological description of the facts which tell us how certain views have been derived from a certain *milieu*. Rather it reaches a point where it also becomes a critique by redefining the scope and limits of the perspective implicit in given assertions ... An analysis based on the sociology of knowledge is a first preparatory step leading to direct discussion, in an age which is unaware of the heterogeneity of its interests and the disunity of its basis of thought, and which seeks to attain this unity on a higher level.
>
> (Ibid., 285–286)

Mannheim's concern, then, is to achieve or constitute a unity that is not itself readily apparent in society. The unity in question involves the general intellectual world, or "total ideology," characteristic of a social group—a unity that is not reducible to the contents of the heads of the individuals involved.

> Although this mental world as a whole could never come into existence without the experiences and productive responses of the different individuals, its inner structure is not to be found in a mere integration of these individual experiences ... As soon as the total conception of ideology is used, we attempt to reconstruct the whole outlook of a social group, and neither the concrete individuals nor the abstract sum of them can legitimately be considered as bearers of this ideological thought-system as a whole. The aim of the analysis on this level is the reconstruction of the systematic theoretical basis underlying the single judgments of the individual.
>
> (Ibid., 58–59)

For Mannheim, the intellectuals to whom this unity appears occupy a unique position in society: as bearers of the intellectual unity of the world of a given social group, they can shape the group as a whole through the claims that they articulate. This "integration of many mutually complementary points of view into a comprehensive whole" comes about because of the "present structure of society" within which "politics as a science is for the first time possible": only the nonpartisan intellectual can appreciate that "opposing views and theories are ... mutually complementary" and can properly and explicitly summarize what individuals occupying other positions in society can only tacitly presume (ibid., 149). By doing so, they drive social progress:

> Attempts at synthesis do not come into being unrelated to one another, because each synthesis prepares the road for the next by summarizing the forces and views of its time. A certain progress towards an absolute synthesis in the utopian sense may be noted in that each synthesis attempts to arrive at a wider perspective than the previous one, and that the later ones incorporate the results of those that have gone before.
>
> (Ibid., 152)[17]

Of course, Mannheim's conception of intellectuals as free-floating nonpartisan observers was an idealization; in practice, the political discourse of his time was just as dominated by partisan claims as ours is. This did not detract from Mannheim's account, however, inasmuch as what he was self-consciously articulating was a vision of how intellectuals *could* function in society—a way of functioning that was made possible by the opportunities presented in the actual role played by

---

17 The similarities between Mannheim's language and Hegel's are far from accidental, and the preceding page in Mannheim's book (Mannheim 1936, 151) makes the link explicit: "Did not Hegel, coming at the end of a relatively closed epoch, attempt to synthesize in his own work the tendencies which hitherto had developed independently?" To an IR reader this may also sound suspiciously like E.H. Carr; on this point, see below.

knowledge in society at the time. Logically, then, the Mannheimian intellectual ought to seek to occupy that nonpartisan space from which a view of the whole might be gained.[18] The encroachment of anything other than the disinterested search for truth into the intellectual or scientific sphere would compromise the integrity of the operation, and therefore produce partial and biased accounts; to the contrary, scientific analyses of society ought to be aiming at producing something that is not classically objective in the sense of being a "view from nowhere," but certainly synthetic by virtue of being located in society but outside of any particular interest within that society.

It is important to note that such a synthesis can and should be the object of scientific critique: not partisan criticism that would simply agree or fail to agree with its values, but scientific critique that could call attention to inadequacies in the synthesis generated by the scientist's own failure to acknowledge and control sufficiently her or his own social conditions. Reflexivity, then, functions as a way of making sure that one's knowledge-claims are as close to being disinterested as it is possible for them to be. As Pierre Bourdieu put it:

> The instrument of objectivation constituted by the social sciences has to be asked to provide the means of rescuing these sciences from the relativization to which they are exposed so long as their productions remain determined by the unconscious determinations that are inscribed in the scientist's mind or in the social conditions within which he [*sic*] produces. And to do this, they have to confront the relativistic or skeptical circle and break it by implementing ... all the instruments that these very sciences provide and so produce the means of countering the social determinations to which those sciences are exposed.
>
> (Bourdieu 2004, 86)

Bourdieu's conception of the epistemic warrant of science is no different in its essentials from Mannheim's, as both posit a disinterested and nonpartisan standpoint as the scientifically superior vantage-point from which to articulate knowledge of society; Bourdieu is, however, more concerned than Mannheim with precisely *how* one approximates that point of view in practice.[19] Reflexivity—

---

18   It is probably worth pointing out explicitly that this holistic strand of reflexivism would strongly disagree with the analyticist notion presented in the previous chapter that different value-commitments and the respective worldly claims that they generate often remain to some degree mutually incomprehensible, although not logically contradictory. In part, this difference stems from the importance of future developments to a holistic reflexivist: the unity of opposed perspectives grasped by an intellectual is *emerging* when she or he articulates it, and that articulation helps dialectically to midwife it into concrete existence. Analyticists do not place such a developmental movement at the core of their methodology, so any future unity that emerges from their scholarship cannot logically be the intended result of a scientific investigation, even if things were actually to happen that way. See Chapter 7.

19   Bourdieu also has a vastly different conception of how science concretely operates than Mannheim or any of the other "traditional" sociologists of science (especially Merton and Lazarsfeld) whom Bourdieu criticizes for not taking tacit practices

often upheld as the most distinctive attribute of Bourdieu's sociology—functions in a way that is quite precisely analogous to the way that falsification functions for a neopositivist: namely, reflexivity underpins or warrants the scientific character of a claim, and provides other scientists with the tools to use in evaluating the claim's status. The difference is that reflexivity is not available to serve as a demarcation criterion for the boundaries of science, since it is a procedure rather than a logical form. *Any* claim can be reflexively criticized by calling attention to the social conditions of its production, and doing so holds out the possibility of improving the claim's scientific status by embedding it in its social context— as when Bourdieu draws on studies of the French university system and the socioeconomic background of people more likely to succeed within it to raise skepticism about the putatively universal character of the knowledge that the system produces (ibid., 91–92).

It might be objected that this kind of reflexivity is internally contradictory, since properly locating a claim with respect to its social conditions of production relies on a knowledge of those social conditions that cannot itself be reduced to the social condition of the researcher: in effect, a context-independent knowledge of context. However, this objection fails to grasp the temporal and dialectical character of reflexivist knowledge, and does not take seriously enough the way that reflexivist researchers intend their claims to function as tools for transforming the very social conditions that they highlight. For reflexivists, it is never appropriate to understand an empirical claim as simply a representation or depiction of a situation or a state of affairs; rather, every empirical claim is dialectically involved in a struggle with its object, and is as such necessarily perspectival. There is no way for a reflexivist to answer a question about whether any particular characterization of social context is *really* accurate, because that question presumes what reflexivists—as monists—deny: that it is sensible to refer to an object as existing outside of all possible references to it. Instead, reflexivists ask: does this characterization of social context, produced with the best and most widely accepted tools presently available to the scientific community, highlight ways in which we fall short of the scientific ideal? Does it provide us with an impetus to criticize our own work reflexively and thus move closer to "an ideally constituted field that would free each of the participants from the 'biases' linked to his or her position and dispositions" (ibid., 114)?[20] If so, then the claim fulfills its proper function, and no more can be required of it than that.

---

rooted in a scientific *habitus* or disposition seriously enough. While fascinating, that substantive debate is less relevant to the point at issue here.

20 Recall from the discussion of logical positivism in Chapters 2 and 3, above, that setting social relations on a properly scientific basis was as much a part of the Vienna Circle project as it is a part of the reflexivist project. The epistemic privilege of science is thus no less pronounced for reflexivists than it was for their logical positivist predecessors; only the contours of "science" are different.

Intellectuals as agents of revolutionary praxis

Of course, not everyone who wrestled with the problem of the intellectuals came to the conclusion that it was possible for intellectuals to bear and articulate a tacit social wholeness. Indeed, the vast majority of reflections on the social status of knowledge in the early part of the twentieth century[21] emphasized the *partiality* of particular intellectual points of view (Abbott 2001a, 62–64). In their seminal book *The Social Construction of Reality*, Peter Berger and Thomas Luckmann imported this sensibility into the American academy by defining the intellectual as "a marginal type ... an expert whose expertise is not wanted by the society at large" and whose "design for society at large ... exists in an institutional vacuum" (Berger and Luckmann 1967, 126). They contrasted intellectuals to the officially sanctioned experts whose social function was to uphold an account of reality in terms of which the dominant social arrangements could be justified and perpetuated; such officially sanctioned experts were, in effect, allied with the prevailing social order, and thus no more nonpartisan or holistic in their grasp of social reality than the dissident—and potentially revolutionary—intellectuals. In such circumstances, reflexivity would function not as a way of preparing the way for a more nonpartisan account of things, but as a way of clarifying whose side a given thinker was on, and whose kind of social order her or his claims upheld.

However, Berger and Luckmann, and their successors, did not press this point so far that the substantive claims of intellectuals became *merely* expressions of the social location of their authors. Reflexivity is not reductionism. Identifying the function of a given intellectual articulation and clarifying its relationship to the dominant social order means neither that intellectuals propounding visions of society are somehow compelled to do so in virtue of their material position in society, nor that the prospective audience for such visions have their reactions to those visions deterministically set by *their* material positions in society. Such naïve materialism—which would make the actual content of particular visions of social life quite irrelevant to any analysis of the role of knowledge in society—has dogged popular Marxism for generations, leading numerous analysts to propound something like a deterministic reduction of knowledge to the functional imperatives of maintaining the capitalist order (for example, Gill 1992; van Apeldoorn 2002). Such a stance raises some tricky epistemic problems for the account of capitalism presumed in such analyses, including the fact that there is something intrinsically and performatively self-contradictory about a scholarly dialectical intervention that loudly proclaims the irrelevance of scholarly dialectical interventions on the grounds that the formulation and reception of intellectual accounts is functionally and materially (over)determined.[22] One might also justifiably ask whether this

---

21   Except in the United States, where the sociology of knowledge was dominated by an emphasis on interpersonal interactions for reasons having to do with the dominance of the "Chicago School" of interactionist sociology (a story related quite neatly in Abbott 1999).

22   I am assuming for the moment that this kind of Marxist scholar is trying to locate her or his work in the reflexivist box, and not in some other philosophical ontology. Scholars

account of capitalism is itself supposed to be holistic or just one among other socially determined perspectives, as either answer would similarly lead to performative contradictions.

It turns out, however, that less deterministic varieties of critical Marxism have considerably better and more defensible answers to the question of how knowledge relates to the social order. Their "critical reflexivist" answers embrace the perspectival character of knowledge, but go on to detail specifically the ways that particular intellectual visions relate to the tacit, or commonsensical, knowledge *already* possessed by the members of the audience to whom scholars are addressing their work. The privileged position accorded to intellectuals involves neither bearing a holistic account of society that transcends and unifies disparate partisan accounts, nor simply expressing a point of view that is inevitably determined by the intellectuals' material position in society. Instead, intellectual activity involves the "critical elaboration" of what the members of a specific group of people in society are already tacitly doing as a component of their daily lives and work. In Antonio Gramsci's terms:

> When one distinguishes between intellectuals and non-intellectuals, one is referring in reality only to the immediate social function of the professional category of the intellectuals ... there are varying degrees of specific intellectual activity. There is no human activity from which every form of intellectual participation can be excluded: *homo faber* cannot be separated from *homo sapiens*.
>
> (Gramsci 1971, p. 9)

As such, what intellectuals do is to seize on "the intellectual activity that exists in everyone at a certain degree of development" and make it "the foundation of a new and integral conception of the world" by rendering that everyday activity explicit. "Each man [*sic*] ... participates in a particular conception of the world, has a conscious line of moral conduct, and therefore contributes to sustain a conception of the world or modify it," and professional intellectual activity is grounded in these everyday activities (ibid.). Intellectual activities, including the social-scientific production of knowledge, should therefore begin with the ways in which people make sense of their everyday surroundings and activities, aligning with particular social groups not by sharing their material circumstances, but by seeking to clarify that group's commonsensical understandings (Bruff 2010).

---

presuming an account of the capitalist order have to determine where their account fits in a philosophical-ontological sense: is it a falsifiable hypothesis, a depiction of a real-but-undetectable causal property, an instrumental analytical device, or a dialectical intervention? As I have discussed in previous chapters, taking the first and third options moves the account away from the revolutionary authority that many Marxist scholars claim, while the second option places extremely high burdens on the would-be critical realist. Taking the fourth option leads to the performative contradiction discussed in the text.

Of course, this is easier said than done, because everyday common sense is far from systematic or even consistent. Thus, a critical reflexivist intellectual concerned to connect her or his position on the existing social order to the views and experiences of a particular social group needs to be attuned to the tensions and ambiguities of everyday understanding. It is not as simple as asking members of a group what they think and then standing on those replies as a foundation for subsequent claims about the social world, because the everyday opinions of ordinary people might be incomplete or even systematically misleading—not because they fail to represent some set of mind-independent "real" social conditions accurately, but because a particular piece of social knowledge may contribute to its own reproduction. It is therefore not sufficient simply to reproduce everyday popular understandings, and instead, a critical reflexivist has to examine how those understandings function in context so as to frustrate the very expectations that they generate:

> The culture industry endlessly cheats its consumers out of what it endlessly promises. The promissory note of pleasure issued by plot and packaging is indefinitely prolonged: the promise, which actually comprises the whole show, disdainfully intimates that there is nothing more to come, that the diner must be satisfied with reading the menu ... The culture industry does not sublimate: it suppresses. By constantly exhibiting the object of desire, the breasts beneath the sweater, the naked torso of the sporting hero, it merely goads the unsublimated anticipation of pleasure, which through the habit of denial has long since been mutilated as masochism.
>
> (Horkheimer and Adorno 1947, 111)

A claim such as this is neither a falsifiable hypothesis nor a disclosing of an undetectable causal power, but rather a provocative observation about the operation of mass culture through a deferral of gratification—which, it happens, is precisely the kind of individual virtue required by a worker engaged in an unpleasant task (ibid., 109). The intellectual observation relates a piece of everyday social knowledge—"present denial brings future benefits"—to its function in reproducing a particular kind of social order, and as such engages in a dialectical process of helping the people who hold that piece of social knowledge to reflect critically on its overall value.[23]

Reflexivity, in this case, is a call for the producers of social knowledge to locate their knowledge-claims in relation to the everyday understandings of particular social groups. The task of an intellectual is not to produce a detached

---

23 Horkheimer and Adorno, like others in the Frankfurt School with which they were associated, often critiqued logical positivism for precisely *not* engaging in this dialectical process. The putative "scientific" neutrality of logical positivist claims, on the critical-theoretical account, shores up the existing social order rather than providing the necessary impetus for revolutionary transformation. But the fact that both logical positivists and critical theorists are seeking to reconstitute society on a scientific basis is striking.

or nonpartisan view of a situation, but instead to contribute to a social group's activities by helping to clarify their existing commonsensical knowledge and to provoke reflection on it. Critical reflexivity is therefore not a way of purifying the social scientist's own view of a situation, but is instead a way of making sure that this view is sufficiently rooted in the concrete situation of the group with whom the social scientist is aligned—the social group whose vision she or he seeks to advance. While there is no necessary philosophical reason that reflexivist intellectuals *have* to be aligned with marginalized or dissident social groups, there has been an historically robust association between this kind of critical reflexivity and subordinate segments of society, perhaps because provoking reflection is less urgent for the preservation of an existing social order than it is for the transformation of that social order.

Indeed, the articulation of a critical reflexivist stance on social knowledge during the early part of the twentieth century—within the Marxist tradition, principally by Antonio Gramsci and especially by members of the Frankfurt School such as Max Horkheimer and Theodor Adorno—was initially wrapped up with demonstrating that socially dominant ideas and the intellectuals who propounded them were perhaps unintentionally reproducing and sustaining the existing social order. The tacit wager was that by unmasking or unveiling putatively universal or general claims as contributing to the advancement of particular groups and their goals, a new kind of intellectual class could be created, one that would more clearly advance the cause of social revolution (Geuss 1981, 38). But irrespective of whether critical reflexivity will or can produce such a class, the philosophical-ontological point remains the same: knowledge-claims, in order to be valid, have to be connected to the everyday understandings of particular groups in society.[24]

Of course, the Frankfurt School tradition is far from the only variant of critical reflexivity that took its cue from Marxism. French intellectuals such as Louis Althusser were equally committed to pursuing emancipatory projects through scientific theory, even though they defined their task as more about the demolition of existing ideologies than about the systematic clarification of a non-elite view of social order. Althusser in particular argued that the development of theory called for a thoroughgoing critique of the "human sciences," which were inextricably bound up with "bourgeois politics and ideology" and aimed to provide a means for

---

24 The issue of whether critical self-reflection will necessarily produce a class of revolutionary intellectuals is a tricky one, involving a series of debates internal to the Frankfurt School project of seeking to disclose tensions in the existing social order so as to advance a critique of that social order that will not be an arbitrary imposition of value-positions from outside the social order (as when, for example, a country invades another country and sets up a political regime more to its liking, justifying its actions on the grounds that its form of political regime is simply and categorically superior to all alternatives). The quest for a sound basis on which to place critiques of the existing social order leads one either in the direction of a "historicist" account of values, or in the (Habermasian) direction of a set of "universal" principles that arise endogenously (for an overview, see Geuss 1981, 92–95). But these more technical matters do not detract from the basic philosophical-ontological point about what warrants a knowledge-claim.

people to adapt themselves to existing social conditions instead of equipping them with the conceptual tools needed to transform them (Althusser 2003, 203–204). Such a critique would involve, in the first instance, an account of "the general political, ideological, and theoretical *conjuncture*" of the time, an account that would "bring out the complex organic relationship between political, ideological, and theoretical problems" and in so doing define the strategic tasks for a Marxist theory of society (ibid., 168). Operating at one step further removed from the practically instantiated ideas privileged by other critical reflexivists, Althusser argued that the task of reflexive theory was to prepare the ground for a genuinely scientific study of society by ensuring that concepts imported from existing ways of studying society were embedded within the proper philosophical and political orientation.

> Whenever a new science is constituted, opening the way to knowledge of a new "continent," a veritable theoretical revolution occurs ... it *imports* a number of theoretical elements (concepts, categories, methods, etc.) into its field, borrowing them from existing scientific or philosophical disciplines outside that field. It puts these theoretical elements to work on the reality of its new object and, in performing this labor, it also rectifies these imported theoretical elements in order to adapt them to the reality of their new "continent" ... [but] there finally comes a moment in which the radical novelty of this object calls into question, not the imported *scientific concepts*, but the grand *philosophical categories* in which these concepts had previously been thought ... it is sometimes necessary to wait a very long time for a favorable conjuncture to offer the theoretical tools adapted to the solution of a long-standing problem.
>
> (Ibid., 176–177)

Althusser's point is that reflexive criticism of the conceptual categories underpinning the use of scientific concepts, much like the criticism of conceptual categories underpinning everyday social practice, can contribute to the production of a science that will further the transformation of society.[25] Similar gestures can be found in Deleuze and Guattari's (1996, 83) envisioning of a "nomadic" science that would "undertake to awaken a dormant concept and to play it again on a new stage," thus encouraging transformation rather than upholding the existing order of things. Although such academic operations take place at a bit of a remove from the lived experience of everyday life, their epistemic warrant is precisely the same as it is for other reflexivists: beginning with practice, critical reflexivist science seeks to clarify logically the tacit assumptions of those practices in order to provoke action.

---

25 Note that for Althusser, as for many other French intellectuals, this connection is also underpinned by his articulation of a close interconnection between philosophy—not just social theory—and politics (Althusser 2003, 212–218). This close connection does not animate other varieties of reflexivist science to the same degree.

Critical reflexivist notions of knowledge such as these sound somewhat similar to the kind of practical grounding in everyday activities recommended by analytical monists. But the everyday activities in question for a reflexivist are not primarily related to a sphere of cultural values, as they would be for analyticist conceptions of knowledge-production; instead, they are the everyday activities of people in the broader society (including philosophers and scientists), and as such, the connection is between knowledge and lived social practice rather than between knowledge and the sphere of cultural values. As I noted in the previous chapter, there is nothing in a monistic position itself that *requires* that the researcher begin with the self-understandings of situated actors, regardless of whether they are ideal-typifying such understandings or critically elaborating them in order to provoke dialectical reflection. Indeed, *on the level of philosophical ontology*, this is one of the most important differences between analyticists and reflexivists, because what warrants a knowledge-claim for an analyticist is its systematic connection to a value-commitment, whereas for a reflexivist what warrants a knowledge-claim is its relationship to everyday practical knowledge and the social group that holds it. It is certainly possible for each of these positions to use the tools of the other: an analyticist might articulate a value-commitment to beginning with everyday understandings and proceed to elaborate an ideal-typical model of everyday understanding, for example, but that would not make her work reflexivist because the warrant for her claims would not simply be the fact that they were connected to a social group's common-sense practices but would instead be the fact that they were connected to an ideal-typical model rooted in a particular value-commitment.

The distinction is subtle, but important. With any scientific claim, it is crucial to ascertain the proper epistemic warrant in order to evaluate the claim; otherwise some facet or factor that one style of research considers quintessentially important might be mistaken for a neat but irrelevant detail, or vice versa. It would not be appropriate to ask a critical reflexivist about her or his analytical model as a condition of evaluating her or his empirical claims, nor would it be appropriate to ask an analyticist to clarify her or his alignment with particular social groups as a condition of evaluating her or his empirical claims. Even if both were working on a similar empirical topic—say, the everyday policymaking process within a foreign ministry—it makes a great deal of difference whether the epistemic warrant for particular empirical claims is the emancipatory potential of the critical self-location of the researcher (Vrasti 2008) or the use of (implicit) ideal-typical models of processes to parse complex empirical situations (Neumann 2007). A simple substantive focus on everyday understandings is insufficient information for ascertaining the philosophical ontology informing a claim, as it is eminently possible to study everyday understandings from a variety of methodological points of view.[26] And only a focus on philosophical ontology, and the epistemic

---

26 Indeed, analyticism and reflexivity are far from the only options; neopositivists and critical realists also have a place in their methodologies for everyday understandings. Here again, philosophical ontology speaks to *how* and not *what* a researcher studies,

warrants to which it gives rise, can help us to determine the proper standards for evaluating the empirical claims in question.

Intellectuals and a diversity of standpoints

Reflexivity might contribute to the achieving of a holistic view of the social world; it might also contribute to the critical clarification of a particular social group's ideas and sensibilities. There is also a third way that reflexivity might warrant a claim in accord with transfactual monism: by helping a social scientist to contribute to the overcoming of a systematic bias or distortion that has repressed or otherwise marginalized the perspective of a particular group. The goal in this case would not be to critically clarify a group's perspective for the purpose of overturning the social order so as to liberate the group in question, but instead to make space for the group's perspective to contribute to a potentially broader grasp of things. And unlike the holistic kind of reflexivity, the aim is not for the social scientist herself or himself to bear or exemplify that broader grasp; rather, the broader grasp in question is the not-yet-achieved outcome of a potential conversation between social groups. The social scientist's role is to promote that conversation, not to foresee its conclusion.

There are many sources one might reference in fleshing out this position, including the writings of Ashis Nandy (1987; 2009) or Tzvetan Todorov (1984). One particularly clear articulation comes from the work of W.E.B. DuBois, who in analyzing the condition of the descendants of African slaves in the United States in the late nineteenth century deployed the notion of the "double consciousness" under which they operated:

> [T]he Negro is ... born with a veil, and gifted with second-sight in this American world,—a world which yields him no true self-consciousness, but only lets him see himself through the revelation of the other world. It is a peculiar sensation, this double consciousness, this sense of always looking at one's self through the eyes of others, of measuring one's soul by the tape of a world that looks on in amused contempt and pity. One ever feels his two-ness,—an American, a Negro; two souls, two thoughts, two unreconciled strivings.
>
> (DuBois 1994, 2–3)

The situation DuBois describes is broadly applicable to the situation of any observer who is situated at the margins of her or his community, forced in a sense to see herself or himself through standards that place her or him in a subordinate position. DuBois did not conclude that such a situation necessitates any kind of radical rejection of the standards of the community, but instead called for a broadening of those standards such that the marginalized could participate equally.

---

even if—as in the case of critical reflexivists—that "how" directs researchers to incorporate a relationship to a specific "what."

Neither repudiation nor uncritical acceptance is called for, as the marginalized individual should not have to give up either of her or his two selves:

> He would not Africanize America, for America has too much to teach the world and Africa. He would not bleach his Negro soul in a flood of white Americanism, for he knows that Negro blood has a message for the world. He simply wishes to make it possible for a man to be both a Negro and an American, without being cursed and spit upon by his fellows, without having the doors of Opportunity closed roughly in his face.
>
> (Ibid., 3)

DuBois especially criticized those activists who preached individual hard work as the key to improving the social conditions of the descendants of slaves in the United States, pointing out that by accepting the notion of individual self-improvement they were blinding themselves to the impact of discriminatory social practices, and that even if particular individuals improved their own situations, the broader social divisions would remain (ibid., 34–35, 101–109). Individual hard work would only lead to self-improvement in the absence of such divisions—in other words, if everyone were white.

However, at the same time, double consciousness implies something more profound than the elimination of arbitrary and discriminatory barriers to entry. The more profound problem is that the articulation of dominant standards privileges, perhaps unintentionally, a set of characteristics and goals associated with and comfortable for the socially dominant group articulating and codifying those standards, thus making the price of entry into the dominant conversation or society a tacit acceptance of a set of alien aims. Sandra Harding (1991, 45) argues that this is precisely the case with dominant notions of objectivity across the natural sciences, which privilege "hierarchical models of causation and control" that are associated, culturally speaking, with "masculine personality traits." Harding is not valorizing women at the expense of men, and she is not arguing that culturally feminine personality traits are preferable to culturally masculine personality traits for the conduct of scientific inquiry (Tannoch-Bland 1997, 161–162). Rather, Harding is calling attention to the peculiar situation produced by the linking of certain goals and characteristics with sets of widely circulated codes of social distinction. Anyone not possessing the "correct" categorical attributes (in this case, gender) will experience double consciousness as a result of the tension between two rival logics: from the dominant standards, a set of goals and characteristics that one should possess, and from the codes of social distinction, a contradictory set of messages claiming that one should not or cannot possess those characteristics or those goals. A science that privileges culturally masculine characteristics and standards, therefore, presents women with a set of unappealing choices: adopt culturally masculine characteristics and goals in defiance of or in tension with the rest of their identities *as* women, or remain outside of the sphere of science altogether.

It is important to keep in mind that the goals and characteristics under discussion here are in no way linked to any sort of innate dispositions of particular persons or groups of people; rather, what is at issue here are cultural codes of meaning and the practices to which they give rise. The question is not whether individual members of under-represented groups *can* adhere to the standards promulgated by the dominant; the issue involves the effects, both on those individuals and on the overall social order, that are produced by the exclusion of sets of characteristics and goals associated with specific groups of people. Harding points out that when it comes to science, chief among these effects is the fact that linking scientific standards and masculine traits increases the potential for bias: grounding scientific accounts, even if only implicitly, "in the lives of men in the dominant races, classes, and cultures" virtually guarantees "partialities and distortions" in those accounts (Harding 1991, 121). The solution to these limitations, as in DuBois' argument, is to highlight the view from the margins, in the hopes of calling attention to those places where the dominant account is unnecessarily narrow. Mary Hawkesworth elaborates:

> Feminist analysis can demonstrate the inadequacies of accounts of human nature derived from an evidentiary base of only half the species; it can refute unfounded claims about women's "nature" that are premised on an atheoretical naturalism; it can identify androcentric bias in theories, methods, and concepts and show how this bias undermines explanatory force; it can demonstrate that the numerous obstacles to women's full participation in social, political, and economic life are humanly created and hence susceptible to alteration. In providing sophisticated and detailed analyses of concrete situations, feminists can dispel distortions and mystifications that abound in malestream thought.
>
> (Hawkesworth 1989, 556–557)

Harding characterizes the incorporation of feminist critique in the canon of science as a step towards "strong objectivity," and argues that the primary benefit of such incorporation is to expand the resources that the scientific community as a whole has for thinking about the world (Harding 1991, 149–151; Harding 2015). Critique is necessary to reveal the blind spots possessed by any science that is unaware of its own social location and conditions of production; this is one of the principal ways that scientific progress happens, as accounts previously thought to be unbiased are shown to have tacit biases that are then corrected by the incorporation of wider points of view (Tannoch-Bland 1997, 162–163; Weldon 2006, 65–66). Precisely because knowledge is generated in a monist manner—not by representing a mind-independent world, but by delineating and explicating a particular vantage-point within that world—the epistemic warrant for a claim must involve a close examination of the perspective animating the claim. And precisely because knowledge is not limited to or limited by experience and observation, on this account, critique can contribute to knowledge by disclosing the conditions that tacitly collaborate to produce certain observations and experiences (Scott 1991).

Another way of putting the point is to suggest that we "provincialize" (as in Chakrabarty 2007) dominant standards of rationality, objectivity, and the like, revealing them to be partial rather than as comprehensively universal as they claim to be. This does not mean that scholars should dismissively criticize dominant standards, but that they should seek to enter into a dialogue with them on a more equal basis—which first and foremost requires knocking the dominant standards off their unreflective perch, from which they appear perspectiveless. The goal in so doing is to transform existing scientific disciplines so as to enable them, and their practitioners, to achieve a broader grasp on the actual world (Hawkesworth 1994, 110). It is that breadth, and the hope of an even more encompassing dialogue in the future, that propels this third variant of reflexivist scholarship beyond the phenomenal and into the transfactual.

Reflexive scholarship in IR

Much of the foregoing discussion should seem familiar to broad readers of contemporary IR scholarship, as there is quite a bit of work in the field that draws on these modes of reflexivity. Unfortunately, however, the terms under which such work is conducted and discussed are somewhat misleading, which generates undue confusion about what makes such scholarship *epistemically* distinct from either opinion or partisan politics. In many ways, the field has not gotten beyond the situation that Wendt lamented in 1992, in which "Science disciplines Dissent for not defining a conventional research program, and Dissent celebrates its liberation from Science" (Wendt 1992, 393). Since the mantle of Science has largely been claimed by neopositivists, critics of neopositivism have often sought to distance themselves from the very notion of science, but in so doing have not been particularly clear about their alternative methodologies—or about tensions between them.

Thus, in a famous article, Robert Cox (1996b, 88–90) distinguished between two types of theory, based on the perspective and purpose that the theory instantiates. On one hand, we have "problem-solving theory," which "takes the world as it finds it, with the prevailing social and power relationships and the institutions into which they are organized, as the given framework for action" and aims to "make these relationships and institutions work smoothly." On the other hand, we have Cox's clear preference, "critical theory," which "stands apart from the prevailing order of the world and asks how that order came about" and is accordingly "directed toward an appraisal of the very framework for action … which problem-solving theory accepts as its parameters." Cox then draws out the reflexivist implications, specifying the relationship between each type of theory and the prevailing social order:

> Problem-solving theories can be represented, in the broader perspective of critical theory, as serving particular national, sectional, or class interests, which are comfortable within the given order. Indeed, the purpose served by problem-solving theory is conservative, since it aims to solve the problems arising in various parts of a complex whole in order to smooth the functioning of the whole … Critical theory allows for a normative choice in favor of a

social and political order different from the prevailing order, but it limits the range of choice to alternative orders which are feasible transformations of the existing world ... In this way critical theory can be a guide to strategic action for bringing about an alternative order, whereas problem-solving theory is a guide to tactical actions which, intended or unintended, sustain the existing order.

(Ibid.)

Cox's argument displays clear reflexivist sympathies, but stops somewhat short of really spelling out the distinctive epistemic warrant for the two types of theory that he designates. Instead, we learn only that theory that places the present in historical context is "critical" while other theory is not, but this gives the reader very little guidance about *how* to go about generating a good critical theory—let alone how to go about evaluating a critical theory. Nor does it provide a compelling reason why neopositivist analyses of relative power concentrations could not be "critical," even though they would rely on robust hypothesis-testing in order to produce and refine their representational claims. If, however, the only thing that differentiates problem-solving and critical theory is their substantive orientation towards the present order, then there is little or no reason that any claim opposed to the present order could not be critical, and that would take critical theory out of the realm of methodology altogether and transform it into something along the lines of a political characterization of a claim's bias or intent. In the absence of any more specific guidance, the misreadings of a scholar such as John Mearsheimer (1994)—who effectively conflates the category "critical theory" with the category "everything that is not neopositivism"—become difficult to oppose on methodological grounds.

The problem here is in no way unique to Robert Cox. Other critical theorists, for instance, Andrew Linklater (2007), provide little more in the way of methodological precepts. In fact, an observer reading through several self-identified works of critical theory in contemporary IR might be forgiven for thinking that the really distinguishing epistemic feature of this kind of work is its indebtedness to a series of Marxist conceptual categories. Cox's own critical-theoretical work (1996a) consists largely of elaborating a Gramsci-inspired account of global hegemony, but provides no compelling set of reasons as to why an analyst not already inclined to this kind of Marxism should adopt categories such as "social forces" and "world order." Likewise, Linklater's characterization of critical theory as an extension of the Enlightenment project of universal dialogue explicitly draws its terminology from Jürgen Habermas' effort to refashion Marxist critique into discourse ethics (see also Lynch 2002). Neither author provides any clear link between critical theory and the use of categories derived from particular strands of Marxist thinking, leading to the implicit equation of critical theory with the use of particular concepts and categories.

As I have argued on many occasions throughout this book, such a linkage makes no philosophical sense. Associations between particular substantive theories and particular methodological perspectives do not arise for compelling logical or intellectual reasons, but because of sociological developments: the dynamics of graduate training, for example (McNamara 2009, 74–76), or the incentives for publication in particular journals (Phillips 2009, 86–88). Such unjustified associations between substantive theory and methodology certainly deprive the field of potentially "important intellectual gains to be made from exploring the underutilized combinations" of substance and approach (Farrell and Finnemore 2009, 64).[27] But even more to the point, by not providing a clearly distinct warrant for empirical claims, critical theorists both miss an opportunity to produce an alternative scientific standard *and* implicitly relieve subsequent critical theorists of the need to do so, since later scholars can simply adopt those established categories and presume that this gives their work a "critical" character. These two problems are closely linked, inasmuch as the lack of a clear set of methodological standards for what makes a theory "critical" simply abandons the ground of such standards to the advocates of other ways of doing science. In a field dominated by neopositivism, this leads to the unfortunate situation in which neopositivist assumptions are deployed as a methodological corrective to the speculations of critical theorists, as though neopositivism had the monopoly on scientific evaluation while critical theory was only good for the promulgation of creative hypothesis (as in Price and Reus-Smit 1998).

The way forward is to focus attention not immediately on the categories and concepts used in making a particular argument, but to start with a systematic effort to clarify the social location from which the argument is being promulgated. Reflexivity, not the use of categories associated with theorists of social revolution, is what differentiates the style of theorizing that Cox prefers from the style that he does not prefer, and it is the effort to locate a theory in context that provides a distinctive way of doing social science. "Critical theory" is a vague notion unless it is linked to "reflexivity," in which case we would have the second of the three modes of reflexivity that I outlined above: a theory is scientifically warranted to the extent that it properly and helpfully clarifies the tacit assumptions of a view of society from somewhere—most likely, from somewhere other than the dominant position—as part of a campaign to transform society. There is absolutely no necessity to use categories such as "hegemony" as a part of doing so, and conversely, using such categories does not suffice to warrant a set of

---

27 Although quite correct in their argument that methodologies and substantive theories are not necessarily linked, Farrell and Finnemore may do more harm than good in continuing to treat "qualitative methods" as a distinctive kind of methodology rather than as a collection of techniques—methods—that could be affixed to a variety of methodological approaches (Farrell and Finnemore 2009, 59), and in conflating analytical pragmatism with critical realism—without specifying that neither critical realism nor analytical pragmatism are at all tied to cross-case covariation as a necessary mark of a causal relationship—on the grounds that both seek to elucidate processes and mechanisms linking causal factors to outcomes (ibid., 66–67). The first step in producing compelling combinations of substance and methodology, I would suggest, is to articulate clearly what different methodologies entail. Absent such clarity, their proposal for a more diverse IPE (International Political Economy) might easily collapse back into the kind of neopositivism that dominates the subfield.

claims. Instead, the standard is dialectical: does the claim, rooted in a systematic clarification of its own perspectival location, contribute to the overcoming of the conditions that it expresses? A good reflexivist claim does, either by removing ideological obstacles to action or by directly contributing to change.

In contemporary IR, this agenda is best and most clearly exemplified by feminist theorists. Far more overtly than most IR Marxist work, feminist scholarship *always* locates itself reflexively. The editors of a recent volume on feminist methodology (Ackerly, Stern, and True 2006, 4) suggest that this is the single most important thing differentiating feminist scholarship from other modes of inquiry: regardless of which techniques of data-collection and data-analysis feminist scholars use in doing their empirical work, and regardless of the concepts and theories with which they work, what unites feminist scholarship (and differentiates it, methodologically, from neopositivism) is the attentiveness of authors working in this tradition to the social location from which they theorize. This attentiveness permits feminists to root their claims in a dialectical process of contributing to the emancipation and empowerment of women through their systematic clarifications of the practical wisdom of those in subordinate positions (Tickner 2006, 28–29). The results of such an investigation are not merely arbitrary opinions, but are instead positive contributions to the transformation of society by helping to prepare the way for a "successor science"—a way of knowing and being that will not rely on gender hierarchies, but will instead achieve a more inclusive standpoint (Hawkesworth 1989, 536).

Thus, when Cynthia Enloe (1996) suggests that IR scholars focus on the margins of society or when Ann Towns (2009) suggests that IR scholars appreciate the links between the "standard of civilization" in international society and the political marginalization of women, this is something considerably more than a recommendation about *what* to study. It is instead a call for altering the way in which we study power in society: instead of confining IR scholarship to the interactions of the powerful—a limitation that tacitly privileges the existing order of things—we should seek to understand how those on the margins are marginalized, precisely because their marginalization makes possible the focus on powerful elites that dominates mainstream IR scholarship. Studying such marginalization means, in the first instance, locating oneself outside of that mainstream, so that the characteristic blindnesses of the perspective from the top of the hierarchy do not obscure the processes and factors that might be perfectly obvious from another point of view. And it is this change of perspective, *not* the specific focus on gender hierarchies, that makes for a feminist methodology, as both feminists (Sjoberg 2009) and non-feminists who analyze gender (Carpenter 2002) acknowledge.[28] Reflexivity affords this change of perspective, by grounding knowledge in a philosophical ontology quite different from other alternatives.

---

28 A queer methodology (Weber 2014) would be similarly distinct from simply an empirical focus on homosexuals, inasmuch as it would focus on the ways that gender binaries marginalize points of view that do not fall neatly into the conceptual either/or of male/female.

Of course, reflexivity is not the exclusive province of feminist IR scholarship. Recent calls to incorporate the global sociology of the IR field into IR scholarship (Büger and Gadinger 2007; Tickner and Wæver 2009) and to work deliberately to make disciplining practices explicit in our empirical work (Beier and Arnold 2005) participate in this same spirit, highlighting reflexivity as a distinct component of generating knowledge about world politics. Post-colonial scholarship (Inayatullah and Blaney 2004; Muppidi 2010) also makes significant strides in this direction, particularly when it seeks to call attention to the unacknowledged traces of colonial categories in the basic conceptual vocabulary of the field. As with feminist work, this kind of scholarship's distinctive epistemic warrant is intimately wrapped up with the embracing both of its own partiality and of its role in promoting some measure of transformation away from existing hierarchies.

One of the challenges with identifying reflexivist IR scholarship, however, is that almost all of the authors I have mentioned would resist being labeled as sharing a methodology in the first place. The peculiar dynamics of the field (and, perhaps, of the social sciences as a whole) have resulted in a situation where the very idea of being explicit and self-conscious about one's procedures of gathering and evaluating empirical data has largely been annexed to neopositivist procedures of hypothesis-testing, and dissidents seeking to do non-neopositivist empirical work have spent considerably more time criticizing those methodological approaches that they do *not* adopt than they have spent articulating an alternative methodology. Not that such scholars have not produced intriguing insights; it is just often unclear precisely *how* they have done so. But abandoning the language of methodology to a dominant neopositivism seems tactically unwise, as it is not clear what it would mean to conduct empirical work without a methodology. Nor is it clear how one would evaluate or critique such work in the absence of some appropriate methodological standards. None of this is to say that reflexivists should have to demonstrate that their work produces knowledge of the sort that can be easily slotted into a neopositivist hypothesis about systematic connections between variables across cases; rather, it is to say that reflexivists have to articulate more clearly *their own* set of methodological standards and then pursue them as consistently and rigorously as neopositivists (and critical realists and analyticists) pursue theirs.[29] I have suggested that thematizing and highlighting the social

---

29 A particularly pressing question in this respect involves the issue of whether and how reflexivist claims can take advantage of results generated by different philosophical ontologies as a way of pursuing their own aims. A case in point involves statistical depictions of an academic field, which might be conceptualized—as Bourdieu (2004, 89–91) apparently does—as a way of enhancing reflexivity by illustrating bias. In Bourdieu's case, the bias involves a systematic association between class origin and how coding schemes are used in research practices. Kathleen McNamara (2009) does something quite similar in her discussion of the subfield of IPE, connecting graduate syllabi with the methods utilized in publications in top-ranked journals. There is an intriguing and thorny philosophical problem here: can someone making a reflexivist argument borrow, in good conscience, empirical results that were produced without any appreciable degree of reflexivity? I am not going to try to give an answer here; for a preliminary exploration and discussion, see Barkin and Sjoberg 2015.

location and function of a claim will yield the greatest epistemic benefits, since this appears to capture the distinctive quality of feminist, post-colonial, and Marxist work—in part by rooting these traditions in the broader philosophical context stemming from debate about Kant's attempt to meet Cartesian anxiety squarely and vanquish it transcendentally.

Along the way, reflexivist IR scholarship might explicitly take up the challenges and limitations of case comparison that I have highlighted in the previous three chapters. By this point it should be readily apparent that there are as many different ways to compare cases as there are methodologies grounded in different philosophical-ontological wagers; there is nothing whatsoever that is methodologically specific about comparing cases, and in particular, there is no necessity that in comparing cases a researcher involve herself in the production of nomothetic generalizations about how causal factors covary across cases. Neopositivists have no lock on the consideration of multiple cases; critical realists can use comparison to help further elucidate the range of effects associated with undetectable causal properties and powers in combination, while analyticists can use comparison in an individuating way so as to highlight the specificity of each individual case.

Analogically, it should be possible to elaborate a distinctly reflexivist kind of comparative practice, although this is a task that has not yet been fully carried out. Two options suggest themselves, however. A reflexivist might compare one's own society with others as a way of de-naturalizing or even dislocating taken-for-granted assumptions (as suggested by Geertz 2000, 16, 77); preliminary steps towards this kind of an "'ethnological' politics of comparison" (Inayatullah and Blaney 2004, 123) can be seen in some post-colonial work. Alternatively, reflexivist comparison might take the form of what Philip McMichael (1990, 391) refers to as "incorporated comparison," which he defines as a "conceptual procedure ... in which the whole is discovered through analysis of the mutual conditioning of parts." Such incorporated comparison, which McMichael develops as a way of setting the analysis of the capitalist world-system on a less doctrinaire basis, holds out the possibility of inductively generating accounts of macro-historical processes grounded in specific case studies, and seems an intriguing fit with the emphasis on dialectical transformation and unfolding developmental process characteristic of many varieties of reflexivism.[30] Regardless, the point remains that reflexivist scholars *should* develop a methodologically grounded form of comparison—or a methodologically grounded opposition to comparison—if for no other reason than to fend off criticisms from neopositivists for whom case comparison is an indispensable strategy of scientific inquiry. Nothing, except perhaps an unfounded dislike for terms such as "science" and "methodology," prevents this methodological elaboration of the reflexivist project in IR.

Indeed, reflexivism lies at the very center of the origin of the IR field. Nothing I have argued in this chapter should be all that surprising to a field that claims

---

30   Thanks to Ian Bruff for suggesting the relevance of McMichael's account of comparison.

E.H. Carr as one of its founders. Carr, famously, derived much of his broad argument about the development of a science of International Relations from Karl Mannheim's discussion of ideology and utopia (Smith 1999, 51–57; Brincat 2009, 584–591). Carr's whole orientation, in *Twenty Years' Crisis* as well as throughout his oeuvre (Molloy 2003), was decidedly dialectical, and a lot of what Carr had to say about the production of knowledge sounds a lot less like contemporary IR realists (who are almost all neopositivists) than it does like contemporary IR Marxists and feminists. Carr's recipe for building a science of world politics involved acknowledging the inevitable tensions and conflicts between utopian and realist moments of theorizing, and proceeding from there to participate in a process of knowledge-production that only makes sense as a contribution to a dialectical transformation of the present. There is very little of the hypothesis-tester about Carr, and his account of the interwar years does not spend time elucidating undetectable causal powers or elaborating ideal-typical models. Rather, he offers his readers only an ongoing and unending set of engagements, the empirical content of which is warranted in terms of their revolutionary effects on the social order:

> Having demolished the current utopia with the weapons of realism we still need to build a new utopia of our own which will one day fall to the same weapons. The human will will continue to seek an escape from the logical consequences of realism in the vision of an international order which, as soon as it crystallizes itself to concrete political form, becomes tainted with self-interest and hypocrisy, and must once more be attacked with the instruments of realism.
>
> (Carr 2001, 87)

7 A pluralist science of IR

Abraham Joshua Heschel is remembered as many things: teacher, religious scholar, mystic, advocate for social justice (Tippett 2009). Throughout his many writings and speeches, one finds a commitment to discussion and dialogue that is quite refreshing to anyone accustomed to thinking of conversations about religion simply as shouting-matches between adherents of different faiths. Instead, Heschel's writing is marked by a profound humility, an ever-present sense of the limitations that inhere in any merely linguistic formulation: no articulation suffices to sum up or exhaust its subject. In consequence, Heschel advocates a wide-ranging conversation between members of different religious communities, the point of which is not to convert others to one's own way of thinking.

> The purpose of religious communication among human beings of different commitments is mutual enrichment and enhancement of respect and appreciation rather than the hope that the person spoken to will prove to be wrong in what he regards as sacred. Dialogue must not degenerate into a dispute, into an effort on the part of each to get the upper hand.
>
> (Heschel 1991, 13)

Of particular concern to Heschel were the ongoing efforts by some Christians to convert the Jews to whom they spoke, on the grounds that Judaism was a partial or incomplete form of Christianity. Against this, Heschel declared:

> Any conversation between Christian and Jew in which abandonment of the other partner's faith is a silent hope must be regarded as offensive to one's religious and human dignity. Let there be an end to disputation and polemic, an end to disparagement. We honestly and profoundly disagree in matters of creed and dogma. Indeed, there is a deep chasm between Christians and Jews concerning, e.g., the divinity and Messiahship of Jesus. But across the chasm we can extend our hands to one another.
>
> (Ibid.)

While scientific methodologies are not exactly articles of faith, and methodological diversity and theological diversity are not precisely the same things despite the almost religious tone of many doctrinaire methodological pronouncements (Schrodt 2006), there are more than a few similarities between the two. Certainly the passion with which partisan advocates of one or another methodology insist on the ultimate rectitude of their preferred way of producing knowledge often reminds one of doctrinal disputes, as does the way in which such advocates not infrequently mistake the forceful pronouncement of their most basic presuppositions for arguments that might warrant those presuppositions—or for arguments that anyone other than those who already believe the proffered doctrine would find at all compelling. Burning at the stake—or its academic equivalent, the viciously gate-keeping peer review—seems the inevitable consequence.[1]

My concern throughout this book has been to move past this kind of holy war by focusing attention on one of its key weapons: the notion of "science." Wielded as though it represented a single, unitary mode of knowledge-production, "science" in a methodological context functions much like "God" does in a religious dispute, as both commonplaces appear to refer to the final court of appeal. If science, or God, stood unambiguously on the side of one or another of the parties to a dispute, the game would basically be over—who could or would stand against science in a putatively scientific field, or against God in a deistic religious context? Better, probably, to remove oneself entirely, and thus leave the field to the dominion of others. And such a move would make a good deal of sense, if and only if either God or science did in fact stand unambiguously on any particular side of a dispute.

Whether God stands unambiguously for or against particular courses of action is a question that should probably be postponed for another occasion. But I believe that the discussion in the preceding chapters has demonstrated quite unambiguously that science does *not* stand for or against any particular mode of knowledge-production that is systematically focused on generating facts about the world, and proceeds in such a way that a community of scientific researchers can collaboratively and publicly work to improve their extant stock of knowledge through the research process. While individual scientific methodologies differ on the precise meanings of these terms, all can agree that scientific research is "systematic," "public," and focused on producing "worldly knowledge." Explicating precisely what each methodology means by these terms, and relating that to the philosophical-ontological commitments underpinning each methodology, has been the overt task of the preceding four chapters, and this in turn has unfolded as part of an overall effort to deprive *any* particular methodology of the ability to claim a uniquely scientific status. Science, instead, emerges from the preceding discussion—a discussion that made use of a variety of literature in the philosophy of science—as irreducibly *pluralist*, fully capable

---

1   I am thinking here specifically of a story related by Dvora Yanow and Peri Schwartz-Shea (2006, ix) about a particularly "acerbic" and dismissive review of a manuscript analyzing methods texts in political science (eventually published as Schwartz-Shea and Yanow 2002). However, I would wager that *any* scholar who has submitted a manuscript that utilized methodological presuppositions other than those preferred by the reviewers has had a similar experience.

of being articulated in at least four different varieties. As a result, "science" ought to stop functioning as a trump-card in our internecine debates, and perhaps we as a field can stop worrying so much about the ultimate status of our knowledge-claims and get on with our primary task of producing knowledge about world politics.[2]

In this way, the perspective of this book broadly supports calls for a "post-foundational IR" in which we as a field abandon the futile quest to articulate a single consistent basis on which to produce knowledge. As Nuno Monteiro and Kevin Ruby put it, "there are no universally accepted PoS [Philosophy of Science] recipes for how international relations should be studied. Philosophical arguments cannot and should not be used to legislate which research questions—or ways of answering them—are legitimate in IR" (Monteiro and Ruby 2009, 42). It is necessary to tread carefully here, however, because the abandonment of a quest for universal foundations does not at all guarantee or even imply that scientific work can proceed in the absence of philosophical foundations specific to that particular piece of work or line of inquiry (Chernoff 2009a, 468–469). Indeed, I would argue, and have argued (Jackson 2009, 461–463), precisely the opposite: the abandonment of a quest for universal foundations should place an obligation on scientific researchers to be even *more* explicit about their philosophical commitments, so that readers can better appreciate the basis on which subsequent knowledge-claims are being advanced.

In addition, only a pronounced explicitness about commitments of philosophical ontology can serve as a defense against the tacit and unreflective reproduction of a dominant set of assumptions. For a variety of historical and institutional reasons, some of which I have sketched in the previous chapters, IR as a field largely labors under the domination of mind–world dualism conjoined with phenomenalism; this informs the neopositivism that constitutes so much of the methodological common sense in the field when it comes to notions such as "explanation," "causation," and even "science." If critics of this methodological common sense were deprived of the ability to discuss these issues, the result would be a continuation of the existing dominance—which is precisely why elites throughout history have sought to control the "public transcript" and to force others to speak using their terms (Scott 1990, 18–19, 203–205). Public language matters, precisely because language is not a neutral instrument, and different vocabularies afford different kinds of legitimate or sensible activity (Shotter 1993a, 121–122). A vocabulary that is not rich enough to allow us to meaningfully discuss differences in philosophical ontology functions in practice as a support for a dominant set of philosophical-ontological presuppositions, and therefore a genuinely post-foundational IR would have to feature *more* discussion of issues

---

2   I am taking for granted the existence of an "us" whose primary task it is to produce knowledge about world politics. Despite continued controversy over whether a distinct field of international studies exists at all, we can certainly point to a series of sociological arrangements that sustain the sense of a field or discipline (Turton 2015); I think that is enough for my purposes here.

in the philosophy of science and their implications for research on world politics, not less.

All of which leads us back to Heschel's notion of ecumenical dialogue. Such a dialogue would proceed from a subtle interplay of similarity and difference: differences of "creed and dogma," but a similarity of attitude or orientation.[3] For theology, the orientation in question is towards the divine; for scientific methodology, the orientation is towards the systematic production of worldly knowledge. But alongside that orientation, differences of "creed and dogma"— different commitments and wagers in philosophical ontology—thrive. Heschel envisioned a dialogue that respects those differences without seeking to dissolve them in some kind of nebulous synthesis, but that simultaneously refuses to let the differences overwhelm the discussion to the point where the interlocutors go their separate ways. Such a dialogue requires a particular kind of public conceptual vocabulary in order to take place at all—a public vocabulary that eliminates rhetorical trump-cards and also provides sufficient clarity about points of difference that facile assimilation becomes impossible. The trick is to set up hard conversations, and not to paper over significant differences.

A more adequate lexicon

Of course, scientific methodology also has one other important advantage over theology when it comes to ecumenical dialogue: unlike theology, methodology is always a *means* toward another end. The cleanest and clearest set of methodological precepts means nothing if it does not fulfill its basic function, which is to enable researchers to produce valid knowledge—"valid" according to the standards internal to that methodology. In Weber's pithy formulation, even though

> the *objective* validity of all empirical science rests exclusively on the ordering of actuality according to categories that are, in a specific sense, *subjective*— namely, in that they depict the *presuppositions* of our knowledge, and are bound up with the presupposition of the *value* of the truth that empirical science alone can give us,

scientific debate always remains something other than the ceaseless clash of value-orientations:

> In the area of the empirical social and cultural sciences, as we have seen, the possibility of meaningful knowledge of what is important to us in the unending fullness of happenings is bound up with the never-ending application of viewpoints of specific and particularized characters, which are all in the last instance oriented by value-ideas. These value-ideas, which are indeed empirically stateable and experienceable as components

---

3   In other ecumenical or "uniting" movements, this similarity/difference interplay is sometimes called a "style" (Walker 2005).

of all meaningful human action, can *not* be grounded as valid on anything empirical ... But all of this should not be misunderstood to mean that the actual task of the social sciences should be a furious hunt for new points of view and new conceptual constructions. *To the contrary*: nothing should be more sharply emphasized here than the proposition that the work of constructing and criticizing concepts, among other means, is *also* in service to a final goal: the knowledge of the cultural significance of concrete historical *configurations*.

(Weber 1999a, 213–214)

In other words, the operation of scientific inquiry means explaining things in the world, and as a result, scientific debate is ineluctably oriented towards the world in ways that theological debate need not be. Rather than an immediate confrontation between divergent values, scientific inquiry makes possible a *mediated* form of contestation—a conversation that, even if it does not lead to any kind of overarching substantive consensus, certainly tamps down the fires of unfettered hostility. Unlike pure wars of elimination, scientific inquiry holds out the possibility of agonism without antagonism.[4]

So the question becomes: what kind of organization of a scientific field can most effectively advance such discussions? How can we simultaneously acknowledge a diversity of philosophical assumptions *and* make it possible for concrete work stemming from those assumptions to occupy a conceptual space in which they might be meaningfully contrasted with one another? The first step, I would suggest, involves the formulation of a vocabulary that is sufficiently rich to describe philosophical diversity within a broadly scientific context; the second step is figuring out what to do with the diversity that we must begin by acknowledging. Throughout this book, I have been primarily working on the first step and developing an appropriate vocabulary, but of necessity the vocabulary that I have been developing is informed by an implicit response to the diversity thus disclosed. Before explicitly discussing the response, I want to make the vocabulary itself clearer.

The conceptual vocabulary that I have proposed for talking about diverse wagers of philosophical ontology within a scientific context is quite similar in spirit and orientation to Thomas Kuhn's later work on scientific change, which became increasingly concerned with fundamental differences in bodies of knowledge. Unlike Kuhn's earlier work, which operated with a very expansive and ambiguous notion of how different "paradigms" differed from one another (Masterman 1970), Kuhn's later work reconceptualized and limited the notion of "incommensurability." Kuhn increasingly focused on irreducible meaning variance generated by semantic differences "between a localized cluster of interdefined terms within the language of theories" (Sankey 1993, 760) and other clusters of terms—a variance that could not be ignored precisely because different sets of terms, different vocabularies, picked out and combined different aspects

---

4   I am indebted to Simon Stow for this turn of phrase.

of phenomena. Kuhn referred to such vocabularies as "lexicons," and argued that a given lexicon was "the long-term product of tribal experience in the natural and social worlds, but its logical status, like that of word meanings in general, is that of convention" (Kuhn 2000, 244). Different lexicons pick out and organize phenomena

> in different ways, each resulting in a different, though never wholly different, form of life. Some ways are better suited to some purposes, some to others. But none is to be accepted as true or rejected as false; none gives privileged access to a real, as against an invented, world. The ways of being-in-the-world which a lexicon provides are not candidates for true/false.
>
> (Ibid., 104)

Just as Kuhn's lexicons are specific to particular scientific communities, the lexicon that I have proposed is, in most of its particular details, specific to the IR community. I have followed the field's founders and have not questioned the notion that IR is a scientific field, but I have also taken seriously the breadth of the notion of science with which they and some of their successors operated. Examining literature in the philosophy of science, I have found support for a typology of ways of doing science that foregrounds commitments in philosophical ontology; in fleshing out that typology, I have identified bodies of IR scholarship that are unified—or at any rate *unifiable*—by their methodological similarities rather than by their substantive foci. The result is a lexicon that enables us, as a field, to have a number of philosophically richer and logically more coherent contentious discussions about world politics. I believe that this lexicon will prove more adequate both in terms of its descriptive accuracy and in terms of its practical payoff for IR scholarship.

Science, broadly defined

The first part of the lexicon involves a redefinition of the term "science" so as to detach it from specific notions such as hypothesis-testing, empirical generalization, the disclosure of deep structures, or a commitment to counterfactual reasoning. Instead, I have followed Max Weber in defining science in very broad terms: the careful and rigorous application of a set of theories and concepts so as to produce a "thoughtful ordering of empirical actuality" (Weber 1999a, 160). This definition yields three constituent components of a scientific knowledge-claim: it must be *systematically* related to its presuppositions; it must be capable of *public criticism* within the scientific community—and in particular, public criticism designed to improve the knowledge being claimed; and it must be intended to produce *worldly knowledge*, whatever one takes "the world" to include. These three necessary components, jointly sufficient, form the broad parameters of the proposed definition of science.

Systematicity is perhaps the most important component of this definition. Without a clear and consistent line from presuppositions to conclusions, it is impossible to evaluate a claim according to any logical or formal standards, and we can easily be left with the kind of unending shouting matches that dominate the opinion pages of major newspapers or the unmoderated discussion forums attached to certain popular websites. If there is no systematic connection between a claim's substantive premises—for example, the behavior of states in anarchy, or the operation of processes within an international bureaucracy—and the empirical conclusions or recommendations that result, then we are in a realm where disagreements that purport to be about arguments can only be disagreements with the proffered conclusions. If our disputes are to be anything other than differences of ex ante beliefs about material power, cultural hegemony, or whatever, the first and foremost thing on which we *have* to insist is that IR scholars make a real effort to connect their conclusions with their premises systematically.

Now, this argument is likely to be uncontroversial for *substantive* premises, but I would argue that it applies even more directly to *methodological* premises and presuppositions in the realm of philosophical ontology. If I do not know whether a claim about patterns of world trade is supposed to be understood as a hypothesis about the causal impact of interdependence (as in Gartzke and Li 2003) or as part of a dialectical intervention to provoke a rethinking of the concept of wealth (as in Inayatullah 1996), then I likely have no real sense of how to evaluate it. Indeed, in the absence of such a systematic connection between methodological premises and the knowledge subsequently claimed, mismatches and misunderstandings are quite likely, as when neopositivists take others to task for not articulating falsifiable hypotheses even as they themselves are taken to task for failing to identify deep structural dispositions or case-specific configurations of factors or for failing to acknowledge their own role in reproducing the system they study. In addition, without a clear sense of how a given methodology warrants and entails specific conclusions, we are left in the same position as those striving in vain to find the logical basis for a conclusion that does not, in fact, have one: all we can do is to agree or disagree with the statement. Methodology connects philosophical premises and substantive conclusions, and if our methodology is not clear and systematic, then there can be no meaningful scientific controversy about a claim.

Alongside systematicity, the notion of public criticism—criticism designed to improve knowledge—stands as another indispensable component of science. Public criticism is implicit in the notion of a systematic connection between premises and conclusions, because if such systematicity is meaningfully to exist in the first place it cannot, by definition, be part of a "private language" comprehensible only to the researcher (Wittgenstein 1953, §243–271). Instead, a systematic connection, especially a systematic *methodological* connection, has to be comprehensible to the relevant research community as systematic, which means that it must explicitly or tacitly use rules and procedures that other members of the community acknowledge as constituting valid logical inference. These rules and procedures, in turn, encompass everything from the precise meaning of a term of art such as "satisfice" to a professional sensibility about the contours of "the literature" and major debates within it. Obviously, these rules and procedures vary over time, but the basic conceptual point is that *at any given moment*, a scientific claim that systematically stems from a clear set of premises is both comprehensible to and therefore criticizable by other members of the relevant community.[5]

The kind of scientific criticism that I have in mind here is not dismissive criticism, but instead the kind of communal engagement with an argument that is intended—intended *publicly*, if not consciously or deliberately—to improve that argument and the knowledge that it warrants.[6] Such scientific criticism is, as far as I can tell, advocated by adherents of *every* kind of scientific methodology, from King, Keohane, and Verba's emphasis on making one's work speak to the concerns of the broader scientific community (King, Keohane, and Verba 1994, 8–9, 15–17) to Wight's call for research that integrates across existing dichotomies of agent/ structure and material/ideational (Wight 2006, 293–294) to efforts to encourage scholars of culture and identity to specify the implicit microfoundations of their arguments (Bates, de Figueiredo, and Weingast 1998). While an uncharitable reading could easily regard all of these critiques as absolutist attempts to eliminate alternative ways of producing knowledge, the logical form of such critiques points in another and more charitable direction: the critic is endeavoring to improve the argument being critiqued, by calling attention to those places where the argument falls short. Coupled with an appropriately broad account of the diverse bases on which scientifically valid knowledge can be produced, public criticism is a healthy aspect of any scientific community.

Finally, science in this broad definition is constituted by an intent to produce worldly knowledge: knowledge that is, in the last instance, referred to the world rather than to something outside of it, such as a set of divinely legislated moral principles. Worldly knowledge is the realm of facts, not of ethical evaluation or mystical contemplation; facts, in turn, are accessible to anyone employing the proper procedures for disclosing them, and depend not on revelation or intuitive insight but on systematic demonstration and public, if technical, argumentation. By "world" I do not mean anything as narrow as the *phenomenal* world, of course; if I did, then critical realists and reflexivists could not fit within the definition of science. Rather, by "world" I mean simply that realm of actuality that a methodology takes to exist, whether that realm of actuality is limited to phenomenal experience or whether it also includes real-

---

5   Some would argue for expanding the boundaries of the community to include everyone potentially affected by the validity of knowledge-claim in question (Dewey 1954). Some would not. I do not want to take a side of that issue; instead I will only point out that "publicity" remains the operative principle *regardless* of the empirical extent of the relevant community.

6   Whether any given scientist involved in a scientific debate is motivated by a desire to help her or his interlocutor improve her or his argument, or is motivated by a desire to undercut the proponent of a claim that rivals her or his own, is quite immaterial to my analysis, which works in the realm of publicly observable intention rather than the private realm of motivation (Anscombe 1963); see also Jackson 2006, 21–26.

but-undetectable dispositional causal powers or yet-to-be-realized dialectical syntheses of divergent perspectives and the social groups that hold them. Every scientific methodology "worlds" in a distinct way, and every scientific methodology limits itself to the near side of the boundary of what it takes to exist, for the simple logical reason that it is impossible to go beyond the world to say precisely where its limits lie.[7] Hence, we have a variety of wagers of philosophical ontology, but wagers that afford and give rise to particular kinds of scientific research—research that is directed, of necessity, at the world and the objects within it.

I propose that these three qualities—systematic, public, and intended to produce worldly knowledge—define a scientific endeavor, differentiating it from other modes of activity such as politics and art. This broad definition maintains the spirit of the skeptical impulse animating scientists from back in the early days of the European Enlightenment (Toulmin 1992); this same spirit can be seen in contemporary scientists and advocates for science such as Carl Sagan, whose words opened this book. But the broad definition does not make the all-too-common mistake of trying to define "science" by looking at a supposedly successful science and extracting a definition from it, and it does not purport to derive from an imagined consensus among philosophers of science about what science is or how it works. I avoid such mistakes because they are *mistakes*: no compelling detailed consensus about science-in-general exists, whether among practicing scientists or among philosophers of science. All that can be defensibly extracted from the wide swath of philosophical commentaries on science is a general sensibility, not a specific set of instructions about how to produce scientific knowledge.

To avoid these mistakes, I began with extant practices of knowledge-production in our field, and set out to reconstruct and formalize those things that they have in common. The resulting definition is of course not suited to disciplining the field by ruling some ongoing stream of inquiry "unscientific," but that was not my goal. Instead, given the amazing diversity of ways that scientists and philosophers of science think about their endeavors, I wanted to articulate a definition broad enough that most of our scholarly ways of "doing IR" would fit within it. Only in that way can the "science question" be put to rest once and for all: by articulating a big enough tent that the overwhelming majority of what takes place in IR scholarship can fit underneath it. This does not mean that every conclusion reached by every IR scholar should somehow be accepted, or that every procedure that every IR scholar engages in is equally

---

7   See Wittgenstein's argument on this point, which I discussed in Chapter 5. Note that the problem of "going beyond the boundary of the world" is a problem that only really shows itself to monists, or to dualist critics of monism; dualists engaged in their own scientific research simply dwell within the world that they envision, a world that according to their philosophical ontology *already* exists outside of mind and cannot therefore be meaningfully "gone beyond" in the first place. Monists, of course, reject this whole philosophical package as nonsensical. But in both cases, the result is worldly knowledge, irrespective of precisely what is meant by "world."

valid—but it does mean that for most claims advanced by most IR scholars, their scientific status should not be in question.

Wagers in philosophical ontology

Putting the "science question" to rest certainly does not mean that we enter a realm where anything goes. To say that any systematic effort to produce worldly knowledge is scientific does not mean that all such efforts are equally successful; nor are they equally systematic, equally open to public criticism, or equally dedicated to worldly knowledge. However, because no two scientific claims necessarily have anything in common beyond their basic intention to produce worldly knowledge systematically—and, more importantly, because scholars disagree about the precise *meaning* of the basic criteria of scientific inquiry— it is necessary to articulate more focused precepts in order to engage critically with actually existing scientific research. Within the broad umbrella of science, researchers make a variety of different commitments, or wagers, about the "hook-up" between the mind and the world, and these wagers demarcate different ways of doing science from one another. To engage in concrete scientific research is not merely to be systematic, open to public criticism, and focused on producing worldly knowledge; it is also to have these three qualities in one of a number of specific ways—to work according to a scientific methodology that incorporates, at its base, some specific philosophical content about the relationship between the knower and the known. There are multiple ways of doing science, and standing under the big tent also means standing in some specific place within the broad universe of scientific methodologies. That specific place, in turn, provides the more concrete operational procedures characteristic of different modes of scientific inquiry.

I have termed the basic philosophical components of a specific scientific methodology "wagers" or "commitments"—I might also have followed Bas van Fraassen (2004b) and called them "stances"—in large measure in order to highlight their formally *ungrounded* character. By this I mean that although they are foundational to particular modes of knowledge-production, they are themselves incapable of being definitively justified—least of all by the scientific methodologies that they entail. Particular ways of enacting the "hook-up" between the mind and the world operate in the background of our concrete and specific procedures for producing knowledge and are tacitly presumed by those procedures; otherwise the procedures themselves would make no sense. But this means that there can be no argument definitively establishing the validity of those particular ways, because any conceivable way that we might go about trying to validate or invalidate a mind–world "hook-up" would *itself* tacitly presume an answer to the question at the outset (Searle 1995, 178). It is simply not possible to submit a world-disclosing ontological assumption to "an ongoing test across its entire breadth" by continual comparison with the results of intramundane practice within the world (contra Habermas 1990, 321), because all such tests would presume an ontology at their very root, reducing an apparent test—whether its results appeared positive or negative—to a tautology. Instead, the only thing that can be sensibly done is to disclose the ways in which particular ways of producing knowledge presume, at least provisionally, the validity of particular wagers about the mind–world "hook-up," and thus require of their practitioners a commitment that is like nothing else so much as an existential leap of faith.[8]

Talking about such wagers of philosophical ontology requires a vocabulary that is precise enough to permit significant differences and similarities between scientific methodologies to come to the forefront. This vocabulary is not a framework for evaluation; it is, rather, an instrument of clarification, helping to make explicit what is ordinarily tacit. The vocabulary that I have suggested and elaborated in the previous chapters revolves around two logical axes: mind–world dualism versus mind–world monism, and phenomenalism versus transfactualism. While not exhaustive of all possible contentious issues in philosophical ontology, I submit that the ideal-typical typology formed by the conjunction of these two axes is sufficient to map out the present diversity of scientific ways of producing knowledge within the IR field, by locating different methodologies at the intersection of different commitments.

		Relationship between knowledge and observation	
		phenomenalism	*transfactualism*
Relationship between the knower and the known	mind–world dualism	neopositivism	critical realism
	mind–world monism	analyticism	reflexivity

Each of the four methodologies named in the table, as has been discussed in greater detail in the preceding four chapters, stems from a particular combination of philosophical-ontological commitments. Neopositivism incorporates a mind–world split and a limitation of knowledge to the realm of phenomenal experience. Critical realism preserves the mind–world split, but allows for knowledge that transcends the phenomenal realm and penetrates behind all possible experience. Analyticism agrees with neopositivism's limitation of knowledge to the phenomenal realm, but dismisses the notion of a mind-independent world as nonsensical. Finally, a focus on reflexivity incorporates both a monist dismissal of the notion of a mind-independent world and a transfactual affirmation of knowledge that goes beyond phenomenal experience. The differences between these ways of producing knowledge lie not in their technical requirements or in the kind of data with which they operate, but rather in their most basic approaches to the design and execution of scientific research.

To be more specific: the four methodologies I have reconstructed in this book differ from one another in the way that they seek to warrant particular knowledge-claims, their understanding of causality and causal explanation, and the use to

---

8   Or—as Nick Onuf (1989, 46), a little less poetically, puts it—a "psychocultural penchant."

which they put comparison across multiple cases. Researchers working within these methodologies, whatever technical procedures they utilize, only generate meaningful results by conforming their knowledge-producing practices to the requirements of research design entailed by the underlying commitments the methodology makes in the realm of philosophical ontology—which in practice means conforming to the precepts and maxims in the following tables.

Methodology	Status of knowledge	Procedure for evaluating claim
Neopositivism	Unfalsified conjecture	Testing of hypotheses
Critical realism	Best approximation to the world	Laboratory investigation or transcendental argument
Analyticism	Useful account	Analytical narrative
Reflexivity	Device for increasing self-awareness	Theorize researcher's own social conditions

First of all, the four methodologies differ widely with respect to what they hold a valid knowledge-claim to consist of, and therefore how a researcher should go about warranting such a claim. Four specific definitions of worldly knowledge thus entail four different operational procedures, and four different ways to design research-projects.

- Neopositivists regard all knowledge-claims as conjectures about the world, never perfectly mirroring the world and therefore always subject to further evaluation and refinement; from this follows the basic neopositivist research-design admonition—test everything!—as well as the immense technical sophistication with which neopositivists have delineated ways of testing conjectures.
- Critical realists, by contrast, regard knowledge-claims as attempts to approximate the mind-independent world by disclosing the deep dispositional properties of the objects within it and regard our knowledge to be the best current approximation that we have; from this follows the maxim that evaluating and improving knowledge means elucidating those dispositional properties either in controlled settings (a laboratory) or through transcendental argument, so as to generate a sufficiently rich depiction of the world.
- Analyticists regard knowledge as a useful account, concerning themselves not at all with the empirical accuracy of the components of their models; such models prove their explanatory value by being utilized to construct an analytical narrative, and for an analyticist this instrumental value is sufficient to warrant a knowledge-claim.
- Finally, reflexive knowledge is also instrumentally valuable, but only insofar as it provokes greater self-awareness and self-reflection on the part of the producers and consumers of such knowledge; from this follows the notion that the validation of a knowledge-claim starts out, of necessity, with the theorizing of the social conditions of its own production.

Methodology	Type of causation	Procedure for causal explanation
Neopositivism	Empirical generalization	Subsume under general law
Critical realism	Dispositional	Inus-complexes
Analyticism	Ideal-typical and configurational	Counterfactuals
Reflexivity	Dialectical	Disclose unresolved tensions

The four methodologies also differ in their understanding of causation and causal explanation.

- For neopositivism, causation is equivalent to an empirical generalization: "X causes Y" means roughly the same thing as "X generally leads to Y," together with the appropriate scope conditions. Increasingly subtle differentiations by neopositivists between different kinds of empirical generality—necessity, sufficiency, proportionality, and so forth—should not obscure the fact that all neopositivist accounts of causation rely on a notion of causality that has generality at its core; nor should they obscure the fact that for any neopositivist, causal explanation means subsuming individual occurrences and instances under some kind of a general law.[9]

- Critical realists reject this emphasis on *empirical* generalization in favor of a focus on the dispositional properties of objects—dispositions that are themselves "general" in that they form the essential core of the object in question, but that do not lead to general empirical laws because of the context-dependent nature of the way that a dispositional property manifests itself in the world. Hence, causal explanation means determining INUS-conditions—combinations of dispositional properties that are Insufficient and Non-redundant but part of a complex that is Unnecessary but Sufficient to bring about an outcome (Mackie 1965)—that are specific to the situation at hand, even though the individual dispositional properties in question may well be found in other situations characterized by other INUS-conditions.

- Analyticists also reject empirical *generalization*, but in favor of logical *generality*—ideal-typical accounts of causal factors, processes, mechanisms, and sequences—which, in their very conceptual one-sidedness, point in the direction of the specific empirical configurations characteristic of particular situations. Causal explanation for an analyticist therefore means using these ideal-typical instruments to pinpoint those moments of historical contingency where things could have gone off in quite another direction, and then weighing the importance of particular factors in producing the outcome that we actually see. Unlike the causal complexes sought by critical realists,

---

9   This is perhaps most apparent in recent neopositivist efforts to draw together all of the various flavors of empirical generalization under the heading of a single unified account of causation (for example, Gerring 2005), but it is implicit in every other neopositivist discussion of causation as well.

an analyticist's case-specific configurations make no claim to completeness, only to adequacy.

- Reflexive methodology is the least focused on causation per se, but to the extent that it is meaningful to define a notion of "reflexive causation" it would have to involve a dialectical interplay between social conditions and explicit efforts to delineate them. For reflexivists, knowledge itself causes and is caused by the operation of broader social forces, and part of the point of theorizing one's own social location is to call attention to the ways in which knowledge is implicated in the social order. A reflexive causal explanation, if it is to be a good one, also foregrounds unresolved tensions within situated knowledge, so as to promote additional dialectical development; in this way, a genuinely reflexive account of any specific object or situation is always an invitation to or a demand for further reflexivity.[10]

Methodology	Type of comparison	Purpose of comparison
Neopositivism	Nomothetic	Test hypothetical covariations
Critical realism	Contrasting	Elucidate causal powers
Analyticism	Individualizing	Specify particular configurations
Reflexivity	De-naturalizing/ incorporating	Provoke social change

Finally, the four methodologies differ in the use they make of the comparative study of multiple cases.

- Neopositivists make the most central use of comparison, because the very logic of neopositivist explanation demands that particular instances be evaluated in terms of their conformity to general laws. This "nomothetic" variety of comparison seeks to test hypotheses about the cross-case covariation of causal factors, and its basic logic is precisely the same whether the comparison in question is small-n, large-n, qualitative, quantitative, or whatever other variant one chooses. In fact, neopositivism can really only accept single-case studies if they are explicitly related to broader generalizations, functioning as "crucial cases" (Gerring 2007), as inputs to a technique for ascertaining prior probabilities for outcomes (McKeown 1999), or as some other component of a broader case-comparative strategy.
- Critical realists, when they use comparison, obviously do not use it to test hypothetical empirical generalizations; rather, they use comparison to bring

---

10 A "reflexivist" account that simply deploys categories in an undialectical fashion is no longer unfolding in a reflexive manner, but has become something else by converting its categories into hypotheses (neopositivism), delineations of causal powers (critical realism), or ideal-types (analyticism). Without the kind of dialectical "folding" whereby an account turns its own logic back on itself to reveal its own contestability—a figure of thought that Stephen White (2000) describes as "weak ontology"—an account ceases to be reflexivist, and becomes, albeit implicitly, something else.

to light the various ways that dispositional properties manifest themselves in the world. This kind of "contrasting" comparison helps a researcher to delineate more precisely the capacities of particular properties, concretely illustrating the ways in which different combinations enable and constrain potential effects. Because the critical realist knowledge-project involves the production of a rich and detailed inventory of causal properties and powers, individual concrete cases function for the critical realist (as they do for the neopositivist) as sites or instances—but as sites or instances for causal powers, not general laws, to show themselves.

- For analyticists, on the other hand, the analysis of specific concrete cases is the whole point of scientific knowledge-production. Analyticists have no problem with single-case studies, since they claim no general empirical validity for their results; instead, the point of a study of some case is to delineate the *situationally specific* configuration of factors that led to the unique outcome actually observed. The inclusion of additional cases in a study does precisely nothing to advance or solidify the epistemic warrant for an analyticist claim, and the only kind of comparison that even makes sense in an analyticist methodology is the kind of "individuating" comparison that focuses attention on the specifics of an individual case.
- Reflexive scholars likewise have no profound epistemic need for comparison, although when they do compare cases they do so for quite distinct purposes: either to ethnologically "de-naturalize" a set of taken-for-granted assumptions about social order by delineating an empirical alternative or to "incorporate" multiple cases into a more holistic view that supervenes on the individual cases. The point of either of these exercises, as with every concrete research practice utilized by reflexivists, is to promote and provoke social change, by unsettling supposedly firm notions and freeing up the possibility of their dialectical transformation.

In all of these, the vocabulary that I have proposed calls attention to the diversity of ways that scientific research on world politics can and does unfold and to the ways in which this diversity is simply not reducible to a single logic of inquiry. The uses of comparison by critical realists, analyticists, and reflexivists are not deficient forms of neopositivist case-comparison; nor are the elucidation of causal powers, the ideal-typification of causal factors and processes, or the dialectical theorizing of social conditions equivalent but bizarre forms of hypothesis-testing. Each methodology stands on its own philosophical ground and, as a result, envisions a distinct and discrete bundle of operational practices for producing scientific knowledge. Thus the lexicon as a whole picks out methodological diversity within the broad category of science.

A constructivist science?

By way of further elucidating the implications of this lexicon for the contemporary IR field, I want to take up briefly the vexing question of the scientific status of IR "constructivism." I focus here on constructivism for two reasons. First, no other identifiable subset of the contemporary IR scholarly literature has worried as long and as loudly about its epistemic standing over the past few years, probably in large part due to the repeated efforts to de-legitimate constructivism as either not scientific or as not yet scientific enough; in a way, constructivists have been on the defensive ever since Alex Wendt's initial effort (Wendt 1987) to delineate a social-scientific approach to putatively unobservable international phenomena such as global social structures, state identities, and symbolic cultural interaction. The second reason for focusing on constructivism is that the condition of possibility for the current discussion about philosophy of science and its methodological implications in the field of IR is, so to speak, the constructivist incursion: although many of the relevant philosophical points had been raised in the field earlier, something about the mid-1980s brought them to the forefront in such a way as to provoke a "third" (Lapid 1989)—or, perhaps, a "fourth" (Wæver 1996), depending on how one counts—great debate. As IR constructivism has made the publication of this lexicon possible, I feel that it is only fair to circle back and tease out the implications of the lexicon for IR constructivism, and in particular for its scientific status.

What might it mean to say, as IR constructivists typically do say, that knowledge —even scholarly, scientific knowledge—is socially constructed? Although older versions of social constructivism emphasized the determination of knowledge and truth by a simple consensus underpinned by social and political factors from outside of the scientific enterprise itself (as in Monteiro and Ruby 2009, 28–30), more recent scholarship has moved well beyond such crude claims and articulated a variety of more subtle mechanisms through which scientific knowledge might be said to be socially constructed (McArthur 2006, 375–380). In so doing, social constructivist scholarship on science has adopted something along the lines of Ian Hacking's famous definition of what it means for something to be socially constructed: "*X* need not have existed, or need not be at all as it is. *X*, or *X* as it is at present, is not determined by the nature of things; it is not inevitable" (Hacking 1999, 6). As such, to say that scientific knowledge is socially constructed is to say that the knowledge that we presently have is not the knowledge that we inevitably would have had in all possible worlds; contingencies can be identified, branching-points at which alternate pathways could have been taken—alternate pathways that would have led, perhaps, to alternate *but equally valid* forms of physics, chemistry, geology, IR, and so on. It is not, however, to say that physicists, chemists, and so on, would or should assent to this claim; "scientific knowledge is socially constructed" is a proposition of the philosophy and history and sociology of science, not a proposition of the specific sciences under investigation.[11]

---

11 Along these lines, see Bas van Fraassen's (2004b, 178–180) distinction between "empiricist" (a philosophical position, opposed in his vocabulary to positions like "realism") and "empirical" (an epistemic policy displayed by producers of knowledge, opposed to policies like "adherence to received wisdom").

On this account, we might expect a "social constructivist" about IR to be someone who argued that our existing knowledge of world politics was not inevitable, and to be engaged in the enterprise of determining those concrete points at which things might have been different. In other words, we might expect "social construction" to function primarily as a term in the study of IR itself, not in the study of world politics. But this is obviously not the case, as a quick glance at various programmatic attempts to define IR constructivism shows: to be a constructivist is to "focus on the social construction of subjectivity" (Wendt 1992, 393); to pay attention to the normative and epistemic interpretations that people impose on objects and on one another as they work through the process of defining their individual and collective identities and interests (Adler 1997, 336–337; Price and Reus-Smit 1998, 266–267); or to ground one's empirical analysis in the intersubjectively established practical world that actors, collectively, establish for themselves (Guzzini 2000, 160–162; Pouliot 2004, 330–332). The common thread in all of these statements is the notion that social construction is a claim properly, or even exclusively, applied to particular objects in the world: in other words, that constructivism is first and foremost a social theory or a scientific ontology, and *not* a methodological claim about the philosophical status and character of knowledge.[12]

IR constructivists thus, if often unknowingly, take after Berger and Luckmann's seminal statement (Berger and Luckmann 1967) about the construction of the world of everyday knowledge and follow in their footsteps by downplaying philosophical considerations to focus on empirical applications. Of course, in so doing, IR constructivists downplay the enormous philosophical and conceptual tensions at the heart of Berger and Luckmann's project, tensions that stem from the authors' attempt to draw simultaneously on a set of phenomenological attempts to dis-solve the Cartesian problem by focusing on everyday experience *and* on a set of sociological claims about the (over)determination of ideas by social location (Abbott 2001a, 61–64). Berger and Luckmann thus took a set of claims designed to reply to Descartes—and, therefore, designed as ways of elucidating the situation of the *knower*—out of their original context and fashioned them into conceptual instruments applicable to their objects of study: people interacting in social situations, living lives shaped and structured by their places in the world. What largely vanishes here—from Berger and Luckmann, but also for most of the scholars that took up the study of social knowledge after the publication of their book—is sustained attention to the situation of the knower *as distinct from* the situation of the research subjects. And this, in turn, opens the possibility that a dominant philosophical ontology at odds with the philosophical presuppositions of the very idea of social construction might be responsible for defining the methodology that one ought to use to research social construction—which is

---

12   IR constructivists inspired by Bourdieu are a partial exception to this charge, inasmuch as they emphasize reflexivity as a necessary principle of valid knowledge-production (for example, Guzzini 2000, 170–172). That said, most IR Bourdieusians do not seem to engage in that much methodological reflexivity in their concrete scholarly work.

precisely what happened in a sociological field dominated by neopositivism (Steinmetz 2005b, 281–285).

Unsurprisingly, more than a little of this tendency can also be seen with respect to IR constructivism. The definition of social construction in terms of the importance of mental and cultural factors in explaining outcomes suggests a certain kind of methodological neutrality for constructivist claims—as though, despite the philosophical sources on which IR constructivists draw when conceptualizing how social actors produce their lived realities, the evaluation of the empirical claims that those constructivist scholars put forth could be seamlessly linked to standards and practices far removed from the original philosophical sources. Thus we have Price and Reus-Smit's advice that constructivists interested in showing that norms matter in world politics should seek to demonstrate "constitutive impact" by ascertaining whether some norm was a necessary condition for a given outcome (Price and Reus-Smit 1998, 282–283); David Dessler's suggestion that constructivists might develop alternative covering-laws incorporating cultural and ideational factors (Dessler 1999, 132);[13] and Ted Hopf's concern to "test hypotheses deduced from a theory of how identity might affect foreign policy choice" against empirical evidence recovered through "deeply inductive interpretivist" techniques (Hopf 2002, xi). Even more explicitly, we have efforts such as Amir Lupovici's articulation of a "methodology for *modernist* constructivist research" (Lupovici 2009, 198) that encompasses cross-case covariation, the generalization of findings from small-n case studies, and even falsifiable hypotheses (ibid., 208–214): in short, all the methodological accompaniments of neopositivism.[14]

Here as elsewhere, in the absence of any sustained attention to methodology properly understood, the default position in IR—whether one is talking about constructivist, rationalist, systemic, individualist, or any other variety of substantive claims—is and remains neopositivism. Let me be absolutely clear: *there is no special philosophical problem with this situation.* As a philosophical ontology, neopositivism is compatible with a wide variety of substantive theories about and scientific ontologies of world politics, and if one wants to be a neopositivist constructivist then there is no logical or philosophical barrier to doing so—the two are perfectly compatible, so long as one does not insist that the philosophical sources from which the operative concepts of ideas and social practices are drawn were somehow intending to generate falsifiable hypotheses

---

13 Dessler, at least, is very explicit about the fact the he is offering suggestions for constructivists who wish to stay within what he calls "positivist social science"—which implies, I think, that there might be a diversity of ways to do social science. I am unclear where other neopositivist-constructivist commentators stand on this issue.

14 Lupovici's use of the adjective "modernist," although calling to mind Emanuel Adler's (1997) functionally similar usage of the term as a shorthand abbreviation for a more precise discussion of a philosophical-ontological position, differs from Adler's usage on substantive grounds: in my terminology, Lupovici appears to mean "neopositivist," while Adler, given his emphasis on reciprocal processes of learning and cognitive evolution, may mean something more like "reflexivity."

or produce general covering-laws pertaining to social action.[15] However, the particular IR use of the term "constructivist"[16] to designate a scientific ontology has resulted in a lot of needless conceptual confusion—a lot of it surrounding the futile and fruitless search for a "constructivist methodology." There is no such thing; there is probably never going to be any such thing; and continuing to focus on "constructivism" as a meaningful category for organizing the IR field is as philosophically nonsensical and practically counterproductive a move as any other attempt to break the grip of an unselfconscious neopositivism has been over the past few decades.

The problem, as Audie Klotz and Cecilia Lynch (2007, 105) acknowledge in their handbook of constructivist research strategies, is that self-identified IR constructivists work with "a wide variety of research designs." Klotz and Lynch thus adopt a strategy of juxtaposition, placing scholarship that treats norms and identities as variables susceptible to inclusion in a testable hypothesis alongside scholarship that works with models of discursive practice or with elucidations of the dispositional powers of structures and agents. Similarly, Dvora Yanow and Peri Schwartz-Shea (2013) gather an even more diverse group of research strategies, many of which highlight the factors usually discussed by IR constructivists,[17] under the heading "interpretivism." As illuminating as these exercises may be in assembling into one convenient location a wide variety of techniques of knowledge-production that do not fit at all comfortably into neopositivist ways of doing research, in a scholarly field dominated by neopositivism they have something of the feeling of a grab bag: a bunch of stuff, parts of which are interesting to particular researchers and not others, and a decisive absence of anything even approximating an overarching, coherent logic of inquiry. In the (perhaps deliberate)

---

15 In fact, to be on the safe side, neopositivist constructivists probably ought to insert a disclaimer explicitly into their theories someplace, something to the effect that although the substantive claims in their work are derived from, or inspired by, particular philosophers and social theorists, they are not really a faithful translation. I imagine such a disclaimer functioning much like the notification that a film is "adapted from" a beloved novel: if placed in a prominent enough location, the disclaimer may prevent anyone from walking into the theater expecting to see the original novel on the screen, and may prevent them from walking out of the theater in protest at alterations to plot, character, setting, and so on.

16 In fairness, the claim that something has been socially constructed is used in fields and domains other than IR, where it is sometimes experienced as "wonderfully liberating" (Hacking 1999, 2) by people who are given license to resist or reject some previously naturalized fact once that fact is revealed to be the (mere) product of social actions and arrangements. In fact, this is about the only meaningful sense in which postmodern IR scholars like Richard Ashley and Cynthia Weber might be categorized as "constructivists," but the resulting tent would be so big that it would encompass basically everyone in the field who did not think that the dynamics of world politics were governed by something like natural necessity (as in Jackson and Nexon 2004). Depending on the specific object in question, almost every IR scholar would likely be a "constructivist" about *some* aspect of world politics.

17 Indeed, some of the chapters in the Yanow and Schwartz-Shea volume are written by IR scholars who are usually described as "constructivists."

absence of a coherent constructivist or interpretivist methodology,[18] works such as these inadvertently prove my point: "constructivism" is a *methodologically* meaningless category in international studies.

As a result, it is very difficult to figure out what "constructivist methods" or "constructivist research strategies" might *mean*. A phrase such as "research on norms" is easy to explicate, because such a phrase makes no methodological pretensions and simply refers to an object of research; similarly, phrases such as "research on the global political economy" or "research on war" would almost certainly gather together scholars and scholarship with different methodological stances, unified only by their focus on a similar empirical domain (even if that domain is conceptualized and studied very differently). So if "constructivist research" were simply equivalent to "research on norms and identities," the phrase might make sense, but the usage "constructivist" *as an adjective* might still lead one to suspect that constructivism named a kind of style of research rather than a collection of objects of research. We would not expect that every IR scholar studying war or the global political economy would or should adopt the same research methods and methodology, because there is nothing in the bare notion of "war" or "political economy" that *necessitates* any particular way of researching the objects in question. Obviously, once a researcher cashes out her or his approach to something by adopting one or another set of methodological precepts, what she or he means by a particular term or concept might vary widely from what another researcher working within a different methodology means by the same term or concept; but what is decisive here is not the substantive research focus but the incorporation of methodological content: a research design, an understanding of causal explanation, and a set of procedures for evaluating claims. To the extent that Lewis Richardson (1960) and Hidemi Suganami (1996) have different concepts of "war," this is obviously not due to "war" *itself*, but to their divergent methodologies for studying war.[19]

Accordingly, since there is not and cannot be any such thing as a "constructivist methodology," it makes no sense to inquire into the scientific status of constructivism per se. As a matter of fact, it makes just as little sense to inquire into the scientific status of realism or neoliberal institutionalism, since they have the same problem as constructivism: they name substantive assumptions about world politics and a number of objects to which those assumptions are thought to adhere, and do not name coherent logics of inquiry (Jackson and Nexon 2009,

---

18 Both the Klotz and Lynch book and the Yanow and Schwartz-Shea volume quite deliberately set aside any notion of a unified logic of inquiry for their projects.

19 This, among other reasons, is why (as I argued in Chapter 2) I think that the notion of "putting ontology first" is such a problematic one: whenever a scholar "puts (scientific) ontology first," he or she is generally smuggling in unacknowledged a methodology with its accompanying *philosophical* ontology. We can only use a concept of an object of study as a way of grounding a field-wide approach to that object if we already agree on what that object is and on what it means to say that the object *is* in one way rather than another—and for my money, such an all-encompassing consensus probably ought to be opposed just in principle, in the name of pluralism. See below.

916–918). But the interminable "is realism making scientific progress?" debate gets its traction from the striking fact that virtually all card-carrying IR realists are neopositivists, and the debate gets its chief irony (and most pointed exchanges) from the fact that Waltz is not a neopositivist (a fact that is abundantly clear from, for example, Waltz 1997).[20] As for neoliberal institutionalists, those most overtly concerned with the scientific status of their research (Keohane and Martin 2003; Legro and Moravcsik 1999) are equally neopositivists, to the point where they misleadingly regard formal models as machines for producing falsifiable hypotheses. The important point, however, is that this general methodological consensus shifts the issue somewhat: instead of the scientific status of realism or neoliberal institutionalism, what these scholars are actually discussing is the scientific status of neopositivist research on interstate balancing or interstate cooperation. Only methodological consensus makes this kind of a discussion meaningful.

However, there is no methodological consensus in constructivism, and there is not likely to be one. Or, rather, given the dominance of neopositivism in the field of IR, if a methodological consensus emerges across constructivism, the result is likely to equate "constructivism" with "neopositivist research on norms and ideas," and to cite the edited volume *Ideas and Foreign Policy* (Goldstein and Keohane 1993) as one of its seminal founding texts. If this were to happen as a result of a process of scholarly debate and consensus-formation, it would be unobjectionable, since there is no compelling *philosophical* or *methodological* reason why norms, ideas, culture, and other intersubjective factors cannot be studied by using a neopositivist methodology. But—and this is my worry—if a methodological consensus is formed as a combination of the deployment of an erroneously narrow definition of "science" against non-neopositivist research and the resulting unavailability of a logically coherent methodological register supporting anything other than neopositivism, then this would be an unmitigated tragedy, *especially in light of the lack of consensus about "science" among philosophers of science*. It is a lie that only the neopositivist way of studying world politics is scientific—a lie that derives some of its power and plausibility, I would argue, from our general lack of familiarity with issues in the philosophy of science and their implications for IR scholarship.

However, by the same token, a decision to conduct research using a non-neopositivist methodology places a particular burden on a researcher: to be clear not only about her or his research methodology, but about where that methodology differs from the still-dominant neopositivist way of doing research. It is not enough to reject hypothesis-testing or cross-case generalizations; the researcher engaging in alternative modes of scientific research has to spell out the warrants for her or his claims in such a way that they cannot be mistaken for neopositivist procedures, and to locate her or his work among the existing bodies of work that utilize a methodology more suitable to the knowledge-production practices that she or he is actually using. The dominance of neopositivism has produced a strange

---

20   See also the discussion of Waltz in Chapter 5.

situation in which even the more forceful critics of neopositivist methodology have a difficult time articulating what they are doing without inadvertently succumbing to the temptation to use an innocuous-sounding phrase such as "structured, focused comparison" (Wiener 2009, 187) while completely glossing over the fact that such a procedure *does not fit, methodologically speaking*, with the balance of their research strategy. This "pseudomorphosis," or distortion produced by trying to articulate a novel approach in a context thoroughly dominated by a different perspective,[21] is a commentary on the relative poverty of methodological language in common use in the field of IR, and the decided slant of that language in a neopositivist direction. Furthermore, the only defensible alternative is to articulate alternatives, and to articulate them as clearly and rigorously as possible.

So the answer to the question of whether constructivism is a science is that non-neopositivist constructivists have their work cut out for them in trying to produce a non-neopositivist science of intersubjective factors and their role in world politics. Just as there is no necessary reason why there would have to be a neopositivist study of such things, there is nothing methodologically speaking to prevent the formation of a "critical realist constructivism," an "analyticist constructivism," and a "reflexivist constructivism." Although some of the relevant conceptual and philosophical spadework has been done already (Onuf 1998; Guzzini 2000; Pouliot 2007; Hansen 2006; Neumann 2002), much remains to be accomplished. Scholars interested in intersubjective factors may have something of a comparative advantage over realists and neoliberal institutionalists in articulating non-neopositivist methodologies, given that the substantive philosophical and conceptual work that they draw on is almost entirely steeped in alternative methodologies, but there is nothing inevitable about this possibility.[22] If something other than neopositivism is to thrive in the study of culture and norms and identities and ideas, committed scholars will have to continue to do the hard work of articulating what those alternative methodologies might look like in an IR context.

---

21 The term "pseudomorphosis" is a mineralogical term for a process whereby a mineral takes on the form of another—a form that it does not normally hold—due to exceptional circumstances; as far as I know, Oswald Spengler (1926; 1928) was the first to use the term in a social-cultural setting.

22 The same might be said of feminists, and of various Marxist and post-colonial theorists: the possibility for articulating non-neopositivist methodologies is certainly quite present, but it has to be concretely enacted in order for it to become actual in the field—and in order for these approaches to resist being either converted into scientific ontologies and assimilated into a neopositivist approach to knowledge-production, or marginalized as non-scientific and therefore having no expectation of systematicity and rigor. The articulation of non-neopositivist methodologies is the best defense against both of these fates, both for these critical theories and for the study of intersubjective factors more generally.

Responding to methodological diversity

Should alternatives to neopositivism thrive, however? The lexicon developed in this book permits a philosophically informed description of different scientific methodologies, but it does not necessarily mandate that these differences be maintained in their purest form. Indeed, one response to the methodological diversity brought to light by my lexicon might be to argue that the field ought to move towards some kind of methodological synthesis, or perhaps a preference for multiple-methodology research. Another response might be that the field should look for reliable ways to evaluate different methodologies against one another comparatively, so that the superior methodology would win out over the others. Against these alternatives, I want to suggest that the proper response to methodological diversity is an *engaged pluralist* attitude (Lapid 2003) that seeks neither to maintain different methodological traditions in their splendid isolation from one another nor to rest content with an eclectic assemblage of notions and concepts drawn from different cells in the typology of philosophical-ontological wagers. An engaged pluralism brings to the foreground specific sets of contentious conversations—conversations that unfold without necessarily resulting in either agreement or stalemate, but instead produce ever-finer differentiations and specifications brought on by the difficult intellectual labor of translation.

It bears repeating that the lexicon I have proposed is a philosophical vocabulary in which methodologies appear in an abstract and purified logical form. Neopositivism, critical realism, analyticism, and reflexivity name four different ways in which scientific research can unfold, not four different self-conscious research traditions or schools of thought within the IR field. In other words, the unit of analysis for this lexicon is the claim, or more precisely, the *argument* supporting and warranting the claim. Methodological categories are not necessarily appropriate for a concrete researcher or even any specific article or book—a given researcher might utilize different methodologies at different times over the course of her or his career, and there is no reason why a single published work cannot contain multiple independent arguments, even if those arguments are themselves drawn from different methodologies.[23] The four scientific methodologies function, so to speak, as ways of specifying the logic of actually existing arguments, and spelling out explicitly what the authors of

---

23   Compare, in this regard, David Marsh and Paul Furlong's (2002, 21) assertion that philosophical wagers and commitments operate at the level of the individual researcher, and not at the level of the argument. I am not sure why the fact that methodologies "reflect fundamental different approaches to what social science is and how we do it" necessarily means that a particular concrete researcher must never change her or his mind about her or his foundational commitments. To use their metaphor, philosophical wagers may not be a "sweater" that we can put on and take off when convenient, but they are not a "skin" that inheres in an individual as a natural fact. I would rather say that methodologies are prosthetic devices like a blind person's cane, allowing us to investigate the world in specific ways (as in Shotter 1993b, 21–23): such prosthetics are more fundamental than sweaters, but are still more easily exchanged than one's skin.

those arguments might have left implicit. To say that a particular argument "is" a neopositivist or critical realist or analyticist or reflexive argument is, therefore, to *reconstruct* that argument along the lines of particular methodology, working from clues in the text about the appropriate methodology to use. Sometimes this is easy to do for an entire work, as when Andrew Moravcsik (1998) spends a great deal of time defining causal variables, specifying the observable implications of particular hypotheses about relationships between variables, and then adducing data to test whether those hypotheses hold up across multiple cases; to reconstruct this as anything other than neopositivism would be simply ludicrous. But in many cases, reconstructing *the* argument of a scholarly work along methodological lines is quite impossible, because the work contains several different arguments that rest on philosophically divergent bases.

The question of methodological diversity, therefore, is a question about a diversity of arguments, not a question about the diversity of research traditions or schools of thought—let alone putative IR "research programmes" or "paradigms." The distinction is important, because methodologically different arguments have different bases in philosophical ontology, and are therefore strictly speaking *incompatible* with one another in the sense that what one regards as decisive another sees as irrelevant. A neopositivist argument places great value on cross-case covariation; other methodologies regard such evidence as suggestive at best and irrelevant at worst. The imaginative elaboration of plausible counterfactuals is critical to analyticist scholarship; critical realist and reflexive arguments do not require this kind of imaginative elaboration, and neopositivist arguments regard counterfactuals to be logically equivalent to comparative cases. And so on. Whole scholarly works, or whole scholarly research traditions, would only face this kind of problem to the extent that they were more or less completely characterized by a single methodology, because the problem of incompatibility is rooted in methodology and in the philosophical-ontological commitments incorporated into different methodologies, and not in particular substantive assumptions.[24]

---

24   In this respect, consider James Rule's (1997, 113–114) argument that the best way for the social sciences to make progress is to stop being so concerned about internal consistency and to focus instead on incorporating the widest possible set of relevant factors into the analysis: "if a Marxist should invoke religious conviction in accounting for the willingness of early Christians to accept martyrdom under the Roman Empire," he asks rhetorically, "has something gone theoretically wrong?" To the extent that we regard Marxism as a set of *substantive* claims about what motivates individual human action (which is a rather tendentious reading of Marxism to be sure), Rule's position makes sense—but only if our methodological goal is to produce a comprehensively compelling account of human action. A consensus on methodology thus affords an integration or inclusion of many different streams of substantive theory under the auspices of that methodology's strategy for producing knowledge. It is, however, quite unclear what if anything it might mean to perform this operation across *different* methodologies, since the only common ground that they share—the broad definition of science—is in my lexicon deliberately not strong enough to permit this kind of integration.

As such, the notion that one could comparatively evaluate methodologies against one another is either completely nonsensical or quite disingenuous. If we were confronted with a neopositivist (Webb and Krasner 1989) and a reflexive (Grunberg 1990) argument about the relationship between hegemony and stability, how would we go about comparatively evaluating them? What standards of evaluation would we use? If we sought specifications of observable implications for the purpose of comparative hypothesis-testing, that would clearly bias the evaluation in favor of the neopositivist argument; if we sought elucidations of the social embeddedness of the researcher, that would clearly bias the evaluation in favor of the reflexive argument. So either a comparative evaluation of these two arguments would be a simple juxtaposition that failed actually to evaluate anything, or it would be a tacit and perhaps hidden positing of the standards appropriate to one methodology as though those standards were not themselves only one of multiple ways of doing science. Either way, there would be no comparative evaluation; there would simply be difference, and perhaps dominance.

This problem also affects proposals for methodological synthesis or for the use of multiple methodologies. Because methodologies differ in such fundamental ways, efforts to synthesize them generally end up privileging one set of methodologically specific standards over others—and using those standards as a procrustean bed into which other methodologies must be made to fit. For example, when David Laitin (2003) proposes a synthesis of large-n correlations, small-n case studies, and formal models into a single recipe for producing social-scientific knowledge, any hint of methodological diversity quickly vanishes as formal models are converted into sources for hypotheses and large-n and small-n work show themselves as means for testing those hypotheses. Similarly, the various calls for the expanded use of "multiple methods" in research design—which, in practice, generally means the inclusion of both large-n and small-n components—rely on a fairly transparent reduction of "comparison" to its neopositivist variant (Ahmed and Sil 2009; Chatterjee 2009).[25] It should be quite unsurprising that synthesis and integration between arguments that all fall into the same methodological category is a fairly unproblematic exercise, because doing away with issues of philosophical incompatibility by definitional fiat has paved the way for a relatively straightforward combination of research techniques. Such syntheses, however, are, in the end, little more than extensions of methodological imperialism under the guise of tolerance.

Standing on the ground of any given methodology, it is reasonably easy to propose and propound a way of conceptualizing scientific research in general that results in the assimilation of alternative methodologies to one's own. Analyticists can transmute any other approach's causal factors and processes into ideal-typical conceptual instruments; critical realists can transform any other approach's claims into partial constituents of its own more realistic accounts; reflexivists can deploy

---

25   The terminology—multiple "methods" instead of multiple "methodologies"—is itself unintentionally revealing.

the results achieved by others in an effort to promote critical self-refection; and neopositivists can make anything into a testable hypothesis. But this tells us precisely nothing about the relative value of any particular methodology, because there are no generally valid reasons vindicating any of these four methodologies over the others. In the absence of any such general vindication, there is simply no *warrant* for this kind of assimilation. Rather than judging an argument by the standards of another methodology, it only makes sense to judge an argument by *its own* methodology, and according to the ways in which that methodology fills out the broad definition of science—systematic inquiry intended to produce worldly knowledge—with specific philosophical-ontological content.

In other words, the only philosophically defensible response to methodological diversity is methodological pluralism. Not methodological *relativism*, as this would imply that it would be possible for different methodologies to come to contradictory conclusions about some matter of fact, but instead, the kind of pluralism of which William James spoke:

> What, in the end, are all our verifications but experiences that agree with more or less isolated systems of ideas (conceptual systems) that our minds have framed? But why in the name of common sense need we assume that only one such system of ideas can be true? The obvious outcome of our total experience is that the world can be handled according to many systems of ideas, and is so handled by different men [*sic*], and will each time give some characteristic kind of profit, for which he [*sic*] cares, to the handler, while at the same time some other kind of profit has to be omitted or postponed … why, after all, may not the world be so complex as to consist of many interpenetrating spheres of reality, which we can thus approach in alternation by using different conceptions and assuming different attitudes, just as mathematicians handle the same numerical and spatial facts by geometry, by analytical geometry, by algebra, or by quaternions, and each time come out right?
>
> (James 1902, 99–100)

James' language may be a bit dated, but his perspective is quite well-suited for a scholarly field characterized by different methodological perspectives and "systems of ideas." Methodological pluralism envisions a situation in which different scientific methodologies generate different bodies of knowledge, each of which is internally justified in distinctive ways, but none of which commands unqualified universal assent. Knowledge remains inextricably bound to the methodology that warrants it, but this does not present a problem so long as each particular claim enjoys the kind of validity conferred by its own methodology: then all the claims are valid, albeit in different ways.[26]

---

26 This argument parallels Donald Davidson's (1973) famous demolition of the idea that relating knowledge-claims to a specific conceptual vocabulary results in a global relativism of "conceptual schemes" (see also Rorty 1981, 308).

A pluralist science of IR thus poses the challenge of dealing with bodies of warranted knowledge stemming from philosophically incompatible methodologies. While it might be feasible to "eclectically" (Sil 2009) take bits and pieces from different bodies of knowledge and explore the ways in which they combine and configure to affect outcomes, this sounds entirely too close to an analyticist methodology to be genuinely pluralist.[27] Instead, the implication of methodological pluralism is that between different bodies of warranted knowledge we have the ongoing challenge of *translation*: literally, the task of making claims comprehensible to speakers of other methodological languages. Because there is no methodologically neutral metalanguage into which we could reliably translate our warranted knowledge-claims and have them be globally understood, methodological pluralism sets up a variety of contentious conversations and efforts to appreciate the insights of alternative ways of producing knowledge while avoiding the temptation to universalize our own modes of conducting scientific inquiry.[28]

Instead of seeking or imposing a methodological monoculture on the field of IR—whether we call this imposition a "disciplining" of the field (Laitin 1995) or the promulgation of a "via media" (Wendt 2000) is, to my mind, quite immaterial—the lexicon that I propose stands firmly on the side of methodological pluralism. This metamethodological sensibility (Shotter 1993b, 21) affords neither clashes of (methodological) civilizations nor the subsumption of diversity into a specious universalism, but calls for dialogical *encounters* between arguments inhabiting different parts of the logical space formed by the combination of basic wagers of philosophical ontology. As Naeem Inayatullah and David Blaney (2004, 17) remind us, the "contact zone" formed when different projects encounter one another admits of many possibilities, "from opacity, repression, and knowledge sought for purposes of domination to a sense of wonder, a desire for understanding and mutual communication, and a joining of social criticisms." As such, surviving an encounter requires entering the dialogue with a firm sense of one's most basic commitments intact, but simultaneously acknowledging that these commitments might themselves be transformed as a result of the dialogue. Striking a balance between stubborn persistence and selective permutation is, I submit, better aided by an abstract and spare delineation of methodological stances than by Inayatullah and Blaney's suggestive but vague admonition always to seek the repressed other within the self. I am not interested in muddying the methodological waters in the field even further than they are already muddied; instead, I am interested in greater precision and ever-finer differentiations, such that scholars become even more

---

27   Also, proposals for "analytical eclecticism" of this sort (for example, Katzenstein and Sil 2008) tend to focus on the combination of factors and mechanisms drawn from a variety of *substantive* research traditions, not so much on the problem of using knowledge that is embedded in different *methodologies*.

28   Echoes of Paul Feyerabend's (1993) argument that a scientific field should cultivate the maximum possible diversity in order to ensure that claims can be compared and contrasted with as many alternatives as possible are entirely intentional.

cognizant of both the strengths *and* the limitations of their ways of producing knowledge.

After all, the only form of "progress" that we ever make in scientific inquiry—especially in *social*-scientific inquiry—involves the more and more comprehensive exploration of the epistemic spaces formed by the logical intersection of our basic commitments (Abbott 2001a, 28–33). In Abbott's terms, the distinctions between basic commitments have a "fractal" character, such that the opposing stances generated by particular combinations of ontological wagers produce, when brought into dialogue with one another, a finer-grained distinction between the stances along their adjacent boundary—but a finer-grain distinction in which commitments are shuffled and recombined in ceaselessly novel ways. Thus, social scientists and historians split into separate disciplinary camps over methodological issues, but subsequent encounters between the two resulted in curious hybrids such as "historical social science" and "social science history" (ibid., 91–93) as each camp sought to (re-)incorporate methodological admonitions that it had started out rejecting, but to repurpose them in its own novel way. The motor of this process is the contingent articulation of core commitments, not for the purpose of erecting eternally unbreachable walls, but for the purpose of productively summarizing the state of play and hastening the state of the next round of dialogue.

It is therefore perhaps not an accident that my metamethodological lexicon includes four categories, since it is placed in a line of descent that runs from a singular-but-vague notion of "science" in the field's early days, through the binary opposition of "explaining" and "understanding" that sought to place each kind of inquiry on an equal footing, methodologically speaking. My lexicon summarizes, in abstracted form, the more subtle differentiation among ways of conducting inquiry that *presently* characterize the IR field; we have outgrown our earlier cocoons, and are now emerging in a more precisely articulated form. I sincerely hope that my lexicon is not the last word on these issues, and I just as sincerely hope that it will need to be replaced at some time in the not-too-distant future as IR scholars climb up the ladder that it provides and then kick away the ladder as their ongoing research overspills its boundaries. As with any lexicon—indeed, as with any methodology, or any argument—mine is a means rather than an end in itself, and the basis on which it should be judged can be nothing other than its practical effect in generating a wide variety of systematic, worldly knowledge about world politics. The issues we study and the problems with which we grapple are too important for us to countenance the categorical dismissal of alien ways of producing knowledge simply because they do not "world" in the way that we are used to worlding, are not systematic in the way that we are used to being systematic, and do not engage in the kind of public criticism with which we are comfortable. To the contrary: "What is urgently needed are ways of helping one another in the terrible predicament of here and now" (Heschel 1991, 22).

Acknowledgments to the first edition

I had no plans to write this book. Yes, I had been complaining for years to everyone in earshot about the philosophical poverty of virtually all of the discussions in the field about research design and the status of knowledge. Yes, I had often quipped that the only thing I really liked about the research manual I had been handed at the beginning of my graduate program—King, Keohane, and Verba's *Designing Social Inquiry*—was the Wassily Kandinsky print on its cover. And yes, I was seemingly incapable of letting an off-hand reference to "positivism" or a casual equation of "variable" and "causal factor" pass by without taking the opportunity to urge the speaker to be more careful in her or his use of terminology. But the idea of writing a book such as this one did not occur to me until Iver Neumann, upon reading a draft of what became my article "Foregrounding Ontology: Dualism, Monism, and IR Theory," commented that he thought that students would find my presentation of the philosophical issues particularly useful, especially because I was reasonably explicit about what these philosophical considerations meant for concrete research practices. Thus was born the idea for a text introducing IR readers to issues in the philosophy of science, and doing so in a way that would improve on earlier discussions.

That conversation may have been the proximate origin of this book, but the perhaps more important factor was a doctoral seminar I taught at American University from 2001 through 2006. In the syllabus for SIS-714, I advised the students that:

> This course is a broad survey of epistemological, ontological, and methodological issues relevant to the production of knowledge in International Relations (IR) understood primarily as an intellectual activity ... Treat this course as an opportunity to set aside some time to think critically, creatively, and expansively about the *status of knowledge*, both that which you have produced and will produce, and that produced by others.

One day during a discussion of Raymond Geuss' *The Idea of a Critical Theory* and how critical theory might relate to other kinds of theory I sketched a 2×2 matrix on the board in an effort to organize some of the issues we were tossing around; at the end of class I decided that the matrix was a pretty good one, and

I copied it down in the inside back cover of my copy of Geuss' book. A few years and a few seminars later, a slightly modified version of that matrix forms the central analytical core of the typology of philosophical ontologies that I have laid out in this book. The name of the course was "The Conduct of Inquiry in International Relations," and even though various curricular changes in the doctoral program have eliminated the course from the catalog, the title—and the spirit of the intellectual enterprise—survives in the preceding pages.

The most important debt that I have incurred while producing this book is to my wife Holly and my children Quinn and Chloe, who have had to put up with interminable protestations about my need to pass on spending time with them in order to read and think and write. Were it not for their support and understanding, I would be utterly incapable of engaging in my scholarly vocation at all, and I am profoundly grateful for their presence in my life.

In terms of professional debts of gratitude, let me first thank Iver Neumann for his initial suggestions that helped to shape the book, and to him and to the other "New International Relations" series editors Jutta Weldes and Richard Little for bearing with me as the book took a bit longer to actually deliver than I had originally, and quite optimistically, hoped that it would take. Nick Onuf provided much-needed words of encouragement when I was bogged down in the minutia of ontological subtlety, as did Dan Nexon; Martin Hall and Thierry Balzacq were among the first people who expressed a genuine interest in adopting the book for course purposes, which helped to keep me on track. Fred Chernoff invited me to present the work-in-progress at Colgate; similarly, Gunther Hellmann and Benjamin Herborth arranged for me to hold a short seminar on the first two chapters in Frankfurt. Subsequent presentations at the University of Delaware, American University, and Johns Hopkins University helped me to refine further the categories and concepts with which I was working. Dvora Yanow and Peri Schwartz-Shea, friends and colleagues with whom I have had numerous stimulating exchanges about research and philosophy over the years, read some early draft chapters, and also invited me to present the whole lexicon at the National Science Foundation-funded Workshop on Interpretive Methodologies in Political Science. The Norwegian Institute of International Affairs hosted me for a three-day seminar as I was working on the book's conclusion; those discussions, together with the discussion surrounding a presentation at the College of William and Mary, were critical in helping me to gather together the threads of the book in a reasonably comprehensive manner. I would like to extend my thanks to everyone who facilitated or participated in those events, as the book bears traces of all of those engagements.

I will confess to some feelings of envy whenever I read in the acknowledgments of a book that the author is profoundly thankful to one or another external funding agency for supporting their research with tidy sums of money, or to institutions to which they were able to retreat while writing. One day I hope to be able to have similar agencies and institutions to thank. In lieu of that, let me thank my students and friends who have had to put up with my being even busier than usual during the time that I was writing this book while juggling a conventional set of professional commitments in teaching and service. Now that the book is done I hope to get you some comments on that thing that you sent me, to hold office hours and meetings in a somewhat less hurried manner, and perhaps even to be available to socialize now and then.

During the crafting of the book, Oliver Lewis invited me to contribute a comment piece to e-IR, which helped me to clarify my thinking and formulate my argument in a more pithy manner. A few outtakes and rough mixes from the book showed up as blog posts on The Duck of Minerva and as longish emails on the "interpretation and method" listserv; the comments that those generated also helped me to clarify things by seeing how the argument was received. I would also be remiss if I did not explicitly reference a number of late-night (and early-morning!) conversations/discussions/arguments with Colin Wight in the bars at a succession of ISA meetings; traces of those sessions show up throughout the text.

During the writing process, my graduate research assistant Josh Jones was an important sounding-board for how the chapters sounded to student ears. Other graduate students, including Tony Rivera, Tamara Trownsell, Kate Goodwin, Jorg Kustermans, Morten Andersen, and Stephanie McDaniel, read drafts and provided feedback. My colleague Celine-Marie Pascale provided an early vote of confidence in the way that the manuscript was unfolding and also connected me with Ian Bruff, whose careful engagement with various draft chapters was invaluable. Robert Adcock likewise read through the complete draft and provided some important observations about areas of nineteenth-century Anglophone philosophy outside of my main areas of knowledge. And at an early stage, Gerard van der Ree approached me about teaching the draft manuscript to his Advanced IR course at University College Utrecht; the feedback that he and his students generated while working through the draft has definitely made this a better book.

At Routledge, Heidi Bagtazo patiently herded the manuscript through the process, and made sure that I was left in the capable hands of Hannah Shakespeare when she went on leave. Harriet Frammingham capably handled the production logistics, from copy-editing to publicity to revisions of the cover layout. Rachel Nishan of Twin Oaks Indexing did her usual admirable job preparing the index. I wish also to acknowledge kind permission granted by the University of Chicago Press for use of the quote by Stephen Toulmin (from *Cosmopolis: The Hidden Agenda of Modernity*, Chicago: University of Chicago Press, 1992) that serves as one of the two epigraphs to this volume. I translated the other epigraph from the German original, Nietzche's *Zur Genealogie der Moral* [On the Genealogy of Morals].

The cover image is from Wassily Kandinsky's *On White II*. As with many of Kandinsky's paintings, the composition illustrates how a number of different elements might be arranged so as to preserve their individuality while still standing in more or less determinate relations to one another. In that way, the picture expresses in visual form something close to what I argue in the book should be true of science as a whole: a kind of engaged pluralism that brings unlike elements into dialogue with one another without fusing them into a specious synthesis. The book's title references not just the doctoral seminar that I mentioned earlier, but should also invoke echoes of Abraham Kaplan's *The Conduct of Inquiry* and John Dewey's *Logic: The Theory of Inquiry*, both of which stand firmly in the lineage leading to the present text.

The book is dedicated to the memory of two of the most brilliant social scientists I have ever had the pleasure to meet and to learn from: Hayward Alker and Charles Tilly. I was never either of their students in a formal way—I never took a class with either man, and neither of them supervised my doctoral work— but both provided me with important and challenging feedback in the early stages of my career. I wish that they could have read this manuscript. I think that Hayward would have pressed me to be both more dialectical *and* more formal throughout, and that Chuck would have urged that I stop being so concerned with ontology and get further into specific empirical implementation. But sadly, both men passed away before I was finished writing. They were exemplary social scientists, equally committed to rigorous inquiry and to the generous invitation of a panoply of skeptical challenges to their own claims. I wrote this book, in the end, in the hopes that the lexicon that it provides might help encourage more of us to follow their example, and that it might contribute to building an IR field in which this kind of social science might flourish. That would be, I think, the greatest possible tribute to them, and to their willingness to mentor a young colleague intellectually who was not, according to the rules of academic parentage, their responsibility— but they were more generous than that, giving of themselves more widely in a way that enriched all of our common intellectual life. Going forward, I hope that we can all do likewise.

Acknowledgments to the second edition

I had no plans to produce a second edition of this book. Yes, there were some passages in the first edition that struck me as being in need of clarification, but nothing so serious as to require a new edition. Yes, there had been critiques of, and critical engagements with, my argument, but I had already responded to those in print, often as part of a symposium or forum on the book.[1] And yes, some things about the global field of international studies had changed somewhat since I first wrote the book, but taking stock of those changes—in particular, coming to terms with the increasing divide between Political Science-dominated U.S. "IR" and international studies as practiced elsewhere in the world—would, it seems to me, take an entirely different book, one that was sociological and empirical where mine was conceptual and philosophical.

So why a second edition, then? The book had already been quite well received, both in the profession (where it garnered two book awards) and, especially, among students. But having taught short, intensive philosophy of science courses for both the European Consortium on Political Research's Winter School on Methods and Techniques and the International Political Science Association/ University of São Paulo Summer School in Concepts and Methods in Political Science and International Relations, I became convinced that I could have done a better job presenting the philosophical backdrop against which the two "wagers" at the typological core of the book arose. Accordingly, in this second edition I have moved some of the material originally at the beginning of each of the core chapters (Chapters 3–6) to an expanded Chapter 2, which mirrors the way I taught those short courses. My students in those courses deserve a great deal of thanks for being the test audience for whom this revised structure was first developed and with whom it was refined. I would be remiss in not acknowledging Lorena Barberia, Derek Beach, Eduardo Marques, Benoit Rihoux, and all of the other people involved in putting those schools together, for including me on the faculty and for giving me the opportunity to recognize that the book could be improved by making it conform more closely to the way I taught this topic. Thanks also to Gerard van der Ree and his students at University College Utrecht, for their feedback on which points in the text were especially thorny and deserved to be

---

1 Such as the one in *Millennium* 41:2 (Jackson, 2013).

reworked in this revised edition. And thanks to Lucas Dolan for copyediting and proofreading assistance.

I had also always been dissatisfied with the use of endnotes instead of footnotes in the first edition of the book. One of my non-negotiable points for producing a second edition was precisely that the publisher would agree to present the book with footnotes rather than with endnotes; the book had always been intended as a "footnotes book" in which the notes played an integral role in the text, and relegating those notes to the back of the book frustrated that intention. Fortunately Nicola Parkin and Craig Fowlie at Routledge had no objections, and indeed, they enthusiastically supported the proposal for a second edition that would present the book the way I had originally planned it, with footnotes.

A perennial request from readers and critics alike is for additional concrete illustrations and detailed discussions of pieces of research using the four methodological styles I explicate here. I love getting this question in a classroom setting, because it affords an immediate opportunity to turn the floor back over to the student: "what do *you* think exemplifies this methodology, and why?" And then one can inaugurate a discussion about the particular piece or pieces of research mentioned, the contours of the particular methodology being illustrated, and the interplay between the two—and between that exercise and the balance of the typology of philosophical-ontological wagers. I did not set out to write a methods manual that would give researchers a set of off-the-shelf tools they could simply pick up and apply; instead I wrote an invitation to think philosophically about the conduct of inquiry in the field, and here as elsewhere, exemplars—paradigms, in the narrow sense—can be a hindrance to understanding. If I have made a contribution, then the categories I elucidate will prove to be helpful opportunities for readers at all levels to clarify their own thinking.

Since the first edition was published I have given maybe three dozen talks on the conception of international studies that I laid out in the book. The fact that the overwhelming majority of those talks were invited by, and delivered to, audiences outside of the United States speaks, I think, for itself. The audiences and discussants at each of those talks gave me helpful feedback and intriguing things to think about, and while I have not responded to every comment in the text—that would be pedantic and distracting—I can honestly say that I have benefited from each engagement with my argument. A particular criticism I encountered more than once involved questioning of my tacit assumption that it was meaningful to speak of a single global field called international studies in the face of the theoretical differences apparent to almost everyone alongside the methodological differences that I sought to make plain. Nevertheless, I persist in my perhaps hopelessly naïve belief that it is possible to constitute the global field of international studies on the basis of our common engagement with the problem of the encounter with difference across boundaries, in a plethora of concrete settings and with a number of different methodological and theoretical perspectives. My hope is that this engagement is sufficient to keep us talking to one another, precisely so that we can play the important role of showing others the motes in the eyes with which they see the world—and perhaps come to recognize the beams in our own.

Bibliography

Abbott, Andrew. 1999. *Department and discipline: Chicago sociology at one hundred*. Chicago, IL: University of Chicago Press.

Abbott, Andrew. 2001a. *Chaos of disciplines*. Chicago, IL: University of Chicago Press.

Abbott, Andrew. 2001b. "From causes to events." In *Time matters: On theory and method*, 183–206. Chicago, IL: University of Chicago Press.

Abrahamsen, Rita, and Michael C. Williams. 2009. "Security beyond the state: Global security assemblages in international politics." *International Political Sociology* 3, no. 1: 1–17.

Ackerly, Brooke A., Maria Stern, and Jacqui True, eds. 2006. *Feminist methodologies for International Relations*. Cambridge: Cambridge University Press.

Adcock, Robert. 2003. "The emergence of political science as a discipline: History and the study of politics in America, 1875–1910." *History of Political Thought* 24: 481–508.

Adcock, Robert. 2007. "Who's afraid of determinism? The ambivalence of macro-historical inquiry." *Journal of the Philosophy of History* 1, no. 3: 346–364.

Adcock, Robert. 2009. "Rethinking classical liberalism in 'progressive' times: The divergent sociologies of Spencer and Sumner." Paper presented at the 2009 American Political Science Association Meeting, Toronto, CA, September 4.

Adler, Emanuel. 1997. "Seizing the middle ground: Constructivism in world politics." *European Journal of International Relations* 3, no. 3: 319–363.

Adler, Emanuel. 2005. "Constructivism and international relations." In *Handbook of international relations*, ed. Walter Carlsnaes, Beth A. Simmons, and Thomas Risse, 95–118. Thousand Oaks, CA: SAGE.

Adler, Emanuel, and Michael Barnett. 1998. *Security communities*. Cambridge: Cambridge University Press.

Ahmed, Amel, and Rudra Sil. 2009. "Is multi-method research really 'better'?" *Qualitative and Multi-Method Research* 7, no. 2: 2–6.

Alexander, Jeffrey C. 1986. *Theoretical logic in sociology: vol. 4. The modern reconstruction of classical thought: Talcott Parsons*. Berkeley, CA: University of California Press.

Alexandrova, Anna. 2009. "When analytic narratives explain." *Journal of the Philosophy of History* 3: 1–24.

Alker, Hayward R. 1966. "The long road to international relations theory: Problems of statistical nonadditivity." *World Politics* 18, no. 4: 623–655.

Alker, Hayward R. 1990. "Rescuing reason from the rationalists: Reading Vico, Marx and Weber as reflective institutionalists." *Millennium* 19, no. 2: 161–184.

Althusser, Louis. 2003. *The humanist controversy and other texts*. Ed. Francois Matheron. London: Verso.

Anscombe, G. E. M. 1963. *Intention.* 2nd edn. Cambridge, MA: Harvard University Press.

Anscombe, G. E. M. 1993. "Causality and determination." In *Causation,* ed. Ernest Sosa and Michael Tooley, 88–104. Oxford: Oxford University Press.

Arabatzis, Theodore. 2006. *Representing electrons: A biographical approach to theoretical entities.* Chicago, IL: University of Chicago Press.

Aronson, Jerry L., Rom Harré, and Eileen C. Way. 1995. *Realism rescued: How scientific progress is possible.* Chicago, IL: Open Court.

Ashley, Richard K. 1983. "Three modes of economism." *International Studies Quarterly* 27, no. 4: 463–496.

Ashley, Richard K. 1984. "The poverty of neorealism." *International Organization* 38, no. 2: 225–286.

Ashworth, Lucian M. 2006. "Where are the idealists in interwar international relations?" *Review of International Studies* 32, no. 2: 291–308.

Austin, J. L. 1962. *Sense and sensibilia.* 2nd edition. London: Oxford University Press.

Ayer, Alfred J. 1952. *Language, truth and logic.* 2nd edition. New York: Dover Publications.

Baehr, Peter. 2001. "The 'iron cage' and the 'shell hard as steel': Parsons, Weber, and the Stahlhartes Gehäuse metaphor in the Protestant ethic and the spirit of capitalism." *History and Theory* 40: 153–169.

Baker, Lynne Rudder. 1993. "Metaphysics and mental causation." In *Mental causation,* ed. John Heil and Alfred Mele, 75–95. Oxford: Oxford University Press.

Ball, Terence. 1976. "From paradigms to research programs: Toward a post-Kuhnian political science." *American Journal of Political Science* 20, no. 1: 151–177.

Banks, Michael. 1985. "The inter-paradigm debate." In *International relations: A handbook of current theory,* ed. Margot Light and A.J.R. Groom, 7–26. London: Pinter Publishers.

Barad, Karen. 2007. *Meeting the universe halfway: Quantum physics and the entanglement of matter and meaning.* Durham, NC: Duke University Press.

Barkin, J. Samuel. 2004. "On the heuristic use of formal modeling in IR theory." Paper presented at the American Political Science Association annual meeting. Chicago, IL, September 2.

Barkin, J. Samuel, and Laura Sjoberg. 2015. "Calculating critique: thinking outside the methods matching game." *Millennium* 43, no.3: 852–71. doi:10.1177/0305829815576819.

Barnes, Barry. 1982. *T.S. Kuhn and social science.* New York: Columbia University Press.

Barnes, Trevor J. 1996. *Logics of dislocation: Models, metaphors and meanings of economic space.* New York: Guilford.

Bates, Robert H., Avner Greif, Margaret Levi, Jean-Laurent Rosenthal, and Barry R. Weingast. 1998. *Analytic narratives.* Princeton, NJ: Princeton University Press.

Bates, Robert H., Rui J.P. de Figueiredo, Jr., and Barry R. Weingast. 1998. "The politics of interpretation: Rationality, culture, and transition." *Politics and Society* 26, no. 4: 603–642.

Baum, Richard, and William Sheehan. 1997. *In search of planet Vulcan.* New York: Basic Books.

BBC. 2004. "The importance of a right-handed shortstop." *h2g2.* April 23. www.bbc. co.uk/ dna/h2g2/A2181467. Accessed 15 April 2010.

Beach, Derek, and Rasmus Brun Pedersen. 2013. *Process-tracing methods: Foundations and guidelines.* Ann Arbor, MI: University of Michigan Press.

Behnke, Andreas. 2008. "'Eternal peace' as the graveyard of the political: A critique of Kant's 'Zum Ewigen Frieden.'" *Millennium* 36, no. 3: 513–531.

Beier, J. Marshall, and Samantha L. Arnold. 2005. "Becoming undisciplined: Toward the supradisciplinary study of security." *International Studies Review* 7, no. 1: 41–62.

Beil, Laura. 2008. "Opponents of evolution adopting new strategy." *The New York Times*, June 4, sec. US. www.nytimes.com/2008/06/04/us/04evolution.html. Accessed 5 June 2008.

Berger, Peter L., and Thomas Luckmann. 1967. *The social construction of reality*. New York: Anchor Books.

Bernstein, Richard J. 1983. *Beyond objectivism and relativism: Science, hermeneutics, and praxis*. Philadelphia, PA: University of Pennsylvania Press.

Bernstein, Richard J. 1992. *The new constellation: Ethical-political horizons of modernity/ postmodernity*. Cambridge, MA: MIT Press.

Bernstein, Steven, Richard Ned Lebow, Janice Gross Stein, and Steven Weber. 2000. "God gave physics the easy problems: Adapting social science to an unpredictable world." *European Journal of International Relations* 6, no. 1: 43–76.

Bevir, Mark, and Asaf Kedar. 2008. "Concept formation in political science: An antinaturalist critique of qualitative methodology." *Perspectives on Politics* 6, no. 3: 503–517.

Bevir, Mark, and R.A.W. Rhodes. 2006. "Interpretive approaches to British government and politics." *British Politics* 1, no. 1: 84–112.

Bhaskar, Roy. 1975. *A realist theory of science*. London: Verso.

Bhaskar, Roy. 1989. "On the possibility of social scientific knowledge and the limits of naturalism." In *Reclaiming reality*, 66–88. London: Verso.

Bhaskar, Roy. 1998. *The possibility of naturalism*. London: Routledge.

Bially Mattern, Janice. 2004. *Ordering international politics: Identity, crisis, and representational force*. New York: Routledge.

Blackburn, Simon. 1994. "The principle of charity." In *The Oxford encyclopedia of philosophy*, 62. London: Oxford University Press.

Blaney, David L., and Naeem Inayatullah. 2010. *Savage economics: Wealth, poverty and the temporal walls of capitalism*. London: Routledge.

Boghossian, Paul. 2007. *Fear of knowledge: Against relativism and constructivism*. Oxford: Oxford University Press.

Bohm, David. 2002. *Wholeness and the implicate order*. London: Routledge.

Bohman, James. 2002. "How to make a social science practical: Pragmatism, critical social science and multiperspectival theory." *Millennium* 31, no. 3: 499–524.

Bourdieu, Pierre. 1990. *In other words: Essays toward a reflexive sociology*. Stanford, CA: Stanford University Press.

Bourdieu, Pierre. 2004. *Science of science and reflexivity*. 1st edn. Chicago, IL: University of Chicago Press.

Boyd, Richard. 1984. "The current status of scientific realism." In *Scientific realism*, ed. Jarrett Leplin, 41–82. Berkeley, CA: University of California Press.

Brady, Henry E., and David Collier, eds. 2004. "Sources of leverage in causal inference: Toward an alternative view of methodology." In *Rethinking social inquiry: Diverse tools, shared standards*, 229–266. Lanham, MD: Rowman & Littlefield Publishers, Inc.

Brincat, Shannon. 2009. "Reclaiming the utopian imaginary in IR theory." *Review of International Studies* 35, no. 3: 581–609.

Brooks, Stephen G., and William C. Wohlforth. 2001. "Power, globalization, and the end of the Cold War." *International Security* 25, no. 3: 5–53.

Brooks, Stephen G., and William C. Wohlforth. 2002. "From old thinking to new thinking in qualitative research." *International Security* 26, no. 4: 93–111.

Bruff, Ian. 2010. "European varieties of capitalism and the International." *European Journal of International Relations* 16, no. 4: 615–638. doi:10.1177/1354066109344379.

Bruun, Hans Henrik. 2007. *Science, values and politics in Max Weber's methodology*. Aldershot: Ashgate.

Bueno de Mesquita, Bruce, and James D. Morrow. 1999. "Sorting through the wealth of notions." *International Security* 24, no. 2: 56–73.

Büger, Christian, and Frank Gadinger. 2007. "Reassembling and dissecting: International relations practice from a science studies perspective." *International Studies Perspectives* 8, no 2: 90–110.

Bull, Hedley. 1969. "International theory: The case for a classical approach." In *Contending approaches to international politics*, ed. Klaus Knorr and James N. Rosenau, 20–38. Princeton, NJ: Princeton University Press.

Bull, Hedley. 1977. *The anarchical society*. New York: Columbia University Press.

Büthe, Tim. 2002. "Taking temporality seriously: Modeling history and the use of narratives as evidence." *American Political Science Review* 96, no. 3: 481–493.

Campbell, David. 2000. *The socially constructed organization*. London: Karnac Books.

Carpenter, R. Charli. 2002. "Gender theory in world politics: Contributions of a nonfeminist standpoint?" *International Studies Review* 4, no. 3: 153–165.

Carnap, Rudolf. 2012. *The unity of science*. London: Routledge.

Carr, David. 1986. *Time, narrative, and history*. Bloomington, IN: Indiana University Press.

Carr, E.H. 2001. *The twenty years' crisis, 1919–1939: An introduction to the study of International Relations*. London: Palgrave Macmillan.

Cartwright, Nancy. 1999. *The dappled world: A study of the boundaries of science*. Cambridge: Cambridge University Press.

Cartwright, Nancy. 2007. *Hunting causes and using them: Approaches in philosophy and economics*. Cambridge: Cambridge University Press.

Cartwright, Nancy. 2009. "What is this thing called 'efficacy'?" In *Philosophy of the social sciences: Philosophical theory and scientific practice*, ed. C. Mantzavinos, 185–206. Cambridge: Cambridge University Press.

Cartwright, Nancy, and Eleanora Montuschi, eds. 2015. *Philosophy of social science: A new introduction*. Oxford: Oxford University Press.

Carus, A. W. 2010. *Carnap and twentieth-century thought: Explication as enlightenment*. Cambridge: Cambridge University Press.

Chakrabarty, Dipesh. 2007. *Provincializing Europe: Postcolonial thought and historical difference (new edition)*. Princeton, NJ: Princeton University Press.

Chakravartty, Anjan. 2007. *A metaphysics for scientific realism: Knowing the unobservable*. Cambridge: Cambridge University Press.

Chase-Dunn, C., and T. Hall. 1997. *Rise and demise*. Boulder, CO: Westview.

Chatterjee, Abhishek. 2009. "Ontology, epistemology, and multi-methods." *Qualitative and Multi-Method Research* 7, no. 2: 11–15.

Chernoff, Fred. 2005. *The power of international theory: Reforging the link to foreign policy-making through scientific inquiry*. London: Routledge.

Chernoff, Fred. 2009a. "Defending foundations for international relations theory." *International Theory* 1, no. 3: 466–477.

Chernoff, Fred. 2009b. "The ontological fallacy: A rejoinder on the status of scientific realism in international relations." *Review of International Studies* 35, no. 2: 371–395.

Christensen, Thomas J., and Jack Snyder. 1990. "Chain gangs and passed bucks: Predicting alliance patterns in multipolarity." *International Organization* 44, no. 2: 137–168.

Clarke, Kevin A., and David M. Primo. 2007. "Modernizing political science: A model-based approach." *Perspectives on Politics* 5, no. 4: 741–753.

Connolly, William. 1989. "Identity and difference in global politics." In *International/intertextual relations: Postmodern readings of world politics*, ed. James Der Derian and Michael Shapiro, 323–342. New York: Lexington Books.

Corbey, Raymond H.A. 2005. *The metaphysics of apes: Negotiating the animal-human boundary*. Cambridge: Cambridge University Press.

Cox, Robert W. 1996a. "Gramsci, hegemony, and international relations: An essay on method." In *Approaches to world order*, 124–143. Cambridge: Cambridge University Press.

Cox, Robert W. 1996b. "Social forces, states, and world orders: Beyond international relations theory." In *Approaches to world order*, 85–123. Cambridge: Cambridge University Press.

Davidson, Donald. 1973. "On the very idea of a conceptual scheme." *Proceedings and Addresses of the American Philosophical Association* 47: 5–20.

Dear, Peter. 2008. *The intelligibility of nature: How science makes sense of the world*. Chicago, IL: University of Chicago Press.

Deleuze, Gilles, and Félix Guattari. 1996. *What is philosophy?* New York: Columbia University Press.

Denemark, Robert A., J. Friedman, Barry K. Gills, and George Modelski, eds. 2000. *World system history: The social science of long-term change*. London: Routledge.

Descartes, René. 1993. *Discourse on method and Meditations on first philosophy*. Trans. Donald Cress. 3rd edn. Indianapolis, IN: Hackett Press.

Desrosières, Alan. 1998. *The politics of large numbers: A history of statistical reasoning*. Cambridge, MA: Harvard University Press.

Dessler, David. 1989. "What's at stake in the agent-structure debate?" *International Organization* 43, no. 3: 441–473.

Dessler, David. 1999. "Constructivism within a positivist social science." *Review of International Studies* 25, no. 1: 123–137.

Deudney, Daniel H. 2008. *Bounding power: Republican security theory from the polis to the global village*. Princeton, NJ: Princeton University Press.

Deutsch, Karl W. 1954. *Political community at the international level: Problems of definition and measurement*. Garden City, NY: Doubleday.

Deutsch, Karl W. 1957. *Political community and the North Atlantic area: International organization in the light of historical experience*. Princeton, NJ: Princeton University Press.

Dewey, John. 1910. *How we think*. New edition. Mineola, NY: Dover Publications.

Dewey, John. 1920. *Reconstruction in philosophy*. New York: Kessinger Publishing, LLC.

Dewey, John. 1938. *Experience and education*. New York: Touchstone.

Dewey, John. 1954. *The public and its problems*. Athens, OH: Swallow Press.

Dowe, Phil. 2009. Absences, possible causation, and the problem of non-locality. "The Monist" 91, no. 1: 23–40.

Dreyfus, Hubert L. 1990. *Being-in-the-world: A commentary on Heidegger's Being and Time, Division I*. Cambridge, MA: MIT Press.

Drysdale, John. 2007. "Weber on objectivity: Advocate or critic?" In *Max Weber's 'Objectivity' reconsidered*, ed. Laurence H. McFalls, 31–57. Toronto: University of Toronto Press.

DuBois, W.E.B. 1994. *The Souls of Black Folk*. New York: Dover Publications.

Duvall, Raymond. 2001. Ideal Types. In *Routledge Encyclopedia of International Political Economy*, ed. R.J. Barry Jones, 703–704. London: Routledge.

Easton, David. 1953. *The political system: An inquiry into the state of political science*. New York: Alfred A. Knopf.

Elias, N. 1991. *The society of individuals*. Oxford: Blackwell.

Elman, Colin. 1996. "Horses for courses: Why not neorealist theories of foreign policy?" *Security Studies* 6, no. 1: 7–53.

Elman, Colin. 2005. "Explanatory typologies in qualitative studies of international politics." *International Organization* 59, no. 2: 293–326.

Elman, Colin, and Miriam Fendus Elman. 1997. "Lakatos and neorealism: A reply to Vasquez." *American Political Science Review* 91, no. 4: 923–926.

Elman, Colin, and Miriam Fendus Elman. 2002. "How not to be Lakatos intolerant: Appraising progress in IR research." *International Studies Quarterly* 46: 231–262.

Elman, Colin, and Miriam Fendus Elman. 2003a. "Lessons from Lakatos." In *Progress in International Relations theory: Appraising the field*, ed. Colin Elman and Miriam Fendus Elman, 21–68. Cambridge, MA: MIT Press.

Elman, Colin, and Miriam Fendus Elman, eds. 2003b. *Progress in International Relations theory: Appraising the field*. Cambridge, MA: MIT Press.

Elster, Jon. 1986. "Introduction." In *Rational choice*, ed. Jon Elster, 1–33. New York: New York University Press.

Elster, Jon. 1989. *Nuts and bolts for the social sciences*. Cambridge: Cambridge University Press.

Elster, Jon. 2000. "Rational choice history: A case of excessive ambition." *American Political Science Review* 94, no. 3: 685–695.

English, Robert D. 2002. "Power, ideas, and new evidence on the Cold War's end." *International Security* 26, no. 4: 70–92.

Enloe, Cynthia. 1996. "Margins, silences, and bottom rungs: How to overcome the underestimation of power in the study of international relations." In *International theory: positivism and beyond*, ed. Steve Smith, Ken Booth, and Marysia Zalewski, 186–202. Cambridge: Cambridge University Press.

Erdelyi, A. 1992. *Max Weber in Amerika*. Wien: Passagen Verlag.

Farrell, Henry, and Martha Finnemore. 2009. "Ontology, methodology, and causation in the American school of international political economy." *Review of International Political Economy* 16, no. 1: 58–71.

Falleti, Tulia G., and Julia F. Lynch. 2009. "Context and causal mechanisms in political analysis." *Comparative Political Studies* 42, no. 9: 1143–1166.

Fearon, James D. 1991. "Counterfactuals and hypothesis testing in political science." *World Politics* 43, no. 2: 169–195.

Feigl, Herbert. 1969. "The Weiner Kries in America." In *The intellectual migration: Europe and America 1930–1960*, ed. Bernard Bailyn and Donald Fleming, 630–673. Cambridge, MA: Harvard University Press.

Ferguson, Yale, and Richard Mansbach. 1996. *Polities: Authority, identities, and change*. Columbia, SC: University of South Carolina Press.

Fetzer, James H., ed. 2000. *Science, explanation, and rationality: The philosophy of Carl G. Hempel*. Oxford: Oxford University Press.

Feyerabend, Paul. 1993. *Against method*. 3rd edn. London: Verso.

Feynman, Richard P. 1988. *QED: The strange theory of light and matter*. Princeton, NJ: Princeton University Press.

Fierke, Karin M. 1998. *Changing games, changing strategies: Critical investigations in security*. Manchester: Manchester University Press.

Fierke, Karin M. 2003. "Language, agency, and politics in a constructed world." In *Language, agency, and politics in a constructed world*, ed. Francois Debrix, 66–86. International Relations in a Constructed World. Armonk, NY: M.E. Sharpe.

Finnemore, Martha. 1996. *National interests in international society.* Ithaca, NY: Cornell University Press.

Finnemore, Martha, and Kathryn Sikkink. 1998. "International norm dynamics and political change." *International Organization* 52, no. 4: 887–917.

Fischer, Markus. 1992. "Feudal Europe, 800–1300: Communal discourse and conflictual practices." *International Organization* 46, no. 2: 427–466.

Flyvbjerg, Bent. 2001. *Making social science matter.* Cambridge: Cambridge University Press.

Foucault, M. 1972. *The archaeology of knowledge.* New York: Pantheon Books.

Foucault, Michel. 1979. *Discipline and punish: The birth of the prison.* New York: Vintage.

Friedman, Gil, and Harvey Starr. 1997. *Agency, structure and international politics: From ontology to empirical enquiry.* London: Routledge.

Friedman, Milton. 1979. "The methodology of positive economics." In *Philosophy and economic theory*, ed. Frederick Hahn and Martin Hollis, 18–35. New York: Oxford University Press.

Friedman, Michael. 1992. *Kant and the exact sciences.* Cambridge, MA: Harvard University Press.

Friedman, Michael. 2000. *A parting of the ways: Carnap, Cassirer, and Heidegger.* Chicago, IL: Open Court.

Galison, Peter. 1990. "Aufbau/Bauhaus: Logical positivism and architectural modernism." *Critical Inquiry* 16 (4): 709–752.

Gartzke, Erik, and Quan Li. 2003. "Measure for measure: Concept operationalization and the trade interdependence-conflict debate." *Journal of Peace Research* 40, no. 5: 553–571.

Geertz, Clifford. 1973. *The interpretation of cultures.* New York: Basic Books.

Geertz, Clifford. 2000. *Local knowledge: Further essays in interpretive anthropology.* New York: Basic Books.

Gell-Mann, Murray. 1995. *The quark and the jaguar: Adventures in the simple and the complex.* New York: Holt Paperbacks.

George, Alexander L., and Andrew Bennett, eds. 2005. *Case studies and theory development in the social sciences.* Cambridge, MA: MIT Press.

George, Jim, and David Campbell. 1990. "Patterns of dissent and the celebration of difference: Critical social theory and international relations." *International Studies Quarterly* 34, no. 3: 269–293.

Gerring, John. 2005. "Causation: A unified framework for the social sciences." *Journal of Theoretical Politics* 17, no. 2: 163–198.

Gerring, John. 2007. "Is there a (viable) crucial-case method?" *Comparative Political Studies* 40, no. 3: 231–253.

Gerring, John. 2012. *Social science methodology: A unified framework.* Cambridge: Cambridge University Press.

Geuss, Raymond. 1981. *The idea of a critical theory.* Cambridge: Cambridge University Press.

Giddens, Anthony. 1984. *The constitution of society.* Berkeley, CA: University of California Press.

Gifford, Don. 1991. *The farther shore: A natural history of perception, 1798–1984.* New York: Vintage.

Gill, Stephen. 1992. *American hegemony and the trilateral commission.* Cambridge: Cambridge University Press.

Goddard, Stacie E., and Daniel H. Nexon. 2005. "Paradigm lost? Reassessing theory of international politics." *European Journal of International Relations* 11, no. 1: 9–61.

Godfrey-Smith, Peter. 2003. *Theory and reality: An introduction to the philosophy of science*. Chicago, IL: University of Chicago Press.

Goffman, Erving. 1959. *The presentation of self in everyday life*. 1st edn. New York: Anchor.

Goldstein, Judith, and Robert O. Keohane, eds. 1993. *Ideas and foreign policy: Beliefs, institutions, and political change*. Ithaca, NY: Cornell University Press

Goldthorpe, John H. 2001. "Causation, statistics, and sociology." *European Sociological Review* 17, no. 1: 1–20.

Goodman, Nelson. 1978. *Ways of worldmaking*. Indianapolis, IN: Hackett Press.

Gould, Stephen J. 2003. *Triumph and tragedy in Mudville: A lifelong passion for baseball*. New York: W.W. Norton.

Gramsci, Antonio. 1971. *Selections from the prison notebooks*. New York: International Publishers.

Grene, Marjorie. 1990. "Perception and human reality." In *Harré and his critics*, ed. Roy Bhaskar, 17–22. Oxford: Blackwell.

Grunberg, I. 1990. "Exploring the 'myth' of hegemonic stability." *International Organization* 44, no. 4: 431–477.

Grupen, Claus. 1999. "Physics of particle detection." *arXiv.org*. http://arxiv.org/abs/physics/ 9906063. Accessed 15 April 2010.

Guilhot, Nicolas, ed. 2011. *The invention of international relations theory: Realism, the Rockefeller Foundation, and the 1954-conference on theory*. New York: Columbia University Press.

Gunnell, John G. 1993. *The descent of political theory: The genealogy of an American vocation*. Chicago, IL: University of Chicago Press.

Gunnell, John G. 2007. "The paradox of social science: Weber, Winch, and Wittgenstein." In *Max Weber's 'objectivity' reconsidered*, ed. Laurence H. McFalls, 58–88. Toronto: University of Toronto Press.

Guzzini, Stefano. 2000. "A reconstruction of constructivism in international relations." *European Journal of International Relations* 6, no. 2: 147–182.

Habermas, Jürgen. 1990. *The philosophical discourse of modernity: Twelve lectures*. Cambridge, MA: MIT Press.

Hacking, Ian. 1983. *Representing and intervening: Introductory topics in the philosophy of natural science*. Cambridge: Cambridge University Press.

Hacking, Ian. 1999. *The social construction of what?* Cambridge, MA: Harvard University Press.

Hafner-Burton, Emilie M., and Alexander H. Montgomery. 2006. "Power positions: International organizations, social networks, and conflict." *Journal of Conflict Resolution* 50, no. 1: 3–27.

Hall, Peter A. 2003. "Aligning ontology and methodology in comparative research." In *Comparative historical analysis in the social sciences*, ed. James Mahoney and Dietrich Rueschemeyer, 373–404. Cambridge: Cambridge University Press.

Hansen, Lene. 2006. *Security as practice: Discourse analysis and the Bosnian War*. London: Routledge.

Hardin, R. 1995. *One for all: The logic of group conflict*. Princeton, NJ: Princeton University Press.

Harding, Sandra. 1991. *Whose science? Whose knowledge?: Thinking from women's lives*. Ithaca, NY: Cornell University Press.

Harding, Sandra. 2015. *Objectivity and diversity: Another logic of scientific research*. Chicago, IL: University of Chicago Press.

Harré, Rom. 1985. *The philosophies of science: An introductory survey*. 2nd edn. New York: Oxford University Press.

Harré, Rom. 1990. "Exploring the human umwelt." In *Harré and his critics*, ed. Roy Bhaskar, 297–364. Oxford: Blackwell.

Hawkesworth, Mary E. 1989. "Knowers, knowing, known: Feminist theory and claims of truth." *Signs* 14, no. 3: 533–557.

Hawkesworth, Mary E. 1994. "Policy studies within a feminist frame." *Policy Sciences* 27, no. 2 (June): 97–118.

Hay, Colin. 2002. *Political analysis: A critical introduction*. London: Palgrave Macmillan.

Hegel, G.W.F. 1988. *Introduction to the philosophy of history, with selections from the philosophy of right*. Indianapolis, IN: Hackett Press.

Heidegger, Martin. 1927. *Being and time*. San Francisco, CA: HarperCollins.

Hempel, Carl. 1965a. "The theoretician's dilemma: A study in the logic of theory construction." In *Aspects of scientific explanation and other essays in the philosophy of science*, 173–229. New York: Free Press.

Hempel, Carl. 1965b. "The function of general laws in history." In *Aspects of scientific explanation and other essays in the philosophy of science*, 231–244. New York: Free Press.

Hempel, Carl. 1965c. "The logic of functional analysis." In *Aspects of scientific explanation and other essays in the philosophy of science*, 297–330. New York: Free Press.

Heschel, Abraham Joshua. 1991. "No religion is an island." In *No religion is an island: Abraham Joshua Heschel and interreligious dialogue*, ed. Harold Kasimow and Byron L. Sherwin, 3–22. Eugene, OR: Wipf and Stock.

Hill, Hugh G.M., Carol A. Grady, Joseph A. Nuth, III, Susan L. Hallenbeck, and Michael L. Sitko. 2001. "Constraints on nebular dynamics and chemistry based on observations of annealed magnesium silicate grains in comets and in disks surrounding Herbig Ae/Be stars." *Proceedings of the National Academy of Sciences of the United States of America* 98, no. 5: 2182–2187.

Hirschman, Albert O. 1970a. *Exit, voice, and loyalty: Responses to decline in firms, organizations, and states*. Cambridge, MA: Harvard University Press.

Hirschman, Albert O. 1970b. "The search for paradigms as a hindrance to understanding." *World Politics* 22, no. 3: 329–343.

Hobbes, Thomas. 1601. *Leviathan*. New York: W.W. Norton.

Hoffmann, Matthew J. 2008. "Agent-based modeling." In *Qualitative methods in International Relations: A pluralist guide*, ed. Audie Klotz and Deepa Prakash, 187–209. New York: Palgrave Macmillan.

Hoffmann, Matthew J., and John Riley. 2002. "The science of political science: Linearity or complexity in the design of social inquiry." *New Political Science* 24, no. 2: 303–320.

Holland, Paul W. 1986. "Statistics and causal inference." *Journal of the American Statistical Association* 81, no. 396: 945–960.

Hollis, Martin. 1994. *The philosophy of social science: An introduction*. Cambridge: Cambridge University Press.

Hollis, Martin, and Steve Smith. 1990. *Explaining and understanding international relations*. Oxford: Clarendon Press.

Hopf, Ted. 2002. *Social construction of international politics: Identities and foreign policies, Moscow, 1955 & 1999*. Ithaca, NY: Cornell University Press.

Horkheimer, Max, and Theodor W. Adorno. 1947. *Dialectic of enlightenment.* 1st edn. Stanford, CA: Stanford University Press.

Horowitz, Alexandra. 2010. *Inside of a dog: What dogs see, smell, and know.* New York: Scribner.

Hume, David. 1977. *An enquiry concerning human understanding.* Indianapolis, IN: Hackett Press.

Inayatullah, Naeem. 1996. "Beyond the sovereignty dilemma: Quasi-states as social construct." In *State sovereignty as social construct,* ed. Thomas J. Biersteker and Cynthia Weber, 50–80. Cambridge: Cambridge University Press.

Inayatullah, Naeem, and David L. Blaney. 2004. *International Relations and the problem of difference.* London: Routledge.

Isaac, Jeffrey C. 1987. "Beyond the three faces of power: A realist critique." *Polity* 20, no. 1: 4–31.

Jackson, Patrick Thaddeus. 2002. "Rethinking Weber: Toward a non-individualist sociology of world politics." *International Review of Sociology* 12, no. 3: 439–468.

Jackson, Patrick Thaddeus. 2006. *Civilizing the enemy: German reconstruction and the invention of the West.* Ann Arbor, MI: University of Michigan Press.

Jackson, Patrick Thaddeus. 2008. "Foregrounding ontology: Dualism, monism, and IR theory." *Review of International Studies* 34, no. 1: 129–153.

Jackson, Patrick Thaddeus. 2009. "A faulty solution to a false(ly characterized) problem: A comment on Monteiro and Ruby." *International Theory* 1, no. 3: 455–465.

Jackson, Patrick Thaddeus. 2013. "Preparing the ground for a more hospitable international relations," *Millennium* 41, no. 2: 367–378.

Jackson, Patrick Thaddeus. 2015a. "Fear of relativism." *International Studies Perspectives* 16, no. 1: 13–22. doi:10.1111/insp.12091.

Jackson, Patrick Thaddeus. 2015b. "Must international studies be a science?" *Millennium* 43, no. 3: 942–65. doi:10.1177/0305829815579307.

Jackson, Patrick Thaddeus, and Daniel H. Nexon. 2004. "Constructivist realism or realist-constructivism?" *International Studies Review* 6, no. 2: 337–341.

Jackson, Patrick Thaddeus, and Daniel H. Nexon. 2009. "Paradigmatic faults in International-Relations theory." *International Studies Quarterly* 53, no. 4: 907–930.

Jackson, Patrick Thaddeus, and Stuart J. Kaufman. 2007. "Security scholars for a sensible foreign policy: A study in Weberian activism." *Perspectives on Politics* 5, no. 1: 95–103.

James, Patrick. 2002. *International Relations and scientific progress: Structural realism reconsidered.* Columbus, OH: Ohio State University Press.

James, William. 1902. *The varieties of religious experience: A study in human nature.* Centenary Edition. London: Routledge.

James, William. 1978. *The writings of William James: A comprehensive edition.* Ed. J.J. McDermott. Chicago, IL: University of Chicago Press.

Janik, Allan, and Stephen Edelston Toulmin. 1996. *Wittgenstein's Vienna.* Chicago, IL: Ivan R. Dee.

Janis, Irving L. 1982. *Groupthink: Psychological studies of policy decisions and fiascoes.* New York: Houghton Mifflin Company.

Jervis, Robert. 1976. *Perception and misperception in international politics.* Princeton, NJ: Princeton University Press.

Jessop, Bob. 1990. *State theory: Putting capitalist states in their place.* University Park, PA: Pennsylvania State University Press.

Joas, Hans. 1997. *The creativity of action.* Chicago, IL: University of Chicago Press.

Johnson, James. 1996. "How not to criticize rational choice theory: Pathologies of 'common sense'." *Philosophy of the Social Sciences* 26, no. 1: 77–91.

Johnson, James. 2003. "Conceptual problems as obstacles to progress in political science: Four decades of political culture research." *Journal of Theoretical Politics* 15, no. 1: 87–115.

Jones, Martin R. 2005. "Idealization and abstraction: A framework." In *Idealization XII: Correcting the model—idealization and abstraction in the sciences*, ed. Martin R. Jones and Nancy Cartwright, 173–217. Amsterdam: Rodopi.

Joseph, Jonathan. 2008. "Hegemony and the structure-agency problem in international relations: A scientific realist contribution." *Review of International Studies* 34, no. 1: 109–128.

Kadvany, John. 2001. *Imre Lakatos and the guises of reason*. Durham, NC: Duke University Press.

Kahneman, Daniel, and Amos Tversky. 2000. *Choices, values, and frames*. 1st edn. Cambridge: Cambridge University Press.

Kant, Immanuel. 1983. *Perpetual peace and other essays*. Indianapolis. IN: Hackett Press.

Kant, Immanuel. 1993. *Grounding for the metaphysics of morals*. Indianapolis, IN: Hackett Press.

Kant, Immanuel. 1999. *Critique of pure reason*. Ed. Paul Guyer and Allen W. Wood. Cambridge: Cambridge University Press.

Kaplan, Morton A. 1969. "The new great debate: Traditionalism vs. science in international relations." In *Contending approaches to international politics*, 39–61. Princeton, NJ: Princeton University Press.

Katzenstein, Peter, and Rudra Sil. 2008. "Rethinking Asian security: A case for analytical eclecticism." In *Rethinking Japanese security*, 249–285. London: Routledge.

Kaufman, Stuart, Richard Little, and William C. Wohlforth, eds. 2007. *Balance of power in world history*. New York: Palgrave Macmillan.

Keck, Margaret, and Kathryn Sikkink. 1998. *Activists beyond borders*. Ithaca, NY: Cornell University Press.

Kedar, Asaf. 2007. "Ideal types as hermeneutic concepts." *Journal of the Philosophy of History* 1, no. 3: 318–345.

Keohane, Robert O. 1988. "International institutions: Two approaches." *International Studies Quarterly* 32, no. 4: 379–396.

Keohane, Robert O. 1998. "Beyond dichotomy: Conversations between international relations and Feminist Theory." *International Studies Quarterly* 42, no. 1: 193–197.

Keohane, Robert O. 2002. *Power and governance in a partially globalized world*. London: Routledge.

Keohane, Robert O., and Helen Milner. 1996. *Internationalization and domestic politics*. New York: Cambridge University Press.

Keohane, Robert O., and Lisa L. Martin. 2003. "Institutional theory as a research program." In *Progress in International Relations theory: Appraising the field*, ed. Colin Elman and Miriam Fendius Elman, 71–107. Cambridge, MA: MIT Press.

Kessler, Oliver. 2007. "From agents and structures to minds and bodies: Of supervenience, quantum, and the linguistic turn." *Journal of International Relations and Development* 10: 243–271.

King, Gary. 2014. "Restructuring the social sciences: Reflections from Harvard's Institute for Quantitative Social Science." *PS: Political Science & Politics* 47, no. 1: 165–172. doi:10.1017/S1049096513001534.

King, Gary, Robert O. Keohane, and Sidney Verba. 1994. *Designing social inquiry: Scientific inference in qualitative research*. Princeton, NJ: Princeton University Press.

King, Gary, Robert O. Keohane, and Sidney Verba. 1995. "The importance of research design in political science." *The American Political Science Review* 89, no. 2: 475–481.

Klotz, Audie. 1995. *Protesting prejudice: Apartheid and the politics of norms in International Relations*. Ithaca, NY: Cornell University Press.

Klotz, Audie, and Cecelia Lynch. 2007. *Strategies for research in constructivist International Relations*. Armonk, NY: M.E. Sharpe.

Knorr, Klaus, and James N. Rosenau. 1969. *Contending approaches to international politics*. Princeton, NJ: Princeton University Press.

Kratochwil, Friedrich. 1989. *Rules, norms, and decisions*. Cambridge: Cambridge University Press.

Kratochwil, Friedrich. 2006. "History, action and identity: Revisiting the 'second' great debate and assessing its importance for social theory." *European Journal of International Relations* 12, no. 1: 5–29.

Kratochwil, Friedrich. 2007. "Of false promises and good bets: A plea for a pragmatic approach to theory building (The Tartu Lecture)." *Journal of International Relations and Development* 10, no. 1: 1–15.

Kratochwil, Friedrich, and John Gerard Ruggie. 1986. "International organization: A state of the art on an art of the state." *International Organization* 40, no. 4: 753–775.

Kuhn, Thomas S. 1970a. "Logic of discovery or psychology of research?" In *Criticism and the growth of knowledge*, ed. Imre Lakatos and Alan Musgrave, 1–23. Cambridge: Cambridge University Press.

Kuhn, Thomas S. 1970b. *The structure of scientific revolutions*. Chicago, IL: University of Chicago Press.

Kuhn, Thomas S. 2000. *The road since structure: Philosophical essays, 1970–1993*. Ed. James Conant and John Haugeland. Chicago, IL: University of Chicago Press.

Kurki, Milja. 2008. *Causation in International Relations: Reclaiming causal analysis*. 1st edn. Cambridge: Cambridge University Press.

Kurki, Milja, and Hidemi Suganami. 2012. "Towards the politics of causal explanation: a reply to the critics of causal inquiries." *International Theory* 4, no. 3) 400–429. doi:10.1017/S1752971912000127

Laitin, David. 1995. "Disciplining political science." *American Political Science Review* 89, no. 2: 454–456.

Laitin, David. 2003. "The perestroikan challenge to social science." *Politics and Society* 31, no. 1: 163–184.

Lakatos, Imre. 1970. "The methodology of scientific research programmes." In *Criticism and the growth of knowledge*, ed. Imre Lakatos and Alan Musgrave, 91–196. Cambridge: Cambridge University Press.

Lakatos, Imre. 1978. "History of science and its rational reconstructions." In *The methodology of scientific research programmes*, ed. John Worrall and Gregory Currie, 102–138. Cambridge: Cambridge University Press.

Lakatos, Imre. 2000. "Lectures on scientific method." In *For and against method*, ed. Matteo Motterlini, 19–109. Chicago, IL: University of Chicago Press.

Lapid, Yosef. 1989. "The third debate: On the prospects of international theory in a post-positivist era." *International Studies Quarterly* 33, no. 3: 235–254.

Lapid, Yosef. 2003. "Through dialogue to engaged pluralism: The unfinished business of the third debate." *International Studies Review* 5, no. 1: 128–131.

Larson, Deborah Welch. 1985. *Origins of containment: A psychological explanation.* Princeton, NJ: Princeton University Press.

Laudan, Larry. 1996. *Beyond positivism and relativism: Theory, method, and evidence.* Bould, CO: Westview Press.

Laudan, Larry, and Jarrett Leplin. 1991. "Empirical equivalence and underdetermination." *The Journal of Philosophy* 88, no. 9: 449–472.

Lebow, Richard Ned. 2010. *Forbidden fruit: Counterfactuals and international relations.* Princeton, NJ: Princeton University Press.

Lederman, Leon, and Dick Teresi. 2006. *The God particle: If the universe is the answer, what is the question?* Boston, MA: Mariner Books.

Legro, Jeffrey, and Andrew Moravcsik. 1999. "Is anybody still a realist?" *International Security* 24, no. 2: 5–55.

Levy, Marion J. 1969. "'Does it matter if he's naked?' bawled the child." In *Contending approaches to international politics*, ed. Klaus Knorr and James N. Rosenau, 87–109. Princeton, NJ: Princeton University Press.

Linklater, Andrew. 2007. *Critical theory and world politics.* London: Routledge.

Litfin, K. 1994. *Ozone discourses.* New York: Columbia University Press.

Locke, John. 1959a. *An essay concerning human understanding. In two volumes, Volume one.* Mineola, NY: Dover.

Locke, John. 1959b. *An essay concerning human understanding. In two volumes, Volume two.* Mineola, NY: Dover.

Lupovici, Amir. 2009. "Constructivist methods: A plea and manifesto for pluralism." *Review of International Studies* 35, no. 1: 195–218.

Lynch, Cecilia. 1999. *Beyond appeasement: Interpreting interwar peace movements in world politics.* Ithaca, NY: Cornell University Press.

Lynch, Marc. 2002. "Why engage? China and the logic of communicative engagement." *European Journal of International Relations* 8, no. 2: 187–230.

Lynch, Michael. 1997. *Scientific practice and ordinary action: Ethnomethodology and social studies of science.* Cambridge: Cambridge University Press.

MacIntyre, Alasdair. 1984. *After virtue.* Notre Dame, IN: University of Notre Dame Press.

Mackie, J.L. 1965. "Causes and conditions." *American Philosophical Quarterly* 2 (4): 245–264.

Mahoney, James. 2003. "Strategies of causal assessment in comparative historical analysis." In *Comparative historical analysis in the social sciences*, ed. James Mahoney and Dietrich Rueschemeyer, 337–372. Cambridge: Cambridge University Press.

Mahoney, James. 2008. "Toward a unified theory of causality." *Comparative Political Studies* 41, no. 4–5: 412–436.

Mahoney, James, and Gary Goertz. 2004. "The possibility principle: Choosing negative cases in comparative research." *American Political Science Review* 98, no. 4: 653–669.

Mahoney, James, and Gary Goertz. 2006. "A tale of two cultures: Contrasting quantitative and qualitative research." *Political Analysis* 14, no. 3: 227–249.

Mahoney, James, Erin Kimball, and Kendra L. Koivu. 2009. "The logic of historical explanation in the social sciences." *Comparative Political Studies* 42, no. 1: 114–146.

Mannheim, Karl. 1936. *Ideology and utopia.* San Diego, CA: Harvest Books.

Marsh, David, and Paul Furlong. 2002. "A skin, not a sweater: Ontology and epistemology in political science." In *Theory and methods in political science*, ed. David Marsh and Gerry Stoker, 17–41. London: Palgrave Macmillan.

Martin, Lisa L. 1999. "The contributions of rational choice: A defense of pluralism." *International Security* 24, no. 2: 74–83.

Marx, Karl, and Friedrich Engels. 1978. *The Marx/Engels reader*. Ed. Robert C. Tucker. New York: W.W. Norton.

Masterman, Margaret. 1970. "The nature of a paradigm." In *Criticism and the growth of knowledge*, ed. Imre Lakatos and Alan Musgrave, 59–89. Cambridge: Cambridge University Press.

McAdam, Douglas, Sidney Tarrow, and Charles Tilly. 2001. *Dynamics of contention*. Cambridge: Cambridge University Press.

McArthur, Dan. 2006. "The anti-philosophical stance, the realism question and scientific practice." *Foundations of Science* 11, no. 4: 369–397.

McCormick, Peter J., ed. 1996. *Starmaking: Realism, anti-realism, and irrealism*. Cambridge, MA: MIT Press.

McCulloch, Gregory. 1995. *The mind and its world*. London: Routledge.

McKeown, Timothy J. 1999. "Case studies and the statistical worldview." *International Organization* 53, no. 1: 161–190.

McMichael, Philip. 1990. "Incorporating comparison within a world-historical perspective: An alternative comparative method." *American Sociological Review* 55, no. 3: 385–397.

McNamara, Kathleen R. 2009. "Of intellectual monocultures and the study of IPE." *Review of International Political Economy* 16, no. 1: 72–84.

McWherter, Dustin. 2012. *The problem of critical ontology: Bhaskar contra Kant*. New York: Palgrave Macmillan.

Mearsheimer, J. 1994. "The false promise of international institutions." *International Security* 19, no. 3: 5–49.

Mercer, Jonathan. 2006. "Human nature and the first image: Emotion in international politics." *Journal of International Relations and Development* 9, no. 3: 288–303.

Michel, Torsten. 2009. "Pigs can't fly, or can they? Ontology, scientific realism and the metaphysics of presence in international relations." *Review of International Studies* 35, no. 2: 397–419.

Miliband, Ralph. 1979. *The state in capitalist society: The analysis of the western system of power*. London: Quartet Books.

Mill, John Stuart. 1874. *A system of logic, ratiocinative and inductive: Being a connected view of the principles of evidence and the methods of scientific investigation*. 8th edn. New York: Harper and Brothers.

Mills, C. Wright. 1967. *The power elite*. Oxford: Oxford University Press.

Mohideen, U., and Anushree Roy. 1998. "Precision measurement of the Casimir Force from 0.1 to 0.9 mum." *Physical Review Letters* 81, no. 21: 4549–4552.

Molloy, Seán. 2003. "Dialectics and transformation: Exploring the international theory of E.H. Carr." *International Journal of Politics, Culture, and Society* 17, no. 2: 279–306.

Monteiro, Nuno P., and Kevin G. Ruby. 2009. "IR and the false problem of philosophical foundations." *International Theory* 1, no. 1: 15–48.

Moon, J.D. 1975. "The logic of political inquiry: A synthesis of opposed perspectives." In *Handbook of political science: Political science, scope and theory*, 131–228. Reading, MA: Addison-Wesley.

Moore, Michael. 2009. "Introduction: The nature of singularist theories of causation." *The Monist* 92, no. 1: 3–22.

Moravcsik, Andrew. 1998. *The choice for Europe: Social purpose and state power from Messina to Maastricht*. Ithaca, NY: Cornell University Press.

Moravcsik, Andrew. 2003. "Liberal international relations theory: A scientific assessment." In *Progress in International Relations theory: Appraising the field*, 159–204. Cambridge, MA: MIT Press.

Morgan, Stephen L., and Christopher Winship. 2007. *Counterfactuals and causal inference: Methods and principles for social research.* Cambridge: Cambridge University Press.

Morgenthau, Hans J. 1946. *Scientific man vs. power politics.* Chicago, IL: University of Chicago Press.

Morgenthau, Hans J. 1985. *Politics among nations.* New York: McGraw-Hill.

Moses, Jonathon W., and Torbjorn Knutsen. 2007. *Ways of knowing: Competing methodologies in social and political research.* London: Palgrave Macmillan.

Muppidi, Himadeep. 2010. *The colonial signs of International Relations.* New York: Columbia University Press.

Nanay, Bence. 2009. "The properties of singular causation." *The Monist* 92, no. 1: 112–132.

Nandy, Ashis. 1987. *Traditions, tyranny and utopias: Essays in the politics of awareness.* Delhi; New York: Oxford University Press.

Nandy, Ashis. 2009. *The intimate enemy: Loss and recovery of self under colonialism.* 2nd edn. New York: Oxford University Press.

Nettl, J.P. 1968. "The state as a conceptual variable." *World Politics* 20, no. 4: 559–592.

Neumann, Iver B. 2002. "Returning practice to the linguistic turn: The case of diplomacy." *Millennium* 31, no. 3: 627–651.

Neumann, Iver B. 2007. "'A speech that the entire ministry may stand for,' or: Why diplomats never produce anything new." *International Political Sociology* 1, no. 2: 183–200.

Neumann, Iver B., and Ole Jacob Sending. 2007. "'The international' as governmentality." *Millennium* 35, no. 3: 677–701.

Neumann, Iver B., and Ole Jacob Sending. 2010. *Governing the global polity: Practice, mentality, rationality.* Ann Arbor, MI: University of Michigan Press.

Neurath, Otto. 1973. *Empiricism and sociology.* Ed. Marie Neurath and Robert S. Cohen. Dordrecht; New York: Springer.

Nexon, Daniel H. 2009. *The struggle for power in early modern Europe: Religious conflict, dynastic empires, and international change.* Princeton, NJ: Princeton University Press.

Nexon, Daniel H., and Thomas Wright. 2007. "What's at stake in the American Empire debate." *American Political Science Review* 101, no. 2: 253–271.

Nickles, Thomas. 1977. "On the independence of singular causal explanation in social science: Archaeology." *Philosophy of the Social Sciences* 7, no. 2: 163–187.

Nietzsche, Friedrich Wilhelm. 1903. "Über Warheit und Lüge im aussermoralischen Sinne." In *Nietzsches Werke*, X: 189–215. 2nd edn. Leipzig: A. Kroner.

Nietzsche, Friedrich Wilhelm. 1967. *On the genealogy of morals.* New York: Random House.

Nietzsche, Friedrich Wilhelm. 1978. *Thus spoke Zarathustra: A book for none and all.* New York: Penguin.

Nietzsche, Friedrich Wilhelm. 1980. *On the advantage and disadvantage of history for life.* Indianapolis, IN: Hackett Press.

Ninkovich, Frank. 1994. *Modernity and power: A history of the domino theory in the twentieth century.* Chicago, IL: University of Chicago Press.

Niou, Emerson M.S., and Peter C. Ordeshook. 1994. "Less filling, tastes great: The realist-neoliberal debate." *World* 46, no. 2: 209–234.

Niou, Emerson M.S., and Peter C. Ordeshook. 1999. "Return of the Luddites." *International Security* 24, no. 2: 84–96.

O'Brien, Dan. 2006. *An introduction to the theory of knowledge.* 1st edn. Cambridge: Polity.

Onuf, Nicholas G. 1989. *World of our making: Rules and rule in social theory and International Relations.* Columbia, SC: University of South Carolina Press.

Onuf, Nicholas G. 1998. "Constructivism: A user's manual." In *International Relations in a constructed world*, ed. V. Kubálková, Nicholas G. Onuf, and Paul Kowert, 58–78. Armonk, NY: M.E. Sharpe.

Oren, Ido. 1995. "The subjectivity of the 'democratic peace: Changing U.S. perceptions of Imperial Germany'." *International Security* 20, no. 2: 147–184.

Orford, Anne. 2014. "Scientific reason and the discipline of international law." *European Journal of International Law* 25, no. 2: 369–385. doi:10.1093/ejil/chu030.

Parsons, Talcott. 1937. *The structure of social action*. New York: Basic Books.

Patomäki, Heikki. 1996. "How to tell better stories about world politics." *European Journal of International Relations* 2, no. 1: 105–133.

Patomäki, Heikki. 2001. *After International Relations: Critical realism and the (re) construction of world politics*. London: Routledge.

Patomäki, Heikki, and Colin Wight. 2000. "After postpositivism? The promises of critical realism." *International Studies Quarterly* 44, no. 2: 213–237.

Phillips, Nicola. 2009. "The slow death of pluralism." *Review of International Political Economy* 16, no. 1: 85–94.

Pickering, Andrew. 1995. *The mangle of practice: Time, agency, and science*. Chicago, IL: University of Chicago Press.

Plato. 1992. *Plato: Republic*. Ed. C.D.C. Reeve. Trans. G.M.A. Grube. 2nd edn. Indianapolis, IN: Hackett Press.

Plotnitsky, A. 1995. *Complementarity*. Durham, NC: Duke University Press.

Polkinghorne, John. 2006. *Exploring reality: The intertwining of science and religion*. New Haven, CT: Yale University Press.

Popper, Karl. 1970. "Normal science and its dangers." In *Criticism and the growth of knowledge*, ed. Imre Lakatos and Alan Musgrave, 51–58. Cambridge: Cambridge University Press.

Popper, Karl. 1979. *Objective knowledge: An evolutionary approach*. Oxford: Oxford University Press.

Popper, Karl. 1992. *The logic of scientific discovery*. 1st edn. New York: Routledge.

Popper, Karl. 1996. *Myth of the framework: In defence of science and rationality*. 1st edn. New York: Routledge.

Poulantzas, Nicos. 2008. *The Poulantzas reader: Marxism, law and the state*. London: Verso.

Pouliot, Vincent. 2004. "The essence of constructivism." *Journal of International Relations and Development* 7, no. 3: 319–336.

Pouliot, Vincent. 2007. "'Sobjectivism': Towards a constructivist methodology." *International Studies Quarterly* 51, no. 2: 359–384.

Powell, Robert. 1994. "Anarchy in IR theory: The neorealist–neoliberal debate." *International Organization* 48, no. 2: 313–344.

Powell, Robert. 1999. "The modeling enterprise and security studies." *International Security* 24, no. 2: 97–106.

Price, Richard, and Christian Reus-Smit. 1998. "Dangerous liaisons? Critical international theory and constructivism." *European Journal of International Relations* 4, no. 3: 259–294.

Putnam, Hilary. 1979. *Mind, language and reality: Philosophical papers, Volume 2*. Cambridge: Cambridge University Press.

Quine, Willard van Orman. 1961. *From a logical point of view: Nine logico-philosophical essays*. 2nd revised edn. Cambridge, MA: Harvard University Press.

Ragin, Charles C. 1989. *The comparative method: Moving beyond qualitative and quantitative strategies*. Berkeley, CA: University of California Press.

Ragin, Charles C. 2000. *Fuzzy-set social science*. Chicago, IL: University of Chicago Press.

Ragin, Charles C. 2008. *Redesigning social inquiry: Fuzzy sets and beyond*. Chicago, IL: University of Chicago Press.

Ray, James Lee. 2003. "A Lakatosian view of the democratic peace research program." In *Progress in International Relations theory: Appraising the field*, ed. Colin Elman and Miriam Fendus Elman, 205–243. Cambridge, MA: MIT Press.

Reisch, George A. 2005. *How the Cold War transformed philosophy of science*. Cambridge: Cambridge University Press.

Rescher, Nicholas. 1979. *Pierce's philosophy of science: Critical studies in his theory of induction and scientific method*. Notre Dame, IN: University of Notre Dame Press.

Rescher, Nicholas. 1997. *Objectivity: the obligations of impersonal reason*. Notre Dame, IN: University Of Notre Dame Press.

Richardson, Lewis F. 1960. *Statistics of deadly quarrels*. Ed. Quincy Wright and Carl C. Lienau. Pittsburgh: Boxwood Press.

Ringer, Fritz K. 1969. *The decline of the German mandarins*. Cambridge, MA: Harvard University Press.

Ringer, Fritz K. 1997. *Max Weber's methodology: The unification of the cultural and social sciences*. Cambridge, MA: Harvard University Press.

Ringer, Fritz K. 2004. *Max Weber: An intellectual biography*. Chicago, IL: University of Chicago Press.

Ringmar, Erik. 1996. *Identity, interest and action*. Cambridge: Cambridge University Press.

Risse, Thomas. 2000. "'Let's argue!': Communicative action in world politics." *International Organization* 54, no. 1: 1–39.

Rorty, Richard. 1981. *Philosophy and the mirror of nature*. Princeton, NJ: Princeton University Press.

Rousseau, David L., Christopher Gelpi, Dan Reiter, and Paul K. Huth. 1996. "Assessing the dyadic nature of the democratic peace, 1918–88." *The American Political Science Review* 90, no. 3: 512–533.

Ruggie, John Gerard. 1998. "Epistemology, ontology, and the study of international regimes." In *Constructing the world polity*, 85–101. London: Routledge.

Rule, J.B. 1997. *Theory and progress in social science*. Cambridge: Cambridge University Press.

Rytovuori-Apunen, Helena. 2005. "Forget 'post-positivist' IR!: The legacy of IR theory as the locus for a pragmatist turn." *Cooperation and Conflict* 40, no. 2: 147–177.

Sagan, Carl. 1997. *The demon-haunted world: Science as a candle in the dark*. New York: Ballantine Books.

Sankey, Howard. 1993. "Kuhn's changing concept of incommensurability." *British Journal of the Philosophy of Science* 44, no. 4: 759–774.

Sartori, G. 1970. "Concept misinformation in comparative politics." *American Political Science Review* 64, no. 4: 1033–1053.

Schiff, Jacob. 2008. "'Real'? As if! Critical reflections on state personhood." *Review of International Studies* 34, no. 3: 363–377.

Schmidt, Brian C. 1998. *The political discourse of anarchy: A disciplinary history of international relations*. Albany, NY: State University of New York Press.

Schram, Sanford, and Brian Caterino. 2006. *Making political science matter: Debating knowledge, research, and method*. New York: NYU Press.

Schrodt, Philip A. 2006. "Beyond the linear frequentist orthodoxy." *Political Analysis* 14, no. 3 (Summer): 335–339.

Schwartz-Shea, Peri. 2003. "Is this the curriculum we want? Doctoral requirements and offerings in methods and methodology." *PS: Political Science and Politics* 36, no. 3: 379–386.

Schwartz-Shea, Peri, and Dvora Yanow. 2002. "'Reading' 'Methods' 'Texts': How research method texts construct political science." *Political Research Quarterly* 55, no. 2: 157 186.

Schweller, Randall L. 1994. "Bandwagoning for profit: Bringing the revisionist state back in." *International Security* 19, no. 1: 72–107.

Schweller, Randall L., and William C. Wohlforth. 2000. "Power test: Evaluating realism in response to the end of the Cold War." *Security Studies* 9, no. 3: 60–107.

Scott, James C. 1990. *Domination and the arts of resistance: Hidden transcripts.* New Haven, CT: Yale University Press.

Scott, Joan W. 1991. "The evidence of experience." *Critical Inquiry* 17, no. 3: 773–797.

Searle, John. 1995. *The construction of social reality.* New York: Free Press.

Shapiro, Stuart L., and Saul A. Teukolsky. 1983. *Black holes, white dwarfs and neutron stars: The physics of compact objects.* 1st edn. Hoboken, NJ: Wiley-Interscience.

Shotter, John. 1993a. *Conversational realities: Constructing life through language.* Thousand Oaks, CA: Sage.

Shotter, John. 1993b. *Cultural politics of everyday life.* Toronto: University of Toronto Press.

Sieferle, R.P. 1995. *Die Konservative Revolution.* Frankfurt am Main: Fischer Taschenbuch Verlag.

Sil, Rudra. 2000. "The foundations of eclecticism: The epistemological status of agency, culture, and structure in social theory." *Journal of Theoretical Politics* 12, no. 3: 353–387.

Sil, Rudra. 2009. "Simplifying pragmatism: From social theory to problem-driven eclecticism." *International Studies Review* 11, no. 4: 648–652.

Sil, Rudra, and Peter J. Katzenstein. 2010. *Beyond paradigms: Analytic eclecticism in the study of world politics.* Basingstoke: Palgrave Macmillan.

Singer, J. David. 1961. "The level-of-analysis problem in international relations." In *The international system,* ed. Klaus Knorr, 77–92. Princeton, NJ: Princeton University Press.

Singer, J. David. 1969. "The incompleat theorist: Insight without evidence." In *Contending approaches to international politics,* ed. Klaus Knorr and James Rosenau, 62–86. Princeton, NJ: Princeton University Press.

Sjoberg, Laura, ed. 2009. *Gender and international security: Feminist perspectives.* 1st edn. New York: Routledge.

Smith, Steve. 1989. "Paradigm dominance in international relations: The development of international relations as a social science." In *The study of International Relations,* ed. Hugh C. Dyer and Leon Mangasarian, 3–27. New York: St. Martin's Press.

Smith, Steve. 1994. "Rearranging the deckchairs on the ship called modernity: Rosenberg, epistemology, and emancipation." *Millennium* 23: 395–405.

Smith, Thomas W. 1999. *History and international relations.* London: Routledge.

Snyder, Jack. 1991. *Myths of empire: Domestic politics and international ambition.* Ithaca, NY: Cornell University Press.

Spengler, Oswald. 1926. *The decline of the West, volume 1: Form and actuality.* New York: Alfred A. Knopf.

Spengler, Oswald. 1928. *The decline of the West, volume 2: Perspectives of world-history.* New York: Alfred A. Knopf.

Sprinz, Detlef F., and Yael Wolinsky-Nahmias. 2004. *Models, numbers, and cases: Methods for studying International Relations.* Ann Arbor, MI: University of Michigan Press.

Spruyt, H. 1994. *The sovereign state and its competitors.* Princeton, NJ: Princeton University Press.

Steinmetz, George, ed. 2005a. *The politics of method in the human sciences: Positivism and its epistemological others.* Durham, NC: Duke University Press.

Steinmetz, George. 2005b. "Scientific authority and the transition to post-Fordism: The plausibility of positivism in U.S. sociology since 1945." In *The politics of method in the human sciences: Positivism and its epistemological others,* ed. George Steinmetz, 275–323. Durham, NC: Duke University Press.

Sterling-Folker, J. 1997. "Realist environment, liberal process, and domestic-level variables." *International Studies Quarterly* 41, no. 1: 1–25.

Sterling-Folker. 2002. *Theories of international cooperation and the primacy of anarchy: Explaining U.S. international monetary policy-making after Bretton Woods.* Albany, NY: SUNY Press.

Stern, Fritz. 1961. *The politics of cultural despair.* Berkeley, CA: University of California Press.

Suganami, Hidemi. 1996. *On the causes of war.* Oxford: Clarendon Press.

Sylvan, David, and Stephen Majeski. 1998. "A methodology for the study of historical counterfactuals." *International Studies Quarterly* 42, no. 1: 79–108.

Tannoch-Bland, Jennifer. 1997. "From aperspectival objectivity to strong objectivity: The quest for moral objectivity." *Hypatia* 12, no. 1: 155–178.

Taylor, Charles. 1995. *Philosophical arguments.* Cambridge, MA: Harvard University Press.

Taylor, Charles Alan. 1996. *Defining science: A rhetoric of demarcation.* Madison, WI: University of Wisconsin Press.

Teilhard de Chardin, Pierre. 2008. *The phenomenon of man.* New York: Harper Perennial Modern Classics.

Tetlock, Philip E. 2006. *Expert political judgment: How good is it? How can we know?* Princeton, NJ: Princeton University Press.

Tetlock, Philip E., and Aaron Belkin. 1996. *Counterfactual thought experiments in world politics.* Princeton, NJ: Princeton University Press.

Tickner, Arlene B., and Ole Wæver. 2009. *Global scholarship in International Relations: Worlding beyond the West.* New edition. London: Routledge.

Tickner, J. Ann. 2006. "Feminism meets international relations: Some methodological issues." In *Feminist methodologies for International Relations,* ed. Brooke A. Ackerly, Maria Stern, and Jacqui True, 19–41. Cambridge: Cambridge University Press.

Tilly, Charles. 1989. *Big structures, large processes, huge comparisons.* New York: Russell Sage Foundation Publications.

Tilly, Charles. 1997. "Means and ends of comparison in macrosociology." *Comparative Social Research* 16: 43–53.

Tilly, Charles. 1998. *Durable inequality.* Berkeley, CA: University of California Press.

Tilly, Charles. 2001. "Mechanisms in political processes." *Annual Review of Political Science* 4: 21–41.

Tippett, Krista. 2009. "The spiritual audacity of Abraham Joshua Heschel." *The spiritual audacity of Abraham Joshua Heschel.* http://speakingoffaith.publicradio.org/programs/2009/heschel/. Accessed 12 December 2009.

Todorov, Tzvetan. 1984. *The conquest of America.* New York: Harper & Row.

Toulmin, Stephen. 1992. *Cosmopolis: The hidden agenda of modernity*. Chicago, IL: University of Chicago Press.

Towns, Ann. 2009. "The status of women as a standard of 'civilization'." *European Journal of International Relations* 15, no. 4: 681–706.

Turner, Derek. 2007. *Making prehistory: Historical science and the scientific realism debate*. Cambridge: Cambridge University Press.

Turner, Stephen. 1994. *The social theory of practices: Tradition, tacit knowledge, and presuppositions*. Chicago, IL: University of Chicago Press.

Turton, Helen Louise. 2015. "The importance of re-affirming IR's disciplinary status." *International Relations* 29, no. 2: 244–250. doi:10.1177/0047117815585888a.

Van Apeldoorn, Bastiaan. 2002. *Transnational capitalism and the struggle over European integration*. London: Routledge.

Van Belle, Douglas. 2006. "Dinosaurs and the democratic peace: Paleontological lessons for avoiding the extinction of theory in political science." *International Studies Perspectives* 7, no. 3: 287–306.

van Fraassen, Bas C. 1976. "To save the phenomena." *The Journal of Philosophy* 73, no. 18: 623–632.

van Fraassen, Bas C. 1980. *The scientific image*. New York: Oxford University Press.

van Fraassen, Bas C. 2004a. *The empirical stance*. New Haven, CT: Yale University Press.

van Fraassen, Bas C. 2004b. "Review: Replies to discussion on 'The empirical stance'." *Philosophical Studies: An International Journal for Philosophy in the Analytic Tradition* 121, no. 2: 171–192.

Vasquez, John A. 1995. "The post-positivist debate: Reconstructing scientific enquiry and international relations theory after Enlightenment's fall." In *International Relations theory today*, ed. Ken Booth and Steve Smith, 217–240. University Park, PA: Pennsylvania State University Press.

Vasquez, John A. 1997. "The realist paradigm and degenerative versus progressive research programs: An appraisal of neotraditional research on Waltz's balancing proposition." *American Political Science Review* 91, no. 4: 899–912.

Vasquez, John A. 1999. *The power of power politics: From classical realism to neotraditionalism*. Cambridge: Cambridge University Press.

Vrasti, Wanda. 2008. "The strange case of ethnography and international relations." *Millennium* 37, no. 2: 279–301.

Wæver, Ole. 1996. "The rise and fall of the inter-paradigm debate." In *International theory: Positivism and beyond*, ed. Steve Smith, Ken Booth, and Marysia Zalewski, 149–185. Cambridge: Cambridge University Press.

Wæver, Ole. 2009. "Waltz's theory of theory." *International Relations* 23, no. 2: 201–222.

Walker, Randi Jones. 2005. *The evolution of a UCC style: History, ecclesiology, and culture of the United Church of Christ*. Cleveland, OH: United Church Press.

Walt, Stephen M. 1987. *The origins of alliances*. Ithaca, NY: Cornell University Press.

Waltz, Kenneth N. 1979. *Theory of international politics*. New York: McGraw-Hill.

Waltz, Kenneth N. 1986. "Reflections on theory of international politics: A response to my critics." In *Neorealism and its critics*, ed. Robert O. Keohane, 322–346. New York: Columbia University Press.

Waltz, Kenneth N. 1996. "International politics is not foreign policy." *Security Studies* 6, no. 1: 54–57.

Waltz, Kenneth N. 1997. "Evaluating theories." *American Political Science Review* 91, no. 4: 913–917.

Webb, Michael C., and Stephen D. Krasner. 1989. "Hegemonic stability theory: An empirical assessment." *Review of International Studies* 15, no. 2: 183–198.

Weber, Cynthia. 2014. "Why is there no queer international theory?" *European Journal of International Relations*, 21, no 1: 27–51. doi:10.1177/1354066114524236.

Weber, Max. 1917. *Wissenschaft als Beruf—Politik als Beruf.* Ed. W.J. Mommsen and W. Schluchter. Tübingen: J.C.B. Mohr.

Weber, Max. 1949. *The methodology of the social sciences.* Ed. Edward A. Shils and Henry A. Finch. New York: Free Press.

Weber, Max. 1976. *Wirtschaft und Gesellschaft.* Ed. J. Winckelmann. Vol. 5. Tübingen: J.C.B. Mohr.

Weber, Max. 1999a. "Die 'Objektivität' Sozialwissenschaftlicher und Sozialpolitischer Erkenntnis." In *Gesammelte Aufsätze zur Wissenschaftslehre*, ed. Elizabeth Flitner, 146–214. Potsdam: Internet-Ausgabe, www.uni-potsdam.de/u/paed/Flitner/Flitner/Weber/. Accessed 15 April 2010.

Weber, Max. 1999b. "Kritische Studien auf dem Gebiet der Kulturwissenschaftlichen Logik." In *Gesammelte Aufsätze zur Wissenschaftslehre*, ed. Elizabeth Flitner, 215–290. Potsdam: Internet-Ausgabe, www.uni-potsdam.de/u/paed/Flitner/Flitner/Weber/. Accessed 15 April 2010.

Weber, Max. 2004. *The vocation lectures.* Indianapolis, IN: Hackett Press.

Weldes, Jutta. 1999. *Constructing national interests: The United States and the Cuban missile crisis.* Minneapolis, MN: University of Minnesota Press.

Weldon, S. Laurel. 2006. "Inclusion and understanding: A collective methodology for feminist international relations." In *Feminist methodologies for International Relations*, 62–87. Cambridge: Cambridge University Press.

Wendt, Alexander. 1987. "The agent-structure problem in international relations theory." *International Organization* 41, no. 3: 335–370.

Wendt, Alexander. 1992. "Anarchy is what states make of it: The social construction of power politics." *International Organization* 46, no. 2: 391–425.

Wendt, Alexander. 1998. "On constitution and causation in international relations." In *The eighty years' crisis: International Relations 1919–1999*, ed. Tim Dunne, Michael Cox, and Ken Booth, 101–117. Cambridge: Cambridge University Press.

Wendt, Alexander. 1999. *Social theory of international politics.* Cambridge: Cambridge University Press.

Wendt, Alexander. 2000. "On the via media: A response to the critics." *Review of International Studies* 26, no. 1: 165–180.

Wendt, Alexander. 2006. "Social theory as Cartesian science: An auto-critique from a quantum perspective." In *Constructivism and International Relations*, ed. Stefano Guzzini and Anna Leander, 181–219. London: Routledge.

Wendt, Alexander. 2015. *Quantum mind and social science: Unifying physical and social ontology.* Cambridge: Cambridge University Press.

Whimster, Sam, ed. 2003. *The essential Weber: A reader.* London: Routledge.

White, Jonathan. 2009. "The social theory of mass politics." *Journal of Politics* 71, no. 1: 96–112.

White, Stephen K. 2000. *Sustaining affirmation: The strengths of weak ontology in political theory.* Princeton, NJ: Princeton University Press.

White, Stephen K. 2002. Review of "Making social science matter," by Bent Flyvbjerg. *American Political Science Review* 96, no. 1: 179–180.

Wiener, Antje. 2009. "Enacting meaning-in-use: Qualitative research on norms and international relations." *Review of International Studies* 35, no. 1: 175–193.

Wight, Colin. 1996. "Incommensurability and cross-paradigm communication in international relations theory: 'What's the frequency, Kenneth?'" *Millennium* 25, no. 2: 291–319.

Wight, Colin. 1999. "They shoot dead horses don't they? Locating agency in the agent-structure problematique." *European Journal of International Relations* 5, no. 1: 109–142.

Wight, Colin. 2006. *Agents, structures and International Relations: Politics as ontology.* Cambridge: Cambridge University Press.

Williams, Malcolm. 2000. "Interpretivism and generalisation." *Sociology* 34, no. 2: 209–224.

Williams, Michael. 1995. *Unnatural doubts.* Princeton, NJ: Princeton University Press.

Williams, Michael C. 2005. *The realist tradition and the limits of International Relations.* Cambridge: Cambridge University Press.

Williamson, Oliver E. 1998. *The economic institutions of capitalism.* New York: Free Press.

Winch, Peter. 1990. *The idea of a social science and its relation to philosophy.* London: Routledge.

Winkler, Kenneth P. 1989. *Berkeley: An interpretation.* Oxford: Oxford University Press.

Wittgenstein, Ludwig. 1953. *Philosophical investigations.* Oxford: Blackwell.

Wittgenstein, Ludwig. 1961. *Tractatus logico-philosophicus.* London: Routledge.

Wohlforth, William C. 1999. "A certain idea of science." *Journal of Cold War Studies* 1, no. 2: 39–60.

Wohlforth, William C., Richard Little, Stuart J. Kaufman, David Kang, Charles A. Jones, Victoria Tin-Bor Hui, Arthur Eckstein, Daniel Deudney, and William L. Brenner. 2007. "Testing balance-of-power theory in world history." *European Journal of International Relations* 13, no. 2: 155–185.

Yanow, Dvora, and Peri Schwartz-Shea, eds. 2006. *Interpretation and method: Empirical research methods and the interpretive turn.* Armonk, NY: M.E. Sharpe.

Yanow, Dvora, and Peri Schwartz-Shea, eds. 2013. *Interpretation and method: Empirical research methods and the interpretive turn.* 2nd edition. New York: Routledge.

Index